XAAS

EVERYTHING-AS-A-SERVICE

The Lean and Agile Approach
to Business Growth

XAAS
EVERYTHING-AS-A-SERVICE
The Lean and Agile Approach to Business Growth

Shantanu Bhattacharya
Lipika Bhattacharya

Singapore Management University, Singapore

 **World Scientific**

NEW JERSEY · LONDON · SINGAPORE · BEIJING · SHANGHAI · HONG KONG · TAIPEI · CHENNAI · TOKYO

Published by

World Scientific Publishing Co. Pte. Ltd.

5 Toh Tuck Link, Singapore 596224

USA office: 27 Warren Street, Suite 401-402, Hackensack, NJ 07601

UK office: 57 Shelton Street, Covent Garden, London WC2H 9HE

British Library Cataloguing-in-Publication Data
A catalogue record for this book is available from the British Library.

XAAS: EVERYTHING-AS-A-SERVICE
The Lean and Agile Approach to Business Growth

ISBN 978-981-121-991-7 (hardcover)
ISBN 978-981-121-992-4 (ebook for institutions)
ISBN 978-981-121-993-1 (ebook for individuals)

For any available supplementary material, please visit
https://www.worldscientific.com/worldscibooks/10.1142/11817#t=suppl

Desk Editor: Sandhya Venkatesh

Typeset by Stallion Press
Email: enquiries@stallionpress.com

Printed in Singapore

Foreword

We have all had similar experiences: to make use of a product, we have had no choice but to buy it. We may want, for example, flexible and regular mobility over medium to long distances, and so we have to buy a car; we may want to drill a few holes to hang up paintings after we move into our new apartment, so we have to buy a drill. Business leaders may want to restructure their balance sheets by moving expenses from capital to operational expenses. Or companies may be reluctant to invest in new technologies for fear that they would become obsolete before they were amortized. Yes, we may often not want to invest in a product, but we may want to pay for its use, or for the experience it may create for us.

Can it be done? Of course, we have always known some form of leasing, and in more recent times, we have witnessed the move towards servitization. First there was Xerox with its extended leasing model for photocopiers, later on we learnt about the case of Rolls Royce or Michelin who did not sell aircraft engines or tyres any more, but the use of these engines, including services such as maintenance, or the use of tyres, including their replacement. In the process, they moved from being companies with a pure product orientation to companies that combined product technology with data collection and analysis. Recently, many companies have switched to Software-as-a-Service (SaaS) operated in the cloud, as opposed to taking licenses on fast evolving software applications on fully owned mainframes.

We knew the stories; we have studied the examples. But we have lacked good conceptual frameworks to shape the future of Everything-as-a-Service, or XaaS as it is called. This is precisely what this book brings to us. Based on a multitude of detailed case studies from many different sectors, and very well-anchored in the literature, Lipika and Shantanu Bhattacharya have developed a practical portfolio of models and tools to go beyond post hoc analysis, to help us to proactively design and implement XaaS-based business models. With their description of the five key elements of a successful XaaS offering in Chapter 1, they immediately help us go beyond the legacy of pure ownership transfer or leasing and primitive servitization. They point out that there is potential also in the nanonization of utility, the promise of continuing innovation through collaboration between the service provider and the users, and the creative use of technology.

The concepts developed in the first chapter lead to an excellent toolbox (BROAD FENCES) to understand, design and evaluate XaaS propositions. In many books where authors provide a set of tools and concepts, one can find a few examples, but often they do not really help the readers in applying them in their own business environment. Here, we have in three chapters a wealth of examples on how the toolbox can be used to probe the feasibility, profitability and potential growth of a XaaS business model. All readers will find at least a few examples that are similar to their own organizations and requirements, and will find inspiration in the detailed case studies. In addition, throughout the book readers will also notice some important recurrent threads. Successful XaaS models always start with the customers and their needs. And this requires deep systems thinking. How to organize for this and how to develop the skills needed to run a great XaaS business is extensively discussed here.

However, this book is more than a "how to" book based on interesting cases. Throughout the manuscript, we discover that it is anchored in a wealth of research in economics and management. Don't be scared though, dear readers. You will not be overwhelmed with academic references. But a practitioner should be comforted that the models and tools presented in this book are based on some of the best research of the last few decades.

The future in most industries is to provide solutions, to offer services, to create experiences. How will it look in your industry? Forecasting is always difficult, but as the saying goes: predicting the future is easier when you shape it yourself. This book provides you with the tools and models to shape your business as a XaaS.

Arnoud De Meyer
University Professor, Singapore Management University

Contents

Contents

Chapter 1

Introduction

Coffee. As a service. Panera Bread, a bakery-café chain in the US, rolled out a new subscription model in March 2020 in the US — customers could get unlimited hot coffee, tea and iced coffee at all US outlets for a monthly subscription fee of $9.[1] Customers in the MyPanera loyalty program could get free refills in-store every two hours. The service was offered using an app. The purpose of the service was to boost customer footfalls and spending at Panera. The chain did a test round for three weeks of the program in a hundred and fifty locations in Nashville, Raleigh, Cleveland and Columbus over a period of three months before launching the service. The test rounds showed that the footfall frequency increased by more than 200% and food orders with the coffee increased by 70%. The renewal rate of the program in the tests was above 90%, hence, the tests were successful in meeting the objectives of the service. Panera's public statement about the service launch lauded the subscription model's ability to separate the utility of the service and the payment. Customers would pay at the beginning of the month, and then enjoy the service without having to worry about paying each time.[2]

---

[1] Tyko, K., "Panera Bread's new coffee subscription program offers unlimited coffee for $8.99 a month", *USA Today*, February 27, 2020, https://www.usatoday.com/story/money/food/2020/02/27/unlimited-coffee-panera-bread-new-coffee-subscription-program/4882655002/, accessed March 27, 2020.

[2] Lalley, H., "Slowed by the pandemic, Panera revisits its coffee subscription service", *Restaurant Business*, June 22, 2020, https://www.restaurantbusinessonline.com/marketing/slowed-pandemic-panera-revisits-its-coffee-subscription-service, accessed August 18, 2020.

The coffee-as-a-service model was offered first by Burger King in March 2019. It offered a small cup of coffee daily to customers for a subscription fee of $5 a month.[3] Its subscription service was also offered using an app, and the objectives of Burger King's subscription plan were also to increase footfalls and increase the food sales with the coffee. The app enabled Burger King to follow an individual's buying pattern of food and drink services over time. What was the fate of the Burger King coffee-as-a-service offering? Some critics pointed to the small cup size as one of the flaws of the offering, others doubted the ability of the plan to significantly increase footfalls.[4] Burger King discontinued the subscription plan after a few months, leading to the conclusion that either the service did not yield the desired outcomes, or the cost made the subscription plan unprofitable.

What is the secret sauce of the as-a-service model? Why does it work for some firms and not for others? The XaaS offering mode (XaaS is the acronym for "everything as a service" or "anything as a service") has become virtually synonymous with cloud computing, which has grown dramatically since its inception with Salesforce's CRM platform. However, when Salesforce first launched its Software-as-a-Service (SaaS) offering for its CRM solution, it was met with a fair degree of scepticism.[5] Marc Benioff had been an employee of Oracle for a number of years and served in various roles like customer support, sales and innovation. He founded Salesforce in 1999 with a mission to replace the licensing model of software with the service offering.[6] His approach was to make software accessible more easily globally, as the diffusion of enterprise software from

---

[3]Taylor, R., "Burger King Launches $5 Coffee Subscription Service", *QS Magazine*, March 2019, https://www.qsrmagazine.com/technology/burger-king-launches-5-coffee-subscription-service#:~:text=On%20March%2015%2C%20Burger%20King,their%20small%20cup%20of%20coffee, accessed March 27, 2020.

[4]Duprey, R., "Burger King's New $5 Coffee Subscription Misses Opportunity to Score Big", *The Motley Fool*, March 26, 2019, https://www.fool.com/investing/2019/03/26/burger-kings-new-5-coffee-subscription-could-be-hu.aspx, accessed March 27, 2020.

[5]Kawamoto, D., "As Salesforce turns 20, looking back at what Benioff built", *San Francisco Business Times*, March 6, 2019, https://www.bizjournals.com/sanfrancisco/news/2019/03/06/salesforce-turns-20-anniversary-benioff.html", accessed March 28, 2020.

[6]Benioff, M. & Adler, C. (2009). Behind the cloud: The untold story of how Salesforce.com went from idea to billion-dollar company-and revolutionized an industry. John Wiley & Sons, California.

Oracle and other leaders in the enterprise software domain was slow. With the licensing model, customers needed to pay high licensing fees upfront, and rapid technology advancements could make the software application obsolete quickly.[7] Hence, many potential adopters of software applications would baulk at licensing the software because of the high initial fees and the rapid obsolescence of the application. Benioff's strategy was to make it easier for customers to access software products by providing them as a service rather than as a product.[8] This concept was very different from how software solutions were sold as bulk packages for enterprise-wide implementation at the time.

Historically, the installation of pre-packaged software solutions involved heavy (multi-million dollar) investments. Often wrapped as a suite of CD-ROMs with individual installations at each computer in the network, such packages took a long time (several weeks) for a customer's IT support department to install across the organization. The cost of the software was typically based on the number of employees of the client organization. In addition to the investment in the software, customer firms were also required to invest in hardware and networking to facilitate the installation of the software, which incurred additional costs. Notably, hardware was expensive at that time — a 15MB hard drive could cost around $2500. Salesforce tried to address these pain points of software purchases by coming up with a service solution that could deliver software products over a cloud and could be purchased by customers through a monthly subscription plan. The idea was to make software a utility that was easy and convenient to use.[9]

[7] Miller, G., "After 20 years of Salesforce, what Marc Benioff got right and wrong about the cloud", *Tech Crunch*, June 18, 2018, https://techcrunch.com/2018/06/17/after-twenty-years-of-salesforce-what-marc-benioff-got-right-and-wrong-about-the-cloud/, accessed March 27, 2020.

[8] Weinberger, M. & Taylor, N. R., "The rise of Marc Benioff, the bombastic owner of Time Magazine who just became Salesforce's sole CEO, has an $8 billion fortune, and owns a 5-acre compound in Hawaii", *Business Insider*, February 26, 2020, https://www.businessinsider.com/the-rise-of-salesforce-ceo-marc-benioff-2016-3, accessed March 28, 2020.

[9] Miller, G., "After 20 years of Salesforce, what Marc Benioff got right and wrong about the cloud", *TechCrunch*, June 18, 2018, https://techcrunch.com/2018/06/17/after-twenty-years-of-salesforce-what-marc-benioff-got-right-and-wrong-about-the-cloud/, accessed March 29, 2020.

The subscription pricing model that was pioneered by Salesforce for software applications had been tried for hardware products in the past as well. Xerox had adopted a similar strategy for offering its 914 copier, and the offering had revolutionized the copier sector. The Salesforce as-a-service model converted non-customers to customers, as it allowed smaller firms with limited budgets to access the tools that they needed to grow their business. By storing all applications and business data on a central hub, businesses got around the high price of physical hard drive space and the need to maintain their own hardware. Moreover, since the solution was available in the cloud, it could be delivered to customers in an agile fashion, with a lower lead time and a lower degree of inconvenience. The installation of the application was much easier from the perspective of the customer, as there were no cumbersome steps like installing software from a set of CD ROMs. Next, typically when software was offered using a productization model, the customer was unlikely to have a close relationship with the provider after the application was delivered to the customer. Customers could request support from the firm either for free or for an additional fee depending on the service model. However, the close contact with the developer was lost. With the XaaS model, the developer–customer relationship was much closer. Since customers could pay per user, they could choose which employees they needed the software for, rather than buying in bulk for the entire organization, thus building flexibility into the purchase.

1.1 CHARACTERISTICS OF SUCCESSFUL XaaS MODELS

What are the key characteristics of successful XaaS offerings? Is it just the change of asset ownership, where the asset ownership is transferred to the provider rather than the customer, and the customer pays for consuming the utility of the asset over time? The asset ownership transfer model has been around for centuries and is more commonly known as renting or leasing the product. Is XaaS just a glorified new name for renting or leasing, which is an age-old way of offering a product? Based on our research, we have identified five key characteristics of XaaS offerings. Asset ownership transfer is indeed one of the critical elements of these offerings, as the transfer of asset ownership to the provider leads to economies of scale and lower costs. We find that the five factors characterizing successful XaaS models are as follows: (i) asset ownership transfer, (ii) change of strategy from offering the best products to being a solutions provider, (iii) nanonization, or a focus on being lean by matching the customer's utility attributes over time, and pricing based on nanonization, (iv) a culture of customer-centricity to create a cycle of continuous innovation, and (v) the judicious use of technology to enable value creation for the customer and the firm, along with the offering of personalized services. Nanonization is the disaggregation of a product into different utility attributes, and the disaggregation of the use of the product into smaller time units. The combination of these five characteristics makes the XaaS model successful. If any of these elements are missing, then the provider may not be successful in the long run. These elements influencing successful XaaS offerings are depicted in Figure 1.1.

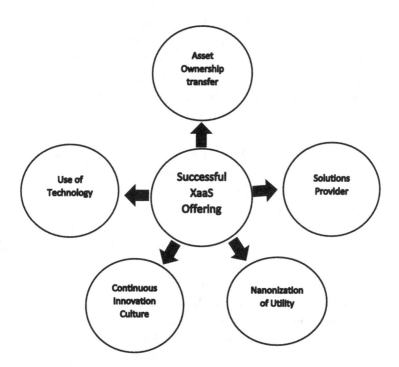

Figure 1.1: Key Elements of Successful XaaS Offering

1.1.1 Asset Ownership Transfer

The transfer of asset ownership enables the customer to make smaller payments for using the product, software or service. Indeed, asset ownership transfer is useful from the customer's perspective in being able to avail of a product's use, as it creates the ability for the provider to be able to accommodate individual customer budgets. From the firm's perspective, the provider does not have to acquire the sum of all its customer's assets to deliver its offering. It can avail of economies of scale or sharing economies for lowering costs for itself and share those savings with the customer. Salesforce does not need to acquire the sum of the customers' processing and data storage capacities. Instead, it can acquire a lower total amount as there will be some resource pooling effects. All customers do not access the service at the same time, so the lower asset capacity should be able to meet instantaneous demand at any point of time. This is one of the core advantages of the sharing economy. Indeed, shared economy offerings also offer often on-demand service and the pay-per-use facility. The sharing economies are obtained by sharing the same set of resources among multiple users. The difference between the XaaS offerings and the sharing economy is that the assets in the XaaS offering are owned by the provider and can be planned and designed centrally for the customers. In the sharing economy, on the other hand, assets are owned by third parties who offer their assets via the platform to customers. The PaaS (platform-as-a-service) model indeed offers some of the business model advantages of the sharing economy. To exemplify the use of the asset ownership transfer model's advantages for Salesforce, let us consider the software's requirements for maintenance and updates. In the productization model, enterprise software maintenance needed regular installation of updates, and often it took support staff weeks to get the scheduling of these installations right. Software maintenance also required hefty maintenance investments by individual users. With a solution on the cloud, this pain point was addressed by allowing updates to run from the cloud conveniently without the costs involved, as the common hosting on the cloud took away the need for individual users to update their own systems. Obviously, the shared resources also enabled customers to adopt the solution without large and risky upfront investments in the software, hardware, implementation, and costs of additional IT staff.

1.1.2 Solutions Provider Strategy

The second key element of the XaaS offering with the productization model is the solutions provider strategy of the as-a-service offering. The contrast between the productization model and the solutions provider model is like the contrast between the make-to-stock and make-to-order strategies. A pure make-to-order strategy starts with the customer: eliciting and validating customer requirements are indeed key. In the pure customization strategy, the provider will need to confirm that the customer indeed wants what s/he states, and there is no gap between what the customer wants and what the provider comprehends. Next, the provider will have to make a rough design of the most appropriate product for serving the customer's needs. If the technology to deliver the customer's needs does not exist or cannot be developed, then the provider will have to either request the customer to change his/her requirements, or else state their inability to design the desired product. At this stage, the provider also shares a price and lead time quote for feasible designs with the customer. Since the final design is not completed yet, the price and lead time quote will have a buffer for unknown factors at this point of time. Hence, purely customized products have significantly higher margins with buffering for two reasons: first, the price is quoted at a point of time when the final design of the product has not been completed. Even if the final design were complete, there could still be unknown factors in the actual making of the product that could increase the cost for the provider. Once both parties have finished negotiating on the design and price of the product, the provider completes the design, builds the product, and delivers it to the customer. Based on this basic differentiation, a purely customized product will very closely adhere to the customer's needs, but will be delivered at a high price and with a delay. In contrast, for a pure make-to-stock policy, the firm will have more product offerings that are manufactured before the customer demand is raised. This implies that the firm will make a set of planned standardized products with different attributes. Customers can choose the product with the attributes at the relevant price point that most closely matches their needs. They will also pay a significantly lower price for the product than pure customized products, as these standardized products are made at scale. The cost of making to stock is lower due to these economies of scale in the manufacturing process; raw materials are ordered in bulk, these materials are processed in bulk, and finished goods are distributed in bulk.

It is interesting to note that before the Industrial Revolution, all manufacturing was done by artisans, with apprentices learning the trade of manufacturing from the master artisan.[10] The artisanal manufacturing era focused on complete customization, with artisans typically making customized goods based on customer requirements. Large-scale mechanization during the Industrial Revolution moved the pendulum from the artisanal manufacturing mode to mass manufacturing, with product standardization as a result. The mass manufacturing shift culminated in Ford's design of the assembly line to make one completely standardized product (Model T). While the coinage of the pendulum effect (the pendulum always swings back) probably did not have the XaaS offering in mind, it is ironic that there is a move in businesses back from the standardized product strategy to the strategy of a solutions provider. The difference is that, in this move, businesses finally seem to have realized that there is a way to achieve both objectives: the desire for customization to closely match customer needs, with the need for lower costs through product standardization. While the entire mass customization philosophy achieved that move by using standardized core assemblies with postponed differentiation, modern IT and hardware XaaS offerings achieve the lower cost base by sharing assets across different customers for economies of scale, and solutions are offered via a menu that customers can choose from.

In the research on solutions provider strategies, the findings are that solutions providers have to combine customer-centricity with product-centricity.[11] The degree of customer-centricity depends on the provider's solutions strategy; there are four components of a provider's solutions strategy. The first component is the solution type: whether the solution is function-specific or industry-specific. An example of function-specific solutions is the CRM solution of Salesforce, while an example of an industry-specific solution is CAD/CAM software for the construction

---

[10] Berg, M. (1991). Artisans and Factory Systems in the Industrial Revolution (No. 2068-2018-800).

[11] Galbraith, J. R. (2002). Organizing to deliver solutions. Organizational dynamics, 31(2), 194.

industry. The second component is the scale and scope of the solution; the more the complexity and features of the solution, the higher the scale and scope. For example, a printer attached to a word processor would have small scale and scope, while a CAD/CAM software for an engineering firm would need software, servers, and services, giving it higher scale and scope. Third, the integration and complementarity between components of the solution determines the nature of the solution. Farming services like the supply of seeds and fertilizers are largely independent of each other, while solutions for cleaning teeth like the toothbrush and toothpaste are complementary. Fourth, the ratio of the provider's revenues from integrated solutions to its total revenues plays an important role in identifying the focus of the provider. The research finds that the organizational structure, the processes used by the provider, the rewards structure, and the skills of the people need to match the solutions provider strategy.

While being a solutions provider is one of the key elements of the XaaS offering, there are some inherent conundrums for a provider in being able to position itself as a solutions provider, on the one hand, and be mindful of customer cost and need considerations, on the other. First, pure customization is a strategy of designing and building a unique product for each customer, while the productization model offers a limited set of products in scale for all customers. Traditionally, this implies that the solutions provider focuses on giving customers extensive choices at a higher price, while mass manufacturers provide customers a few solutions to choose from, but at a lower price. For the XaaS model to provide solutions while being mindful of costs, XaaS providers typically use multiple tactics. First, by sharing a fixed set of assets between a large set of customers, XaaS providers get economies of scale. Hence, the asset ownership transfer is key for the success of the as-a-service offering, otherwise it could not be both a solutions provider and a cost-conscious provider. Second, XaaS offerings often use the concept of mass customization, where the core product or asset is standardized for all customers. The provider then designs many add-on features that can be offered to the customer complementarily with the core asset. Customers may be offered these add-on features as a part of the service bundle, or as standalone components. Third, the organizational structure and the people skills within the organization play a critical role in making XaaS offerings successful. The organizational structure and people skills should be designed to be aligned with the rewards system and the processes used to deliver the solutions provider strategy.

To chart Salesforce's solutions provider strategy, Salesforce started with the productization model by developing a standardized solution for the customer relationship management (CRM) software. The understanding was that most organizations used software applications to manage their sales data. The early product development and marketing was focused on making the CRM software easy to use. CRM applications were built with the intention of enabling businesses to automate their marketing, sales process and customer service and support. In addition, they also allowed customers to manage their sales force staff more effectively through sales force automation, marketing automation, document management, analytics, and custom application development. From the software perspective, the original CRM software was basically a barebones structure, which was simple and easy to use and did not require a setup.[12] Users could just login to the CRM system and use its functionalities. Initially, the CRM software was offered free to the first few users, followed by aggressive marketing strategies to build a client base, with the initial customers providing word-of-mouth support. A key feature of the initial word-of-mouth marketing strategy was to sell the customer's success story.[13] Once the free users had a positive experience from the CRM software, they became the sales agents who could promote the software via word-of-mouth feedback about the product. For the initial rounds of user validation, Salesforce used salespeople across organizations as free users, who could then influence others in their organization to try the product.

In the first year of its launch, Salesforce did not create much of a stir in the market. Despite the significant value proposition of the CRM, many enterprises failed to deploy CRM applications successfully due to a

---

[12] Bielawski, S., Kempe, C., McDaniel, A., Tate, A. & Harrison, J. S., "Case Study, Robins School of Business, University of Richmond", January 2015, https://robins.richmond.edu/documents/Salesforce.pdf, accessed March 30, 2020.

[13] Brian O'Connell, "History of Salesforce: Timeline and Facts", *The Street*, February 27, 2020, https://www.thestreet.com/technology/history-of-salesforce, accessed March 29, 2020.

variety of reasons. First, CRM solutions available in the market were expensive. They also had a high cost of implementation, leading to an apprehension in trying Salesforce's SaaS offering even though its usage was priced much lower. Second, it was difficult to implement a CRM system uniformly across an organization owing to its functional specificity, and typically CRM software saw low rates of adoption outside sales divisions. Third, most players in the market at the time regarded cloud services as a fad that would pass, and not an effective solution for CRM. Salesforce used aggressive marketing strategies to overcome the initial apprehensions. A key to its offering was the low cost of accessing a CRM solution, and this was attractive to small and medium firms. Gradually, larger firms started to notice how easily and quickly the platform was able to enable migration of customers, and that then drove large-scale adoption of Salesforce solutions.[14]

Following the early adoption, Salesforce began offering solutions to allow customers to tailor important characteristics of the solution to meet their unique requirements without the use of significant IT resources. These solution offerings began Salesforce's transformation journey from a productization model to that of a solutions provider. The solutions were enabled by a set of application programming interfaces, or APIs. The APIs permitted customers and independent developers to write their own code that could then be wrapped and synchronized with the Salesforce CRM to integrate and interact with existing third-party and legacy systems.[15] This helped organizations avoid system silos and allowed them to build interoperability between their legacy systems and the Salesforce CRM. Hence, Salesforce began using mass customization techniques for letting customers and third parties design customized modules with their standardized core software.

The solutions approach is being adopted in other industries like shipping as well. Maersk is the largest container shipping line globally and has been historically known for offering shipping services. Over the last few years, Maersk has evolved into an integrated end-to-end solutions

---

[14] Salesforce, The Complete History of CRM, https://www.salesforce.com/ap/hub/crm/the-complete-crm-history/, accessed March 30, 2020.

[15] Shah, H., "How Salesforce Built a $13 Billion Empire from a CRM", FYI Blog, https://usefyi.com/salesforce-history/, accessed March 29, 2020.

provider. It has expanded its repertoire to include finance and insurance, data analytics, inland logistics, cross-border and other related services. Maersk's objective is to have a suite of complete end-to-end services for retailers, manufacturers and other supply chain partners. The end-to-end solutions suite enables Maersk to unlock more value from global logistics operations compared to its traditional shipping revenues. Maersk's integrated suite of solutions also enables customers to have the advantage of a one-stop shop to access all their logistics needs, rather than searching for providers of each individual service.[16]

1.1.3 Lean Approach for Meeting Customer Needs: Nanonization of Customer Utility

The third key characteristic of successful XaaS offerings is their ability to unpack the utility that customers derive from their offerings across individual attributes, and over time. These customer needs are then met with matched offerings by the provider that are targeted specifically at those attributes, and at the right time. This lean matching of customer needs leads to a lower degree of waste, the lean matching is achieved by the targeted offering of solutions attributes towards specific customer needs. We refer to this lean matching of XaaS offerings by the unpacking of customer utility into individual attributes as the nanonization of customer utility. This entails two important steps: the unpacking of utility from individual attributes of the product or the bundled service set, and the unpacking of customer utility over time. Almost all airlines offered only full service to customers two decades ago, hence, customers were sold a consolidated ticket for their flight, and were offered seating on a first-come, first-served basis, meals and baggage services. Even if customers only carried handbags and did not want to consume the meal offered by the airline, they had to pay the standard ticket price. Budget airlines began recognizing that different customers had preferences for different service attributes. Some customers were interested only in flying to the destination, they did not need baggage services, seat

---

[16] Maersk, Logistics Solutions, https://www.maersk.com/logistics-solutions, accessed April 5, 2020.

selection and meals. Other customers would desire baggage services and travel insurance, but would not desire seat selection and meals. Budget airlines then separated the bundled services of flying to the destination along with baggage services, seat selection, travel insurance and meals to a set of individual standalone services that were offered in conjunction with the flying service. Customers could choose the elements of the service that they desired. The airline had to ensure that each standalone service was offered at a price point that provided positive customer surplus to the customer for the bundle elements that they chose.

The nanonization of the pricing mechanism with the utility offered by the provider is key. Providers of XaaS offerings use either the subscription or the pay-per-use mechanism for nanoizing the prices charged to customers. In the pay-per-use mechanism, customers only pay for the services that they use when they use them. In the subscription mechanism, customers pay for the right to use the services they need for a fixed period. While it is important for providers to ensure that customers attain more value than the price they pay, the provider should control the variable and fixed costs for offering each service element in the bundle. The variable cost of the additional services should be lower than the prices offered for those services, and the fixed costs must be controlled so that the XaaS offering is profitable for the provider. Hence, the nanonization of customer utility has to be done with twin objectives in mind: customers should derive more value than the price of each of the services, and the firm has to derive value by ensuring that the price of each service is higher than the costs of offering that service. In a product with multiple attributes or in a service bundle, providers integrate the costs of all components of the product or service and charge a consolidated price for the entire bundle. In this process of unpacking of utility, the budget airline should go over the design of each sub-element of the service in detail, to ensure that customers derive utility from those services, which should be offered profitably by the airline at the right price points. For instance, budget airlines must have doubtless considered whether they could charge customers for the right to board the plane earlier, or for using the washroom facilities as standalone services. Based on their analysis, the budget airlines decided (wisely) not to charge customers for these services. Services that did not add customer value had to be eliminated or redesigned. Similarly, service processes during the flight and value creators like seat width had to be redesigned to be aligned with the need for providing customer and firm value. This elemental analysis of the different attributes of the service is referred to as the nanonization of the utility attribute space.

While the process of nanonization of the utility attributes of the service is easier to understand, there is a concomitant need for managing the nanonization of the customer utility across time. Let us consider the example of Farming-as-a-Service (FaaS) provider, Trringo. Trringo is the largest services provider in India of agricultural equipment. It is a part of the Mahindra Group, which is one the largest industrial conglomerates in India.[17] Trringo began with offering the "Tractor-as-a-Service" concept to smallholders in India, the Mahindra group being the largest manufacturer of tractors in the country. While 45% of India's workforce is engaged in agriculture, the diffusion of tractors in India is still at a very low level of about 1 tractor per village on average. The obvious root cause is that tractors are expensive, and smallholders cannot afford the initial outlay for the farm equipment. Addressing this ground reality, Trringo has grown by leaps and bounds. Its offerings of tractors and mechanized farm equipment have grown dramatically through a distribution network of more than a hundred hubs from where the farming equipment can be rented. The offerings are organized as a franchise model, where Trringo franchisees lease tractors from Trringo at a fixed rental price, and Trringo maintains them.[18] The tractors are then offered to farmers on a pay-per-use basis, along with the driver. The excess profit over the rental price is retained by the franchisees. In this manner, Trringo increases the rural business activity in addition to the farm equipment available via the rental service offered by it.

---

[17] Sangwan, S., "Trringo — A First of Its Kind Tractor and Farm Equipment Rental Business", *Entrepreneurs Disrupt*, 14 March, 2017, http://bwdisrupt.businessworld.in/article/Trringo-A-First-of-Its-Kind-Tractor-and-Farm-Equipment-Rental-Business-/14-03-2017-114346/, accessed April 1, 2020.

[18] Bain, "Indian Farming's Next Big Moment: Farming as a Service", https://www.bain.com/contentassets/cb61f701eb1b4923bb41a8a70f04a290/report_indian_farmings_next_big_moment_-_farming_as_a_service.pdf, accessed April 1, 2020.

Trringo offers farmers the use of an entire suite of farm equipment, including tractors, reapers, cultivators and tillers.[19] While it can offer a one-stop shop of bundled services in a subscription model, Trringo chose to go down the path of offering individual standalone services like budget airlines, or the choice of a bundle. In addition to the nanonization of the utility attribute space, Trringo also exemplifies the unpacking of utility over time. Farmers in India typically plant and cultivate crops in their farms twice a year: the summer (kharif) crop, which is harvested in autumn, and the winter (rabi) crop, which is harvested in spring. Tractors are used for various parts of the agricultural process. For example, tractors can be used for soil cultivation before planting seeds, they can be attached to disc harrows for tilling, with a planter for seeding, or for clearing fields after the harvest.[20] Hence, tractors can be used on the farm for various activities throughout the farming process. In contrast, reapers are used only during the harvesting process. Similarly, disc harrows and planters are used only at specific times on a farm, hence, the demand for most farm equipment apart from tractors is very seasonal.

What impact does the seasonality of demand and hence seasonality of farmer utility of farm equipment like reapers, planters and disc harrows have on the farming-as-a-service offering? First, while reapers, tillers and disc harrows can be procured from each of the distribution hubs and used by farmers on a pay-per-use basis, there is a huge variability in the utilization of these equipment over the year. During the season before the planting, disc harrows will be in high demand from all farmers. After the tilling process, they will no longer be used for a period of 5–6 months. During the seeding time, planters will be in high demand, and then will not be used for the same duration. Reapers will be used only during the two harvesting periods every year. If the asset base at each distribution hub is fixed, to balance the temporary imbalance between demand and supply during the time the equipment is in demand, Trringo can potentially

---

[19] Singh, S. (2017). How Inclusive and Effective are Farm Machinery Rental Services in India? Case Studies from Punjab. *Indian Journal of Agricultural Economics*, 72(3), 230–250.

[20] Rostelmash, "Tillage equipment", https://en.rostselmash.com/uploads/product_media/546b3b627094dRSM_Versatile_Tillage.pdf, accessed April 1, 2020.

practice surge pricing, i.e., price the equipment high when the demand is high. This enables only those smallholders with high utility to use the equipment during those times, but farmer surplus would be lowered by surge pricing. Can Trringo think of other methods to manage the fixed seasonal assets to balance the needs of farmers with the seasonal use of equipment? The soil and climate in regional clusters are like each other, but they could be reasonably different for dispersed geographical locations. Could Trringo use a lower fixed asset base across all their hubs, and then transport equipment from one hub to another, when the demand at the first hub was over, and the demand at the second hub was about to start? In other words, Trringo could smooth demand for the equipment by studying the data of the patterns of usage of equipment at different points of time in different regions. It could then share equipment across regions with negatively correlated demand for that equipment. Another option for Trringo is to work in close partnership with farmers to practice crop rotation more frequently, this could also smooth demand for the equipment. However, Trringo would need to ensure that farmers also derive value from crop rotation.

The above examples demonstrate the challenges and the importance of the nanonization of customer utility across the attribute space and over time. Customers are heterogeneous in their preferences for service attributes and over time. When a firm is used to designing and building products, it tries to provide some form of utility to a large set of heterogeneous customers. However, individual customers may not need all the features of the product, nor do they necessarily need to use the product very often. Manufacturing products with many different features and functionalities tend to make products more expensive. Customers may choose not to buy complex and expensive products if they do not find the utility provided to be worth the price, or if they do not intend to use the product often. The implication is that customers would accept less functionality if the product would be significantly cheaper, and it could be offered at the time when the customer had a high utility for it. Having a nanonized view of the service attributes that customer's care for and the time when they have the highest utility for the functionality of the product would convert non-customers to customers in many cases. A careful consideration of heterogeneity in the preferences and time-based patterns of customer utility would enable the provider to create better value for customers and for itself.

1.1.4 Use of Technology for Creating Customer and Provider Value

Providers can use technology for enhancing customer value and their own operations and profitability in many ways. Customers have several touch-points with the provider in the service process, which can be identified by mapping the customer journey. The customer journey outlines all the interactions with the provider and then captures the experiences of the customer in these interactions — from awareness through post-sales support and repurchase. Depending on the design of the customer journey, the provider can have various online and offline touchpoints with the customer. The judicious use of technology at these touchpoints can enhance both the customer's experience and provide the firm with invaluable data to personalize the services for the customer. Both Panera Bread and Burger King interfaced with the customer for their coffee-as-a-service offering with an app. However, the monitoring of customer usage of the service can be done by offline methods as well. Indeed, providers often share a physical card with a date stamp with customers for the accrual of loyalty points. Each time that the customer accesses the service, the card gets physically stamped. The offline solution works as well as the app in terms of monitoring the usage of the service by the customer to ensure that the customer does not avail of the same service multiple times across different outlets. However, the role of the app in this case is not only monitoring the customer's usage of the subscription service. Panera Bread and Burger King can also get data about the customer's orders of food with the coffee, and the number of times that the customer visits outlets to redeem the service. This provides the chains with data about customer buying behaviour and the food orders they typically make. This automated data collection of customer behaviour can then be analyzed by AI algorithms and any patterns that customers exhibit in their ordering behaviour can be identified. These patterns can then be used to personalize suggestions for the customer on their next visit, or to share promotion details that customers could potentially be interested in. Trringo interacts with its customers via an app, a website and calling interfaces. Their app platform has won several awards like the IDC Digital Transformation Award. It helps Trringo in two-way communication: learning about customer demand, analyzing patterns of usage for different equipment, and in sharing information about their services with customers.

The technology interfaces also help the provider in making their own procurement and operating processes efficient, as the data from the app can be aggregated, and used for minimizing waste in procurement and operational processes. For Panera Bread and Burger King, the use of the app also alleviates the need to carry the physical card each time to the store. Physical assets like cards have other challenges: the need for replacement cards if they are lost, and loss of efficiency from checking if the customer has already availed of the allowed number of service offerings for the day. Hence, the judicious use of technology can help in digitizing the collection of data, the processing and analyzing of the data, and enhance the set of offerings for customers. The transformation of offline paper-based workflows into automated, digital work streams can eliminate most human intervention, improve the quality and reliability of the data, and also keep the customer informed of the services that they have availed. While billing for services, the app helps the customer to check if s/he availed of the service as often as stated in the bill. Data entry process automation can save invaluable time, for instance, in healthcare-as-a-service applications, doctors can scan past reports, prescriptions, drug allergies straight into the medical records of the patient. The automation applications are much easier if they are standardized across providers; indeed, the administrators of many global healthcare systems are working towards standardized interfaces for healthcare records.

In Salesforce's SaaS journey, one of the key elements of Salesforce's widespread acceptance was its ability to provide its customers with data of customer interaction history that became critical to its success. The decision-makers in most customer organizations of enterprise software adoption are the heads of the respective IT departments. They can either poll employees for usage data of the use of enterprise software systems, or they can get that data from the provider. By providing a periodic update of the use of its software by the employees of the customer, Salesforce was able to get buy-in from decision-makers by showing the degree of repeat access of the solution by the customer's employees. In addition, Salesforce provided customers with data about the use of the software by different departments of the customer organization. The cloud-based contact management of Salesforce enabled different functions within the customer to collaborate with each other. This data enabled IT heads of customer organizations to monitor internal collaboration. Finally, Salesforce enabled customers to create knowledge management systems for CRM by allowing their employees to share customer insights for key accounts.

The offering of hardware products in the service mode can also use technology effectively in enhancing the service process. MAN is a large manufacturer of buses, trucks and other mobility products in Germany, with a mix of product and service offerings. The service offerings are typically charged based on the pay-per-use model. Since the distance travelled is strictly verifiable on the odometer, MAN charges customers based on the distance they travelled.[21] The service contract also offered uptime guarantees, fuel efficiency enhancement and programs for driver training. MAN installed IoT-based sensing devices in their vehicles, which enabled them to conduct a holistic analysis of the interactions between the various systems in their vehicles with the operating conditions of the vehicles. This analysis helped them recommend best practices to their customers for the usage of their vehicles to improve fuel efficiency and reduce costs. The ongoing learning process was also incorporated by MAN in their design processes of the vehicles, enabling them to make better vehicles that would match the road and weather conditions, and driving patterns of their customers. In addition to the aggregated data that helped in recommending best practices for operation and design principles, MAN could also obtain personalized driving data for the operation of their vehicles. This personalized usage data enabled MAN to make individualized recommendations to drivers. For example, some drivers kept the engine running for extended periods of time after the vehicle stopped, leading to fuel efficiency loss. Other data like driver speeding behaviour were used by MAN in their driver training programs to hone their skills.

---

[21] Lyden, S., "Is Truck-as-a-Service the Future of Fleet Management?", *Field Service Digital*, June 28, 2016, https://fsd.servicemax.com/2016/06/28/truck-service-future-fleet-management/, accessed April 3, 2020.

1.1.5 Continuous Innovation Cycle

One of the most differentiating features of the XaaS offering is the relationship between the customer and the provider. In the productization model, the relationship between the customer and the provider is transactional, the interaction ends at the point of the delivery of the product. However, in the as-a-service offering, the customer has recurring usage of the service on the platform. While customer support is typically also offered in the productization model after the sale is made, the customer only contacts the provider when s/he finds defects and/or has operating issues with the product. If the warranty period is over, the provider is under no obligation to resolve any operating issues, and may charge for any additional service. In contrast, in the as-a-service offering, the provider and the customer have a continuing relationship. Hence, the knowledge of the customer's business context, operating conditions and business goals and practices is critical for the provider in designing subsequent services after the first offering. The relationship is key to the acquisition and retention of the customer, as if the provider does not solve pain points of the customer on an ongoing basis, the customer can vote with their feet at any point of time. The ideal benefit of the provider–customer relationship is the co-creation of additional services over time to benefit both parties.

After Salesforce had built a significant user base with its CRM service offering, it began offering further value to customers by adding other cloud-based solution components to its repertoire. The objective behind offering other services was to look for ways to nurture a growing ecosystem. Over time, Salesforce introduced the AppExchange platform, where third-party developers could create their own apps and sell them to other users within the Salesforce community. In 2006, Salesforce enhanced services in its ecosystem by releasing the on-demand programming language Apex, which allowed third-party programmers to write and run code on Salesforce's shared architecture.[22] In 2008, Salesforce released an

---

[22] Mycustomer, "Salesforce.com Announces Apex, the World's First On-Demand Programming Language and Platform", October 9, 2006, https://www.mycustomer.com/marketing/strategy/salesforcecom-announces-apex-the-worlds-first-on-demand-programming-language-and, accessed April 5, 2020.

official platform for developers called Force.com, as its first Platform-as-a-Service (PaaS) offering.[23] Force was one of the first PaaS-based services launched in the market. It allowed third parties to deploy apps on Salesforce's architecture. Additionally, it created a new revenue stream for Salesforce, as users of the platform were not necessarily CRM customers, but independent developers who used the platform for building software applications. Salesforce also expanded its core offerings beyond a CRM by acquiring other SaaS companies and remodelling their solutions to fit the company's suite of offerings. By offering more cloud services, it was able to cast a wider net and bring in more users into the Salesforce platform, adding to the attractiveness of its ecosystem. As the cloud grew, Salesforce saw more success. To showcase its continuous innovation and evolving suite of services, Salesforce launched an annual event for its customers called the Dreamforce conference.[24] At the Dreamforce conference, Salesforce set a tradition of announcing new products and ideas every year. The conference served a dual purpose in that it became the cornerstone on which the Salesforce community was grown, and existing customers retained. It also created the much-needed enthusiasm and buzz around the cloud concept.[25] While the early success of Salesforce attracted many competitors to launch their cloud businesses, Salesforce has continued to maintain market dominance as the incumbent by constantly reinventing itself.

The success of Salesforce is often attributed to its leadership position in CRM software; however, in addition to that offering, the SaaS mode of offering was critical for Salesforce's success in the early days. Its growth

---

[23] McCarthy, B., "A Brief History Of Salesforce.com: 1999–2020", SalesforceBen.com, March 13, 2020, https://www.salesforceben.com/brief-history-salesforce-com/, accessed April 7, 2020.

[24] ThomasNet, "Salesforce.com Announces Dreamforce 2007, the On-Demand Conference of the Year", May 30, 2007, https://news.thomasnet.com/companystory/salesforce-com-announces-dreamforce-2007-the-on-demand-conference-of-the-year-520467, accessed April 7, 2020.

[25] Michael Krigsman, Culture and customer loyalty: A Salesforce.com insider shares secrets to software success, ZDNet, December 5, 2019, https://www.zdnet.com/article/culture-and-customer-loyalty-a-salesforce-com-insider-shares-secrets-to-software-success/, accessed April 7, 2020.

strategy was driven by a two-pronged approach of introducing new services in the SaaS and PaaS domains. Salesforce continually spread its net wider by acquiring other companies to create an ecosystem that forged its dominance in the market. The viral marketing and network growth effect are due to the persistently evolving value proposition and Salesforce's extended commitment to making software more accessible. The evolution of the XaaS model from a solutions provider providing access to services without the need to install expensive assets to a model that uses usage data for continuous innovation has led to the "strategic partner" model for XaaS providers. The strategic partner enhances the competitiveness of its customers by integrating the customers' needs in its innovation process. The continuous evolution of the provider's services to enhance the customer's competitiveness leads to a long-term symbiotic relationship between the provider and the customer.

1.2 HISTORY OF XaaS

While Salesforce made the moniker of "as a service" offering popular, the first firm in modern times to use almost the entire set of characteristics of successful XaaS models in its business offerings was Xerox. Today, the brand name Xerox is literally synonymous with photocopying, to the extent that in many countries, customers use the term "Xerox copies" to mean photocopies. Xerox began as the Haloid Photographic Company. Its origins were in the manufacturing of photographic paper and equipment. It designed and developed its first photocopier in 1959 and called it the 914 copier, as the copier could copy sheets as large as 9 by 14 inches.[26] Given Xerox's expertise in paper processing because of its origins, Xerox's printer could print on plain paper, while competitors needed special paper supplies for photocopying. The competitors' models were using the complementary assets pricing model, where the base copier was sold for a modest $300. The competitors made higher margins on the special paper supplies that were marked up significantly (the razor and blade

---

[26] Mehta, S. N., "The office copier turns 50!", Fortune, January 22, 2010, https://archive.fortune.com/2010/01/21/technology/xerox_copiers.fortune/index.htm, accessed April 11, 2020.

model). The competitors' products were also slow even for that era — they had a capacity of making between 3–15 copies every hour. The 914 was a disruptive copier design that produced high quality images on plain paper, with a capacity of making 7 copies every minute.[27]

The catch was that the manufacturing cost of the copier was a princely sum of $2,000, but the need for consumables in the form of paper supplies was lower (consumables like toner were still needed for the 914). The high manufacturing cost created a problem for the commercialization of the technology. The copier had its advantages in the operating phase, but the capital expense of the product was very high. Most offices that used copiers were comfortable with the concept of slow copying, and utilized copiers only for important official copying. Most other documents were passed around hand to hand. The need for copying capacity at the speed of 7 copies per minute was unthinkable at that time, with critics questioning the need for copying so many pages in the first place. The economics of the product made its early diffusion hard. Xerox tried to get partners to market the new 914, but was turned down by Kodak, General Electric and IBM. IBM consulted with Arthur Little and Co., who concluded that while the copier was useful for specialized copying solutions, it was not a suitable product for offices, as the cost of the copier was too high given that offices typically made only a few hundred copies a month.

Xerox finally decided to market the copier itself, by offering it as a service. The terms of the service were that the monthly leasing cost was $95, and the cost to copy beyond the first 2,000 copies would be 4 cents for each copy. The contract for the service was designed cleverly, as most customers thought they would not go to the limit of 2,000 copies per month, given that their existing use was less than a third of that number. Xerox would provide maintenance services for the copier, and the lease could be terminated with a half-month's notice. While Xerox would recover the product's cost within the first two years of the leasing service, customers could also get access to higher copying capacities with lower operating expenses as the copier could print on plain paper. Xerox's bet

---

[27] Chesbrough, H. & Rosenbloom, R. S. (2002). The role of the business model in capturing value from innovation: evidence from Xerox Corporation's technology spin-off companies. *Industrial and corporate change*, 11(3), 529–555.

was that once customers were used to the lower inconvenience costs of printing on plain paper, they would not worry so much about the operating costs and would use the copier much more frequently. The bet turned out to be right; the demand for photocopying shot up dramatically, leading to a CAGR of 41% year-on-year for the 914. Xerox went from an enterprise with a few million dollars of revenue to a 2.5 billion $ enterprise in 1972.

Xerox had a monopoly on the copier market for more than a decade and went on to increase the capacity for photocopying dramatically in subsequent years. However, their foray into the copy-as-a-service model was interrupted by regulatory authorities. In 1972, the Federal Trade Commission (FTC) initiated an anti-trust motion against Xerox to break up its monopoly. Xerox settled with the FTC in 1975 to share its IP with competitors for a court mandated royalty. They had to offer the 914 for sale in addition to leasing it, and customers could buy consumables like toners as well as maintenance services from competitors.

Why did Xerox start the asset ownership transfer model for photocopiers? As they say, necessity is the mother of invention. Xerox adopted the "as a service" model as the cost of copier ownership for the customer was too high. Thus, the "sell the copy, not the copier" strategy was an outcome of the customer's budget constraint. Moreover, in addition to the hesitation in making a large investment in a copier machine, customers feared that the technology of the copier could evolve and change over the longer term. Hence, it made sense for them to lease the machine and replace it with a newer version when a new technology was available without the huge investment. Xerox offered other solutions like maintenance and servicing because they could charge customers 4 cents a copy beyond 2,000 copies a month. If the copier broke down, and stayed damaged for an extended period, Xerox would lose money as customers would not be able to make more than 2,000 copies a month. Hence, with the XaaS offering, Xerox aligned its own incentives with those of its customers; if the machine broke down frequently for long periods of time, the customer was inconvenienced and Xerox lost revenues. The biggest success of Xerox's model was the nanonization of the customer utility bet; its forecast that customers would make copies more often was the cornerstone of its offering. Customers derived a continuous utility from photocopying, and the utility of making copies was higher with the 914, as it used plain paper. Office managers did not need to worry about ordering specialized photographic paper. In terms of the customer profile, Xerox targeted large firms as its core market segment, as it felt that large copier machines installed in these firms would have high profit margins per unit. For large firms, the copier served as a pooled resource for a large set of office workers. Also, most of the larger offices did not care as much about the price of copying, while they did care about the need for 100% up-time on their machines. Soon, customers began making copies of documents for referencing and recording purposes, which they did not do earlier owing to the high cost of photocopying. The missing element of Xerox's copy-as-a-service offering was the lack of continuous innovation, as it did not need to invest in either at the time. Its product was so successful that it created a monopoly. While it used technology solutions to ascertain the number of copies being made, the design of the 914 and Xerox's offering stayed stable till 1972, when Xerox's monopoly was ended by the FTC.

What are the advantages of the leasing and servicing models in a monopoly? First, customers will have to make leasing payments in perpetuity to the provider, since customers are paying for the right to use the product. They will also not have the choice of switching products unless they have other options to break the monopoly. Hence, the revenue streams that Xerox accrued over the 13 years from 1959 to 1972 were more than three or four times the amount it would have made from selling the product at a reasonable margin (say with a price of $2500–$3000). Second, since Xerox also controlled the supply of consumables like toner, it controlled the ecosystem offering, and could potentially only offer the copying service as a bundle. While it is easier to make toner than the copier as the design is much simpler, owning the ecosystem by being a solutions provider acts as a barrier for entry to competitors. Xerox could potentially claim that any maintenance for offices who acquired external non-Xerox toners would not be covered by the maintenance contract, as the external toner was of lower quality. It is harder for competitors to reverse engineer leased machines, as the machines are only available at customer or franchise locations. Hence, leasing equipment is a better option than selling the equipment in a monopoly. The research consistently shows this to be the case for the above reasons.[28] We will compare productization and XaaS models in a competitive environment in Chapter 4 to investigate if leasing performs well in a competitive environment. We now summarize the early history of renting or leasing as a precursor to the XaaS offering.

1.2.1 Early History of XaaS

The early history of servitization can be traced back to the period of 2000 BC, when records of the leasing of agricultural land, equipment, cattle and water sources exist in ancient Sumer. Similarly, leasing laws are found in the laws of Hammurabi at the period of around 1760 BC. In Greek history, Aristotle made references to leasing, and there are also references to leasing in the records of the Roman Empire.[29] In more recent times, among the earliest firms to use leasing for offering services was Bell, the parent of AT&T. Bell introduced their telephone services in 1877 as a service, where the telephone unit was rented to customers along with the facility of calling services.[30] While leasing is just one element of the XaaS offering, it is critical as the maintenance of asset ownership with the provider has the advantage of customers being able to use the product, without committing to owning the product.

In the commercial sector, after Bell, one of the most well-known offerings using leasing was that of radios in the pre-World War 2 period, at a time when radios had the pride of place as a source of communication and public entertainment. Radio Rentals was a British firm that began operations in 1930 in Sussex. Since the cost of acquisition of radio sets was high in those days, Radio Rentals realized the appeal of renting rather than selling radio sets to customers. The budget impact of radio sets at the

---

[28] Balasubramanian, S., Bhattacharya, S., & Krishnan, V. V. (2015). Pricing information goods: A strategic analysis of the selling and pay-per-use mechanisms. *Marketing Science*, 34(2), 218–234.

[29] Elliott, J., "History of Equipment Leasing", Leaseworld.org, July 18, 2016, https://leaseworld.org/2016/07/18/history-of-equipment-leasing/, accessed April 15, 2020.

[30] Wikipedia, "Bell Telephone Company", https://en.wikipedia.org/wiki/Bell_Telephone_Company, accessed April 15, 2020.

time was high for most customers, and the market size for sold radio sets was limited. The rental model worked well for the firm, and by 1936, the firm was being traded publicly with over fifty thousand customers. Just like Xerox, one mainstay of Radio Rentals's model was its ability to integrate its offering with other elements of the ecosystem. The firm acquired Mains Radio Gramophone in 1945, which was a manufacturer of radio sets, leading to a vertically integrated offering with a reasonable payback time.[31] After two decades of operating as a renter of radios, Radio Rentals saw the potential of television sets replacing radios as the primary family source of communication and entertainment. The firm began renting television sets in 1953. It also manufactured the television sets itself, though it maintained its name as Radio Rentals. The model was hugely successful in the U.K. and Australia, as it was believed to be more efficient to rent a television that could eventually break down or run into problems than to buy it outright. As expected, maintenance services were bundled with the television set. From the customer's perspective, the rental model had notable advantages: the first of which was the high variety of television sets offered, the second advantage was that for price conscious customers, used television sets could be rented for lower prices. The monthly rent paid by users was either kept steady or reduced over time for the first few years, and customers willing to pay in advance were offered a discount. Perhaps the maintenance services contributed in a big way to the draw of the unit: the television sets would break down often, and faulty sets were repaired or replaced by Radio Rentals at no charge quickly. Knowing the importance of providing round-the-clock service, Radio Rentals maintained mobile vans stocked with spare parts in large cities. The firm still exists today but has merged since to be a part of Boxclever.[32]

The leasing model of yesteryear has morphed to the XaaS world today by adding many salient features to the leasing model. Although, the modern XaaS moniker has primarily been reserved for applications in cloud computing, the number of instances where products and integrated services are being offered using the XaaS mode has multiplied. We now

---

[31] Grace's guide to British Industrial History, Mains Radio Gramophone, https://www.gracesguide.co.uk/Mains_Radio_Gramophone, accessed April 15, 2020.

[32] Boxclever, "About Us", https://www.boxclever.co.uk/who-we-are, accessed April 15, 2020.

describe the characteristics of XaaS offerings in the IT, general product and integrated service domains.

1.2.2 IT Service Offerings Under XaaS

The IT offerings under the XaaS mode on the cloud have burgeoned beyond the original SaaS set of offerings (Figure 1.2 shows the range of completely in-house to completely outsourced solutions).[33] The most popular services in the IT domain in the XaaS mode are the SaaS, PaaS (platform-as-a-service) and IaaS (infrastructure-as-a-service) offerings. However, the list of IT offerings in the XaaS mode has been growing to include other service offerings such as Storage-as-a-Service (StaaS), Desktop-as-a-Service (PCaaS), Security-as-a-Service (SECaaS) and Disaster Recovery-as-a-Service (DRaaS). The list is endless, as firms can keep adding to the services they offer on the cloud. The cloud computing offering is one of the fastest growing ways of offering software services.

One of the distinctions between the IaaS, PaaS and SaaS offerings is the degree of outsourcing offered by the provider. In the SaaS offering, the

					Self-Managed
					Provider Supplied
Traditional On-Premises IT	Colocation	Hosting	IaaS	PaaS	SaaS
Data	Data	Data	Data	Data	Data
Application	Application	Application	Application	Application	Application
Databases	Databases	Databases	Databases	Databases	Databases
Operating System	Operating System	Operating System	Operating System	Operating System	Operating System
Visualization	Visualization	Visualization	Visualization	Visualization	Visualization
Physical Servers	Physical Servers	Physical Servers	Physical Servers	Physical Servers	Physical Servers
Network & Storage	Network & Storage	Network & Storage	Network & Storage	Network & Storage	Network & Storage
Data Centre	Data Centre	Data Centre	Data Centre	Data Centre	Data Centre

Figure 1.2:   Distinction between Cloud Computing Offerings

Source: Gartner https://www.zdnet.com/article/xaas-why-everything-is-now-a-service/.

---

[33] McLellan, C., "XaaS: Why 'everything' is now a service", ZDNet.com, November 1, 2017, https://www.zdnet.com/article/XaaS-why-everything-is-now-a-service/, accessed April 18, 2020.

firm may outsource its data storage as well to the SaaS provider, but for reasons of security, most firms prefer to manage their own data. However, all other services like the application itself, the databases and operating systems and other services are outsourced to the provider. In the PaaS model, the infrastructure, the operating system, and databases are out-sourced, but the application is hosted by the customer, the customer uses hardware and software tools from the provider. In the IaaS model, net-working, virtualization and storage are sourced from the provider, but the software component including databases and the operating system are hosted by the customer. For the IT-challenged reader, the traditional on-premises IT system is similar to owning your own home and all the furni-ture and fixtures, while the SaaS concept is akin to living in a hotel, the furniture and all other bells and whistles are owned by the hotel, you pay only based on your consumption of services. The IaaS and PaaS models are like renting your home but owning some of your furniture.

One of Amazon Web Services (AWS)'s most popular IaaS services is the Amazon Elastic Compute Cloud (EC2).[34] The elastic description comes from the ability of Amazon to scale the number of servers needed to support the customer on number-of-requests basis. For instance, if a fashion e-retailer uses AWS EC2 services for hosting their e-commerce website, at times of high traffic (number of visitors) at the website, AWS will add more servers in real time to make sure that the time to access the service (latency) for the customers of the e-retailer is low. At other times, when the traffic at the website is low, AWS will allocate a smaller number of servers to the e-retailer. The elasticity of the capacity offered to the customer means that the customer will only pay for the capacity that is needed at that point of time to manage instantaneous demand. The server capacity adjusts itself to the demand requirements.[35] Obviously, IaaS offerings are based on pooling economies, and when different firms in different sectors use the infrastruc-ture services, the demand of these services should likely be uncorrelated.

---

[34] Kardon, L., "An Introduction to Amazon EC2", Pagely, June 25, 2019, https://pagely.com/blog/amazon-ec2/, accessed April 20, 2020.

[35] Shpanya, A., "Three ways to optimize for Amazon's pricing strategy", Econsultancy, March 18, 2016, https://econsultancy.com/three-ways-to-optimize-for-amazon-s-pricing-strategy/, accessed April 21, 2020.

AWS can automatically allocate a higher number of servers to those customers who are experiencing high traffic, and a smaller number of servers for other customers. If servers are operating at different levels of utilization (ratio of demand to capacity), then smart IaaS systems should route new traffic to the server that has the maximum idle capacity, leading to fastest service. This enables IaaS providers to serve the needs of multiple customers with a limited server capacity.

The PaaS model is often used for integrating customized solutions with standardized solutions from providers, where the customized solution is hosted by the customer, and the standardized solution is hosted by the provider. Oracle provides an example of working with Cummins Engines on a PaaS solution for procurement.[36] Cummins had an ERP solution from Oracle, but needed a collaborative procurement platform for all their purchasing employees around the world to source large number of items together for quantity discounts in purchasing. The legacy systems of Cummins that managed the procurement process were different at different locations. Cummins was looking for an integrative platform to integrate all the data available at the locations, so that all local business leaders had access to the same information. Oracle worked with Cummins in creating a supplier information database with price and quantity quotations. Each part had a lot of information with technical specifications, all these datasets had to be uploaded in addition to the price and quantity information. The final output would enable the procurement managers of Cummins to negotiate with their suppliers on joint procurement, or separate procurement outcomes of groups of components coming from each supplier. Oracle worked with Cummins to streamline the request for quote (RFQ) process in the application that Cummins would host, and possibly integrate with Oracle's ERP system cloud offering for seamless operations.

In addition to the IaaS and PaaS offerings, the desktop-as-a-service model is getting more and more popular for enterprises. Rather than buying office computers for individual use, enterprises prefer to use the PCaaS option (PC or desktop-as-a-service). Enterprises can contract for

---

[36] Duane Erautt, Platform as a Service (PaaS): Key Benefits and a Case Study, CSS, Feb 1, 2020, https://cssus.com/news/platform-as-a-service-paas-key-benefits-and-a-case-study/, accessed April 21, 2020.

getting office computers for all their personnel at a lower price, and not have to worry about obsolescence if the next generation of processors is introduced. Disaster Recovery-as-a-Service (DRaaS) is also getting increasingly popular. This service is a risk mitigation offering that protects the customer's data and insures the specific utility from the application in the event of disruption from an external event. External events may be caused by natural disasters, or an intended hacking or cybercriminal event. Providing backup in the event of a disaster allows the business to operate smoothly even if unforeseen events occur and is an important part of enabling business continuity planning (BCP). For instance, in June 2017, Maersk's global operations were badly affected when a cyberattack organized by Petya hacked into Maersk's IT assets around the world, causing major disruption to Maersk's operations.[37] Large firms are usually targeted by cybercriminals with ransomware, in this case, the hard drives of all the computers were encrypted. The DRaaS option ensures business continuity in the event of such outages.

1.2.3 Product Offerings Under XaaS

The name "everything as a service" is broad enough for the inclusion of other services as well. Buoyed by the success of the XaaS offerings in the IT sector, many providers offer other kinds of services with physical assets. A well-known offering is the concept of space-as-a-service that has been pioneered by firms like WeWork (the residential offering of WeWork is WeLive). WeWork is a provider of commercial and office spaces, and WeLive is a provider of residential spaces. The offerings of both firms are similar: WeWork brands itself as the workspace of the future, with flexible workspaces that are based on the principle of co-working and networking. WeWork's app uses skill-based profiles to match co-workers in a given space to maximize networking.[38] One of the key differences between

[37] Greenberg A., "The Untold Story of NotPetya, the Most Devastating Cyberattack in History", Wired 22 August, 2018, https://www.wired.com/story/notpetya-cyberattack-ukraine-russia-code-crashed-the-world/, accessed April 23, 2020.

[38] Zeitlin, M., "Why WeWork went wrong", *The Guardian*, 20 December 2019, https://www.theguardian.com/business/2019/dec/20/why-wework-went-wrong, accessed April

leasing and XaaS is the offering of flexible on-demand services by XaaS; WeWork's tenants do not need to pay for pre-specified long-term leases. In fact, landlords often lease out units to WeWork, and WeWork obtains tenants for the space. This model mitigates the demand risk of the landlord from having to acquire tenants directly. One of the key offerings of WeWork to landlords is the aggregation of demand. In the leasing model, the lessor typically provided a pre-specified term of the lease in the contract with concomitant penalty clauses for breaking the lease early.[39] In contrast, in the housing-as-a-service or the space-as-a-service model, the flexibility offered in terms of the duration of commitment on the part of the lessee is even higher. The lessee effectively adopts the pay-per-use model in contrast to the subscription model of leasing. It goes without saying that the risk of getting enough lessees to fill up their working spaces lies with WeWork, if WeWork cannot get enough demand, then their financial model has a high amount of risk. The space-as-a-service offering has similar risks to hotels and airlines: a single unfilled office seat represents lost revenue for the given day. However, WeWork has not used yield pricing yet, like airlines and hotels to balance capacity and demand.

A second key difference is the degree of agility, innovation and responsiveness provided in the Office-as-a-Service model: WeWork uses the data from their app in terms of the usage of their space to continuously innovate on the suite of services offered to make the co-working experience more meaningful. In addition to the office spaces, WeWork also offers other associated services like cafes and canteens, community spaces to foster innovation, and partnership opportunities with other local firms. The degree of flexibility offered by WeWork is based on four primary models: hot desks for short-term on-demand use; dedicated desks for dedicated firms, so that co-workers belong to the same organization; private office spaces that are equipped with accessories like furniture and can accommodate different team sizes; and customized build-outs, where firms using the spaces can have conference facilities, laboratories and

---

25, 2020.

[39] Sen, C., "The Pandemic Should Be WeWork's Moment", Bloomberg Business, September 15, 2020, https://www.bloomberg.com/opinion/articles/2020-09-15/wework-was-built-for-post-coronavirus-flexible-work-demands, accessed October 1, 2020.

other customized features. WeWork's space-as-a-service model has been heavily scrutinized recently, and its stakeholders have scrutinized the operating model closely over the last two years. We will analyze WeWork's offering in Chapter 4 with the BROAD FENCES model that will be developed later in this book and provide recommendations for WeWork's operating model.

In the Furniture-as-a-Service set of offerings, IKEA is one of the biggest players in the furniture market who announced their foray into the as-a-service market last year. IKEA's motivations include making their offerings more affordable for customers, increasing the convenience factor for moving, and using the circular economy in the furniture market.[40] Ahrend also uses the furniture-as-a-service model to create a sharing platform for office furniture solutions.[41] In designing their furniture solutions, Ahrend uses modularity, easy assembly and disassembly as their design values. Hence, repair, refurbishing and reuse of their office furniture extends the lifecycle of the materials.[42] Ahrend also works closely with its suppliers. The design of any line of furniture products begins with design meetings with suppliers so that common design values are adhered to.

The office furniture market is predicted to reach a hundred billion dollars globally in 5 years, hence, the value derived for individual stakeholders has been analyzed closely. One of the main value additions of the furniture-as-a-service offering is the reuse of materials: a lot of metal, plastic, wood and filling is used in furniture. Traditionally, about 80–90% of furniture material is wasted, as furniture is disposed even when it is of usable quality. From the customer's perspective, there is a huge mobility consideration for young firms, just like mobility is an important

---

[40] Thomasson, E., "IKEA to test furniture rental in 30 countries", Reuters, April 3, 2019, https://www.reuters.com/article/us-ikea-sustainability-idUSKCN1RF0WY, accessed May 1, 2020.

[41] Ellen MacArthur Foundation, "Bringing office furniture full circle", https://www.ellenmacarthurfoundation.org/case-studies/bringing-office-furniture-full-circle, accessed May 1, 2020.

[42] Robotis, A., Bhattacharya, S., & Van Wassenhove, L. N. (2005). The effect of remanufacturing on procurement decisions for resellers in secondary markets. *European Journal of Operational Research*, 163(3), 688–705.

consideration for young individuals. Start-ups are typically constrained for funds, and depending on the funding cycle, the office space needed, the number of employees and the funds available vary dramatically. With resource constraints, it does not make sense for young firms to invest a large amount into office furniture and décor; it may also not send the right message to investors. Ahrend wants to promote responsible office furnishing practices. Its model is that firms that want to exit their current office furniture contract can return their used furniture to Ahrend at any point of time. It will refurbish and reuse the furniture, reupholster sofas and other soft furniture, and offer these furniture pieces to other customers. Ahrend has worked with organizations like KLM to reuse old furniture seat material for table-top resurfacing. The furniture-as-a-service model promotes the circular economy, helps in reducing the contribution of used furniture to landfills, and creates economic value for young organizations. The customer pays for the period that they use the furniture and payments are typically collected on a monthly basis. Hence, furniture can be added or returned based on monthly staffing changes. Maintenance services are included in the contract, via a QR code which is tracked by Ahrend. Ahrend also works closely with customers by visiting them every two years and can change the furniture depending on the customer needs. It also has a database that tracks furniture quality at every visit, so that furniture reuse can be planned. A study by the MacArthur Foundation estimates that Ahrend may have saved over 4,000 tonnes of materials by using their circular economy design principles. The firm's profitability by increasing the lifecycle of furniture is also higher, as they get payments from customers in perpetuity with a lower cost base from reusing furniture.

The circular economy model in use by Ahrend shows another advantage of the asset ownership transfer model: the higher potential for using the circular economy for lowering costs from shared assets. In general, for technology-based systems, the system advances are dictated by some limited core technologies like processors and specific components like RAM memories. Most other parts of the technology-based systems are durable with longer lifecycles. Maintaining the ownership of the core assets enables providers to reuse components, leading to lower costs with higher environmental benefits. Xerox has always had a high degree of circular economy use, as only parts of the copier that enable mechanical movement need replacement. However, casings and durable components can be used from one generation of machines to the next, and materials used in short lifecycle components can be recycled to make new components.[43] The circular economy benefits of XaaS offerings that are enabled by asset ownership transfer can be one more source of sustainable competitive advantage.[44]

In the logistics space, providers have created an entire suite of on-demand services like Logistics-as-a-Service, Transport-as-a-Service and Warehousing-as-a-Service. The move towards 3rd party logistics (3PL) and 4PL meant that manufacturing firms were searching for solutions where they could focus on core activities like design and manufacturing. Some customers still prefer an integrated model where they can design their own complementarities, e.g., Walmart has an integrated logistics system to manage their just-in-time deliveries from manufacturers.[45] Other firms have realized that having a best-in-class logistics capability needs a high scale, and 3PL and 4PL providers achieve that scale by offering logistics services to a large number of customers. In the logistics space, Volvo has been one of the manufacturers who has been engaging in the autonomous truck development race. Volvo has struck a deal with Bronnoy Kalk AS, which is a mining major in Norway, to offer six fully autonomous trucks.[46] The trucks will operate in a secluded area between the mine and the stone crushing area that are separated by 3 miles. Tests have been concluded and services will be offered from this year (2021). Volvo will own the trucks and offer them to Bronnoy Kalk under a "per

---

[43] Bhattacharya, S., Guide Jr, V. D. R., & Van Wassenhove, L. N. (2006). Optimal order quantities with remanufacturing across new product generations. *Production and Operations Management*, 15(3), 421–431.

[44] Bhattacharya, S., Robotis, A., & Van Wassenhove, L. N. (2019). Installed base management versus selling in monopolistic and competitive environments. *European Journal of Operational Research*, 273(2), 596–607.

[45] Robinson, A., "Walmart: 3 Keys to Successful Supply Chain Management any Business Can Follow", Cerasis, https://cerasis.com/supply-chain-management/, accessed May 1, 2020.

[46] MacDuff, A., "Breaking new ground" Volvo Trucks, January 30, 2019, https://www.volvotrucks.my/en-my/news/magazine-online/2019/feb/bronnoy.html, accessed May 1, 2020.

ton" of limestone delivered contract from the mine to the stone crusher. While mobility companies have offered their services on a per-km traversed basis, this will be the first instance where the provider of autonomous trucks will be charging the customer based on the cargo delivered. The motivations for Volvo are like those of other XaaS providers: customers are wary of paying high upfront costs for acquiring assets, along with the associated costs of hiring qualified drivers and maintenance costs. By collaborating with Bronnoy Kalk on an output-driven metric, Volvo is using the XaaS model to charge the customer based on the value created for the customer. The XaaS offering mode is also a way for Volvo to test its autonomous trucks' performance, as the operations will be in a limited area with limited risk in the form of human traffic. Autonomous vehicles need significant amounts of training data for their self-driving algorithms to be refined, and this collaboration with Bronnoy Kalk could help Volvo test its autonomous trucks' commercial readiness. The data generated could also be invaluable in providing a test case for scaling the autonomous trucking business for Volvo, as the global autonomous road cargo business could hit a billion dollars by the end of the year.

1.3   OVERVIEW OF THIS BOOK

The intent of this book is twofold: to provide an overview to the reader of what makes XaaS offerings attractive, and how to design and grow XaaS-based offerings. XaaS offerings have different value propositions and different economic value for the customer and methods of value extraction for the provider compared to firms using the productization model. While the nomenclature of these offerings has originated from IT applications, as we see from the various hardware applications, these offerings are not limited to the IT context. This book aims to adopt a unified framework across different application domains to seek a better understanding of as-a-service offerings. We draw ideas and techniques from our own research as well as other researchers in the academic and practice domains to create this unified framework.

The XaaS model has a number of USPs that have been mentioned in this chapter: the asset ownership transfer from the customer to the provider, the change in the provider's strategy from a one-size-fits-all productization strategy to a solutions provider strategy with built-in customer choice, the nanonization of the customer's utility over attribute space and time with concomitant pricing design choices, the use of technology for enhancing customer and provider value, and a commitment to continuous innovation to creating value for the customer and the provider. While these are broad, overarching themes of XaaS offerings, we will do a deep dive into each of these themes to provide examples and design principles of how providers can achieve success in these broad themes. The book will provide a "How to" guide to design and develop successful XaaS offerings, and then grow them over time. The book endeavours to offer entrepreneurs and leaders of firms intending to offer XaaS offerings with a toolkit to assess and ideate about the design of their offerings. The book will also provide a toolkit for existing XaaS providers to grow their offerings. The "How to" toolkit is divided into parts: we first develop a model of the various ingredients of successful XaaS offerings at the micro-operational level, we call this model the BROAD FENCES model. The design, development and growth model will focus on different elements of the micro success factors at different points of time in the XaaS offering diffusion process. The FPG (Feasibility, Profitability, Growth) model will describe the sequential focus of providers on different micro elements of the XaaS offering over the service lifecycle. The FPG model will be summarized in the XaaS Staircase as a tool for easy visualization of the design, development and assessment of XaaS offerings.

The remainder of the book is organized as follows. In Chapter 2, we will do a deep dive into the customer perspective on XaaS offerings. We will start with an overall customer utility model that dissects the value of the offering for the customer and deconstructs the utility into different parts that measure customer value in the service attribute space and over time. The nanonization of the service offering to be lean will be evaluated from the viewpoint of the customer, along with the implications of the asset ownership transfer model. The XaaS offering may not be suitable for all customers as noted in this chapter. Many customers still prefer to own their assets for products, software and services offerings. The characteristics of customer segments who would be interested in XaaS offerings will be elucidated in this chapter as well, along with the benefits of risk sharing between the provider and customer, and a description of residual risks of the XaaS offerings. Customer utility from the one-stop shop model of the solutions provider will be analyzed, along with the advantages of technology use and the ability to keep pace with technology advancements using the XaaS model.

XaaS offerings are usually offered either through subscriptions for unlimited or limited use during a certain period, or through performance-based contracts (output driven contracts), or via usage-based contracts (actual metered use of services). Each of these different modes of offering the as-a-service concept has their advantages and disadvantages. We will start with the motivations of pricing and contracting in Chapter 3 and then delineate when to use each of these pricing schemes. The concept of verifiability of a measure will be introduced, along with technology metering solutions that enable the verifiability of measures that can be included in contracts. We will highlight some typical XaaS contracts that are used in practice and assess the risk division of these contracts between the provider and the customer. We will conclude Chapter 3 by identifying good contract designs that enable close and continuous relationship building and strategic partnership between the provider and the customer.

No provider works as an island. It always needs to have vendors of components and resellers to aid in the delivery of its XaaS offerings. Design and operating principles of XaaS offerings must be adopted by partners as well, and risks must be shared by partners for impactful delivery. In Chapter 4, we will identify the best practices for providers to work with partners in the design and delivery of their offerings. We will also revisit the success factors of XaaS offerings from the provider's perspective and demonstrate how providers can work with partners and customers to offer shared value to all parties. The element of competition gives customers a choice in the adoption of as-a-service offerings and it significantly changes the trade-offs for providers in the solutions to be offered, and pricing and contract models. We will outline steps needed for as-a-service offerings to adjust to competition by suggesting competitive strategies in contrast to operating as a monopolist.[47] While the customer also

---

[47] Bhattacharya, S., Krishnan, V., & Mahajan, V. (1998). Managing new product definition in highly dynamic environments. *Management Science*, 44(11-part-2), S50–S64.

values sustainability from a societal awareness perspective, providers can gain economies of scale and environmental benefits from using design principles for reuse and leveraging the circular economy in their offerings. Hence, this chapter will also add insights into provider strategies for taking advantage of the circular economy in enhancing the value for customers and lowering their own cost base. Based on the analysis of customer perspectives, pricing and contracts and provider attributes, we will develop the BROAD FENCES model in Chapter 4. Further, we will suggest methods for providers to use individual drivers of the BROAD FENCES model to enhance their offerings for the customer and for themselves. To illustrate the use of the model, we will take a case study approach and exemplify the use of the BROAD FENCES model with the case studies. The sequential focus on the different elements of the BROAD FENCES model will be then discussed in the FPG model and we will propose principles for enhancing the growth of XaaS offerings using the FPG model. Finally, we have developed a visualization tool called the XaaS Staircase for the easy visualization of the application of the FPG model. The FPG model and the XaaS Staircase will be illustrated with case studies in Chapter 4.

While providers may adopt some of the five characteristics of firms with successful XaaS models, our research shows that the organization structure of the firm plays a critical role in successfully achieving these five characteristics. In Chapter 5, we will highlight the characteristics of high-performing organizations in achieving the XaaS success factors. We will begin with a description of the research on processes and process characteristics that align different organizational structures with different firm strategies. We will contrast the organizational structure of firms that adopt a differentiation strategy with those that adopt a focused strategy. The implications of the distinction will be discussed, and we will outline why neither pure differentiation nor pure standardization is suitable for XaaS offerings. Successful organizations mix elements of both these organizations along with other changes to deliver high performance. We will showcase successful organization structures, and then share best practices for rewards systems and process design from the mix of these structures. We will also highlight the role of lowered complexity and hierarchy in organizational structures and posit that the move to flat structures with rich information sharing and an alignment of the different elements of the XaaS offerings is the right solution.

While organizational structures are the hardware of aligning the business strategy, internal structure and XaaS offerings, the software in the form of people skills and organization culture is equally important for impactful as-a-service offerings. Chapter 6 will outline the people skills needed for agile service offerings and provide recommendations for developing these skills internally. The needs of a proactive organizational culture and promoting a role mobility orientation will be discussed. People skills can be again divided into hard (functional) and soft (behavioural skills), we will identify ways for assessing and developing these skills. The research has found extensively that resistance to change is an important inhibitor of agility. Developing the ability for rapid iteration and experimentation among one's employees is critically important for continued growth. We will suggest ways of growing the ability to experiment, iterate, and conclude with a discussion of the needs and approaches for growing an entrepreneurial and collaborative mindset in the organization.

Chapters 7, 8 and 9 will provide illustrative case studies of the BROAD FENCES and FPG models along with their visualization with the XaaS Staircase in different industry sectors. Chapter 7 will highlight the application of our toolkit to the offerings from the world of products, while in Chapter 8, we will analyze the set of IT offerings using the XaaS model. It is probably the easiest to achieve economies of scale for XaaS offerings in the IT sector, thereby enabling rapid business growth. However, there has been a mixed bag of results for XaaS offerings in the IT sector as well. We will showcase some best practices for achieving the XaaS success factors by analyzing the results of all our case studies at the aggregate level. Chapter 9 will adopt a similar approach to analyze unbundled services offerings and delineate best practices for service-offering firms who are considering using the XaaS model for providing a broader degree of consumer choice. We will summarize the best practices for each sector at the end of the chapter.

Chapter 10 will conclude the book with a brief discussion first of the theory of the firm, the reasons for the firm's operations and its existence and boundaries as posited by Coase in his seminal work on the theory of the firm. We will place the XaaS offering in the context of this theory, and at a micro level, demonstrate how the XaaS model changes the role of the firm (provider), its boundaries and relationships with partners. The XaaS success factors will be revisited from the firm's and customer's perspectives, and the growth potential of these business models across industries will be assessed. Finally, we will share some of our forecasts for the growth of XaaS models in different industry sectors.

Chapter 2

The Customer Perspective on XaaS

In this chapter, we start by developing a unified framework of customer choice between the XaaS and productization (selling products) modes of firm offerings. In creating this unified framework, we have drawn from the practitioner and academic research from different fields like computer science and IT, economics, marketing, strategy, finance, accounting and operations management. IT professionals will be familiar with the concepts of network congestion and data security from shared services. Economists will recognize the grounding principles of utility theory, and accounting professionals will be well-versed with the trade-offs between the capital expenses (capex) and operating expenses (opex) models. Our approach is largely indifferent to the domain of application: the customer choice model should be applicable across the gamut of IT applications, products and services. We believe that the unified framework of customer choice is a good starting point, as informed customers make their decisions taking all these factors into account, rather than thinking from a siloed perspective.

What are the factors that customers consider when they decide to buy or lease products, services and software? Looking at individual decision-making perspectives into the mode of access of these assets can provide valuable insights into the customer perspective on XaaS offerings. The leasing business is the precursor to the servitization model, as ownership is maintained by the lessor, but income and utility from any asset accrues to the lessee, and in return, the lessee pays the leasing fee. Read any book or article on the subject, and the answers to these questions always start with "It depends", leading to the nuanced thoughts in conventional wisdom on leasing versus buying. For instance, the earliest leased assets like agricultural land had a mix of ownership models, with some farmers owning their farms and transferring them to the next generation. Other farmers leased the land and paid leasing fees. Farming has traditionally been a family profession, and most early documents on both practices had a marked preference for ownership. If you chose to lease the farm and continued farming activities for generations, you would potentially be paying leasing fees on it in perpetuity. If the leasing fee was tied to the output of the farm, and the output was observable and verifiable (clear measures of the output could be checked by both the lessee and the lessor), then any risk attached to the output could be shared between the lessor and the lessee. If, however, the leasing fee were fixed, then the risk arising from any variability of the output of the farm would be borne by the lessee only, regardless of whether s/he owned the farm or was leasing it.

The decision of home ownership versus leasing or renting is more complex and emotional.[1] Home ownership provides the owner with access to growth in the underlying asset value, as any increase in real estate prices accrue to the homeowner. Conversely, the homeowner also faces the risk of property prices depleting if the region has an economic downturn. The homeowner does need to have access to the capital needed to purchase the home, so associated attributes like creditworthiness and the budget for the down payment are prerequisites for purchasing the home. Payments made on mortgages contribute partially towards increasing the home equity of the owner. From the financial perspective, home ownership provides the homeowner with potential tax deductions for the mortgage, but also exposes the owner to property taxes depending on the location of the home. The homeowner is also responsible for the upkeep and maintenance of the home; depending on the condition of the home, the cost of maintenance, insurance and renovation can be significant. From an emotional perspective, home ownership enables a person to put down roots in a region, make changes to the home that reflects the family's tastes and lifestyle, while leasing restricts the customization of the home to the owner's taste. Home

---

[1]Hoffman, W., "Renting vs owning: 4 headaches of homeownership", *AsiaOne Money*, February 28, 2020, https://www.asiaone.com/money/renting-vs-owning-4-headaches-homeownership, accessed May 4, 2020.

ownership also gives the owner a sense of security, stability, the sense of belonging to a community and good old-fashioned social status.

Conversely, leasing the home makes it easier to switch homes and jobs, as the lessee has a limited term of lease, and hence, moving is much easier. The benefit of not being locked into an illiquid investment like real estate enables lessees to be more mobile in their career prospects. Unlike the budgetary requirements for home ownership like the down payment, the credit history requirements for leasing are much less daunting. The lessee does not increase his/her equity from rental payments, and there is no appreciation of property prices that accrues to the lessee. However, the lessee has the advantage that they have a fixed payment to make every month without any variability dictated by fluctuating mortgage rates. While homeowners are exposed to maintenance and upkeep costs, the lessee is covered from maintenance risk, as the landlord is expected to bear all the maintenance costs. The lessee does not get tax benefits or costs as well, as rents are not tax deductible, though at the same time, there is no property tax exposure for lessees. The cost of renter's insurance, if any, is usually included in the rent, making the payments for the lessee much more predictable. The risk of property value increases in the region works in the opposite direction for the lessee as compared to the homeowner. When property prices in the region increase, home ownership is more attractive as capital gains accrue to the homeowner, while they increase the potential rent to be paid by the lessee for the next term of lease. Finally, the issue of transaction costs favour the lessee: homeowners pay significant costs for executing the transactions of buying (and selling) their homes, these costs can be to the tune of 2–10% depending on the country or region of residence. The transaction costs for lessees are significantly lower, as the cost of certifying rental contracts is much lower than the cost of stamp duty and the like.

How do most people resolve this dilemma? There is a marked tendency to favour home ownership especially for individuals who intend to reside in a region for a longer term. Conversely, individuals with careers that are more mobile and who stay in one place for shorter periods of time seem to favour leasing.[2] There are many financial arguments to be made

---

[2] Kneuven, L., "8 reasons why buying a house is better than renting, according to people who have done it", *Business Insider*, August 30, 2019, https://www.businessinsider.com/personal-finance/why-buying-a-home-is-better-than-renting, accessed May 6, 2020.

on both sides of the divide. However, the emotional benefits of home ownership seem to outweigh the gains from moving easily to another residence and region, especially for individuals with a long-term horizon.

The purchase or lease of cars is another interesting decision. The leasing of cars has grown significantly over the last few decades. While car ownership also has similar issues to home ownership in terms of the budget effect (making the down payment on the car and monthly payments if the car is bought on a loan) and increasing asset equity, there are a number of other issues that are highlighted in owning or leasing a vehicle. A vehicle owner uses the same vehicle over its lifetime, the performance of the vehicle degrades over time, leading to more frequent maintenance requirements over time. In contrast, a vehicle lessee has a fixed term for the usage of the vehicle and can hence switch to leasing a new car with potentially higher performance. Products like cars exhibit performance improvements from technology improvements in components like engines, as well as manufacturing technologies, leading to lowered costs of providing the same level of performance. From the financial perspective, the vehicle owner is responsible for sourcing his/her own maintenance, insurance and repair services, while the lessee typically gets all his/her financial components lumped into one single payment. This results in the total cost of ownership (TCO) to be lower for purchased vehicles than leased vehicles, especially for larger fleets, as individual components like insurance and financing can be sourced more cheaply.[3] There will be a premium charged by the lessor for the one-stop solution in leasing, however, the transaction and administrative costs for the lessee are lower.[4] The monthly lease payments for the lessee may also be lower than the monthly loan payments of the car owner, depending on the term of the car ownership loan. While the lessee has to return the car at the end of the lease term if the lease is an operating lease, the lessee has the option of purchasing

---

[3] Rotary Lift, "Leasing vs. Buying: The Advantages Depend on Your Fleet Size", *Rotary*, January 11, 2018, https://blog.rotarylift.com/leasing-vs.-buying-the-advantages-depend-on-your-fleet-size#:~:text=In%20general%2C%20fleets%20of%20more,fleet%20instead%20of%20lease%20it.&text=This%20may%20come%20as%20a,with%20fleets%20in%20that%20range, accessed May 7, 2020.

[4] Clark, J., "Is it smarter to buy or lease a car?", https://auto.howstuffworks.com/buying-selling/buy-or-lease.htm, accessed May 7, 2020.

the vehicle at a pre-specified contractually agreed price if the lease is a capital lease, mimicking the effects of car ownership. Effectively, the capital lease mechanism provides the lessee with the option of switching to car ownership at the end of the term if s/he so desires, the price premium for the leasing option can be interpreted as the option price for this flexibility.

From the financial perspective, if the car is also used for business purposes, then the lease can be deducted as a business expense, while, in the case of car ownership, the value of the car can be depreciated. So there are financial benefits to both leasing and purchasing. If the lease for the car has a dual tariff structure, where the lessee can drive the car up to a pre-specified maximum (usually 10,000–15,000 miles) annually, then the lease payments can pile up for vehicle users who drive a lot, compared to those who own their vehicle. Hence, the decision to buy or lease also depends on the pricing model being offered. Next, one of the big unknowns in vehicle acquisition is the quality and the reliability of the vehicle. This is not as important a question in the acquisition of a new vehicle but is of paramount importance in the acquisition of a used vehicle. There is substantial research to show that the possibility of purchasing a "lemon" often is the critical driver to the decision to lease the vehicle.[5] Leasing exposes the lessee to a substantially lower degree of quality risk than the decision to purchase the car.[6] While there are a number of services like mechanics and organizations like Auto Lemon Detectors who can provide inspection services to grade the quality of a used car, the quality risk of purchasing a used car is still significant.[7] The leasing option provides an important mitigating factor to quality risk. Finally, while owned cars can be customized in many ways including enhanced aesthetic and performance attributes, leased cars have specified contractual clauses that limit the ability of the lessee in customizing the car.

---

[5] Johnson, J. P. & Waldman, M. (2003). Leasing, lemons, and buybacks. *RAND Journal of Economics*, 247–265.

[6] Johnson, J. P., Schneider, H. S., & Waldman, M. (2014). The role and growth of new-car leasing: Theory and evidence. *The Journal of Law and Economics*, 57(3), 665–698.

[7] Auto Lemon Detectors, "Lemon Busters", https://autolemondetectors.org/, accessed May 7, 2020.

We now analyze the offerings of HaaS (housing-as-a-service) and CaaS (car-as-a-service) to understand the customer perspective on XaaS offerings beyond the benefit of asset ownership transfer that leasing provides. In the Housing-as-a-Service (HaaS) domain, WeLive adopts a similar co-living principle as its counterpart WeWork in the office space domain. One of the key reasons for the growth of co-living is that you can get access to facilities you would want to use, but not want to own.[8] The co-living facilities are primarily private bedrooms in upscale dormitories with common facilities like living rooms, kitchens, gyms and utility rooms. The model is like the old-fashioned "roommate" arrangement in a university dormitory, however, key features such as connectivity, cleaning services and social events are also offered. The bedrooms can either be furnished or unfurnished, and flexible terms of contract vary from short-term on-demand models to longer horizons. WeLive interacts with the customer set using an app, which measures the usage of the facilities, and repairs and other services are billed through the app. The primary market segment of WeLive is the large set of younger millennials working in the technology sector, as they have a higher need for housing mobility. Firms with similar HaaS offerings include Startcity, Common and Quarters, all of whom have similar living arrangements, and they use technology to enhance the customer interface.

What makes individuals pick the HaaS model as their residential choice?[9] One factor in favour of the HaaS model is the budget effect: housing prices have been growing faster than wages in many large cities globally, especially in cities with booming economies. The emotional aspects of home ownership like starting a family and putting down their roots in a region do not appeal to the demographic picking the HaaS choice. The constituents of this market segment are typically single, and are likely to move quickly, as they are mobile in their careers. Given their

[8] Hansen-Bundy, B., "A Week Inside WeLive, the Utopian Apartment Complex That Wants to Disrupt City Living", GQ, February 27, 2018, https://www.gq.com/story/inside-welive, accessed May 8, 2020.

[9] Jacobs, H., "Inside WeWork's WeLive, where millennials squeeze into tiny apartments to take advantage of perks like Sunday dinner, daily happy hours, and morning yoga", *Business Insider*, December 20, 2017, https://www.businessinsider.com/wework-welive-wall-street-co-living-photos-tour, accessed May 8, 2020.

lack of a family structure, the social interaction opportunities afforded by the co-living model are more attractive to this demographic. While living with roommates can offer a similar experience, sharing rooms requires informal social contracts of shared cleaning and cooking duties. In WeLive and other similar firms, these services are provided as add-ons or in the basic contract, reducing the need for enforcing informal social contracts. Billing through the app is an added utility, as lessees do not need to worry about mundane things like getting coins for their laundry.

The CaaS (car-as-a-service) or MaaS (mobility-as-a-service) offering is also picking up steam. The features of the CaaS or MaaS model have many similar features to the HaaS model, ranging from flexibility of the time horizon to the introduction of innovative associated services with the core mobility service. The budget effect plays an important role: the cost of owning a car is high, the average owner of a car in London spent about 600 pounds a month in 2019 on their car as the TCO.[10] For drivers who use their vehicles relatively less frequently, the on-demand services afforded by the CaaS and MaaS models represent a higher utility over the car ownership option. Hence, the expected frequency of usage is an important factor for adopters of XaaS models; customers with lower frequencies of usage prefer the XaaS model over buying the asset. Obviously, in larger cities, micro-mobility-as-a-service, or the offering of e-scooters and bicycles on demand, competes with the CaaS offering.

Unsurprisingly, the first movers in the CaaS and MaaS models were car rental organizations like Hertz and Avis, along with new age sharing firms like Zipcar. In addition to the short-term rentals that firms like Hertz offer, they also began offering subscription or membership models where members could use their offered vehicles on-demand as often as they wanted to, for a pre-specified period. Zipcar (eventually acquired by Avis) offered vehicles on a subscription model in city locations using a dual tariff model. Members would pay an annual subscription fee and would be provided an electronically encoded membership card called the Zipcard.

---

[10] McKinsey and Company, The future of mobility is at our doorstep, https://www.mckinsey.com/~/media/McKinsey/Industries/Automotive%20and%20Assembly/Our%20Insights/The%20future%20of%20mobility%20is%20at%20our%20doorstep/The-future-of-mobility-is-at-our-doorstep.pdf, accessed May 8, 2020.

Each time a member wanted to use a car, s/he could access the Zipcar platform to find a car located in a garage close to them. The cars were offered on an hourly service basis. If the member chose to use a car for a couple of hours, they could pay with a credit card that was associated with their membership instantaneously, and go and wave their Zipcard in front of the driver-side door. The on-board computer would recognize the booking for those two hours and enable the car to be unlocked and the engine to be operated. The member would return the car to a pre-agreed garage, which could be the same as where the car was picked up.[11]

The CaaS and MaaS model providers are not limited to car rental companies. Ford launched the Ford Canvas program in 2017, based on a subscription model to its customers. By 2019, Ford had enrolled about 4,000 subscribers into the Canvas program across the cities of San Francisco, Dallas and Los Angeles.[12] Was it a case of exponential growth leading to a sustainable new stream of revenues for Ford? Hardly. In 2019, Ford sold the Canvas business to Fair with an undisclosed mix of equity and fixed fee. Fair has had more success with the subscription model (Fair has 45,000 subscribers across the US) using an app. Car2Go also exited the MaaS model this year in many cities, though it continues with the model in others. In its exit statement, Car2Go referred to a mis-estimation of the investments and resources it needed to make its MaaS offering successful.[13]

Notwithstanding the inability of the Ford Canvas program or Car2Go to have a universally successfully model, firms like Canoo have not been discouraged from rolling out ambitious MaaS models. Canoo's offering is the use of an electrical vehicle with a range of 250 miles per charge-as-a-service in Los Angeles and San Francisco. The offering is based on a subscription model with a fee upfront and a monthly charge for unlimited

[11] Hart, M., Roberts, M. J., & Stevens, J. D. (2003). Zipcar: Refining the business model. *Harvard Business School Case* 803–096, January 2003. (Revised May 2005.).

[12] Wayland, M., "Ford sells monthly vehicle subscription service to Fair", *CNBC*, September 12, 2019, https://www.cnbc.com/2019/09/12/ford-selling-monthly-vehicle-subscription-service-to-fair.html, accessed May 8, 2020.

[13] Hawkins, A. J., "Share Now, formerly Car2Go, is leaving North America", the Verge, December 18, 2019, https://www.theverge.com/2019/12/18/21028517/sharenow-car2go-leaving-north-america-bmw-daimler-cities-date, accessed May 9, 2020.

access, and includes all associated services like insurance, maintenance, taxes and unlimited mileage.[14] Selfdrive.ae is a UAE-based firm that offers a micro-lease service with other services included in variable lease term schemes ranging from monthly schemes to 3 years.[15] Customers can make bookings for the micro-lease service online, and the lessor can switch cars every month with the service, providing the customer with multiple car models to drive.

2.1 CUSTOMER UTILITY MODEL

Now that we have seen some examples of trade-offs for well-known products like residential and office spaces and vehicles with the selling, leasing and XaaS models, we can start deconstructing the factors that customers use in their choice of adoption of different models. To do so, we will first elucidate the building blocks of value of an offering to customers. In economic theory, this value is represented by the term "customer utility". The term utility in the economic context derives from the notion of satisfaction from the use of a product or a service. Jeremy Bentham was a philosopher who introduced utility as a property of a good or a service that provided positive benefits like pleasure and happiness, and prevented negative effects like unhappiness to the customer of the good.[16] John Stuart Mill elaborated on the concept of utility, and expanded on the theory of utilitarianism.[17] The theory describes the different components of utility that developed intrinsic and extrinsic value from a product or service, or the desires and actions of individuals. Hence, within economics, the concept of utility is used to represent the worth or value of a product or service,

---

[14] Deibel, M., "Canoo: Build for Mobility as a Service", Productasaservice.net, December 15, 2019, https://productasaservice.net/canoo-build-for-mobility-as-a-service/, accessed May 9, 2020.

[15] Selfdrive, "Selfdrive.ae Launches "Microlease" — UAE's First Car Subscription Platform", *PR Newswire*, September 30, 2019, https://www.prnewswire.com/ae/news-releases/selfdriveae-launches-microlease---uaes-first-car-subscription-platform-300926155.html, accessed May 9, 2020.

[16] Bentham, J. (1996). *The Collected Works of Jeremy Bentham: An Introduction to the Principles of Morals and Legislation*. Clarendon Press.

[17] Mill, J. S. (1910). Utilitarianism, Liberty, Representative Government. London: Dent.

and the measurement of utility is based on a utility function that measures the individual's value from a product or a service given a set of choices. Samuelson developed the notion of utility further by measuring utility through indifference curves for individuals from different goods based on the available resources, production functions (ease of production) and the individual preference ordering of customers.[18] In modern economics, the notion of utility is often expressed as the maximum value the customer is willing to pay for a good, also known as the customer's reservation price for the good. The customer's reservation price for a good includes all the benefits, satisfaction and value that the customer derives from the good, hence, it is the maximum price that s/he is willing to pay for the good. The concept of reservation price draws an equivalence between the concept of utility (satisfaction from using a good) to the financial value of the good to the customer. We will use this definition of utility for understanding the customer's choice process between buying the good or using it as a service.

Let us consider the simple example of a customer's choice of mechanism in accessing a book: the customer can either buy it from the local bookstore or borrow it from the local library. If the book is a whodunit, most of the value from reading the book is likely to be limited to the first time that the customer reads the book, as the identity of the perpetrator and the process of uncovering this perpetrator is the key value from reading the book. Once the reader knows the identity of the perpetrator and the methods used by the protagonist in uncovering the identity of the perpetrator, the satisfaction or value derived by the reader from reading the book the second time is significantly lowered. Hence, if the book is expensive and it is available in the local library, the reader would prefer to borrow the book from the local library and not buy it. There are multiple factors that influence his/her choice: the reader will read the book only once, the book is expensive to buy, and it is available for a smaller fee or no fee (if the library is public) at the local library.

Let us now assume that the book is available at both the local bookstore and the local library, but the book has engineering factors of

---

[18] Samuelson, P. A. (1956). Social indifference curves. *The Quarterly Journal of Economics*, 70(1), 1–22.

conversion between different scales, and the customer is an engineer who uses this book multiple times for the purpose of his/her work. Even if the book is expensive, the customer will need to make multiple trips to the local library each time s/he needs to refer to the book, hence, in this case, the customer will prefer to buy the book, so that it is readily available to him/her. The utility from reading the book does not diminish over time, as the conversion factors in the book will help the customer each time to the same degree, thereby making his/her work more efficient. Also, if the customer purchases the book, s/he does not incur the inconvenience of having to go to the library each time s/he needs to refer to the book. Hence, customers are more likely to buy reference books that will be used multiple times and are more likely to rent pulp fiction books that they will read only once or twice.

A similar observation can be made about other categories of products and services as well. Let us consider the choice of buying or renting a movie DVD. If the movie is one of the run-of-the-mill latest movies that have been released, the customer will likely watch the movie only once, hence, renting the movie once makes more sense. If, on the other hand, the movie is a classic, or a kids' movie like *The Jungle King* that children watch multiple times with the same rapt attention as they watched the first time, it may be better to buy the DVD. As many parents know, making multiple trips to rent the same DVD may not be the most sensible decision. Similarly, if a firm's employees usually work remotely from home, but need to go to the office occasionally to meet clients or suppliers, then the firm is better off adopting WeWork's pay-per-use model. In this case, the firm pays for each occasion that their employees use WeWork's facilities. If, on the other hand, the employees need to work closely together every day as there is a substantial amount of teamwork involved in their roles, then the firm is better off signing a longer term contract with WeWork, where the employees can use WeWork's facilities on a sustained basis.

We will now elaborate on the factor of inconvenience that differentiates the experience of buying a product from renting it as a service. As can be seen from the book example above, if the service is offered in the XaaS mode on a pay-per-use basis, the utility from using the service each time is lowered owing to this inconvenience factor. Henceforth, we refer to this set of inconvenience costs as the "deal transaction costs".[19] In the choice of buying the book or borrowing it from the library, the reader has to go to the library each time to borrow the book, enter his/her customer details like the membership number, and then return the book to the library at the end of the borrowing period. Buying the book also has its associated transaction costs: if you buy the book from the brick-and-mortar bookstore, you must go there physically. If the customer buys the book online, they must enter their membership and payment details and then wait for the book to be delivered to their home. However, it is important to note that when buying the good, these costs are incurred once. In contrast, when the customer uses the book as a service, these transaction costs are incurred each time the customer accesses the product or the service in the pay-per-use model. Hence, the deal transaction costs from buying a good can be bundled with the price of the book, which is paid once. In contrast, the transaction costs from using a good as a service must be borne each time the good is used. A similar observation can be made about renting DVDs, apart from the inconvenience of having to make two trips to the local DVD rental store, there is also a higher degree of inertia in returning the DVD.

An additional mental or behavioural cost imposed when using a service in the pay-per-use mode is the "ticking meter effect", which has been well documented in the research.[20] When you take a taxi, if you are offered a fixed fee to go to your destination, your satisfaction from the ride is typically higher. The reason is astoundingly simple: you have the comfort of knowing how much you are going to pay, so you can enjoy the scenery and your favourite music on your trip. In contrast, if you are paying by the meter, you are more likely to be watching the meter and thinking about why is it taking you so long to get to your destination, rather than having a relaxed trip. When customers make calls on an unlimited time plan, they talk about the weather, the game last week, the number of new COVID

---

[19] Balasubramanian, S., Bhattacharya, S., & Krishnan, V. V. (2015). Pricing information goods: A strategic analysis of the selling and pay-per-use mechanisms. *Marketing Science*, 34(2), 218–234.

[20] Lambrecht, A. & Skiera, B. (2006). Paying too much and being happy about it: Existence, causes, and consequences of tariff-choice biases. *Journal of marketing Research*, 43(2), 212–223.

patients in their country and the implications for the reopening of the economy. In contrast, if they call on a pay-per-minute plan, they stick to business, and the respondent is likely to find the caller's behaviour to be curt, as the caller is constantly aware of the steadily increasing bill for the call. The research findings also consistently find support for the ticking meter effect. For instance, if customers are asked if they prefer to have flat fee pricing or pay-per-use pricing for the same average charge, customers prefer flat fee pricing, as it lowers the uncertainty of the payments that they have to make. Hence, the ticking meter effect also adds to the deal transaction costs of renting a product.

Taken together, the utility from a service can be expressed as the sum of the utilities from using the service each time. This utility can be represented as the multiplicative product of the number of times the service can be used, and the average or expected utility each time the service is used. If the pay-per-use model is used, the transaction costs associated with the pay-per-use model reduce the expected utility per use compared to buying the product or the service. The reservation price (financial equivalent of the utility) can then be represented by the multiplicative product of the frequency of usage (the number of times the product or the service will be used), and the expected utility per use of the product or the service (with the deal transaction cost factored in).

The decision to adopt a particular mechanism in utility theory depends critically on the customer surplus, i.e., the difference between the utility that the customer accrues from a product or a service, and the price that the customer pays for it. The customer surplus represents the net value of the product or service to the customer, i.e., the difference between the value that s/he derives from the product or service, and what s/he pays for it. Note that the utility that the customer gets from a product or the service can be represented by the reservation price that s/he is willing to pay for the product or the service. Hence, the customer surplus can be modelled as the difference between the reservation price of the product or the service for the customer, and the actual price that s/he pays for the product or the service. Obviously, customers will choose the mechanism (buying or using the product or service on a pay-per-use basis) with the higher customer surplus. In the choice between renting or buying the core asset and then signing other contracts for associated services, customers choose the mechanism that has a higher difference between the utility accrued and the price paid for the product or service.

For the example of the book postulated earlier, the reservation price of the whodunit is largely the utility that the customer derives from reading the book for the first time, with the utility contributions from reading the book subsequent times being substantially diminished. Hence, the customer surplus of the whodunit is the difference between the utility of reading the book and the rental price of the book under the renting mode, and the difference between reading the book and the sales price of the book under the buying mode. Given that rental prices are typically a small fraction of the sales price of a book, renting the whodunit yields a higher surplus for the reader. On the other hand, since the engineering conversions book is read multiple times by the reader, s/he pays the price of buying the book (and any associated transaction costs just once). However, the price of the rental of the book and the transaction costs are borne multiple times. Hence, the reader of the engineering conversions book is more likely to purchase the book.

2.2 OBSOLESCENCE OF TECHNOLOGY, PRODUCT LIFECYCLE, TIME OF HORIZON

We use this framework of customer surplus to analyze the impact of factors like the duration of the product lifecycle and the risk of technology obsolescence on the customer's choice between buying or adopting the XaaS offering for accessing an asset. When the asset lifecycle is short, or the risk of technological obsolescence is high, the number of times that the asset can be used is limited to the time horizon that the next generation of the asset is introduced. At that point of time, owing to compatibility issues (other users migrating to the next generation), the expected utility of the product or service is significantly reduced. The Software-as-a-Service (SaaS) model is a good example of the value of the service model when obsolescence of the software is a major concern. The SaaS model of software applications is typically offered to customers using a cloud computing approach, where users do not need to install the software locally and can access the application on the Internet. Most developers of software applications use the agile model of software development, where the first application that is commercially released has most of the features available, and most of the bugs have been fixed. Given the high-velocity environment of the software application world, firms do not have the luxury of waiting to develop a perfect application and launch it into the market. Instead, using the agile approach, firms prefer to launch applications commercially when they have a reasonable viability, and they subsequently launch patches that enhance the functionality and reduce the number of bugs of the application.

For users to keep pace with developments by adopting the latest software applications in the buying mode, they would need to purchase licenses to subsequent generations of the application and install those in their own hardware. This would mean that the frequency of usage would be lower, and they would need to pay the purchase price of each generation, lowering their customer surplus. Purchasing software licenses for each generation also imposes search costs on the user. The user must keep abreast of developments in the application domain and make the decision to purchase the license for the next generation at the appropriate time. Hence, the SaaS model typically sees more upgrades compared to the distribution of software through licensing means. From the developer's perspective, the costs of distribution of the upgrade are negligible, and they can migrate customers to the upgraded version of the application with the best quality and the most features seamlessly. If one customer identifies a bug that causes that customer's system to crash, the developer has to do an individual study of whether the environment of the user had a role to play, or whether the developer's software was at fault. In contrast, if a bug is identified on the cloud, it is painfully obvious that this issue can occur for other users as well, hence, troubleshooting software bugs is easier in the SaaS model. In the SaaS offering for upgraded versions, all customers benefit from the latest version. In contrast, in the selling of individual licenses, the developer can potentially contract with individual users for patches, which does not benefit the larger user community. The issue of maintenance of upgraded software is also harder for the license model, as the IT staff of the individual business must schedule the installation of the upgrade, leading to delays in typical upgrade installations. In contrast, the maintenance of the upgrade schedule in the SaaS model is the developer's responsibility. The developer should ideally have an upgrade calendar that is shared with users, this minimizes any disruption for users from the upgrade. For instance, Oracle's Help Centre maintains an upgrade calendar that is shared with clients, this enables client workforces to prepare in advance for the upgrade.[21]

The 2018 State of IT Report by Spiceworks on IT spending and new trends in technology showed that XaaS offerings (Figure 2.1) like IT auto-mation, SDS/virtual SAN, IaaS, PaaS, SDN and Hyperconvergence are getting increasingly popular.[22] These applications are typically offered using the XaaS model and were among the top new technologies that had either been adopted, or firms intended to adopt them in the next year. The State of IT Report by Spiceworks was conducted by surveying over 1,000 IT professionals. This shows that XaaS offerings are a helpful way of keeping abreast with new technology. Customers can adopt new technolo-gies quickly without having to incur the transaction costs of purchasing the license and installing the software each time on their own hardware. Having the provider host the application enables the user to have quick access to each subsequent generation, hence, the burden of keeping abreast of technology advances lies with the developer of the application. Hosting the application on the user's own hardware may also have hard-ware upgrade implications and increase the TCO for the user. On the other hand, using the SaaS model enables the user to pay only for basic hard-ware, and hence, keep their customer surplus higher. Another benefit of the SaaS model includes more focused resource allocation on the part of the user; the user does not have to take care of the on-boarding process for the application, which is the responsibility of the developer. Since the developer does the on-boarding processes for multiple users, the devel-oper enjoys significant economies of scale in on-boarding processes, enabling them to pass on some of the savings to the user. The use of the SaaS model also provides users with the benefit of complementarity — developers provide applications using a standardized set of protocols and

[21] Oracle, "Managing Release Updates", https://docs.oracle.com/en/cloud/saas/service/18c/facca/managing-release-updates.html#managing-release-updates, accessed May 13, 2020.
[22] Spiceworks, "The 2018 State of IT Report", https://www.spiceworks.com/marketing/state-of-it-2018/, accessed May 15, 2020.

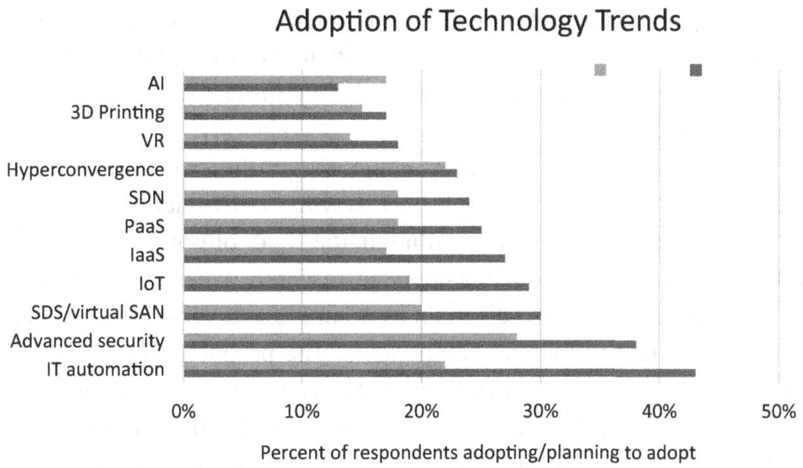

Adoption of Technology Trends

Figure 2.1: Proportion of Firms that have Adopted or Intend to Adopt New Technologies
Source: State of IT Report 2018 by Spiceworks.

interfaces, which enables users to integrate applications with other applications provided by the same developer or other developers.

2.3 COMPLEMENTARITY AND BUNDLING

A good example of the use of XaaS model in the customer space is the offering of cell phone plan services by most providers today. While the service is not labelled by the XaaS moniker, cell phones are among the customer products with the shortest lifecycles, with product generational changes happening in less than a year. Most cell phone providers have bundled plans that include the cell phone, along with calling, messaging and data services. For plans with a higher degree of usage, the price of the phone is substantially discounted for the customer with plans that have a higher calling, messaging and data usage frequency. While cell phone plan providers also offer calling, messaging and data-only plans with no basic phone included, those plans are typically not popular with users. For standalone service subscriptions, users must buy their own cell phones, which get obsolete very quickly. Having to buy each subsequent generation of cell phones lowers the customer surplus significantly. Most customers prefer to adopt inclusive cell phone plans that offer the phone and calling, messaging and data services in an inclusive plan, as that lowers the impact of obsolescence of the base equipment (the phone) on the customer surplus.

The cell phone service plan example above illustrates one of the big advantages of the XaaS model over buying individual products and services — the critical role of bundling in the XaaS offering. The bundling strategy has been studied extensively in research, where firms combine products and services and sell them as a bundle at a substantial discount, rather than selling individual components. The products and services are typically complementary to each other but can also be standalone offerings that do not offer complementary benefits with other components in the bundle. The discounting is typically offered owing to economies of scale; when firms bundle components, the individual components of the bundle offer savings to the firm, which can be passed on to the customer. For example, cell phone service providers have a fixed capacity for offering calling and data services. This capacity will be used to a lower extent if calling and data plans are offered separately. By using an integrated set of resources for calling and data, the firm pools the risk of usage by separate customers and maximizes the utilization of their capacity by using the bundling strategy. The bundling strategy can be offered by the firm in distinct forms: offering the option of either standalone services or as a bundle, this form of offering is known as a mixed bundling strategy. Cell phone providers typically also offer this bundling package, where customers can choose to have a calling plan and data plan separately. The other form of bundling is known as pure bundling, where customers can only avail of the bundle, and cannot avail of the separate services as standalone services. This form of bundling is more restrictive and may run afoul of anti-trust laws.

The use of mixed and pure bundling is an important advantage of the XaaS model. In the car-as-a-service model, typically, the usage of the car is bundled with maintenance and insurance, as it provides a one-stop shop for customers. Hence, the XaaS model can lower the transaction costs of renting or leasing by bundling services together. In contrast, the purchasing mode of products would need customers to source associated services with their products in an opportunistic fashion. Bundling also reduces the transaction costs associated with bill payments and not just search costs for services, as the payments for different services can be rolled into one consolidated payment. In the WeLive case, we see that laundry and other utility services are offered via an app, and customers can get one consolidated bill at the end of the month.

We have illustrated the customer choice model between the purchasing and pay-per-use modes. We now differentiate between the purchasing and subscription modes. As stated before, the XaaS model is offered with one of two pricing schemes: subscription models which enable the customer to use the service as often as needed on a fixed fee, and pay-per-use models, where customers pay for the service each time that they use it. How does a customer choose between buying a product or leasing it using the subscription model (where they can use the product as many times as they want during the period of the subscription)? It turns out that the frequency of usage (number of times that the product or service will be used) and the expected utility per use are critical factors in this decision as well. For instance, while the usage frequency per period is common across both models (the product or the service can be used as often as the customer wants in both the buying and the subscription models), the time horizon for the decision is the key differentiating factor between the two models. For example, in the home-as-a-service model, the customer will make payments in perpetuity if s/he uses the HaaS model. In contrast, if the customer buys his/her home, s/he will make either a lumpsum payment, or s/he will make monthly payments on a mortgage but build equity in the home. Hence, the period that the product/service will be used becomes the key factor, the frequency of usage is dependent on the period of usage. The utility per use will get translated into a utility per period, and the trade-offs related to obsolescence of the core asset will apply in the same fashion. For instance, if the asset depreciates quickly over time, the depreciation in value is akin to obsolescence, while if the core asset appreciates in value over time, that asset appreciation would move the customer towards the purchasing mode. The use of bundling in the HaaS model with a long lease will again reduce the transaction costs associated with the XaaS model.

2.4 SWITCHING COSTS AND LOCK-IN RISK

Another factor that influences customer choice for XaaS offerings are the switching costs from one offering to another, and the risk of lock-in. The switching cost factor typically works in favour of the XaaS model, and against the purchasing mode. Switching costs are defined as the financial, compatibility and psychological costs of switching from one provider to another. As an example of financial switching costs, most cell phone service providers charge an early termination fee that is defined in the contract. A top US cell phone services provider charges up to $350 in total for early termination, which is prorated based on the number of months left in the contract.[23] Hence, the later in the contract that the customer cancels the subscription, the lower the amount that s/he has to pay, as the termination fees for the provider decreases at a rate of $15 per month. Similarly, a top cable services provider charges $10 for each month left in the contract as an early termination fee.[24] The switching cost can also be the time and effort required by the customer to change providers, and includes search costs and the costs of disruption for switching from one provider to another of the regular business during the switchover. For example, some software applications have a high degree of learning associated with the operation of the application. If customers want to switch from one application to another with similar functionality, the time and effort needed to master the new application would be a significant hindrance to switching. Next, there are also interoperability issues with switching applications, as the current application may be seamlessly integrated with other applications. Any effort to switch to another application would require investments in time and effort in making the new application work in consonance with the rest of the system.

Firms may often introduce switching costs on purpose to lock-in customers to their products and services. In addition to the financial penalty

---

[23] Verizon, "My Verizon Wireless Customer Agreement", https://www.verizon.com/legal/notices/customer-agreement/#:~:text=If%20your%20contract%20term%20results,completion%20of%20the%20contract%20term, accessed May 17, 2020.

[24] Starhub, "Starhub's service specific terms and conditions: Starhub TV", https://www.starhub.com/content/dam/starhub/legal-notices-and-terms/consumer/starhub-tv.pdf, accessed May 17, 2020.

cost examples postulated earlier, firms may introduce interoperability issues for developers who make independent applications for their platforms. The anti-trust motion against Microsoft for promoting the use of the Explorer and reducing the functionality of other browsers on computers running on the Windows Operating System is an example of deliberate switching costs.[25] These interoperability issues were introduced to induce customers to use the Microsoft's applications as a bundle. Typically, the higher the degree of market power of the provider, the higher is the ability to induce switching costs.

A related issue to switching costs in choosing between the options of the SaaS model and purchasing licenses for software applications is the risk of vendor lock-in. Research studies have found that the risk of provider lock-in is significant in cloud computing applications, as unlike applications in the B2C space, applications in the B2B space have a lower degree of standardization.[26] The cloud computing environment has a higher degree of proprietary standards, leading to lower interoperability and portability when moving from one provider to another. Hence, when applications move from local hosting to being hosted on the cloud, the risk of being locked into a provider is amplified.

While there are specific examples of providers in some XaaS offerings having higher switching costs and the risk of provider lock-in compared to adopting the purchasing mode, in general, the XaaS offering is better off on the issue of switching compared to the purchasing mode. For instance, comparing home ownership and the HaaS model, homeowners typically have a much higher investment in their homes, making the home a more illiquid asset. Similarly, for services like the cell phone-as-a-service or the car-as-a-service offerings, adopting the service offering involves getting locked in for the term of subscription. At the end of the lock-in period, the customer can switch to another

---

[25] Weiser, P. J. (2009). "Regulating interoperability: Lessons from AT&T, Microsoft, and Beyond", *Antitrust Law Journal*, 76, 271, available at https://scholar.law.colorado.edu/articles/454.

[26] Opara-Martins, J., Sahandi, R., & Tian, F. (2014). Critical review of vendor lock-in and its impact on adoption of cloud computing. In International Conference on Information Society (i-Society 2014) (pp. 92–97). *IEEE*.

provider. The existence of secondary markets makes it easier for adopters of the purchasing mode to switch as well. However, secondary markets usually only exist for hardware assets. Secondary markets for software applications are very limited or non-existent, as technology lifecycles are very short, and licenses are not transferable. Secondary markets for hardware products may also have a high depreciation (with the exception of homes), as technology products, cars and other physical assets have a high value when new, and tend to either depreciate or go obsolete very quickly.

Since customers do not acquire assets upfront, the risk of trying out the service in the XaaS mode is relatively low. Many providers offer a free trial for their cloud-based products to entice customers to try out their products. For instance, Huawei offers their elastic cloud servers and databases to customers for free for 1,500 hours over the first 12 months.[27] In the IaaS space, iland offers customers a free 30 day trial of their hosted IT infrastructure, including access to 24-hour support and advanced security features.[28] This enables customers to sign a longer term contract if they are satisfied with the performance of the product.

The advantage of lower switching costs and risk of lock-in results in a higher responsiveness and agility for XaaS offerings. For instance, since the SaaS provider hosts the application, if there are significant drawbacks in the functionality of the software, users can communicate these drawbacks to the provider. The provider can add those functionalities in modules to the application and upgrade the application. While firms selling licenses can improve their software as well by introducing software patches, the user may need other hardware and software assets for the upgrade patches. Centralizing the asset requirements on the part of the developer makes it easier to quickly roll out innovations in an agile mode. In contrast, having the software hosted in a decentralized fashion

---

[27] Huawei, "Huawei Cloud: Free Trial", https://activity.huaweicloud.com/intl/en-us/free_packages/index.html?utm_source=google_intl&utm_medium=cpc&utm_campaign=%E8%B0%B7%E6%AD%8C-%E6%96%B0%E5%8A%A0%E5%9D%A1-%E4%BA%A7%E5%93%81&utm_content=%E6%96%B0%E5%8A%A0%E5%9D%A1-product-server&utm_term=Cloud%2BServer&gclid=EAIaIQobChMI0KiSh5PL7gIViQ4rCh0rGQyFEAAYASAAEgI5A_D_BwE#section-3, accessed May 17, 2020.
[28] Iland, "Take a free 30-day trial", https://www.iland.com/free/, accessed May 18, 2020.

makes it harder for developers to achieve the same degree of agility. One of the touted advantages of the XaaS offering is the move for users from transactions to experiences. The XaaS mode enables the developer to make changes and improvements in a centralized fashion. Hence, the user can focus on benefiting from the experience of using applications provided with minimal effort. This centralized effort also leads to significant economies of scale, leading to system costs being lowered. Rather than having to make individual investments on the part of users, the developer can make centralized investments for all users, leading to lower systemic costs.

2.5 BUDGET EFFECT

Next, we look at the budget allocation of the firm into purchasing assets versus the need to focus the use of assets for core business purposes.

A study by Deloitte in the Monitor Deloitte report on the growth of the services economy and the concomitant growth of the XaaS offering space in the ASEAN region has found that customers have focused less on acquiring physical goods as a percentage of the total household expenses over the last two and a half decades (Figure 2.2).[29] Instead, customers have spent more money on services and experiences, indicating that as customers grow wealthier, their propensity to acquire permanent ownership of goods declines. They prefer to allocate a higher share of household expenses to consuming services that are non-inventoriable (hence, the higher share of experiences). Similarly, the Monitor Deloitte report finds a trend among corporate entities in the ASEAN region to have fewer illiquid property, plant and equipment (PPE) assets as a percentage of total assets (the vertical bars in Figure 3 represent the range of PPE assets to total assets of individual firms). The mean proportion shows a decrease from 31% in 2001 to 23% in 2017. Hence, firms are adopting more asset-light models and are outsourcing more business activities.

---

[29] Deloitte, "Everything as a Service: A new era of value delivery", https://www2.deloitte.com/content/dam/Deloitte/sg/Documents/strategy/sea-so-everything-as-a-service.pdf, accessed May 20, 2020.

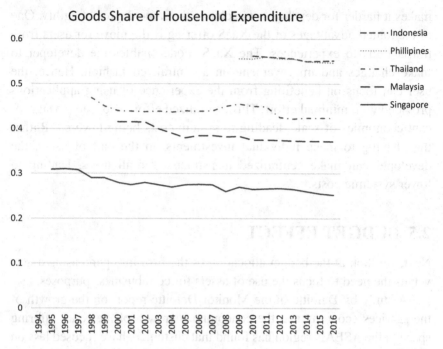

Figure 2.2: Decreasing Household Share of Expenses on Goods Acquisition from 1994–2016

Source: Monitor Deloitte analysis.

The budget aspect has multiple components, such as the access to capital and the need to free resources for core activities, and the debate on whether it is better to have one's own capital assets, or whether it is better to outsource non-core activities as operating expenses. The access to capital is an important issue for SMEs in the B2B world, and for the proportion of budget allocated to the acquisition of goods in the B2C world. The adoption of enterprise resource planning (ERP) systems is a good example to illustrate the budget effect. Most businesses would agree that ERP systems help in automating repeated operational tasks like inventory management and payroll accounting, and in making them more efficient. ERP systems also reduce the amount of resources needed for routine activities, thus freeing up expensive resources and time for more value-added

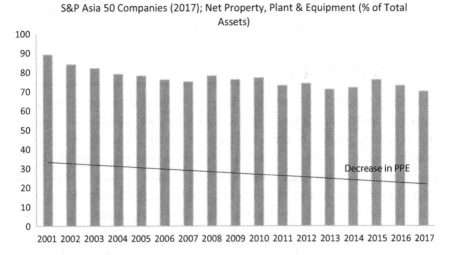

Figure 2.3: Decreasing Corporate Share of Plant, Property and Equipment (PPE) as % of Total Assets from 2001–2017

Source: Monitor Deloitte analysis.

activities. Among the most widely used features of ERP systems are financial control and reporting, and order entry and purchasing, while the use of other features for integrating operational activities is mixed for different firms. However, the adoption of ERP systems was high among larger firms in the early diffusion of ERP systems, while the adoption of these systems in the SME space was lagging. The most obvious reason for the slow adoption of ERP systems in SMEs obviously is the budget effect. In the initial diffusion of ERP systems, most developers offered these systems with licenses to host the software internally in the client's organization, there were very few early SaaS offerings of ERP systems. The CRM system of Salesforce was among the first offerings in the SaaS domain, and since then, the adoption of ERP systems by SMEs has been growing.

In the B2C space, the budget impact of purchasing a product can push customers towards the SaaS model as well. Models such as Zipcar in the cars-as-a-service space have grown precisely for this reason: they enable customers to access car services in the city on demand, without the need for a car loan. Car loans are expensive as the underlying asset depreciates quickly, and the interest rate for a car loan is typically higher than that of a mortgage, as a house keeps its value better than a car.

2.6 CAPEX VS OPEX

The XaaS model also lets users keep their limited resources for core activities, and turn their resource needs for non-core activities into operating expenses, so that businesses can have a better handle on the gross margin needed for gross profitability. In the income statement, the gross profit of the business (sales minus cost of sales or variable costs) is the overall profit of the business without considering fixed costs. By turning non-core activities from fixed costs to variable costs (capex to opex), the business has a better handle on its profitability. The trouble with fixed costs is that they are accrued regardless of the volume of sales, hence, it is difficult for the business to ascertain if the current underlying business model is profitable. If the capital expenses (capex) can be turned into operating expenses (opex), the gross margin of the firm is a better indicator of the underlying profitability of the firm, and the business can have a better handle of changes that need to be made.

The research is unanimous that in cloud computing the opex model dominates the capex model, in that businesses have a better understanding of how their profits are impacted by the costs of IT systems. These advantages of adopting the opex-heavy model using the XaaS mode for assets over the capex-heavy mode of purchasing extend to other XaaS offerings as well.[30] The first advantage of the XaaS offering is from the lower cost of centralized resources when applications are offered to multiple customers, leading to economies of scale, and hence, lower opex for customers. Medium to large-sized businesses would spend millions on acquiring resources for data centres for which they needed equipment, real estate, investments in software, along with hiring an IT team for operating and maintaining the centre. In contrast, Amazon could offer data centre services to a large set of firms, which gave Amazon

---

[30] Rafique, K., Tareen, A. W., Saeed, M., Wu, J., & Qureshi, S. S. (2011). Cloud computing economics opportunities and challenges. In 2011 4th IEEE International Conference on Broadband Network and Multimedia Technology (pp. 401–406). *IEEE.*

economies of scale in offering these services. Amazon would also have to acquire a smaller set of resources to serve all the users than if each user acquired resources themselves, owing to resource pooling. The lower costs from the economies of scale enable providers like Amazon to pass on some of these savings to customers, leading to operating expenses for users.

For accounting, capex acquisitions of fixed assets are considered a part of property, plant and equipment (PPE), which is a part of the non-current or long-term assets of the firm. Since long-term assets are used to create value for the firm over a longer horizon, these investments must be depreciated or amortized over the lifetime of the asset. Assets like systems, servers and workstations are considered to be a part of the PPE if they are acquired, even if the lifecycle of these assets is fairly short, and hence, they have to be depreciated at a high rate. Given the high velocity environment of the IT space, frequently, the asset is outdated before the lifecycle that the firm has accounted for it. The tax benefits of these investments are prorated over the lifecycle of the asset, hence, accounting for these assets as the opex model leads to better tax advantages.

If software applications are sourced using the SaaS model, the operating expenses of these applications are tax deductible for the year, as the firm is only liable for taxes on the profits it makes, and the operating expenses lower the tax outlay of the firm. The opex model also reduces the need for onerous investments in space and equipment, and the need for a large IT team for operating and maintaining systems. Next, since the operating expenses for SaaS applications are stable and predictable, the financial planning and control of the firm is easier. The risk of running over the IT budget is borne by the provider, and the customer does not run the risk of paying much more for IT operations than was initially forecast if the customer has a steady usage pattern. Similarly, the lifecycle prediction forecast of the IT assets is no longer a risk, as that is also borne by the provider. If the IT assets get obsolete earlier than planned, the customer can either upgrade to the next generation earlier, or switch providers if the provider's solution is not keeping abreast of the latest technology offering. Third, the estimation of the capacity risk is borne by the customer in the own IT asset model. If the required capacity turns out to be lower, then the customer has made a higher investment in capacity, which is wasted. If the required capacity turns out to be higher, then there could still be wasted investments. In IT applications, you cannot add fractional servers, investments in capacity are discretized, as you need to add server capacity in an integral stepwise fashion, rather than in a continuous mode. In contrast, in the SaaS model, you only pay for the capacity you need in the pay-per-use mode, or up to a fixed known quantity in the subscription mode. Fourth, the risk of business cycles requiring lower capacity in bad times and hence leading to overinvestment is no longer existent. In business downturns, the usage of the application is lowered and, hence, payments are lowered in the pay-per-use mode. Finally, there is the agility advantage of the opex model, in that the system can be up and running when the application is outsourced in a shorter period. The capex model has the added disadvantage of a longer lead time for the receipt of delivery of the assets, and the need for installing and integrating all the assets before they become operational. Some of the more intangible benefits of cloud computing include global accessibility, and 24-hour support. The expenses of 24-hour support for one's own IT assets are higher. However, the security needs for global access to one's own IT assets may be lower.

Some additional issues to consider between the capex and opex models are the opportunity costs and disposal costs of assets and the cash flow associated with acquiring assets versus paying for them per use. Acquiring own IT assets involves an opportunity cost if the firm is acquiring them with its own cash, as that money could have been invested in other opportunities with potentially higher returns. If the assets are being acquired by financing them, then the firm is potentially adding the weighted average cost of capital (WACC) to the annual operating expenses of the firm in the form of annual interest payments, which lowers the firm's profitability. Similarly, many IT assets like electronic equipment have disposal costs associated with them, as regulations for the disposal of electronic equipment are stringent in many countries. The SaaS model dominates the own assets model for both opportunity and disposal costs. Finally, cash flow considerations for businesses dictate that any early payment for the acquisition of IT assets that are depreciated or amortized over a longer period negatively impact the cash conversion cycle. Businesses would ideally like to pay suppliers for equipment as late as possible and get paid by customers as early as possible for the best cash flow results to stimulate growth. The acquisition of IT assets would mean that the customer pays upfront, leading to an early lumpsum payment to suppliers, while it would be generating returns on that investment over the IT assets lifecycle. This leads to cash flow problems as investments are made way before those investments can generate returns. In contrast, with the XaaS model, firms only pay for the use of IT assets in the period that they consume them. Hence, the payments to suppliers are made much later, and closer to the payments made by customers, leading to a shorter period for which the firm must finance its operations, and better cash conversion cycles.

In comparing the total cost outlay from the acquisition of IT assets versus adopting the XaaS model, it is useful to use the TCO methodology.[31] The TCO is the set of complete costs associated with operating an asset (however, it does not consider if the benefits from that asset are different from buying or using the XaaS mode). It is a very useful analysis when comparing the options of IT asset acquisition with that of adopting the XaaS mode. The set of total costs includes all direct costs associated with the assets like the cost of acquisition. It also considers indirect costs like consumables for maintenance, insurance, installation and transition for the assets, security and disaster recovery costs, the costs of support internally. Finally, the costs associated with the workforce that is needed for maintaining the assets should also be considered. Hence, the TCO approach intends to estimate all the costs associated with adopting either approach (IT asset acquisition or XaaS) over the entire asset lifecycle.

For mass market products, the research on the buying versus the XaaS model is mixed about the TCO. For instance, many studies have compared the TCO of owning cars with the CaaS model. For cars, the Kelley Blue Book provides various components of the TCO like fuel, insurance, maintenance and typical repair costs and depreciation.[32] Most studies find that the TCO is higher for the CaaS model versus the car acquisition model, while a few studies find that buying cars has a higher TCO. Surprisingly,

[31] Mouritsen, M. (2013). Is your organization managing or mangling its technology assets? *Strategic Finance*, 94(7), 35.

[32] Kelley Blue Book, "Total cost of ownership", https://mediaroom.kbb.com/total-cost-ownership, accessed May 21, 2020.

for cars, a very high frequency of usage might push customers towards the CaaS or the leasing model if these models are offered on a subscription basis rather than on a pay-per-use basis, as the costs of maintenance are borne by the provider. Hence, users who drive their cars with moderate frequencies would find that the TCO for car ownership is lower, while users with very high frequencies of usage would prefer to use the CaaS model. Users with very low frequencies of usage might prefer to use sharing economy solutions like Uber, Zipcar and Grab or good, old fashioned taxis. Users with low frequencies of usage do not have a positive customer surplus from the car if they buy it, owing to the cost of acquisition. It is noteworthy that the sharing economy is also an example of the XaaS model, where the firm does not acquire its own assets, but has asset owners use their platforms to provide the basic service. Most users of Uber and Grab have low frequencies of usage; hence, they prefer not to buy cars or lease cars, but to pay as they go.

2.7 ONE STOP SHOP: MAINTENANCE AND INSURANCE

The inclusion of maintenance and insurance as a one-stop shop model of the CaaS mode is well known, and is an important element of the technology XaaS offerings as well. However, in the B2B vehicular services space, one particularly interesting offering is the tyres-as-a-service (TaaS) model. Interestingly, the tyres-as-a-service model was first offered in 2000, when Michelin launched its Michelin Fleet Solutions (MFS) program.[33] While Michelin has always been known for its innovation in its core product offering (for instance, Michelin was the creator of radial tyres), the MFS was the first example in the tyre sector of a servitization mode of offering. The MFS solution was intended for truck and passenger bus operators, where Michelin offered the service of tyre maintenance and tyre insurance to fleet operators (Michelin would maintain the tyres and replace them if damaged). However, the initial foray of Michelin into the XaaS world

---

[33] Ulaga, W., Dalsace, F., & Renault, C. (2010). Michelin Fleet Solutions: From Selling Tires to Selling Kilometres. IMD case study, 510-103.

failed, both for internal and external reasons. Customers interpreted the offering of a maintenance and insurance service by a tyre manufacturer like Michelin as a signal of poor tyre quality. Internally, Michelin's own sales and marketing staff were not convinced about this model, as they were focused on new tyre sales. They had a similar conclusion about the offering: sending the signal that new tyres would be packaged with a maintenance and insurance bundle sent the wrong signal to customers. This is an important lesson for bundling various services together in the XaaS mode — customers have to be convinced that the quality of the underlying product asset is good, and the additional maintenance and insurance services are offered for lower transaction costs and peace of mind for the customer. Michelin had proposed an additional fee for the bundling of the maintenance and the insurance service. While this is quintessential Monday-morning quarterbacking at its best, Michelin would have been better off if they had proposed a higher price for the bundle with the maintenance and insurance services. In this case, they would have been signalling the opposite message: their tyres were of high quality and they were convinced that fleets would need lower maintenance and insurance. An additional reason for the failure of the MFS service was that Michelin had to develop an extensive network of servicing stations for the offering, the cost structure of the servicing network and the maintenance services made the profitability of the new services venture questionable.

However, while the failure rankled internally in Michelin, it tried the services model again in 2013 with Michelin Solutions for commercial vehicles. In its second foray into the XaaS model, Michelin decided to use technology to design a suite of services that would offer value to the customer. In addition to offering maintenance and insurance services, Michelin used IoT technology to launch the Effifuel system for fuel efficiency. The system used internal sensors to collect data on tyre pressure, fuel consumption and road conditions like temperature and the speed of the truck. These data were analyzed in a cloud solution to provide recommendations for reducing fuel consumption and reducing tyre wear and tear for better tyre management. It also provided target savings to fleet operators to reduce fuel expenses, with an SLA for the savings tied into the contract. The results of the offering have been significant: fleet operators have lowered their annual fuel consumption by 2.5 litres for every 100 km, representing an average savings of more than 3,000 euros over a distance of 120,000 km. Additionally, the carbon emissions of the trucks have been lowered by 8 tonnes, representing better environmental compliance.

By using data analytics effectively, Michelin has integrated technology into their offering to reduce costs for fleet operators, proving that customer solutions designed by them have shared value for the customer. There is more general buy-in for the solutions approach internally at Michelin now, and obviously, increased profits from the services component. The Michelin Fleet Solutions example illustrates three important points about the XaaS model: first, the solutions approach must generate visible and verifiable value for the customer. Ideally, pilot tests should estimate this customer value, along with clear directions on how this value can be unlocked. Second, bundling value-based services like maintenance and insurance as a separate package can cause doubts in the customer's mind about the product's quality when offered with new products. If the price of services like maintenance and insurance is bundled with the product, the value proposition of hassle-free usage is made better. Of course, this concept does not extend to all services, indeed some services like customer analytics can be sold as an independent value proposition. The different components of the services that are bundled together or unbundled may signal different messages to customers, hence, firms take a nuanced approach in offering service bundles or standalone services to customers. Third, a better integration of the different services offered by the firm to the customer using technology can have complementary effects on the firm's cost base and on the customer's value proposition. Hence, integrating the operational efforts behind different services can be symbiotic for the firm and the customer.

The one-stop shop (total solutions provider) methodology that the XaaS model provides is one of the main value propositions of the XaaS offering. To make this value proposition salient (especially with services like maintenance and insurance) is challenging and rewarding. In addition to the technology behind the integration, design concepts like design for serviceability and design of quality for XaaS offerings are key in ensuring value for the customer and the firm. We review those methodologies next.

2.8 DESIGN FOR SERVICEABILITY AND DESIGN FOR QUALITY

The concept of design for serviceability has been around for some time, and though it will not exactly qualify as a cutting-edge methodology now, sometimes vintage old wine in a new bottle does deliver the right notes to the palate. All of us who have worked at white collar jobs have opened innumerable doors and twiddled with knobs on a copier to find that elusive jammed sheet of paper and pulled out sheet after sheet and closed the door finally, only to see the copier is still jammed. The concept of design for serviceability (DFS) was probably invented for copier warriors: the product should be designed in a way that service engineers should be able to repair and do preventive maintenance easily. Ideally, users should be able to troubleshoot and fix small problems easily. The objectives of DFS are to maximize availability and the mean time between failures (MTBF) and minimize the down time of the asset or application, or the mean time to repair (MTTR).[34] While the concept applies to the selling of the product along with a maintenance contract, the incentives of the purchasing model are not well-aligned with the customer. In contrast, in the case of the Copier-as-a-Service mode, the incentives of the provider and the customer are designed to be aligned. When the manufacturer of the copier sells the copier to the customer along with a maintenance contract, the manufacturer makes money from the sale of the copier, and from the maintenance contract. In the case of purchased copiers by the customer, the maintenance of the copier is governed by service level agreements (SLAs), which act as a constraint. So the manufacturer has to ensure that the copier is repaired within a few hours of receiving the maintenance call from the customer, but the manufacturer does not lose any money from the downtime of the copier or from a lower availability, both of which hurt the customer. In contrast, the copier-as-a-service mode operates typically on a payment for the number of copies made. If the downtime of the copier when it breaks down is high, or if the copier breaks down frequently, the customer can make less

---

[34] NPD Solutions, Design for serviceability/maintainability, https://www.npd-solutions.com/dfs.html, accessed May 19, 2020.

copies on the copier. This lowers the revenues of the provider, giving the provider an incentive to reduce the frequency of breakdowns and the downtime during breakdowns. Hence, in the copier-as-a-service mode, the incentives of the provider and the customer are better aligned.

While the DFS concept is very detailed, a brief overview is as follows.[35] When the underlying asset fails, the diagnostics should be as easy to do as possible; IoT sensors can play an important role in hardware products. While we have focused on the hardware context with the copier example to illustrate the need for DFS, in the software context, ideally, small problems should be easily diagnosable by the user or the local IT team. Diagnostics are almost universally done (in both hardware and software) by applying a signal to individual modules and checking the response of that module. If the response of the module is not the specified response, then that module needs to be repaired. For integrated architectures, this diagnosis is harder to do, hence, modular design architectures are a must for DFS. Ideally, the diagnostic capability must be inbuilt in the system for local users and maintenance staff on the ground to be able to run quick diagnostics. In exceptional cases, the diagnostics may be conducted remotely, or by specialized servicing equipment. Next, items that fail more frequently should be physically accessible the fastest, so that the repair process can access these modules first. The equipment should also be accessible easily, so that service can be done quickly. Simplification of the design is obviously needed, as there are fewer diagnoses needed and lower spare inventories required. Standardized design is very useful, as modules can be reused in software, parts can be commonly sourced with economies of scale in hardware, and fewer parts can be used to service more equipment. For the sake of safety, high voltage terminals or sharp edges should require special access. Parts should be capable of assembly only in one way, so that if users try to assemble them any other way, it quickly becomes obvious that the assembly has not been done correctly.

The design for quality (DFQ) principle works in a similar way to the DFS concept, in that the product should be designed to be operated as

---

[35] Gobbo Junior, O. & Borsato, M. (2020). A Method to Support Design for Serviceability in the Early Stages of New Product Development. *International Journal of Computer Integrated Manufacturing*, 1–16.

easily as possible, without requiring much support, and the product should be designed to be reliable. The communication to customers about the reliability of the product also needs to be designed carefully. For instance, if Michelin sells the tyres to customers, and then offers a service package for maintenance and insurance, Michelin makes money off the tyres and then off the maintenance package separately. However, if Michelin charges customers for the number of kilometres that the tyres are used for, then Michelin has aligned incentives with customers, as if the tyre is damaged and needs to be changed, then the truck will be idle for the tyre downtime. Michelin will lose money in that case, just like the customer. Hence, the DFQ principle and the XaaS offering are aligned from the provider and the customer's perspectives.

The principles of the DFQ framework are similar to those in the DFS framework. For example, simplification and standardization are two basic principles that overlap between the two methodologies. Anecdotally, it has been observed that assembly accounts for 9 out of 10 defects, as parts are designed usually in most commercial products today to have Six Sigma quality (the failure rate of components are in parts per million, or ppm). Hence, easy assembly and easy testing of product functionality are key principles in the DFQ framework. A number of quality problems also arise from the interface of design and manufacturing. Hence, concurrent or simultaneous engineering in product development and the agile methodology in software development are key to identifying design quality problems early. The concept of design thinking runs parallel to the agile methodology in being able to capture the voice of the customer early in the design process. Reusing tried and tested modules in software is an essential element of the DFQ toolkit in software, as they have been debugged and tested extensively in the field before. The need for robust design is also emphasized in the DFQ framework; components and the assembly should be functional in a higher range than the design specifications, and the field conditions that products are designed for should be as varied as possible. Failsafe techniques should be applied as often as possible, as in the DFS method.

The solutions provider approach of the XaaS mode requires that all components of the solutions fit with one another as seamlessly as possible. The DFS and DFQ frameworks enable this seamless integration by designing different elements of the offering together, hence, the principles of DFS and DFQ can be used for the effective design of service bundles in the XaaS context.

2.9 XaaS FOR GOVERNMENT OBJECTIVES

So far, we have looked at the XaaS mode of offering primarily from the commercial viewpoint. However, the XaaS mode of offering is getting increasingly popular as a way of offering government services as well. The Gartner CIO survey of 2019 found that over 80% of new government initiatives in most countries will be offered in the XaaS mode by the year 2023.[36] Governments are increasingly adopting digital services and the survey found that 53% of digital initiatives that have been designed are being implemented currently. An impressive fraction of 39% of the senior government leaders surveyed reported that cloud applications of digital initiatives would be the area where they would invest the most resources over the next 4 years. Gartner concluded that while data security and governance on the cloud remain concerns for many senior government leaders, they are getting comfortable with the data security measures being implemented by cloud providers. The current bottleneck for the implementation of government digital initiatives is not the capability of the providers, but rather, the readiness of the government agencies themselves. The Gartner survey finds that while some governments have leaders who are digitally ready, several of them do not have the people skills required for the successful implementation of these initiatives. Gartner posits that CIOs need to either transform the skills of existing leaders or add more external employees with the requisite skills. As an example, the migration from the own data centre to the cloud will require agile design teams who could move ideas to implementation using external cloud resources more quickly. The scope of government IT projects will also change, as the objectives change from automating basic services like bill

---

[36] Hippold, S., "Gartner Predicts By 2023 Over Half of Government IT Workers Will Occupy Roles That Don't Exist Today", *Newsroom, Gartner*, March 6, 2019, https://www.gartner.com/en/newsroom/press-releases/2019-03-06-gartner-predicts-by-2023-over-half-of-government-it-w, accessed May 22, 2020.

payments for public utilities to more social projects like enhancing inclusion and digital ethics. The profiles of the government IT leaders need to change from IT savvy employees to system designers and social scientists. The IT skillsets of government leaders currently are typically in legacy systems like mainframes, and they will need to acquire skills in emerging technologies like AI, machine learning, deep learning, IoT and the blockchain.

Specifically, regarding the XaaS mode, Gartner finds that government leaders are interested in cloud services primarily because of the lower capex outlay for these offerings. Governments had made huge investments in acquiring, enhancing and maintaining large IT systems in the past, and with the fast-paced changes in technology, the shift from the capex model to the opex model is attractive for them. The scalability and agility of the XaaS mode from the pilot to the launch makes it easier for governments to adopt the XaaS mode, as both small local offerings and nationwide initiatives are enabled by the XaaS mode. While XaaS does offer responsiveness, the challenge for government agencies could be that IT experts are not involved in project discussions, and agency leaders may contract directly with XaaS providers. Gartner identifies two pitfalls of this approach: first, agency leaders may lack the IT expertize and knowledge to negotiate contracts and SLAs with XaaS providers. There may also be benefits to centralizing the access to the solutions, which may be lowered with individual agency leaders acting entrepreneurially. Second, even if the solution is implemented, there will be a need for agency IT teams to be involved to provide local support. Gartner recommends that government CIOs actively build an internal capability for working with XaaS providers for negotiating contracts, and understanding the project needs and the provider's capabilities.

2.10 XaaS FOR IP SERVICES

An interesting example of a corporate offering that serves the objectives of governments and regulatory authorities is the patent aggregation model offered in the XaaS format. Why do governments adopt and operate Intellectual Property (IP) protection regimes nationally and globally? The objective of IT protection is to encourage innovation, firms who engage in

R&D must be able to monetize their investments. If investments in innovation are not protected for a period, competitors can reverse-engineer innovative product and service designs and offer copied offerings, leading to the innovator not being able to get the fruits of their investments. When IP cannot be protected, investments in innovation suffer due to the free-rider effect. In the pharmaceutical industry, for instance, the cost of R&D projects can run into billions of dollars, and the process of drug development from concept to regulatory approval can take up to 10 years. At the same time, the number of compounds that make it from the concept stage to the approval stage is less than 1%. Without an appropriate IP protection regime, pharmaceutical firms would not have an incentive to invest in R&D for treating diseases. Hence, IP protection acts as a mechanism that governments can use to encourage investments in innovation by the private sector. In many industry sectors, the IP protection laws protect genuine assets built by the innovator for a limited period, enabling the firm to develop a platform for growth and continually invest in innovation. These innovations may not just be in the core product or service, but in the way the product or service is delivered or accessed, as innovations pervade all areas of operations.

While the protection of innovation is indeed socially optimal, IP protection regimes can be misused as well. Strong empirical evidence suggests that often, non-practising entities (NPEs) can acquire patents and then use legal machinery to coerce firms to pay for patent infringement, as the domain of a patent is often blurred. These NPEs have a business model of monetizing their owned IP primarily by legal means, and are referred to as patent trolls in the practitioner literature.[37] Since it is hard to determine the value of patent infringement, patent trolls rely on the legal system to extract high punitive fees from the alleged infringer of their IP. The research on IP trolling activity estimates that trolling litigation has cost over 80 billion dollars in losses directly and indirectly, and reduced the spread of technology advances.[38] This makes practising firms careful

[37] Ipeg, "The NPE ("Patent Trolls") Minefield", 2014, https://www.ipeg.com/the-npe-patent-trolls-minefield/, accessed May 22, 2020.
[38] Lee., T. B. "Study: patent trolls have cost innovators half a trillion dollars", arsTECH-NICA, September 20, 2011, https://arstechnica.com/tech-policy/2011/09/study-patent-trolls-have-cost-innovators-half-a-trillion-bucks/, accessed May 24, 2020.

in their use of innovations, resulting in excess legal activism, increased search costs, and lowered innovation and social welfare. Most NPEs acquire their IP in secondary markets. While governments are aware of the risks of having secondary markets for patents, the value of patent trading is high as it creates liquidity for innovation. Often, patents are generated by universities and research organizations who are NPEs, and having a secondary market for IP enables them to monetize their investments in innovation. Hence, closing secondary markets down to limit patent trolling is not a viable option. The costs of monitoring legal activism is high, hence, identifying serial patent trolling behaviour is hard, making the control of patent trolling a challenge.

In this environment, XaaS providers of IP rights can play an important role in matching the needs of firms, society and the government, and can regulate the negative impact of patent trolls. These providers can be divided into three categories: (i) defensive aggregators, who acquire IP rights in the open market and then use a subscription model to offer the entire patent repository for legal protection of subscribers, (ii) offensive aggregators, who acquire patents and offer them to customers on a pay-per-use basis, with the objective of obtaining licensing fees for access to specific patents, and (iii) IP advisory firms, who offer consulting advice on IP acquisition, management and technology transfer.[39]

Defensive aggregators have used subscription models effectively to distribute IP more widely, and control patent trolling behaviour. RPX was the pioneer of defensive aggregating in the patent intermediary world. It followed the strategy of acquiring patents, and then using them defensively by offering them to all firms with a subscription model.[40] RPX has a stated objective that it will never use its patent portfolio to generate money using patent litigation. Their patent portfolio is strictly meant for defensive purposes. Firms that have subscribed to RPX's patent portfolio

---

[39] Wang, A. W. (2010). Rise of the patent intermediaries. *Berkeley Technology Law Journal*, 25, 159.

[40] RPX, "RPX Introduces First Defensive Patent Aggregation Service", November 25, 2008, https://www.rpxcorp.com/about/news/rpx-introduces-first-defensive-patent-aggregation-service/#:~:text=RPX%20Corporation%20is%20the%20first,%2Dpracticing%20entities%20(NPEs), accessed May 26, 2020.

services pay an annual subscription fee, and they can use the portfolio for defending themselves against litigation for any patent infringement. Hence, RPX acts as a shield against patent trolls, and helps firms focus on their core missions of innovating and adding value to products and services for customers.

How does RPX generate value for firms, the government, and customers with its Patents-as-a-Service (PaaS) offering? The research has shown that the PaaS offering indeed helps make innovation markets more efficient from the government's perspective.[41] First, firms get protection against litigation by patent trolls. Since RPX has access to a substantial patent pool that subscribers have knowledge of, they can find similar patents that enable them to defend themselves against litigation. Second, if RPX acquires a patent, they share that patent with all firms within their subscriber pool, whereas if a practising entity like a technology firm acquires a patent, they will ideally use it for their own operations only. From that perspective, RPX helps to distribute the innovation more globally to many firms, leading to all those firms using that innovation in their products and services. This also leads to greater customer welfare, as all the products adopted by customers are influenced by the innovation. Since multiple firms can use the innovation in their products and services, customers benefit from products with higher functionality. The competitive environment controls price increases by the firms using the innovation, enabling more customers to acquire products and services that use the innovation.

From the government's perspective, the social welfare of the innovation system, as represented by better customer value, higher competition, more innovation usage and less patent litigation is enhanced. The incentives for firms to engage in R&D are maintained, as if they sell their IP to defensive aggregators like RPX, they get some value for that IP. However, does the defensive aggregation model of sharing innovations hinder the use of patents and innovation as a differentiating mechanism from

---

[41] Agrawal, A., Bhattacharya, S., & Hasija, S. (2016). Cost-reducing innovation and the role of patent intermediaries in increasing market efficiency. *Production and Operations Management*, 25(2), 173–191.

competition? In other words, why would firms innovate if patent aggregators like RPX bought their IP, and then distributed the IP to all firms operating in that business using RPX's subscription model? The short answer is "No", practising firms still have an incentive to pursue innovation. RPX's defensive aggregator approach works for a selective class of patents. Our research shows that defensive aggregators typically acquire incremental innovation patents, and not radical innovation patents, which are more likely to provide market differentiating ability. Hence, firms engaging in R&D for significant market differentiation will not sell their IP to RPX, but use it themselves for obtaining competitive advantage in their products and services. This leads to an incentive for firms to engage in developing radical innovations. Patent trolls also do not have access to radical innovation IP, as those patents are well-known in the market, hence, the bidding pressure on those patents is very high, even if those patents are sold in secondary markets. The RPX example demonstrates that when used effectively, firms that operate with the subscription model in market mediating roles like IP distribution can help smooth market functioning. The goal of the XaaS mode of offerings is to share applications across multiple firms, the higher the subscriber base, the better.

There are other examples of the pay-per-use mode of solutions offerings in the IP market as well, showing that XaaS offerings are not limited to products, services and software, but can extend to the offering of critical assets such as IP as well. InnoCentive is a XaaS offering that uses its platform to crowdsource innovations for clients. It was set up by Eli Lilly as an open innovation platform where firms could provide innovation "challenges" to any "solvers" who would bid to solve those challenges. The reward money for the challenge is announced with the challenge, and InnoCentive has developed a system to ensure that clients pay the reward money to solvers who provide meaningful solutions to the challenges. The average award for a solution is $20,000, with some challenges having awards of more than five times that figure.[42] The InnoCentive concept is

---

[42] Wikipedia, InnoCentive, https://en.wikipedia.org/wiki/InnoCentive#:~:text=The%20 average%20award%20amount%20for,%2420%20million%20in%20the%20process, accessed May 28, 2020.

very similar to other firms in the sharing economy who provide XaaS offerings on a pay-per-use basis, without the resources to provide the service themselves. However, the InnoCentive model (and the model of many other innovation sharing platforms) does have some constraints. First, a lot of emphasis is laid on the interest and participation of skilled solvers. Not every challenge will have a large set of solvers bidding to sole the challenge. The quality of the solution critically depends on the ability and skills of the solvers, just like Uber and Grab depend on an external resource of drivers with cars participating in their platform-based services. Designing the right incentives for the solvers is critical to the sustenance of the model. The gig economy equivalent of the reward system may not be sustainable. Some challenges need experts with multiple skills to collaborate for success, yet the InnoCentive model relies on individual solving skills and does not encourage collaboration between solvers yet.

2.11 XaaS CHALLENGES OF SHARED RESOURCES

So, will XaaS be the only game in town? The challenges facing the XaaS mode of offerings derive from some of the same factors that make them more efficient compared to the own asset model. One of the salient features of the service-based offerings is that a common set of capacity resources of the provider is used to serve a large set of customers. The economies of scale from pooling multiple customers accessing the same resources enable the scalability of these models. However, if a large set of customers tries to access these services at the same time, the resulting network congestion can cause the services to slow down or break down.[43] Hence, the usage of shared resources has its own set of challenges to manage. On a highway, traffic often flows smoothly for some part of the highway, and then owing to maintenance work, one lane is shut down. This causes the traffic flow to slow down dramatically, as the capacity of the

---

[43] Barney, D., "The Great Cloud Bottleneck: How Capacity Issues Can Kill Your Cloud Project", Redmondmag, December 6, 2011, https://redmondmag.com/articles/2011/12/01/cloud-bottleneck-issues.aspx, accessed May 30, 2020.

highway just got reduced by one lane. The impact of one lane shutting down is higher on a two-lane highway than a four-lane highway. Similarly, online systems have a finite capacity, this systemic capacity is given by the slowest part of the system or the bottleneck. The bottleneck may be caused by different resources: sometimes communication links may be the bottleneck, at other times, a poorly designed system can cause one part of the network to be clogged. Faulty devices may cause this impact as well, causing all traffic to be routed to the lower number of functioning devices (this is like the lower number of lanes on the highway temporarily). Any glitch in the operation of the bottleneck in shared resources lowers the available capacity for all users, leading to the need for judicious management of these shared resources.

The demand on the network is the other side of the picture. The utilization of the system is the ratio of the demand on the network to the current network capacity. If the demand on the network increases, for a fixed capacity, the utilization increases, causing congestion effects. A network with a utilization of up to 60% at a given point of time should function reasonably, but when the utilization approaches high figures like 80–90%, the network slows down dramatically, leading to latency (delay in accessing the network). Latency can also be caused intentionally. Cyberattacks that cause repeated requests of the network can cause the network to slow down, leading to denial of service requests, and packet (data) losses. In addition to latency, other key performance indicators (KPIs) of XaaS offerings that matter due to network congestion are bandwidth (flow rate of information), throughput (the amount of data that is transferred per unit time), and data storage and retrieval times.[44] The latency, bandwidth and throughput of a system are related by a relationship known as Little's Law — the amount of packets in the system is the product of the bandwidth and the time taken in the system, given by the latency of the system. For example, if it takes a car two minutes to go through a tunnel and the number of cars entering the tunnel every minute (flow rate) is ten, then the number of cars in the tunnel at any point of time is twenty.

---

[44] NetApp, "What is XaaS (anything as a service)?" https://www.netapp.com/knowledge-center/what-is-anything-as-a-service-xaas/, accessed May 30, 2020.

There are techniques that can be used by providers to lower network congestion. Data security measures can be used to differentiate between genuine users and cyberattacks. Backoff protocols in high congestion, fair queueing to equalize capacity usage for different requests in prioritization are other examples of congestion-reducing measures.[45] In some systems, where the digital signature of requests can be verified, intentional prioritization for some packets ahead of others using admissions control can also be used under high utilization. Hence, capacity planning on the provider's part is critical to ensuring a high quality of service. In extreme cases, latency may advance to the next stage of the system breakdown or outage, causing lost time on the system. Typically, service outages are rare events, caused by multiple causes that are like those causing latency due to network congestion. They may be caused by simple issues such as a power system outage with no backup due to a general lack of backups, cyberattacks, or software bugs. Both network congestion and system outage are well-known challenges. To provide guarantees against both problems, providers typically offer service level agreements (SLAs) that specify the guaranteed uptime of the system, and the quality of service (bounds on latency) with their service contracts.

Interestingly, network congestion issues are common to all XaaS offerings with shared resources and are not limited to software or computer infrastructure issues alone. Ridesharing services like Uber and Grab routinely face congestion during office hours in the morning and evening, as the utilization of the system (the ratio of service requests to the number of cars available) peaks during office hours. At these times, riders must wait for a long time to receive service. The response of the ridesharing services to this temporary mismatch of service capacity and demand has been to implement "surge" pricing, which gives priority to the customer who is willing to pay the highest price for the service at that point of time. The surge pricing concept is like yield pricing or revenue management schemes used by services like airlines and hotels, who increase prices

---

[45] Cisco, "QoS: Congestion Management Configuration Guide, Cisco IOS XE Release 3S", January 21, 2018, https://www.cisco.com/c/en/us/td/docs/ios-xml/ios/qos_conmgt/configuration/xe-3s/qos-conmgt-xe-3s-book/qos-conmgt-oview.html, accessed May 30, 2020.

during times of peak demand. One simple solution to reducing the impact of congestion for hardware services is to schedule the arrival times of requests: scheduling lowers the variability of arrivals, and makes it easier to apportion a fixed amount of capacity for multiple demand requests. While scheduling requests may not be feasible for online XaaS offerings, providers can share their scheduled maintenance times with clients so that clients can plan their use of the service outside of these maintenance times.

A second challenge for XaaS providers is the limited range of customization that they can provide. While offerings under the XaaS umbrella indeed provide solutions, the customization offered is from a limited set of resources that are designed by the provider to be mixed and matched. Hence, complete customization to the requirements of the user cannot be achieved under the umbrella of shared resources. For instance, in the space of ERP systems, many large organizations have their own solutions that have been custom-built for them. In contrast, features can be added to ERP offerings under the XaaS umbrella, but the core product is still the offering of the provider, so any customization must be around the core offering. While WeWork and WeLive offer the options of customizing the office and the residence to the standardized fit-out, a potential homeowner can buy land and build his or her home from scratch. Hence, customized offerings under the XaaS umbrella must be developed around the core offering of the provider, while asset ownership allows the option to design the complete product specifically for the esoteric needs of the customer.

In addition to design customization limitations, the as-a-service set of offerings may also be exposed to inadequate performance risk. While SLAs can be designed for KPIs like the uptime of the system and the latency, it is hard to design SLAs for every KPI. In addition, if the SLAs are not met, penalty clauses for subpar performance may not be written into the contract. There also may be hidden costs associated with the adoption of as-a-service platforms, as some service aspects may be tacitly assumed by the user without adequate coverage from SLAs. If those aspects are not mentioned explicitly, the provider may charge for the offering of those features. Negotiating as-a-service contracts has pitfalls for both the user and the provider, as neither party may be fully aware of the expectations of the other. Experienced professionals on both sides of the table would be aware of these issues and would likely negotiate various contingencies into the contract. Some standard customer support problems may also arise, as customer support capacity works in a similar way to system capacity. If a lot of customers are reaching for customer support at the same time, the quality of the service is lower. However, there are standard SLAs like the time to pick up the call and first-time resolution that can be written into the customer support contract.

The security of data in cloud applications has traditionally been one of the most discussed challenges of cloud computing. While data can be stored in the user's storage facilities as well, cloud computing provides users with the option of storing their data in the provider's data centres. Both parties are responsible for ensuring data security. Providers install features for ensuring that their client's data and applications are securely stored, and users must ensure that their administrative and authentication measures cannot be misused to gain entry into the provider's data centres. However, cloud storage centres have had security issues in the past. Cloud Security Alliance lists the following threats: abuse of cloud computing access, insecure interfaces, abuse of data by the employees of the provider, shared technology, intentional data loss and account hijacking.[46] Cloud computing providers often do not have detailed checks on the identity of customers. As is often the case, they provide free trials without verifying customer details. This enables malware developers and other organizers of cyberattacks to create accounts for the use of the provider's facilities, and then using this access for illegal activity. The application programming interfaces (APIs) may not have secure access designed to the same extent as other parts of the system, causing another source of access for cybercriminals into data centres. Users do not know the profiles of the employees of the provider, and there have been cases where the provider's employees have breached the data security of the users. Cloud computing typically combines different resources like storage and processing together. Illegal access to the processing or other units can also

---

[46] Cloud Security Alliance, "CSA Releases New Research — Top Threats to Cloud Computing: Egregious Eleven", September 8, 2019, https://cloudsecurityalliance.org/press-releases/2019/08/09/csa-releases-new-research-top-threats-to-cloud-computing-egregious-eleven/, accessed May 30, 2020.

provide access to the storage units. Cybercriminals can cause intentional data loss by deleting key elements like identifier numbers of user accounts, which leads to the entire data losing its value. Finally, accessing the password and second factor authentication of one genuine user can provide access to the shared resources of the cloud provider. Cloud providers can implement several security features like data isolation or segregation that prevents systemic access to user data from illegal access to one cloud resource. However, cybercriminals are also evolving in their attack methods on data security. While data security issues do exist for own IT asset operators as well, security features are designed to block all external entry, and physical assets are owned by the operator. Second, access to both processing and storage resources are not shared, hence, they can be more tightly controlled than for cloud providers whose systems are accessed by multiple users.

We summarize the key points made in this chapter related to the choice of customers between acquiring assets and using them as a service to obtain utility.

2.12 SUMMARY

We now have a nuanced lens for understanding the choice between XaaS and productization offerings for customers. These factors range from the strategy of being offered customized solutions versus a standardized asset, the initial budget outlay to the total cost of operation, the inclusion of various risks from both of the offering modes, and the time to set up and start using either offering. The factors also include customer characteristics like how often the customer intends to use the core product or service, the utility they derive from each usage and the associated deal transaction costs, and the capex and opex accounting, costs and flexibility factors.

The factors influencing customer choice between the XaaS offering and buying the product and acquiring services separately are summarized in Table 2.1.

From the financial and accounting perspective, we see that customers are constrained by the budget effect. If the initial outlay for availing of a service is high, customers will prefer to pay as they go. The choice of the opex against the capex framework relates to the availability of financing

Table 2.1: Factors Influencing Customer Choice of XaaS Offering and Product Selling Models

Factor	XaaS (Solutions provider)	Selling (Product + Services)
Budget effect	Opex based	Capex based
Solutions approach and customization	Solutions developed along standard core, one-stop shop model, customization is cheaper	Full customization possible at higher cost, can add best-in-class services to core offering
Risks of asset valuation, quality, capacity, budget overruns, DFS/DFQ, switching costs	Usually lower	Usually higher
Obsolescence of product/service and time of horizon	Usually better for shorter horizons and technology lifecycles	Usually better for longer horizons and durable assets
Frequency of usage	Ideally low to moderate	Ideally high
Expected utility per use	Better for diminishing utility from repeated use	Better for steady utility over multiple uses
Deal Transaction costs	Low search costs, high repeated transaction costs	High search costs, one-time transaction cost
Complementarity and bundling	Higher benefits	Lower benefits
Agility and cash flow	Higher benefits	Lower benefits
Economies of scale from shared resources	Higher economies, congestion effects, data security a concern	Low economies of scale, low congestion, and low security concerns

options, the tax accounting benefits, the need for the visibility of core operations being profitable, the impact on cash flow and the TCO. While the financial and accounting factors are important components of customer choice, they must be superimposed with strategic decisions like should the firm be investing scarce resources on non-core activities? Is the firm better off sourcing for individual service add-ons themselves after acquiring assets, or is it better to have a one-stop shop from where all services can be sourced? In addition to the financial and strategic implications, decision-makers must weigh the risks associated with the lifecycle of the underlying product or technology, and their own strategic direction. If the customer intends to operate in the business for a long time, then the acquisition of underlying assets may make sense, as the depreciation or the amortization would be done over a longer time horizon. However, if the underlying technology has a short lifecycle, then the risk of obsolescence must be considered. There may be other sources of asset valuation risk, for instance, real estate assets appreciate in many parts of the world even in inflation-adjusted terms, while macroeconomic boom and bust cycles may lower valuations of durable assets as well. The risks of quality, servicing, budget overruns and variable payment schedules have also to be considered in making this decision.

From the economics and marketing perspectives, customer characteristics differ for different product and service classes. Some products like books and films may provide temporal utility, while others may have more durable utility. Depending on the access characteristics to the services and the associated search costs for different services, customers may make different choices based on the offering mode. The solutions provider approach has its advantages as it provides convenience in the form of a one-stop shop for all associated services. Indeed, data analytics and improving technologies make it imperative for the provider to rejuvenate their set of offerings over time. By offering products bundled with services or bundled services, providers may find that the utility to customers is more than the sum of the parts of individual services. Sharing resources across multiple customers indeed helps in creating economies of scale; however, the operational measures of latency, bandwidth and throughput must be managed well.

Perhaps the most widely stressed advantage of the XaaS mode of offering is the agility it provides customers. We conclude the chapter by pointing out that the agility advantage is indeed critical for the contemporary world. However, by absolving the customer of multiple risks to enable agility, providers have the added responsibility of engaging in continuous innovation to ensure sustained customer value. Sustained competitive advantage from the XaaS mode of offering is only feasible if this continuous innovation cycle can be perpetuated.

Chapter 3

Pricing for the XaaS Model

The pricing of XaaS offerings (like the pricing of any good) is one of the most important factors that customers consider before making their decision to adopt the product, service or software. The reader should note that the actual value of an offering to a customer is the difference between his or her value and the price charged. This difference is called the customer surplus (discussed in Chapter 2). Let us consider the offering of a general product, service or software first to develop insights into the trade-offs in pricing. These insights are very basic. From the customer's perspective, his or surplus depends on the price of the offering, thus, obviously, the lower the price, the higher the customer surplus. However, from the provider's perspective, the pricing decision is more nuanced: if the provider prices the offering at a low value, the number of customers adopting the offering will be high. In this case, the provider's sales will be high (equal to the number of customers adopting the offering), however, the margins (price minus variable cost) will be low. On the other hand, if the provider prices the offering at a high value, the margins will be high, but the sales will be low, this basic understanding of pricing applies to all situations. The provider's gross profits are the product of the sales and the margins, from which the provider subtracts its fixed costs to get its net profit before tax. Obviously, the provider should choose the price that maximizes this net profit figure if the provider is focused on maximizing its profits.

However, there are several other considerations in addition to profits maximization that the provider needs to factor into its pricing decision. The first consideration is the varying of price over time. The provider may want to change its pricing policy over time due to multiple reasons. For instance, the provider may want to increase the customer base to begin with in the early phase of the offering, this helps in increasing the number of customers adopting the offering.[1] Once the provider has reached a critical number of customers who have adopted the offering, the provider may want to increase its prices to maximize profitability.[2] This approach is known as penetration pricing. The penetration pricing strategy has the advantage of creating a loyal customer base early and increasing network and word-of-mouth effects for rapid diffusion of the offering. Hence, creating awareness and expediting the diffusion of the offering is helped by penetration pricing. The provider may also have alternative monetization methods like advertising revenue that depends on the size of the customer base. Having a high customer base enables the provider to charge a higher advertising rate based on the size of the market, and hence, penetration pricing helps to increase this base as well. However, customers may not like the increased price for the same offering over time, and may either choose to switch providers, or not use the offering in the future if their customer surplus is negative. The pricing of the entire set of online offerings on the Internet in the early days was designed around this principle. Providers offered services like search for free and monetized their offerings from alternative sources like advertising. In the products category, the pricing strategy of complementary assets (like razors and blades) is based on this strategy. The provider may want to offer the base asset (the razor) at a low price to get customers to adopt their product, and then price the complementary asset (the blade) at a high margin to increase their profitability over time.

On the other hand, if the offering has a high awareness to begin with, and there is a large base of customers who are interested in the offering, the firm may price the offering high early on. This enables the firm to get a high margin from the customers with a high utility from the offering and

---

[1] Jan Haemer, "Skimming or Penetration Pricing?", Simon-Kucher & Partners, April 17, 2019, https://www.simon-kucher.com/en-sg/blog/skimming-or-penetration-pricing, accessed May 30, 2020.

[2] HUANG, Jianhui. Pricing Strategy for Cloud Computing Services. (2014). 1-133. Dissertations and Theses Collection (Open Access), Singapore Management University. Available at: https://ink.library.smu.edu.sg/etd_coll/103

who want to avail of the offering early. After the customers with the high utility (and correspondingly high reservation price) have adopted the product or the service, the provider can subsequently lower the price for the customers who have the next highest levels of utility from the offering. This price decrease continues over time, until all customers who have reasonable utility from the offering adopt it. This pricing strategy is known as the skimming strategy. The provider skims the top end of the market first, and then continues lowering prices until it hits steady state where a large share of the market has adopted the offering. The skimming strategy is used in the offering of books. Most books are offered at a high price early in the form of hardcover books, and over time, the price of the book is reduced, until the price hits a certain level.[3] At that point of time, the softcover version of the book is introduced at a much lower price point. While the aesthetics and reading pleasure of the hardcover version of the book are higher, the content of the softcover is the same. The same strategy is also used for pricing offerings that lose value quickly because of obsolescence. Providers of PC systems, cell phones and other technology products use the skimming strategy.

Finally, for customer staple goods, most retailers use the strategy of constant pricing with some promotions thrown in every now and then. The constant pricing strategy is known as everyday low pricing (EDLP). The EDLP strategy has been used famously by Walmart to signal to customers that they would not have any additional customer surplus from timing their purchases.[4] Other retailers use promotions for a variety of reasons: to clear excess inventory, to attract customers to visit their stores and buy other goods, to reward loyal customers, or to encourage customers to try a product for the first time.

Hence, there are different decision-making models and objectives for pricing: maximizing the profits of the firm, increasing the customer base first and then levelling off at the profit maximizing price leading to a

---

[3] Bhattacharya, S., Krishnan, V., & Mahajan, V. (2003). Operationalizing technology improvements in product development decision-making. *European Journal of Operational Research*, 149(1), 102–130.

[4] Walmart, Key Messages, https://cdn.corporate.walmart.com/33/df/a80e565641f5ad6 b1c2437fc4129/walmart-key-messages.pdf, accessed June 1, 2020.

penetration strategy, or differentiating between the willingness of customers to pay, leading to a skimming strategy. Of course, this is a small subset of pricing strategies, there are several other objectives of pricing that we will consider later in this chapter. The price points under each of these different strategies would be different at any point of time owing to the different objectives, and the value provided to customers.

3.1 PRICING MODELS OF XaaS OFFERINGS: FLAT-FEE, SUBSCRIPTION AND PAY-PER-USE PRICING

While it has been empirically observed that most providers in the as-a-service offering space use either pay-per-use (also known as "pay as you go", or "pay for resources"), subscription models (use the services as often as you want for a fixed period, similar to a lease) or performance-based contracts, the underlying trade-offs of these pricing models have a common set of economics. The nanonization of services under the XaaS mode of offerings also enables the nanonization of pricing. We will demonstrate the pricing benefits aligning with the nanonization of customer utility over the attribute space and over time. We will begin by comparing the pay-per-use, subscription model and flat-fee pricing (selling the asset model) first to develop insights into the strengths and weaknesses of these pricing models. Pay-per-use pricing and performance-based pricing are similar, with the difference that the provider charges for resources used in the pay-per-use pricing model, and charges for some kind of output that matters to the customer in the performance-based contract. The subscription and pay-per-use pricing models have an important advantage over flat-fee pricing: there is no need for massively discounting the asset at the end of the lifecycle of the asset.[5] The drop of prices at the end of the horizon is observed very clearly for technology assets, however, it is a ubiquitous phenomenon, and is seen whenever a provider replaces a generation of assets with the subsequent one.

---

[5] Robotis, A., Bhattacharya, S., & Van Wassenhove, L. N. (2012). Lifecycle pricing for installed base management with constrained capacity and remanufacturing. *Production and Operations Management*, 21(2), 236–252.

For the development of the insights, we will consider a small example first. Our simplified example will consider only the utility of the customer and the price, and the impact on the provider's profits. For this simplified model, we ignore all other effects including the fixed and variable cost of the offering. Consider a provider who can offer a service to a set of 4 customers: Andrew, Bonnie, Charles and Daisy. The provider will either offer them the service in the pay-per-use mode, or in the monthly subscription mode. Andrew and Charles have an expected utility per use of $40 (reservation price equivalent of utility, hence the value of the service) and Bonnie and Daisy have an expected utility per use of $60. Andrew and Bonnie expect to use the service 5 times in a month, and Charles and Daisy expect to use the service 10 times in a month. If the provider offers the service to them in the pay-per-use mode, the four customers have a deal transaction cost of $1 for each time they must access the service. For brevity, we can assume that the provider operates in a monopoly, i.e., there is no competitive offering in the market.

If the provider offers the service to them in the pay-per-use mode, then the provider will either charge a price of $38.99 or $58.99 for the following reasons. If the provider offers the service at a price of $38.99, then the surplus for Andrew and Charles is $0.01 (the utility of $40 minus the price of $38.99 and the deal transaction cost of $1), and the surplus for Bonnie and Daisy is $40.01 ($80 − $38.99 − $1). Since all four of them have a positive customer surplus, each one of them will adopt the service. If the provider charges a price of less than $38.99, all four of them will still adopt the service, as they have higher customer surpluses, but the provider's profits will be lower, hence, the lower price will be suboptimal. If the provider charges a higher price than $38.99, then Andrew and Charles will not adopt the service, as they get a negative surplus. If the provider charges a price of $58.99, only Bonnie and Daisy will adopt the service as their customer surplus is positive ($0.01). Andrew and Charles will not have a positive customer surplus ($40 − $58.99 − $1 = −$19.99) for the higher price. If the provider charges a higher pay-per-use than $59, none of them will adopt the service. Table 3.1 summarizes the impact of pricing on the adoption and the profit contributions of the four customers.

Table 3.1:   Sales and Profits from Pay-Per-Use Example

Pay per use price	Customers adopting	Profits
$38.99	A, B, C, D	$38.99 (2 \times 5 + 2 \times 10) = 1169.70$
$58.99	B, D	$58.99 (5 + 10) = 884.85$

To estimate the profits, it is easy to see that if the price is $38.99, then all four of them adopt the service. Andrew and Bonnie expect to use the service five times in a month, so the expected profits from each of them is 38.99×5, and since Charles and Daisy expect to use the service 10 times in a month, the expected profits from each of them is 38.99×10. If the provider charges the higher price-per-use of $58.99, then only Bonnie and Daisy adopt the service, yielding profits of 58.99×5 and 58.99×10, respectively.

As can be seen from Table 3.1, if the provider uses the pay-per-use mode, then the optimal price-per-use is $38.99, all four customers adopt the service and the highest profit is $1169.70 for the provider. If the provider increases this price-per-use to $58.99, then only two customers (Bonnie and Daisy) pay the higher price, and while they give higher margins to the provider, the lower participation in the market leads to a lower profit of $884.85. What if the utilities per use of the market were more skewed? For instance, what if Bonnie and Daisy had a utility-per-use of $100 instead of $60? In that case, the two potential price points to consider would be $38.99 and $98.99. If the provider wanted all four customers to avail of the service, then it would price the service at $38.99 and get a profit of $1169.70 as before. However, if the provider prices the service at $98.99, then Bonnie and Daisy would give the provider a profit of $98.99 \times (10 + 5) = \$1484.85$. Hence, in this case, the provider would be better off ignoring Andrew and Charles, and pricing the service high for only Bonnie and Daisy to use.

First, this little example illustrates the trade-off between sales and price described earlier in the chapter. If the provider prices the offering at a low level, it will sell to a larger set of customers, but at a lower margin per customer. If it sets the price high, it will sell to a smaller set of customers, but at a higher margin. This demand elasticity with respect to price is true of all goods and the modes that they are offered in, whether the modes are flat-fee pricing, pay-per-use or subscription. The optimal pricing strategy for the provider depends on the degree of dispersion or skew of the utility-per-use if the provider offers the service in the pay-per-use mode. If the skew of the market is significant (customers differ significantly in their utilities-per-use), then it may be optimal to ignore the customers with low utilities and target the customers with high utilities. In this case, the provider prefers to get the high margins from a smaller set of customers. If the degree of skew is low (the utilities-per-use of customers are close to each other), then in that case, the provider prefers to set the price lower, and attract a larger customer segment.

Next, we derive the profits for the provider if it used a subscription mode of offering. Let us revisit our example to identify the optimal price for the subscription mode. We first compute the total utilities of all four customers. The total utility of the customer for the month is the multiplicative product of the utility-per-use and the number of times the customer expects to use the service in the month. Hence, Andrew has a total utility of $40 \times 5 = \$200$ per month from using the service, Bonnie has a utility of $300, Charles has a utility of $400, and Daisy has a utility of $600. As before, the only prices the provider needs to consider are $199.99, $299.99, $399.99 and $599.99. The profits from the subscription mode of offering as a function of the price are tabulated in Table 3.2.

At the price of $199.99, all four customers would adopt the product, as their net utility over the month was higher than the subscription price. At the price of $299.99, Andrew would not avail of the service as his expected utility was $200; the other cases are derived similarly. We make two observations in the use of the flat-fee subscription example. First, the optimal price for the subscription fee is $299.99, and the provider would expect only Bonnie, Charles and Daisy to adopt the service at this price.

Table 3.2: Sales and Profits from Flat-Fee Subscription Example

Subscription price	Customers adopting	Profits
$199.99	A, B, C, D	$199.99 \times 4 = 799.96$
$299.99	B, C, D	$299.99 \times 3 = 899.97$
$399.99	C, D	$399.99 \times 2 = 799.98$
$599.99	D	599.99

Hence, there is some impact from the demand elasticity of price as before. However, note that the optimal profit for the monthly subscription is lower than the optimal profit from the pay-per-use offering.

Is this insight generalizable, or is it a function of the numbers used in this example? Our research shows that this insight is indeed generalizable, in a monopoly, the pay-per-use mechanism dominates the subscription mechanism and the flat-fee pricing in the productization model (we shall elaborate on this later). Why does the pay-per-use mechanism do better than the subscription mechanism in extracting customer utility for the provider always? The pay-per-use mechanism nanonizes customer utility along the dimension of frequency of usage perfectly, and along the mechanism of utility-per-use imperfectly. The customer's utility is determined by both the usage frequency and the utility-per-use. The key insight is that the pay-per-use mechanism discriminates perfectly among customers on the dimension of the frequency of the usage by nanoizing value from each use, but the subscription mechanism and the flat-fee mechanism do not. To understand why the pay-per-use mechanism is better, it is instructive to compute the customer surpluses for all four customers under the optimal prices of the two modes (please see Table 3.3).

In the pay-per-use mechanism, at the optimal price, all four customers adopt the offering. The users with the lower utilities-per-use (Andrew and Charles) can use the service. However, the pay-per-use mechanism

Table 3.3: Customer Surpluses for Optimal Pay-Per-Use and Subscription Prices for Example

Mode	Customer	Customer's surplus
Pay-per-use	Andrew	$(40 - 38.99 - 1) \times 5 = 0.05$
	Bonnie	$(60 - 38.99 - 1) \times 5 = 100.05$
	Charles	$(40 - 38.99 - 1) \times 10 = 0.10$
	Daisy	$(60 - 38.99 - 1) \times 10 = 200.1$
Subscription	Andrew	Does not adopt
	Bonnie	$300 - 299.99 = 0.01$
	Charles	$400 - 299.99 = 100.01$
	Daisy	$600 - 299.99 = 300.01$

extracts almost all the value from them, leaving them with very small customer surpluses. Bonnie and Daisy have higher utilities per use, so they are left with some surplus (about $300 in total). Some total value is lost in the deal transaction costs, with neither provider nor customer extracting that value. In the subscription mechanism, at the optimal price, Andrew is not being served, so his needs are unmet by the provider. Bonnie's utility is extracted almost fully, but Charles and Daisy have some customer surplus. The total customer surplus in the pay-per-use mode is $300.30, while the total customer surplus in the subscription model is $400.30. Hence, the pay-per-use mode extracts the value from the customer more efficiently, while serving a higher set of customers (Andrew is not served in the subscription mode).

This is exactly how the pay-per-use mechanism works better than the subscription mode or the flat-fee pricing modes in the XaaS offerings. The pay-per-use mechanism nanonizes the customer's utility from the service along two dimensions: utility-per-use and frequency of usage. Hence, the pay-per-use mechanism is a lean mechanism, as it discriminates perfectly along the frequency of usage; there is no "waste" for the provider on the utility-per-use dimension. While the nanonization of the pay-per-use mechanism along the dimension of utility-per-use (customers with higher utilities per use will have some surplus) is not obvious, it is obvious that pay-per-use discriminates perfectly along the frequency of usage dimension. Customers with different usage frequencies but the same utility-per-use (like Andrew and Charles) will have their entire customer surplus extracted by the provider. In the extreme case where all customers have the same utility-per-use but different frequencies of usage, the pay-per-use mechanism has zero loss of efficiency in pricing: it can extract the entire customer surplus of all customers.

A comparison of selling the product using flat-fee pricing versus offering the service in XaaS mode as a subscription provides very similar insights to the presentation above. The subscription model nanonizes the customer's utility over time, whereas selling the product bundles the utility-per-use and frequency of usage into one common utility framework. Smallholders, who are customers of Trringo, the agricultural equipment provider, cannot afford to buy reapers, disc harrows and planters as they are too expensive. However, they find all three sets of equipment useful if offered access to them on a subscription or pay-per-use model. They will subscribe to the planter just before the seeding season, the disc harrow well before the seeding season, and the reaper during the harvesting season. At other times, they will not subscribe to the services. The nanonization of the utility model over time (offering equipment monthly) enables smallholders to subscribe to the service when they need it, overcoming the hurdle to pay a large sum to acquire the equipment.

How does the XaaS offering nanonize the pricing based on utility-per-use? Note that when IT assets or products are sold, they are sold based on a flat fee, for all the functionality and features offered by the product, regardless of whether the customer needs it or not. Hence, the productization model uses a blunt instrument of creating one product with a certain set of functionalities, features and performance. Different users get different utilities from the product. In contrast, the XaaS offering can be offered as an unbundled set of services, where customers can choose to combine the computing or software facilities with maintenance in the SaaS model, or the driving of the car with insurance in the CaaS model. The unbundling of different features nanonizes the utility-per-use; customers only pay for the services that they want. If they want a higher degree of a certain function, then the provider can potentially mix and match components to offer that higher degree of performance for that function, at a correspondingly higher price. The utility-per-use in this example was a monolithic entity, but in practice, the utility-per-use is a combination of different functions, features, and performance. While in theory, the unbundling of the utility-per-use can offer a higher degree of discrimination on that dimension, perfect nanonization is only possible in a negotiated pricing model with the customer. While we have observed negotiating one-on-one pricing in our observations in the XaaS sector, the standardization of most offerings has resulted in prices being strictly based on pre-determined menus of functions and performance. Negotiated pricing models typically involve customer acquisition related to one-time discounts; however, as we point out later, they create a reference point and should be avoided. Hence, pay-per-use perfectly nanonizes pricing on frequency of usage, and moderately on the utility-per-use in practice.

Of the four customer profiles presented in the example, Andrew represents the SMEs of the world. He has a low utility-per-use and a low frequency of usage. In the past, in a world without XaaS offerings, Andrew's low overall utility meant that most providers ignored his needs, and Andrew went unserved. Most SMEs who considered adopting ERP systems did not have a bundled utility in a reasonable timeframe to justify buying an in-house system, hence they did not adopt offerings with flat fees. However, today the nanonization of the ERP offering has increased the diffusion of ERP systems among SMEs. In general, the nanonization of XaaS offerings has turned customers with Andrew's profile from non-participants to customers; while they do not represent huge value as an account, they do not require much maintenance either. Offering customers with Andrew's profile the standardized version of different solutions modules brings them into the customer base, and they provide a stream of revenue without clogging the provider's resources. Their frequency of usage is typically smaller and, hence, their contribution to the utilization of the provider's resources is smaller, as they have fewer employees and customers. However, if the provider has many potential customers in the SME segment, their combined utility makes it worthwhile for the provider to target customers with Andrews's profile. Hence, from the social perspective, the XaaS mode of offering has been particularly useful for customers with Andrew's profile, as they can now access services that they could not earlier.

At the other extreme, Daisy represents the large key accounts of most XaaS providers. She has a high utility-per-use and a high frequency of usage. Customers like Daisy demonstrate the 80/20 rule for XaaS providers; 80% of the business revenue comes from 20% of the customers like Daisy. The services offered by the provider are part of the core competence of customers like Daisy. Since they have a high utility, they need more customized solutions that they are willing to pay for; hence, customers like Daisy should be strategic partners for the XaaS provider. Their needs today will be the needs of other customers like Andrew, Bonnie and Charles tomorrow; hence, providers should work with strategic partners like Daisy to know their pain points. These pain points can be used for developing continuing solutions in an agile manner to be rolled out to the market in the future. At the risk of over-generalizing, customers like Charles are typically large organizations, but the services of the provider are non-core to their business, hence, they derive a high utility from the services, but use them infrequently. In many cases, customers like Charles represent growth customers who could use the provider's services more frequently if they were convinced of their value. Bonnie represents customers who are either in sunset businesses or hypercompetitive business sectors. Hence, they use the services frequently, but do not derive a high utility from them. The provider should have value from serving them as they represent a steady flow of revenue.

Our discussion has assumed so far that customers are able to estimate their usage frequency in the future, and the provider is able to estimate them as well. While this estimation can be done with a certain degree of accuracy at the aggregate level both by the provider and the customer, beyond customers like Daisy, it is hard to do this estimation at the individual level. What is the impact of uncertainty in the estimation of usage frequency on the part of the customer or the provider? Our research shows that surprisingly, the risk of usage frequency estimation works in different directions for the customer and the provider. From the customer's perspective, the impact of any risk from the uncertainty of estimating his/her usage frequency moves the customer in the direction of flat-fee pricing or subscription pricing. Of course, the preference is governed by the price-per-use, subscription price and flat-fee price; if all else stays the same, the customer is more likely to move towards subscription and flat-fee pricing owing to estimation uncertainty of the usage frequency. The driver of this preference is risk-aversion in decision-making, the risk profile research finds that most decision-makers are risk-averse. Subscription pricing eliminates the uncertainty effect at the period level, and flat-fee pricing eliminates the impact of uncertainty of usage frequency at the lifecycle level. When customers are unsure of how often they will use the service, any uncertainty makes them move in the direction of the flat fee at the period or the lifecycle level. This effect has been corroborated experimentally as well. Surprisingly, for providers, our research confirms the reverse effect: customers' and provider's usage frequency uncertainty makes the provider prefer the pay-per-use mechanism even more. The insight is that the provider can pool the usage estimation risk across different customers: some customers will use the service more, and others will use the service less. When offered the flat-fee or subscription pricing options, the provider must lower the flat fee or subscription price to account for the impact of uncertainty on net customer utility. However, when using the pay-per-use pricing methodology, the provider's risk is pooled across customers, and hence, the provider will keep the same level of profits as in the case when customers could predict their usage frequencies accurately. Hence, the pay-per-use mode of pricing is even better under uncertainty from the provider's perspective, and the provider can lower the price-per-use to entice customers to use the pay-per-use mode of pricing.

3.2 HYBRID MODES OF PRICING

There are hybrids of flat-fee and price-per-use models that are employed in practice as well. In general, two-tariff pricing schemes are more difficult to evaluate by customers, but they add a fine-tuning element for the provider. The hybrid models are as follows: in the first mode, the provider charges a fixed fee per period with a limit for the number of times that the service can be used for the period. Any usage beyond this pre-specified limit is charged at a price-per-use. A simple example of this model is the Xerox mode of offering the 914, which was described in the first chapter. Xerox charged a fixed fee of $95 per month and offered copying up to 2,000 copies per month for no additional charge. The model of charging copies in the Xerox model is known as the freemium model, where the first few usage occurrences are not charged, and only usage beyond a pre-determined limit is charged.[6] In Xerox's case, for any copy beyond 2,000 copies per month, customers were charged 4 cents per copy.

Does the freemium model (fixed fee up to a limit and additional uses charged a price-per-use) perform better than the pay-per-use and the subscription mechanisms? If fixed cost and variable costs of operation are not included, the simple answer is "No"; in terms of being able to extract customer surplus efficiently, the pay-per-use mechanism dominates the hybrid pricing scheme. Surprised? It seems reasonable that a two-part pricing scheme should work better than a single pricing scheme. The answer is that the simple price-per-use mechanism regulates payments better owing to its frequency of usage discrimination effect. Why do

---

[6]Bragg, S., "What is Freemium Pricing?", *AccountingTools*, February 7, 2021, https://www.accountingtools.com/articles/2017/5/16/freemium-pricing, accessed July 16, 2021.

providers use the hybrid mode then? Providers use the hybrid mode to justify the fixed cost of the asset. Note that the 914 copier costs $2000 to produce, it was the most expensive copier to produce of its time, owing to the advanced technology that enabled it to print on plain paper. If Xerox used a price-per-use only, customers with very low usage frequencies would be able to lease the machine from Xerox and would then print only a few copies a month. This would mean that Xerox's payback time would be very high, maybe even beyond the lifetime of the printer. Serving customers with very low usage frequencies did not make sense for Xerox, as the resources were not shared. Each customer of Xerox had a dedicated machine at his or her office, hence, the costs of the copier machine had to be recouped by Xerox. When resources cannot be shared, and the investment in the dedicated equipment must be recouped by the provider, the hybrid model of the fixed fee plus a price-per-use beyond a pre-specified limit is indeed optimal. This is the reason that the first hybrid mode of pricing is used. The return on investment (ROI) on the initial investment is based on the combination of the fixed fee and the price-per-use. What did commercial customers who could not afford $95 per month for copying services and students do when they needed to copy documents? Entrepreneurs like Paul Orfalea saw the opportunity presented. Orfalea started a chain of office services called Kinko's.[7] Kinko's charged a few cents to copy per page, but they had the advantage of sharing resources across multiple customers, hence, the economics made sense for their business model. Kinko's was eventually acquired by Fedex and rechristened as Fedex Office.

This is another important insight for XaaS pricing: when resources can be shared to have moderate to high utilization, the pay-per-use mode indeed works the best. When resources are dedicated to one customer, the provider must eschew offering the services to low usage frequency users, and it should offer its services only to some customers with moderate to high frequency of usage. The provider should then charge a fixed price for recovering its investment in the dedicated resource and charge a

---

[7]Yiwen Chan, Kinko's founder explains how 'business is an art', September 11, 2012, https://www.thedp.com/article/2012/11/kinkos-founder-explains-how-business-is-an-art, accessed June 1, 2020.

price-per-use beyond a pre-specified limit to benefit from a high frequency of usage of the customer. In this case, the risk of low usage frequency is passed on to the customer. Any upside from high usage frequency is charged by the provider.

The second hybrid pricing mode is that users are charged a price-per-use up to a certain pre-specified limit, and then any usage beyond that limit is not charged. While this mode is used in practice, this pricing mode should be regarded more as a reward system rather than as an incentive aligning pricing mode for the customer. This pricing mechanism does not provide optimality for any known objective, but rewards customer loyalty. The mechanism is akin to airline frequent flyer miles, where flying for a certain number of pre-specified miles gives the customer the right to fly another set of miles for free. High-frequency users of the service like Charles and Daisy will contribute lower revenues from this mechanism, but it enhances their motivation to continue using the service.

3.3 PRACTICAL CONSIDERATIONS: UNITARY ANALYSIS OF PRICING

There are many methods for pricing services in practice: cost-plus pricing, value-based pricing, competitive pricing and time-variant pricing are some examples. These methods use some or all factors of the demand sensitivity to price, the fixed and variable costs of offering the service, the value to the customer and the degree of competition in a combination. The analysis of the example shown in Tables 3.1, 3.2 and 3.3 used the notion of value-based pricing, which requires the provider to estimate the value of the service to the customer. The value of the service should be estimated as the multiplicative product of the utility-per-use and the expected frequency of usage of the customer. The value-based pricing method is indeed the starting point of determining the price of most service offerings. In contrast, in the productization model, most firms use the cost-plus model as the basis of pricing. In practice, how does one determine the utility-per-use and the frequency of usage of the customer? This requires the nanonization of the value of the service's competition, either from existing competitors, or by estimating the effort required by the customer to set up the assets for the service internally. This is more of an art than a science. Estimating a dollar equivalent for a customer's utility-per-use will have some error by default, though there are a number of ways of reducing this error. For instance, in a competitive market, estimating the value of a service is easier to do, as the provider can compare the differentiation of the service to that of the competition.

In a monopoly with a brand new offering, the provider needs to start with the next best alternative: if the customer were to acquire the assets internally and avail of the service, how much would that cost the customer? How often would the customer use the assets over his/her lifetime? Dividing the total cost of ownership (TCO) by the expected number of times of usage would be a rough-cut starting point for the analysis of the nanonized value or utility-per-use, as the customer's next-best alternative is to acquire assets for himself/herself. The customer would also have the costs of installation, maintenance, insurance; hence, all those costs need to be considered in estimating the TCO. The price of the provider will have to be lower than the nanonized value for the customer for the latter to adopt the service. The lower price must be supported by the provider, either by lower costs from economies of scale for shared assets, or cost of capital for dedicated assets. While these methods of nanonized customer value estimation will have some degree of error, in our observations, it helps the provider get the pricing decision within a certain reasonable range.

From his days at Oracle, Benioff had a broad idea of how much customers paid for developing their components for the various functions of a CRM system. When Salesforce introduced their CRM solution in the SaaS mode of offering, Benioff used this knowledge to estimate the value of a CRM product to the customer.[8] CRM systems offer functionalities like order entry and tracking, lead time quotation and other aspects, Salesforce had to start with a rough cut analysis of the TCO of customers building their own solutions. It could then estimate the nanonized value roughly by considering the number of employees of typical customers, and the number of times employees used CRM software in a given time period (as an estimate of the frequency of usage). Xerox had a radical new

---

[8]Brian O'Connell, "History of Salesforce: Timeline and Facts", *The Street*, February 27, 2020, https://www.thestreet.com/technology/history-of-salesforce, accessed June 3, 2020.

offering in the form of the 914 copier, as it could copy on plain paper, but it knew how much existing copiers cost (about $300), the number of copies large offices made each month at the time (about a 1,000), and how much the office spent on consumables like wet paper. Of course, Xerox also bet that since the cost of making a copy was lower for customers with the 914, they would make many more copies with the 914, giving them a higher estimate of frequency of usage for the 914. Xerox had to start off by determining how much customers paid to make a copy with their legacy machines, along with the hassle of ordering specialized consumables like wet paper. This provided a rough-cut estimate of the utility-per-use of the customer, as Xerox would need to provide higher utility-per-use for customers to switch to the 914. WeWork typically acquires office space by leasing them from existing developers. WeWork can estimate how much the customer would have to pay to design and develop their own office space if they contracted directly with the developer. One of WeWork's core offerings is that customers with flexible work-from-home policies could use WeWork's on-demand space model. WeWork would need to incorporate those savings into their utility-per-use and frequency of usage estimates.

This rough-cut analysis is not easy, but it is critical for the pricing decision. Service providers must start with this rough-cut analysis of estimating the nanonized value of their services first. The pricing decision will build on this nanonized value by sharing savings from economies of scale and technology innovation with customers. Customer research is important to fine-tune the pricing levels, but the initial rough-cut analysis helps to get the reasonable range of acceptable prices. In our own observations, providers who do not start with this rough-cut analysis are not successful with their offering, as they get their pricing decisions wrong by an order of magnitude. If the price is too low, they never break even. If they price too high, customers do not even consider their offering. Customers will do a breakeven analysis, either cursorily or in depth when considering a service, by comparing how much it would cost to do it themselves. If they do not see the value of the offering, they will not avail of it, as they fear paying very high margins.

Before we provide the key modifications that providers need to make to the value-based pricing model in practice, it is useful to understand the key objectives of cost-plus and demand elasticity pricing. As stated earlier, cost-plus pricing is the dominant mode of pricing for product offerings. The provider first estimates the total fixed cost for serving a customer base, and the unit variable cost of manufacturing the product — there are standard techniques to do this in the accounting literature. For competitive situations, techniques like target costing are used where the provider works backwards from the market price to arrive at a target cost, and then designs the product to have the target cost at the variable cost of manufacturing. The objectives of cost-plus pricing are to ensure the provider breaks even in the worst case and makes optimal profits in the best case. The provider estimates the total market size that will be served, the fixed costs of serving the market, and then adds a margin to the variable cost. The margin will ensure the provider breaks even for low market adoption (covers the fixed costs and variable costs for the low market size) and provide a high profit if the market adoption is high. Hence, the key decision to be made in the cost-plus method is the margin; if the margin is high, the adoption will be low, and if the margin is low, the adoption will be higher due to price sensitivity of demand. Demand elasticity models do the same. They add a margin to the cost to maximize profits, the provider then checks if the optimal profits cover the fixed costs of operation.

For the best-in-class XaaS providers, nanoizing the unit of analysis to the unitary level is critical for the pricing decision, as the provider also has to account for variable and fixed costs in their value-based pricing decision. The decision on the level of modularity for the pricing analysis starts with estimating the profitability of the lowest self-sufficient and independent module that offers the complete suite of the offering. When the provider needs dedicated assets to serve the customer (e.g., copier services cannot be shared for large offices, such customers need their own dedicated copiers), the unit of analysis is the individual dedicated asset, and the corresponding customer. For instance, Xerox had to do the first-cut analysis at the copier level for the 914 copier, as copiers could not be shared, hence, the operations of each individual copier had to be profitable. For car leasing services, offering the services of each individual car must be profitable. We call this lowest self-sufficient and independent module of the service that offers the complete suite of services as the nanonized module.

For the pricing of the services of the 914 copier, Xerox started with the following objectives: their price had to be such that customers would switch to their product from the competing products. Next, they had to be able to recover their costs from producing and servicing copiers and make some profits if the volume of leased copiers was above the planned break-even quantity. To recover the cost of the copier, Xerox could not serve offices with very low usage frequencies with the copier, as they would never recover the cost of the copier from customers who made a very small number of copies. Hence, Xerox chose a leasing fee of $95 per month, which would enable the cost of the copier ($2000) to be recovered in about 21 months, without considering the other variable costs like the consumables (toner), the maintenance and other services. For providers offering services with dedicated assets to each customer, a fixed fee is an important component of the service pricing model. Without the fixed fee, the investment in the dedicated asset cannot be recovered. For Xerox, considering the other costs would extend the payback or breakeven period of the copier beyond the 21 months. The additional cost of 4 cents per copy beyond 2,000 copies enabled this breakeven period to be earlier at the copier level. Since the lifecycle of the copier machine was long, any revenues after the first two years approximately would result in profits for Xerox. The prices charged by Xerox would also need to cover the organizational fixed costs beyond the copier, as Xerox had additional organizational fixed costs.

For car leasing, similarly, the price offered for the lease must account for the depreciation costs of the car, the maintenance costs, and the fixed costs beyond the operation of the car. Hence, for dedicated assets, the fixed fee for the fixed asset and the price-per-use must be low enough for customers to avail of the service (lower than the reservation price). At the same time, the service must be profitable for the provider (cover all fixed and variable costs, and then yield a profit). Hence, car leasing providers typically use a combination of a fixed fee and pay-per-use price per km that covers the fixed costs, the variable cost for most customers with reasonable usage, and then provides a profit for the provider after considering organizational fixed costs.

For providers who provide locational based XaaS offerings with shared resources, the nanonized module is the location of each offering.

The sharing of resources for these providers is typically resource-specific. For example, WeWork will have to ensure that their pricing models will provide positive customer surplus for customers who use their services over developing their own office space. They will also need to ensure that the pricing model covers the variable costs of leasing the office space from the developer, and any other variable and fixed costs that they incur at the locational level. The profits made from each individual location also must be high enough so that they are above the fixed costs of WeWork at the organizational level. In offering their Furniture-as-a-Service model, Ahrend will have to ensure that their revenues are higher than their costs at a local level, and their economies of scale from reusing furniture at multiple locations gives them enough savings to cover the fixed costs at the organizational level.

For providers in the IT sector offering the XaaS model, and providers where resources beyond localized or personalized assets are shared, making pricing decisions at the nanonized module level is even more critical. IT providers often have unbalanced system offerings with excess resources of one kind of asset, and fewer of the other. It is well known in process analysis that a chain only performs as well as its weakest link. Data centres typically have multiple assets: servers, computing resources, networking routers, switches, storage area networks and backups for memory, security applications, communication links and software. For IT providers offering services in the XaaS mode, they first need to define a nanonized module for analysis for a given number of customers. For the nanonized module, the capacity of the module and the number of customers the module can serve are linked by the Quality of Service (QoS) constraints that are defined in the SLAs with customers. The step of defining a module requires the provider to have a mix of different applications and functions that they will support. For example, the provider may offer a B2B client who offers fashion goods using e-commerce with web software access for the customers of the client, data analytics on customer demographics and so on. Each of these offerings will need different shares of the provider's assets. By making some assumptions on the nature of the mix, like the ratio of the total of each service like web access and data analytics, the provider should first balance the acquisition of resources in the module as far as possible. Given the balanced capacity of the module and the typical

•

mix of services, the provider can estimate the utilization of the module. From the utilization, using tools from queueing theory and heavy traffic approximations, the provider can estimate the service quality metrics like latency and bandwidth. The total number of customers that can be supported by the nanonized module will be determined by the QoS targets to be set by the provider in the contract SLAs.

The total fixed costs of the module will be shared across the customers with varying frequencies of usage. Typically, apart from maintenance and a few other consumables, IT services have very low variable costs. The price of the services (along with the capacity) should be designed at the modular level for the first acquisition of resources, and subsequent additions of joint resources can be done based on the scaling of the demand for the service. If the price is set too low, then a large number of customers will pay for the service, but the latency of the service will be high and the bandwidth will be limited, leading to the QoS constraints not being satisfied. If the price is set too high, the usage will be low, and the provider will not have the ability to recoup its investments in the resources. This balancing of capacity and pricing is key to the success of the IT XaaS offerings. Our observations in practice show that this is best done at the modular level. The pricing of some of the services may be lower than if they were offered as standalone services, but if they increase the value of other complementary services, the lower prices are justified.

To illustrate the above-mentioned method, let us consider the setup of services of a new budget airline (yes indeed, budget airlines meet the requirements of qualifying as a XaaS offering). The airline starts with a set of routes that they will fly on based on estimations. They will need a detailed analysis of the demand on the different routes, the number of flights on each route, the staffing needs and fuel and other variable costs. Based on the number of seats, the airline will set the price to make a profit under certain assumptions. While each flight does not need to be profitable for the airline (feeder routes can be run unprofitably as they enable economies of scale on hub-to-hub routes), the airline can test the utilization and profits at different price levels to know if their offering is profitable. Future additions of capacity on new and existing routes can be tested by marginal analysis on the existing capacity.

Our observations in practice show that while seemingly trivial, the nanonized module of pricing analysis is another key element of the successful pricing paradigm for XaaS offerings. This is particularly true for IT XaaS offerings; after all, the nanonized module pricing analysis for personalized and localized shared services like Xerox and WeWork is intuitive. In our observations, all successful pricing policies have well-identified nanonized modules for pricing, this nanonized model has three main advantages. First, organization fixed costs have economies of scale; as the provider's volume grows, the same pricing level typically increases the provider's profitability. Second, IT assets should typically be added in a stepwise fashion. The provider should first be able to meet existing customer needs with the existing modules with a high confidence interval on the QoS constraints (the constraints should typically be satisfied 99% of the time or higher). When the QoS constraints are close to the limits, the provider should add another module for the next set of new customers. Hence, this process makes the capacity acquisition process structured, and the pricing model stable. Third, the joint optimization of capacity and price enables the provider to offer the service with little excess resource costs (though the provider may add some resource redundancy to maintain a high QoS). As stated above, the dominant pricing mode for IT XaaS offerings is the price-per-use mode based on per unit time or resources consumed, as that is the most efficient mechanism for unlocking customer value. IT infrastructure offerings in the XaaS mode can have huge savings from economies of scale, therefore shared resources are becoming the default model for IaaS offerings. Economies of scale for other IT as-a-service offerings are also high. Typically, providers with failed pricing policies price too low as their analysis does not account for fixed costs at the nanonized module level or at the organizational level. In badly planned cases, prices do not cover provider variable costs at the nanonized module level. We do not see providers often in practice who price too high, but in the rare examples that we have seen, reducing prices seem to have a salutary effect on market acceptance. However, increasing prices has a mixed effect on the customer.

While there do exist mathematical models for determining the pricing of XaaS services, in our experience, almost all providers determine nanonized pricing solutions with extensive simulations. The use of

"What if" scenarios and sensitivity analysis to assumptions is best done with simulations, real-life pricing problems are too complex to be modelled and solved using optimization models. Simulation has the added advantage of testing both the average profitability and robustness with sensitivity analysis. We have seen well-performing providers using both simulation and optimization methods for testing the robustness of their pricing solutions. In our judgement, simulation is the right tool to be used with optimization model solutions acting as robustness checks for comparing with the results of the simulation model.

3.4 TIME-VARIANT PRICING

Should providers practice penetration pricing or skimming? Should providers practice time-variant pricing? While the hedged answer "it depends" does apply to some extent in this case, the answer does tend in the direction of penetration pricing. There may be arguments to be made in favour of penetration pricing, for example, over time, inflation increases the costs of resources. If the provider passes on the effect of increased resource and operating costs due to inflation to customers, and if those increases are in a reasonable range, customers do not switch typically, as these are industry effects. Competitor pricing will also increase over time due to inflation, so as far as the increases are benchmarked with the market, penetration pricing is acceptable.

On the other hand, the practice of discounting services early on for customer acquisition is fraught with many risks. First, it creates a reference point for the customer, if prices are increased later, the customer surplus reduces over time, causing a higher churn rate among customers. Similarly, pricing services initially aggressively for the market for customer acquisition and market share gain sets customer expectations, it may be difficult to increase prices later. Second, while it seems that relationship-specific discounts are confidentially negotiated, there are no secrets in efficient markets. Other customers will ask for similar discounts. Third, the signalling effect to the customer is that the discount is needed to justify the value offered by the provider. Discounting is a form of negative value signalling. We recommend that rather than discounting services initially to attract customers, providers offer more value to customers to acquire them. This may be in the form of a free trial for a short period to all customers, so that customers can try out the service to ascertain its value to them. Second, we recommend that instead of negotiating prices freely with customers during acquisition or for retention freely, the provider offer two or three categories of service bundles, such as "Basic", "Premium" and "Pro", which are offered at three distinct price points. This takes away the need for negotiating for individual services; users with high price sensitivity can avail of standardized solutions in the basic bundle, while users with high customization and functionality needs can avail of the professional bundle. The acquisition of customers can be eased by offering the customer the choice of paying for a lower tier but availing of the higher tier for a short period of time. The features in the three bundles are known, so the customer can try out the features in the higher bundle, and decide if s/he wants to continue paying a basic price, or move up to the premium and pro levels. If the provider offers multiple tiered bundles, discounting for customers will be limited to asking for more functionality at a lower price. The provider can reward long-term users with the free use of a higher category bundle for a period that is based on the duration of the relationship. Tying any sops to the offered services is better for customer acquisition and long-term retention than the initial discounting of the service.

Examples of the use of skimming pricing strategies are rare (lowering the price over time), an obvious driver that would drive price skimming is competitive entry. It is well known that competitive entry drives the prices down of existing providers in the market as customers have more choice. Hence, competitive markets tend to reflect the degree of competition in pricing. Other reasons driving a skimming strategy could be economies of scale, where the provider's cost base is lowered by the addition of more scale and more customers. While this is a good reason to lower prices in the form of shared savings with customers, we do not see examples of this in practice. Rather, economies of scale encourage providers to hold their prices steady over longer periods of time and then pass on cost increases due to inflation to customers.

In sharing economy examples, we see dynamic or time-variant pricing that is driven by revenue or yield management. Ridesharing firms like Uber and Grab change their prices over the course of the day to reflect momentary imbalances between supply and demand. At peak hours, the price of the ride increases and decreases as the congestion driven by higher demand eases during the off-peak hours. While in theory, other providers that acquire their own assets could also practice yield management, we do not see examples of yield pricing in practice in IT XaaS offerings. Sharing economy providers like Uber and Airbnb are balancing a fixed supply of assets beyond their control with the demand, while IT-as-a-service providers have the resources under their own control. Customers would expect that providers in IT settings would acquire more resources to improve their QoS in response to varying demand patterns over time, rather than practising dynamic pricing to balance demand with capacity.

3.5 COGNITIVE ASPECTS OF PRICING AND COMPETITION

Beyond the measures of profits, market share and managing the imbalance between capacity and demand, pricing must take other considerations into account. The pricing of the service should be easily understood by the customer, and the pricing model should be perceived as fair. Beyond the ease of understanding and fairness, customers should be able to predict their monthly spend, they should have a choice of price and features, and should not fret about pricing when using a service. The price-per-use, subscription and flat-fee modes are all low in terms of complexity; however, with multiple price-functionality menus, the choice between mechanisms becomes more complex. If the provider offers menus on the price–functionality continuum, it should limit the number of choices so that it does not cognitively overburden the customer. Fair pricing means different things to different people, but generally, price-per-use or pricing based on resources consumed is fairer than flat-fee pricing. This fairness arises from the notion of consumption: if the customer consumes more of a certain resource, s/he finds it palatable that s/he pays more for the resource. If an air ticket from New York to Singapore is priced higher than an air ticket from New York to London, it is perceived to be fairer than a scheme where you fly to all destinations from New York for the same list price. The predictability of the monthly spend are highest for subscription models where the customer pays a flat fee regardless of his/her usage. Obviously, the subscription fee model is preferred by users who have a high frequency of usage. A customer who has a cup of coffee once a month is not likely to find Panera Bread's all-you-can-drink monthly coffee subscription model to be attractive. However, the subscription model has the benefit of taking away the ticking meter effect — you do not need to worry about having to meter your usage as the more you use, the more you pay. Finally, another soft insight about pricing in international markets is that the provider should bear the currency risk and price in the local currency. While customers can convert currencies as efficiently by punching in a few numbers on a calculator, the cognitive ease of understanding of services in the local currency is higher. This enables customers to overcome cognitive hurdles of price comprehension and compare value from the service to the price more easily.

3.6 COMPETITIVE PRICING

We have discussed competition and its effect earlier on pricing. Competitive markets indeed have lower pricing regardless of the offering mode. However, is there any specific effect of competition on the offering mode? To answer this question, let us consider and compare the customer surplus from the same offering that is offered by two competitors: one competitor offers it in the pay-per-use mode, while the other competitor offers it via a subscription mode. In a competitive environment, the two competitors will price in a way that the customers self-select the pricing mode that is preferable for them. We will develop a very simple model that enables us to understand the impact of competition on the pricing mode. Let us assume that the number of times a customer will use the service is N in the given time frame for the subscription mode, the utility-per-use is U, the deal transaction cost is D for repeated usage, and the prices in the pay-per-use mode and subscription mode are p and $S,$ respectively. It is important that p and S are an equilibrium pair of prices; we will assume that p and S are an equilibrium pair of prices for this example (explaining the notion of equilibrium prices is beyond the scope of this book, the reader may refer to any game theory primer for understanding the concept of equilibrium prices).

Then the customer surplus from the pay-per-use offering is $N(U - D - p)$, since the customer gets a utility-per-use each time of $U - D$, which is the difference between the utility-per-use and the deal transaction cost that accrues to the customer for each use. The customer surplus for every use then is $U - D - p$, since the customer pays a price of p for each use. Since the customer uses the service N times in the period, the customer surplus for the period is $N(U - D - p)$. In contrast, in the subscription mode, the customer only pays once, hence, his/her customer surplus is $NU - S$. Which mode will the customer prefer? Setting $NU - S > N(U - D - p)$ shows that if $N > S/(D + p)$, the customer will prefer the subscription mode, and the customer will prefer the pay-per-use mode if $N < S/(D + p)$. Hence, if both the subscription and pay-per-use modes are offered, high-frequency usage customers will prefer the subscription mode, while low frequency usage customers will prefer the pay-per-use mode.

This insight is supported by the customer surplus figures in Table 3.3. We see that for Andrew and Bonnie, their customer surplus is higher for the pay-per-use offering, and for Charles and Daisy, their customer surplus is higher for the subscription offering. While the optimal prices in Table 3.3 are not in equilibrium under competition, the insights hold for equilibrium prices as well. As can be seen from the customer surplus, users with high usage frequencies prefer the subscription mode (as can be seen from the Panera Bread subscriber list of coffee addicts), they pay a flat fee for the period. The pay-per-use mechanism extracts the utility of high-frequency usage customers efficiently, but the subscription mode leaves more value on the table for them. For low frequency usage customers, the subscription price is too high for them to adopt the service, but they get some positive surplus from using the pay-per-use mode infrequently. This shows that the distribution of value between the provider and the customer is critical in retaining high-frequency users in a competitive environment. In a monopoly, customers have no choice, and hence, providers can extract a higher value from customers. Apple changed the music industry with its famous 99 cent per song strategy, as it gained widespread acceptance from customers who were forced to buy complete CDs earlier, even though they wanted to listen to one or two songs per album. However, in a competitive environment, customers have a choice, and the retention of high-frequency, high-value customers becomes critical. In a competitive environment, the flat-fee structure of the subscription mode leaves more value for the customer, hence, the subscription mode is preferable in competitive pricing. Spotify has successfully challenged Apple for dominance in the music industry with its subscription model.

Netflix's pricing scheme for its on-demand streaming services is the subscription model, where customers pay a moderate flat monthly subscription fee to access all of Netflix's movie, seasonal and original content offerings. From the cost perspective, Netflix's cost base is primarily fixed, as it licenses content from other providers in the form of licensing fees, and it bears the cost of its own original content by amortizing the content over time. The licensing fees are typically region specific and not volume dependent, i.e., the fees do not depend on the number of customers who have watched the licensed content. Netflix paid north of 13 billion dollars in 2018 for its total licensing and own content costs.[9] In contrast, other providers have multiple modes of monetization of their streaming services: they collect revenue in the form of advertising time, flat subscription fees and hourly fees for content access over a pre-specified limit. In contrast, Netflix uses the subscription model only, as customers like the ability to access content without having to worry about the ticking meter effect and monitoring how much content they have accessed. From the provider's perspective, Netflix has high economies of scale. As its subscriber base grows, the content costs are amortized over a larger customer base, and the costs of streaming services like servers decrease over time due to the larger base.

This is a critical insight for competitive pricing. While in the monopoly, the pay-per-use mechanism is ideal for the provider as it efficiently extracts the customer surplus, it does not leave any value for customers on the table. On the other hand, the subscription mode does not extract customer surplus as efficiently as the pay-per-use mode, but it leaves customer value on the table. In a competitive setting, the high-frequency users like Charles and Daisy will plump for the subscription mode, and

---

[9]Tainer, D., "Netflix's Original Content Strategy Is Failing", *Forbes*, July 19, 2019, https://www.forbes.com/sites/greatspeculations/2019/07/19/netflixs-original-content-strategy-is-failing/?sh=3ac937e03607, accessed June 3, 2020.

the low frequency users like Andrew and Bonnie will chose the pay-per-use mode. The loss of high-frequency users to the subscription mode and the lower prices-per-use from competition significantly lower the attractiveness of the pay-per-use mode in a competitive environment. Our research shows that the existence of competition switches the profitability for the provider in terms of choice of mode. Since Charles and Daisy have a higher utility from the service and hence a higher willingness to pay, in a competitive market, the provider should switch from a pay-per-use mode to a subscription mode as the subscription mode will be adopted by the high-frequency users. The provider offering the subscription mode has higher profits compared to the provider offering the pay-per-use mode.

The same insight also applies in a monopoly where high-frequency users have a choice of either designing and building their on-premises solution or adopting the solution as a service from the provider. If the lifecycle of the assets is very long, then the on-premises model is preferable for high-frequency users whose core business uses the service. They will have a higher customer surplus from an on-premises solution. However, given that in IT, assets have a finite lifecycle, in practice, the customer surplus for the on-premises solution is limited as the lifetime and, hence, the number of times the customer will use the service (N) are limited. Trying to justify the high cost of IT assets and recoup their investments is one of the reasons that large firms tend to stick to legacy solutions for longer than smaller and more nimble competitors who adopt XaaS offerings.

3.7 PERFORMANCE-BASED XaaS CONTRACTS

Performance-based contract (PBC) is an outcome-based contracting method that changes the basis of contracting from input parameters (like usage of resources) to the output of the service from the customer's perspective.[10] The outcomes can be measures like quality of the process that the provider is responsible for, or the outcome of the usage of the customer. The contract may contain financial and non-financial incentives in

---

[10] Wikipedia, Performance-based contracting, https://en.wikipedia.org/wiki/Performance-based_contracting, accessed June 2, 2020.

the form of bonuses and penalties if certain pre-defined output measures are not met. In general, PBC governance enables verifiable results when input measures are not easy to observe or verify. The objectives of PBC-based relationship governance are to ensure the strategic alignment of the provider and the customer, by providing both parties with incentives to work along the same dimension. For example, the availability (proportion of uptime) of the provider's service can be verified by technological means. If the availability is contracted on, the customer's utility is higher, and s/he can avail of the service for longer periods of time. Hence, incentivizing the provider to have a high availability incentivizes both the provider and the customer.

What does the verifiability of a contract mean? A contract is not verifiable when the metric that has been contracted on cannot be verified in a court of law by reasonable means. This could be a result of the metric's lack of a commonly accepted and defined scale, or the lack of ability to have a measurement of that metric. For instance, customer satisfaction can be measured on scales of 1 to 10, but there is a fundamental difference in terms of each person's measurement of satisfaction. Two different people may experience the same service but assess it very differently, as their expectations of the service were very different, hence customer satisfaction is not verifiable. The distance travelled by a car on the other hand is verifiable, as it is recorded on the odometer, the verifiability of the distance can be ascertained by checking if the odometer is faulty or not.

The notion of verifiability in services contracts is important, as contracts are frequently designed with metrics that are not verifiable. For example, in consulting and in outsourcing IT projects, the dominant model for contracting is the time and materials contract.[11] They are also used at times in construction projects. Time and materials contracts are based on reimbursing the costs of the materials used by the provider, and the time spent by the employees of the provider, on the project at a pre-specified rate. However, time and materials used in a project can be monitored only at a high cost to the satisfaction of both parties, and they cannot be verified in a court of law. The basic advantage of time and materials

---

[11] Chen, Y. & Bharadwaj, A. (2009). An empirical analysis of contract structures in IT outsourcing. Information Systems Research, 20(4), 484–506.

contracts was that they enabled the customer to change the job scope easily. Since the customer bore the risk of effort on the part of the provider, the customer was free to make as many changes as s/he wanted. Most providers set standardized rates for time and materials; hence, it was easy to compare the cost structures of different providers to make provider selection choices. However, effort is not verifiable; the provider and the customer had to jointly decide on monitoring for the time and materials contracts. Monitoring the time and costs of materials is expensive, and any boilerplate system of monitoring increased the project costs. The provider has the incentive to slow their activities down for more billable hours, this problem could be alleviated somewhat by adding bonuses for finishing at or ahead of schedule. If disputes arose, it was difficult to resolve them in a court of law. For example, customers had to prove that due diligence was not done in procurement, and multiple supplier quotations may not have been obtained.

There are many examples of performance-based contracts that are used in practice in XaaS contracts. The example of Volvo Trucking in Chapter 1 is a good example. Volvo contracts with Bronnoy Kalk on the amount of tonnes of limestone that their autonomous trucks ferry from the mines of Bronnoy Kalk to the stone crusher.[12] Volvo could alternatively also have contracted on the number of km driven on the trucks used by Bronnoy Kalk, or by the number of hours that Bronnoy Kalk had the trucks dedicated to its use. How should Volvo choose the right metric to contract on? If Volvo had chosen the time that Bronnoy Kalk had their trucks for their use, Bronnoy Kalk would carry the risk of the utilization of the trucks. For instance, if an accident or inclement weather shut down the mines for a short period, Bronnoy Kalk would still have to pay Volvo for that time. Hence, the incentives between Bronnoy Kalk and Volvo would not have been perfectly aligned, Volvo would still be paid for the time that Bronnoy Kalk could not utilize the trucks. What if one of the autonomous trucks broke down? Volvo would still be paid for the time that the truck broke down under a time-based contract unless it was specified

---

[12] Volvo Trucks, "Volvo Trucks provides autonomous transport solution to Brønnøy Kalk AS", November 20, 2018, https://www.volvotrucks.com/en-en/news-stories/press-releases/2018/nov/pressrelease-181120.html, accessed June 3, 2020.

that Volvo would only be paid for the time the trucks were functioning properly. On the other hand, when the contract is based on the number of tonnes of limestone ferried from the mine to the stone crusher by the truck, Volvo bears the risk of the performance of the trucks, and other forms of environmental risk. Bronnoy Kalk could ferry small quantities of limestone without worrying about full truck load economies to the stone crusher if the capacity of the mine was lower than that of the stone crusher, to enable a just-in-time use of the stone crusher. The trucks would make multiple trips for ferrying a small number of tonnes of limestone, resulting in a high utilization of the trucks but in low revenues for Volvo.

Rolls Royce made the slogan "Power by the Hour" popular in the airline industry over 20 years ago by offering pioneering as-a-service offerings to airlines. Their offerings were based on the performance of their engines, and other airline services that they offered like instrumentation.[13] Their as-a-service offerings became the gold standard for the industry and other engine manufacturers like General Electric, and Pratt and Whitney also climbed onto the Power by the Hour bandwagon. The Power by the Hour approach to contracting for engine services maintenance with airlines aligns the incentives of the airline to Rolls Royce by setting payments based on the number of hours that the engine was used for in flying. The service demonstrated Rolls Royce's commitment to efficient performance of the engine with minimal downtime by ensuring that the engine would remain operational, and the downtime from engine problems would be as close to zero as feasible. In addition to the alignment of incentives, Rolls Royce also committed to a fixed maintenance cost routine, as it would do scheduled maintenance on the engine at fixed intervals of time to ensure the airworthiness of the engines. From the airline's perspective, the Power by the Hour indeed enabled them to make the maintenance schedule and the cost of maintenance predictable. However, it also exposed Rolls Royce to the business cycle uncertainties of the airline sector, as when the airline sector could not operate (e.g., during the

---

[13] Knowledge@Wharton, 'Power by the Hour': Can Paying Only for Performance Redefine How Products Are Sold and Serviced?, February 21, 2007, https://knowledge.wharton.upenn.edu/article/power-by-the-hour-can-paying-only-for-performance-redefine-how-products-are-sold-and-serviced/, accessed June 3, 2020.

pandemic), Rolls Royce would also not be paid for the service of their engines.

The Amazon Elastic Compute Cloud (EC2) is another example of shared risk with customers. Amazon provides "elastic" capacity that is dynamically adjusted to the needs of the customer.[14] For example, an e-commerce provider will pay higher amounts for usage when many customers visit its website hosted by Amazon, and will pay lower amounts if the number of customer visits is low. While the notion of capacity adjustment is laudable from the viewpoint of the customer, the customer's business risk is shared by Amazon.

Why do Volvo, Rolls Royce and Amazon share their customer risk by offering performance-based contracts? First, if the resources are shared across multiple customers, it is easier to mitigate business risk of customers, as the businesses of different customers in different sectors are not perfectly correlated, leading to diversification benefits. Amazon's resources are indeed shared, hence, sharing customer risk for them is not as risky a proposition as for Volvo and Rolls Royce, whose resources are dedicated. Adopting PBC governance for dedicated resources makes the provider a strategic partner for the customer, but also exposes the provider to a high variability in revenues from the customer's risk. As mentioned in Chapter 1, Volvo may be using the Bronnoy Kalk relationship as a test case in a safe environment for their autonomous trucks, so even if the trucks chalk up a lot of kilometres for low revenues, Volvo may gain from the testing. In Rolls Royce's case, they may not have taken a pandemic-caused severe downturn for the entire airline industry into consideration in their as-a-service offering. The use of PBC governance over resource usage-based metrics may make it easier for customers to adopt the service as well, as customers can see the alignment with their own businesses. In contrast, usage-based metrics often include metrics like processor time that may be obscure for the customer. Sometimes, outcome-based contracts are seen to be fairer as well, for instance, should Xerox charge by the papers entered in the copier and toner usage (inputs), or on the number of good copies made? If usage-based metrics are used, then the results of

---

[14] Dynamic scaling for Amazon EC2 Auto Scaling, AWS, https://docs.aws.amazon.com/autoscaling/ec2/userguide/as-scale-based-on-demand.html, accessed June 5, 2020.

defectives (jammed paper copies) are the responsibility of the customer, while with output-based metrics like fair copies, the risk of quality is borne by the provider. In the Xerox case, since the quality of the output is influenced by Xerox's maintenance services, fairness may dictate that only good copies be charged.

A second advantage of PBC-based relationships is that there is a higher degree of visibility for the customer on the verifiable metrics, rather than usage-based metrics that are monitored by the provider. Ideally, the metrics should be easily visible and understandable by both parties. Usage-based metrics are usually skewed in terms of visibility towards the provider. In contrast, since the provider is responsible for the maintenance of the resources, outcome-based metrics like the number of good copies can be checked by the provider during maintenance. In many cases, the provider can use technologies like IoT-based devices in the assets that share the metrics with both the provider and the customer in real time. As a best practice for PBC governance, the provider and customer should ideally contract on more than one metric. Contracting on only one metric places a high bar in terms of aligning the incentives of the two parties. Contracting on multiple metrics would be better in terms of providing a safety net if a measuring instrument was found to be faulty, or if the sole metric was not perfectly aligned with the interests of both parties.

A very interesting application of performance-based contracts is the set of gain sharing or shared savings contracts. These contracts can be very useful as additional contracts in the XaaS context to align providers and suppliers. A large travel management customer (for confidentiality, we shall call this customer Travelcountry) used to offer their own customer support services (CSS) initially, but they found that offering CSS was expensive, and not their core competence.[15] As a result, it switched to a customer support services provider (for confidentiality, we will call the provider as WNX). When Travelcountry switched to WNX as their CSS provider, it designed a standard contract where WNX was paid for each

---

[15] Bhattacharya, S., Gupta, A., & Hasija, S. (2014). Joint product improvement by client and customer support center: The role of gain-share contracts in coordination. *Information Systems Research*, 25(1), 137–151.

call that Travelcountry's customers rated as satisfactory (solved their issues). WNX's performance was good and Travelcountry's customers reported a high degree of satisfaction with WNX's services. However, Travelcountry observed that it did not have data on customer pain points with its web service any more. Initially, when it offered its own CSS, Travelcountry could use customer problem data for improving its web services. Hence, Travelcountry approached WNX and asked it to share what Travelcountry customers' pain points were in the calls that WNX was receiving. WNX pointed out the incentive incompatibility for itself: if it shared pain points with Travelcountry, then Travelcountry would fix those issues in their website design. This would result in a lower number of customers calling the CSS provider, leading to a drop in revenues. In response, Travelcountry and WNX designed a gain share or shared savings contract. Travelcountry would offer WNX a bonus for any call reductions that would result from WNX sharing customer pain point data with it. The bonus was designed in such a way that at the very least, WNX's revenues would not drop, and if the call volume dropped significantly, WNX's compensation would be higher. WNX was incentivized now to share customer pain point data with Travelcountry, and Travelcountry's web services design was improved further.

Gain sharing or shared savings contracts are another example of the alignment of incentives between providers and customers in XaaS contracts. Often, the differing incentives for the provider and customer that are based on verifiable data, like call volume in a call centre, arise from the nature of the contracted metric. By designing an additional gain share contract, the provider and the customer can overcome the incentive misalignment that is caused by focusing on a metric like call volume only.

While we have outlined several advantages of PBC contracts, these contracts have their disadvantages as well. One of the disadvantages of PBC governance is that contracts with customers must be negotiated on a one-on-one basis with customers, and hence, it is hard to scale with many customers. Each customer has their own specific industry features and aligning the pricing with each industry for providers of services like IaaS, PaaS and SaaS will be hard. Second, customers have to note that while the incentives of both parties may be easier to align in PBC contracts, the margins will have to reflect the business risk and other forms of operational risk of the customer in steady state. Volvo Trucks may agree to a lower price per tonne of limestone delivered by Bronnoy Kalk as of now to take advantage of the testing benefit of their autonomous trucks. However, in the long run, Volvo Trucks would change the margin of the contract for other cargo delivery applications if their autonomous trucks were approved for commercial applications.

The use of technology in pricing can enhance the implementation of PBC contracts. IoT applications in driving have enabled performance-based pricing for Volvo Trucks and Michelin Solutions. In the refrigeration-as-a-service space, ISA has used IoT technologies for remotely monitoring temperatures in refrigerators globally in real time.[16] Enhancing the connectivity offered by IoT has enabled ISA to streamline repair and maintenance offerings. ISA partnered with Telenor for the connectivity and cloud services needed for ISA in providing cold chain management services. For commercial refrigeration users, the steady maintenance of optimal temperatures enhances their ability to buy in larger quantities and streamline procurement processes. The maintenance of a controlled temperature environment is critical for reducing food waste. The investments by ISA were recouped in a few months, hence, IoT solutions can be very effective in terms of the return on investment. The online remote system of ISA generates alarm notifications when temperatures of their serviced refrigerators move outside the control limits, providing the ability for quick reaction. The IoT devices also provide data for ISA to conduct preventive maintenance at regular schedules to prevent problems before they occur. The temperature controls can also consider the local weather pattern changes to adjust the refrigeration settings accordingly. The system can generate reports for checking compliance by regulatory authorities, and check energy efficiency of the product. Component level knowledge can enable ISA to design inventory policies for spares and other parts in warehouses. ISA partners with local providers for providing their services, like installation and maintenance, and works closely with the local provider for monitoring the quality of the provided services. The services

---

[16]Telenor, Reinventing refrigeration with IoT, https://www.telenorconnexion.com/iot-case/isa-smart-refrigeration-with-iot/, accessed June 7, 2020.

are priced with SLAs that guarantee metrics like machine downtime and temperature control ranges.

Technology solutions can also enable customized pricing and solutions. 3D printing is currently being used extensively in the medtech sector for making surgically implanted devices and cosmetic products like invisible braces. The advent of 3D printing solutions has enabled surgically implanted devices to consider customer physical features in real time, as automated solutions can be used to have surgically implanted devices printed within a few hours. Surgical instruments can also be printed quickly, and design iterations can be assessed and tested within a few hours. The functional needs of implanted devices and surgical instruments can be quickly tested after printing. 3D printing solutions can also make accessibility of equipment easier to hard-to-get locations like space stations and combat zones. While 3D printing is commercially viable today only in a small number of sectors, increased research on materials and printing processes can lower costs significantly. When commercially viable, 3D printing can make the productization model obsolete; providers can sell customized designs of various products and get them printed at the local printers.

3.8 SUMMARY

The effect of nanoizing the pricing policies of as-a-service offerings has been as important for providers as the ability to nanonize the value of the service to the customer. In the past, by using the leasing model, providers could nanonize the value of the service to customers over time partially by offering a bundled price in the form of a leasing fee. This helps to partially explain the popularity over time of leasing; customers only pay for the service if they use the asset. The ability of the provider to nanonize the value and, concomitantly, the pricing of the service has been critical to the rapid growth of XaaS offerings. The lean matching of customer usage with provider revenues enables customers to pay only for what they use and enable providers to extract customer utility more efficiently.

While there are several pricing methods like cost-plus pricing, demand elasticity pricing, value-based pricing and competitive pricing, we find that the research and practice in XaaS pricing are aligned. Value-based or usage-based pricing which meters pricing based on the value and the usage of the customer is the best mode of pricing in a monopoly.[17] Value-based or usage-based pricing can nanonize the pricing to price the product with perfect efficiency for the frequency of use, and with a high efficiency for the expected utility-per-use. Providers can nanonize the pricing along the usage frequency dimension by charging customers for resource usage — the lower the usage frequency, the lower the payments made by the customer. Hence, usage-based or metered pricing charges the customer per usage instance. It converts non-customers who previously could use the service infrequently and hence could not afford to pay flat fees to customers. Providers can provide multiple bundles of services at different pricing levels to discriminate between customers on the utility-per-use dimension. While firms in the productization model could also provide multiple bundles in the form of low-end and high-end products, these bundles had to be pre-configured, and customers could not choose individual functions. Nanoizing the pricing offering by enabling access to functions in different bundles allows providers to nanonize the pricing along the utility-per-use dimension. Value-based pricing based on metering usage extracts value efficiently from customers, and hence, the provider profits are higher, and the customer surplus is lower. Hence, value-based pricing that is metered by the usage frequency is optimal for the provider in a monopoly. If the resources are shared, then the provider should use usage-based metered pricing only without any additional flat-fee component, as even low-frequency users can access the service and provide revenues to the provider. The provider does not need to recoup fixed costs specifically from any customer, as there are no dedicated resources for any customer.

In contrast, if the provider needs to associate dedicated resources for the service of individual customers or organizations (e.g. for office copiers or cars), then the provider should use a flat fee in conjunction with a price-per-use. The flat fee enables the provider to recover the fixed cost of the

---

[17] Balasubramanian, S., Bhattacharya, S., & Krishnan, V. V. (2015). Pricing information goods: A strategic analysis of the selling and pay-per-use mechanisms. *Marketing Science*, 34(2), 218–234.

dedicated resource and allows the customers to use the product for free up to a pre-specified limit. For usage beyond the limit, the provider should charge the customer on a price-per-use basis. For rewarding loyal customers, the provider can use a hybrid pricing model that rewards high-frequency users. The pricing model charges customers a price-per-use for usage up to a pre-specified limit, and then any usage beyond the limit is not charged. The key insights from the chapter are summarized in Table 3.4.

Including the impact of fixed and variable costs requires a careful assessment of the different objectives of pricing: providing customers with positive customer surplus, getting fixed costs recouped in a

Table 3.4:   Best Practices for XaaS Pricing

Environment	Best practices for pricing
Monopoly, shared resources	Value pricing based on pay-per-use
Monopoly, dedicated resources	Value pricing based on flat fee and free usage up to a limit, then pay-per-use for usage beyond the limit
Loyal customers	Pay-per-use up to a limit, then free usage beyond the limit
Inclusion of fixed and variable costs	Pricing and capacity analysis at the level of the nanonized module — smallest independent asset core for complete suite of services
Estimating customer value in monopoly	Start with estimated frequency of usage from number of employees, estimate utility-per-use by dividing TCO of acquiring own assets by the estimated frequency of usage
Estimating customer value in competition	Differentiated value provided by service vis-à-vis competition
Tool for real-life pricing	Simulation
Time-variant pricing	Increase prices for inflation adjustment over time, offering customer more value for customer acquisition, preferable to discounting
Pricing in competition	Subscription-based pricing
Customer usage hard to measure	Performance-based contracts
Measurement of usage tool	IoT technology

reasonable period of time, and making profits with the inclusion of all costs. For the purpose of setting prices in the real-life setting, the provider should design prices with a modular set of resources that is self-sufficient to provide the entire suite of services, we call this module the nanonized module. For copiers and cars, this nanonized module is the individual asset of the copier and the car, for localized service providers like WeWork, this nanonized module is the office space at a specific location. For IT XaaS service offerings, the design of the nanonized module with a planned set of customers enables the provider to design prices, capacity and QoS levels for the module. After the nanonization of pricing, the unitary analysis of pricing is probably the most important takeaway of this chapter. While it seems trivial, we repeat that this unitary analysis at the nanonized level is often not done at the right level of detail, leading to pricing problems as the provider scales its operations. These problems may be in leaving too much value on the table for the customers, or the provider pricing itself out of the market.

To nanonize the pricing, the estimation of the value of the customer is important. The chapter provides important insights into this estimation process. For estimating customer value, the provider can begin with the number of employees of the customer, and a rough-cut analysis of each employee's usage of the service. For the utility-per-use, in a monopoly, the TCO (total cost of operations) of the customer is the total cost estimate of all fixed and variable costs if the customer wanted to set up the services internally. The expected utility-per-use can then be estimated by dividing the TCO by the estimated usage frequency of the customer. In a competitive environment, the expected utility-per-use can be determined by comparing the value provided by the provider when benchmarked against the competitor's offerings. The estimation of the utility-per-use is a critical element of the pricing, as the estimate of the utility-per-use acts as a ceiling for the price-per-use. The difference between the utility-per-use and the price-per-use multiplied by the frequency of usage represents the customer surplus. In terms of setting initial prices, the firm should use simulations as the right tool for this decision. While we have seen both simulation and optimization models, the problem is too complex for optimization models to have a rich enough solution. Our experience is that both models can be used in conjunction for providing robustness checks, and optimization tools are used as input for final decisions with simulation models.

While we do see time-variant pricing in practice and, being a recommended practice in research, we see time-variant pricing as being more useful in sharing inflation adjustment increases over time with customers. Our observations on both practice and research indicate that discounting creates negative externalities from the perspective of customer expectations and customer retention. Hence, we discourage the practice of discounting for customer acquisition from a pricing perspective. Rather than using discounting, we encourage providers to provide free trials and other methods of showcasing the value of their services for customer acquisition. We also do not see providers sharing savings with customers in practice, rather providers would increase prices later to benefit from the savings from economies of scale. In competitive environments, we find strong evidence that subscription-based pricing is a better mode of acquiring and retaining high-frequency customers. Hence, in a competitive environment, the dominant mode of pricing should be subscription-based pricing; usage-based pricing is adopted by low-frequency users. The key difference between monopoly and competitive environments is the customer surplus; pay-per-use extracts utility better and, hence, is the better pricing mode in a monopoly. However, in a competitive environment, the subscription mode leaves more surplus for the customer, and hence, a higher customer surplus. Hence, the dominant pricing mode shifts from usage-based pricing in a monopoly to a subscription-based mode in a competitive environment.

Finally, the role of technology in metering usage and other outcomes is key in XaaS offerings; providers can use technologies to make contracts more verifiable and visible to customers. If customers can monitor their usage and find the metrics easy to understand and explain internally, then usage-based pricing can have a higher buy-in among customers. An alternative is to explore performance-based contracts which contract on customer metrics and align the service provider's incentives to improve the service with the customer's business incentives. In addition to offering better metering services for usage and suggesting metrics for aligned incentives, technology can also enhance the ability of the provider to offer better customer-oriented services in the future.

Chapter 4

Divide and Conquer: Disaggregating Products and Services

In this chapter, we present a method for the provider to plan and evaluate if its offering is suitable to be launched in the XaaS mode. Our method divides the evaluation into a three-stage model: first, the provider evaluates if the offering is feasible to be launched in the XaaS mode. Following the evaluation of feasibility, the provider next should assess the profitability of its offering in the XaaS mode. If the assessment of the first two stages yields a positive evaluation for the provider, the provider should then evaluate if it can grow its offering sustainably in steady state. The three-stage model should be evaluated based on several factors that have been presented in the first three chapters of the book, we call the model based on these factors as the BROAD FENCES model. The BROAD FENCES model looks at various aspects of the nanonization of the offering to determine its suitability as a XaaS offering. The model further disaggregates the analysis of the factors into three stages (feasibility, profitability, and growth), and conducts the analysis based on their importance in each of these stages.

For the evaluation of the provider's offering, it is useful to understand the differences between the XaaS mode and the productization model from the provider's perspective. We first present the differences between the two extreme models by understanding the differences from the provider's perspective in marketing their offerings in the two modes, followed by an analysis of procurement and execution of the offering in the two modes. We also describe the differences of the two modes in a competitive environment and elucidate the benefits of the circular economy for as-a-service offerings.

4.1 MARKETING XaaS OFFERINGS

How is the marketing of XaaS offerings different from that of marketing products? Given that products are sold with the assumption of one main transaction with the customer over a longer lifetime, the role of revenue generation and marketing of products is different from that of services. Since the XaaS offerings involve repeated transactions, revenues from each customer are generated as a stream due to the nanonization of customer utility and pricing. The focus in product marketing is to generate awareness of customer needs and fulfil those needs as closely as possible. In contrast, for services, the focus is on relationship marketing and building trust. To understand the value of relationship building and trust, and identify the economic value of customer retention, we first develop some insights with the concept of customer lifetime value (CLV).[1] Very simply, the customer lifetime value is the amount of net present value (NPV) that the customer generates for the provider, after subtracting the customer acquisition cost. We will develop the concept of customer lifetime value with a simple example. Let us consider the market for the service to consist of just two market segments: Alpha customers and Delta customers. We can consider that the characteristics of the constituents of the individual segments are like each other. The Alpha customers have a utility-per-use of $41.01 for each use of the service, and if they adopt the service, they use the service 5 times every month. Delta customers have a utility-per-use of $61.01 for each use of the service, and if they adopt the service, they use the service 10 times every month. The deal transaction cost for each customer in both segments is $1 for each time they use the service. We assume that the provider wants customers from both segments in its target market, hence, it can price the service at $40, as the price offers a positive customer surplus for both segments ($0.01 for Alpha customers

[1] Jain, D. & Singh, S. S. (2002). Customer lifetime value research in marketing: A review and future directions. *Journal of Interactive Marketing*, 16(2), 34.

and $20.01 for Delta customers) for each use. The provider's marketing staff meet once with customers for acquisition, the cost of customer acquisition, including the demo, trial and other costs, can be assumed to be $1,000 per customer. After the meeting, 10% of Alpha customers and 20% of Delta customers convert to the service. We assume that further meetings do not change the minds of customers, hence, one meeting is all it takes for customers to make up their minds about adopting the service.

The customer acquisition cost (CAC) is defined as the ratio of the average cost of contact to the conversion rate of customers. Intuitively, if the provider spends $10,000 sending catalogues to a 1,000 customers, and acquires a 100 of them, then the cost of acquiring each of the 100 customers is $100 (the total amount for sending catalogues of $10,000 divided by the number of customers who adopted, viz. 100). From the above data, it is easy to see that the CAC for Alpha customers is $10,000, as for every 10 Alpha customers that the marketing staff meets, on average, one will adopt the service (the conversion rate of Alpha customers is 10%). In contrast, for every five Delta customers that the marketing staff meets, two will adopt the service (as the conversion rate is 20%). Hence, the CAC of Delta customers is $5,000. The customer acquisition cost is a simple metric that can be estimated roughly, it includes the average cost of marketing efforts per customer. Hence, it can be estimated by the total marketing budget divided by the number of target customers that the marketing effort reached out to. The total marketing budget can be used on online advertising as well. While it is hard to isolate the impact of different parts of the marketing mix to know which efforts have had the highest hit rate, the CAC provides a broad estimate of customer acquisition cost across different methods. In practice, individual controlled experiments can be conducted to find the customer acquisition cost through different channels.

The next steps in CLV analysis involve the computation of the payback period for a customer segment and the total customer value over the horizon for the service offering. For this example, we set the horizon as a period of 5 years, and we assume a discounting factor of 5%. Tables 4.1 and 4.2 show the payback period and the customer lifetime value for Alpha and Delta customers over the horizon.

The profit per customer is calculated by the revenues generated per customer in the segment (multiplicative product of price-per-use,

Table 4.1:   Customer Lifetime Value and Payback Period for Alpha Customers

Alpha customers	Year 1	2	3	4	5
Profit per customer	$40 \times 5 \times 12 = 2400$	2400	2400	2400	2400
NPV (discounted)	2400		2280	2166	2057.7	1954.815
Cumulative profits (after CAC)	−7600	−5320	−3154	−1096.3	858.515

Table 4.2:   Customer Lifetime Value and Payback Period for Delta Customers

Delta customers	Year 1	2	3	4	5
Profit per customer	$40 \times 10 \times 12 = 4800$	4800	4800	4800	4800
NPV (discounted)	4800	4560	4332	4115.4	3909.63
Cumulative profits (after CAC)	−200	4360	8692	12807.4	16717.03

frequency of usage per month and number of months in the year). The discounted NPV is obtained by multiplying profits of Year 2 by 0.95, year 3 by 0.95^2, and continuing in a similar fashion for subsequent years. The cumulative profits are obtained by adding the profits of the first two years in the second year, the first three years in the third year and so on.

With the parameters used in the example, it is easy to see that the payback period for Alpha customers is 5 years (the first year when the cumulative profits turn positive), while the payback period for Delta customers is Year 2. The CLV for the offering for Alpha customers is $858.51, while that of Delta customers is $16,717.03. From this analysis, it is easy to see that the provider should be focused on Delta customers, as they provide more lifetime value, and their cost of acquisition is lower. Given the minimal timeframe of the offering of 5 years, the payback period of Alpha customers is too high, the acquisition of Alpha customers can be justified only if the service lifetime was significantly longer than 5 years. Second, we have not included variable costs in the example; if the variable costs are substantial, then Alpha customers would not be providing value worth their acquisition over the timeframe. Typical maintenance costs of XaaS offerings include the cost of maintenance and the cost of consumables. Including those costs would lower the profit margin from each customer. Next, the CLV analysis is indeed sensitive to the parameters that are being tested. The provider can use sensitivity analysis to investigate if there are other methods that can be used to acquire Alpha customers. For instance, in the example, the cost per meeting with the customer is high at $1,000 per meeting relative to the revenue generated, and the conversion rate of customers is low at 10%. If there were other methods of attracting customers with lower cost like online automated demos, or a higher conversion rate like free trials, then the provider could potentially use those methods to acquire Alpha customers and have a corresponding lower CAC, justifying the acquisition of Alpha customers.

An important addition to the model would be to incorporate a churn rate, i.e., acquired customers would have a positive chance of discontinuing the service in subsequent years. Other factors that could be included in the model would be the costs of continued customer contact like informing them of updated services every year, and the need for obtaining their feedback and letting them know of additional services. If we assume a survival rate (retention rate of customers) of 80%, our analysis would yield the results for the CLV in Table 4.3.

As can be seen from the analysis with the churn rate, the CLV for the Delta segment drops by over 57% with an annual churn rate of 20%. While the payback period is still the second year, a customer drop-off of 20% per year results in the lifetime value of the customer dropping by more than half, as the average time horizon each customer uses the service reduces from 5 years to a lower figure of 3.36 years. The payments from the customers every year drop accordingly.

From our observations in the industry, we conclude that providers focus a lot on acquiring customers, but they pay relatively little attention to the retention of customers. After the customer has been acquired, the provider needs to invest in relationship marketing with the customer to understand

Table 4.3: Customer Lifetime Value and Payback Period for Delta Customers with Churn Rate

Delta customers	Year 1	2	3	4	5
Profit per customer	$40 \times 10 \times 12 = 4800$	4800	4800	4800	4800
Survival rate	100%	80%	64%	51%	41%
NPV (discounted)	4800	3648	2217.98	1078.83	419.74
Cumulative profits (after CAC)	−200	3448	5665.98	6744.81	7164.55

how to retain customers, as the successful retention of customers can yield a sustainably profitable model. Relationship marketing focuses on both customer acquisition and retention through a mix of structural and customer community-based marketing activities.[2] We will first showcase the relationship marketing campaign of Dollar Shave Club (DSC) as one of the models for relationship marketing effort. The DSC model was a pioneer in the shaving-as-a-service offering space and has been widely accepted as one of the iconic examples of relationship marketing.[3]

The shaving razor market has been dominated by Gillette for many years. They have about a 50% market share in the US, with Edgewell's Schick and Wilkinson Sword being the closest competitor with a market share of about 14%.[4] The dominant position of Gillette and Edgewell's brands meant that they could influence the upgrading and adoption of new razor and blade models every 4–5 years. They achieved this by a combination of creating a larger inventory of the next generation of razors and pricing older and newer generations in close proximity.[5] The price points and margins of the leaders were considered to be high, and potentially, new entrants could gain market share by pricing their products at a lower value. However, manufacturers with cheaper razors and blades that offered basic functionality did not have the brand image or the distribution capabilities of the market leaders. The image of shaving with branded expensive equipment was assiduously built by the market leaders, by having top sports stars and icons in other fields as their endorsers.

How did DSC break into this fiercely competitive market? DSC was co-founded by Mark Levine and Michael Dubin in 2011.[6] At the outset,

[2] Das, K. (2009). Relationship marketing research (1994–2006): An academic literature review and classification. *Marketing Intelligence & Planning*, 27(3), 326–363.

[3] Glazer, E. (2012). A David and Gillette story. *Wall Street Journal*, April 12, 2012, https://www.wsj.com/articles/SB10001424052702303624004577338103789934144, accessed on July 16, 2021.

[4] Shameen, A., "The Edge Malaysia, Tech: How direct-to-consumer firms are disrupting retail", February 26, 2020, https://www.theedgemarkets.com/article/tech-how-directtoconsumer-firms-are-disrupting-retail, accessed June 10, 2020.

[5] D'Aveni, R. A., "Strategic Supremacy through Disruption and Dominance", MIT Sloan, April 15, 1999, https://sloanreview.mit.edu/article/strategic-supremacy-through-disruption-and-dominance/, accessed June 10, 2020.

[6] Booth, B., "What happens when a business built on simplicity gets complicated? Dollar Shave Club's founder Michael Dubin found out", *CNBC*, March 24, 2019,

the marketing of DSC was about highlighting the utility of the razors as opposed to the image of the endorsers. They achieved this by claiming that most of the high cost of the branded razors was associated with the heavy advertising spend of the leaders on the global icons they used as their endorsers. However, the distribution capabilities of the market leaders were hard to replicate. Most other competitors with cheaper products had assumed that customers would acquire their shaving needs at the local brick and mortar retail store. In contrast, DSC recognized that trying to replicate the distribution capabilities of the market leaders would not be feasible. Instead they chose a relationship-based direct marketing approach to attract customers. The cost of customer acquisition was purposefully kept low. DSC's offering was a subscription model where customers would get their razors free of charge, and blades would be charged at $1 every month with shipping and handling costs.[7] The membership of the subscription was not charged, and all subscribers were part of the DSC community. Rather than building on the image of the iconic endorsers, they built a community on a hip, witty and cool image.

DSC has continued with the subscription model. Today, they offer shaving and showering products in their subscription model. Their starter shaving set consists of the razor, shaving scrub, butter and aftershave along with the cartridge at a cost of $5. Their cartridges are expected to last for two weeks, and every two months, they ship a shaving package consisting of supplies for two months for a payment of $39.99. DSC is not vertically integrated, but buys its supplies from third-party sources like Dorco, and distributes them through a mail-order system.[8] In terms of Customer Lifetime Value, DSC recognized that the stream of revenues from continuing subscriptions would eventually become a profitable model. The subscription model makes use of a behavioural bias, where

https://www.cnbc.com/2019/03/23/dollar-shaves-dubin-admits-a-business-built-on-simplicity-can-get-complicated.html, accessed June 15, 2020.

[7] PabloBotero, "Online retailing and the Dollar Shave Club", *Digital Initiative*, November 18, 2016, https://digital.hbs.edu/platform-rctom/submission/online-retailing-and-the-dollar-shave-club/, accessed June 15, 2020.

[8] Solomon, S. D., "$1 Billion for Dollar Shave Club: Why Every Company Should Worry", *The New York* Times, July 26, 2016, https://www.nytimes.com/2016/07/27/business/dealbook/1-billion-for-dollar-shave-club-why-every-company-should-worry.html, accessed June 15, 2020.

customers are more likely to pay on a continuous basis if the spend on a certain category is predictable. In Chapter 3, we had posited that the productization model is preferred when pay-as-you go methods introduce uncertainty in payment schedules. However, with the subscription model of the shaving-as-a-service offering, DSC made the payments for shaving predictable with the subscription model, while when customers buy their own shaving kits, the payment schedule is variable, depending on when the customer replaces their cartridge blades.

It is ironic that DSC's subscription-based shaving-as-a-service offering borrowed the concept of low acquisition cost from the very industry incumbents it was competing with. It is well known that the leaders in the shaving industry had sold razors relatively cheaply and had high profit margins on blades, as the blades constituted a repeated set of transactions with the customer. DSC used the same concept but extended the benefits of relationship marketing with the membership in the club and adopted the subscription model to structurally lock in the stream of revenues. Their target market was primarily students and young professionals who would appreciate the utilitarian value of good and inexpensive shaving equipment, and their online marketing efforts were targeted at digital channels to reach out to this demographic. The viral marketing and community-building efforts of DSC have paid off as it has not used advertising in the traditional sense for customer acquisition. Their initial customer acquisition efforts were limited to online videos, which were spread virally. For subsequent acquisitions of new customers, DSC relies on word-of-mouth marketing and referral marketing, limiting itself to relationship marketing efforts. The relationship marketing investment is showcased by the "Bathroom Minutes" periodical, which has funny anecdotes from customers, grooming advice and humour columns.[9] In July 2016, Unilever acquired DSC for $1 Billion, which was about 5 times DSC's annualized revenues in 2016. DSC had a market share of 8% in the US in 2018.[10]

---

[9]Wegert, T., "Dollar Shave Club Wants to Keep You Reading on the Toilet", *Contently*, May 26, 2015, https://contently.com/2015/05/26/dollar-shave-club-wants-to-keep-you-reading-on-the-toilet/, accessed June 15, 2020.

[10]Primack, D., "Unilever Buys Dollar Shave Club for $1 Billion", *Fortune*, https://fortune.com/2016/07/19/unilever-buys-dollar-shave-club-for-1-billion/#:~:text=Unilever%20announced%20on%20Tuesday%20evening,%2Dbased%20business, accessed June 15, 2020.

DSC's success has spawned competitive models from Harry's and Gillette, which have introduced their own subscription club versions for their offerings.[11]

The Dollar Shave Club has some important lessons for relationship marketing efforts for XaaS providers. First, the efforts of retention do not have to be borne by the provider only. If the provider can offer value for its existing customers, the existing customers can offer similar value by assisting in acquiring and retaining customers. A community of customers can provide word-of-mouth and referral viral marketing; indeed, in the diffusion of ERP systems, this community benefit was structural in nature. Large OEMs were the early adopters of ERP systems, but their benefits from these systems were limited if did not lead to an integration with the systems of Tier 1 suppliers. Many Tier 1 suppliers were large entities in their own right, but subsequent integration with lower tier suppliers was hard owing to the budget effect. The XaaS mode of offering ERP systems enabled smaller suppliers to avail of ERP system services, the OEM acted as a viral marketing agent of the provider by encouraging a large share of the supply chain to adopt the ERP system it operated with. Without the integration of ERP systems in the chain, the benefit of adoption was limited for individual customers owing to interoperability issues — it was hard to coordinate supply chain activities with OEM ERP systems having to liaise with legacy systems at smaller suppliers.

DSC's marketing efforts have had a very small advertising spend associated with them. Instead, they focused on word of mouth and referrals for acquiring new customers and use the periodical and online content for retaining existing customers. The repeated interactions model of the XaaS offering makes it critical that providers use all resources including existing customers to help them in acquiring and retaining customers. The customer journey mapping process can help the provider in understanding how to make their acquisition and retention processes more effective and efficient. The customer journey map can be summarized as a series of steps starting with the awareness of the need, the search process for providers, a

---

[11] Danielsson, M., "Gillette vs. Harry's vs. Dollar Shave Club: What's the Difference?" Investopedia, July 24, 2019, https://www.investopedia.com/articles/investing/022016/razor-wars-gillette-vs-harrys-vs-dollar-shave-club.asp, accessed June 15, 2020.

comparison of different providers, followed by the adoption decision.[12] Following the adoption, customers make decisions on whether to stay with the provider (retention) and advocacy (recommend the provider to others). Providers can use net provider scores (NPS), which is a measure of the proportion of customers who would recommend them wholeheartedly to the total number of customers, to show high levels of customer satisfaction. Referral programs, where the provider gives a discount to other members of the customer's ecosystem, can be used as advocacy measures. The provider can use relationship marketing techniques as shown in the DSC example to communicate more effectively with new customers in the awareness, search and comparison phases of the customer journey.

How is relationship marketing for XaaS offerings different from the marketing efforts of the productization model? First, the best practices in the marketing of XaaS offerings have most characteristics of marketing services, which have differences with marketing products. The first difference is while products are tangible, services are intangible. This difference in marketing effort exists even if services are offered with dedicated resources to the customer. For example, when providers offer copy-as-a-service or cars-as-a-service, they often offer dedicated copiers and cars to individual customers. Hence, the copy-as-a-service or cars-as-a-service offerings provide the tangibility of the core asset to customers in the as-a-service mode as well. However, even if resources are dedicated, the marketing of the tangible good as a product is different from the service offering. For instance, when selling a car, a provider is likely to customize the marketing messages around the driving experience, durability and longevity of the car, and features like the safety and the image of the car. In contrast, the durability and longevity of the car do not matter to the customer if s/he is using the car as a service, so the marketing messages to as-a-service customers have to be tailored differently. For services that are offered with shared resources, e.g. in the online IT offerings space, this difference is exacerbated, as customers do not even see the tangible assets,

---

[12] Lisa Ross, "Customer Journey Mapping — Six Steps to Creating the Complete Customer Journey Maps", Invesp, May 14, 2020, https://www.invespcro.com/blog/customer-journey-maps/, accessed June 15, 2020.

they use the service as and when required. It is well known that product marketing is a combination of the product, price, promotion and placement (4Ps). In addition to these four factors, services marketing adds the elements of process, people and physical evidence (the 7Ps of marketing services).[13] Processes for services marketing have to be structured and standardized as far as possible, otherwise relationship marketing can be very expensive if individual customers have to be reached in unique ways. The DSC example uses the "Bathroom Minutes" magazine and online videos and information to reach the required degree of standardization. While we will elaborate on the people skills and customer support of the People aspect (the 6th P) in Chapter 6 of this book, customer relationship management is an important element of the People factor. Finally, the 7th P (physical evidence) stresses on the need to demonstrate value to the customer. This can be done by having existing customers spread awareness by word of mouth, NPS and referrals, and by various methods of customer feedback.

The needs of agile execution and coordination for XaaS offerings with partners are presented next.

4.2 AGILE XaaS PROCUREMENT AND USER INTERFACE EXECUTION

We now provide an overview of the provider's capability needs to be able to coordinate with vendors and users to offer the XaaS offering effectively. One of the requirements of XaaS offerings is the need for agile execution as stated in Chapter 1. Since the ideal XaaS offering will have continued customer retention and value, the objectives of as-a-service offerings are aligned with the agile execution mode of developing services. The hallmark of generic agile processes is that they always operate in a flux: at no stage can the provider say that its internal processes have reached the target, as the target is constantly evolving. Just as in design thinking, customer needs are assessed and ranked, and the basic

---

[13] Cowell, D. W. & Communication Advertising. (1984). *The Marketing of Services.* London: Heinemann.

functionality of the offering along with other add-on functionalities and features that are delighters are identified. To develop the basic functionality, agile processes add required functions and features in an iterative fashion with collaborative and cross-functional teams in distinct phases called sprints. In each sprint, different elements of the basic functionality are designed and added to the offering and tested for integration. When the provider is satisfied that it has enough functionalities and features to gather meaningful customer feedback, it first works with lead users for testing. Lead user feedback is incorporated into the second iteration and the second iteration's functionality is determined. After the offering has been tested repeatedly and the customer expresses satisfaction with the offering, the first version is launched. Agile execution prioritizes continuous innovation with discipline. Customer requirements are continuously monitored and the as-a-service offering is constantly redesigned to be more aligned with customer expectations to provide customer value. Designing XaaS offerings with the agile methodology enables the provider to prioritize high value features, hence, increasing the nanonized utility-per-use and the potential price that can be charged. The speed of launch is also quicker as the additional functionality required by customers is being offered in a nanonized format, the provider need not wait to add all required functionalities in the service. Finally, the agile process makes the fixed cost of the XaaS offering lower as non-productive effort is reduced, and the potential design flaws are captured and rectified early in the design process. The improved flexibility and visibility provided by agile processes are critical for being able to design, develop and monitor XaaS offerings.

While designing the offering, one of the key steps is incorporating agile procurement steps early in the development process. Agile procurement has two distinct components: the first is the selection of vendors in an agile manner in the design process. The second is the procurement of component quantities in an agile fashion based on observed demand. The concept of lean agile procurement deals specifically with the selection of vendors and co-opting them early in the design process.[14] The key difference in approaches in the lean agile model of procurement with the

---

[14] The Lean Procurement Canvas, Lean Agile Procurement, https://www.lean-agile-procurement.com/lean-procurement-canvas, accessed June 20, 2020.

traditional model of procurement is the integration of the vendor in the design process. The traditional approach has the provider deciding the outcomes of the design process. The provider then identifies the functionalities of key components of the solution required, followed by the selection of the vendor(s) with the components that offer the closest functionality to the desired functionality by the provider. In contrast, in the lean agile procurement framework, the provider starts with a rough sketch of the outcomes from the customer's perspective, and then approaches multiple vendors for solutions that achieve those outcomes. The vendors can provide feedback on the outcomes as well, but the provider has the final say on the outcomes. The provider finalizes the outcomes based on the feasible set of technologies and components from the different vendors. The process requires the provider to interact with vendors in the design process, evaluate the strengths and weaknesses of the solutions provided by the vendors, culminating in the selection of one vendor.

The lean agile procurement process starts off with the setting up of a cross-functional procurement team.[15] The cross-functional team defines the broad outcomes required of the solution. In the second stage, the team shares the broad outcomes of the desired offering with the vendors in advance, and the vendors prepare for their briefing with the provider by designing a single solution, or multiple potential solutions. The third stage involves the provider's cross-functional team meeting with the different vendors, and then having extensive meetings with all the vendors for a few days evaluating their solutions. In this stage, the provider's team can also refine the broad outcomes that they had planned earlier based on the vendors' feedback. For instance, in some cases, the vendors may inform the provider that the current state-of-the-art technologies cannot support the outcomes or will be too expensive for the provider's offering to be successful commercially. Based on the iterative discussions, the provider's team will check the different vendors' solutions first for feasibility. Infeasible solutions (and corresponding vendors) will be eliminated from the selection process. In the fourth stage, the provider can select one of the vendors' solutions and qualify it for the procurement, or

---

[15] Ruau, M., "Approach-Lean Agile Procurement (LAP)", Scoop.it!, January 20, 2020, https://www.scoop.it/topic/devox/p/4114393592/2020/01/20/approach-lean-agile-procurement-lap, accessed June 20, 2020.

it can move further and ask them for a proof of concept prototype that can be tested. This process continues until one vendor is selected. The longer the selection process, the higher the potential payment for the non-selected vendor gets, to compensate it for its effort in participating in the discussions. However, incurring this additional screening cost is important, as it lowers the probability of having to switch vendors at a later stage. The lean agile procurement process has been found to reduce the lead time of vendor and solution selection dramatically to a matter of a few weeks in practice. It also improves the quality of the solutions eventually offered by the provider.

The procurement of resource quantities (either shared or dedicated) for the offering should also be ideally synchronized to demand for make-to-stock environments in an agile manner. While the synchronization of procurement with demand is obvious in the make-to-order model (procurement starts after the order is placed), it is harder to achieve in the make-to-stock model. In the productization model, this agile execution philosophy was first demonstrated by the United Colours of Benetton. The example is famous today for its showcasing of production quantity agility.[16] Benetton used to compete only based on colour, it did not have too many sizes, fits or fabric choices. Initially, Benetton would procure apparel in multiple colours. The demand for apparel is primarily a function of season, the main collections are the Fall and Spring collections. Fall collections tend to be darker in colour, with fewer patterns used, and heavier fabric. In contrast, Spring collections tend to be peppier and more colourful, with lighter fabric and more design patterns. Before the advent of the agile supply chain, Benetton had a high lead time for making its apparel. It would procure fabric from different parts of the world and had stitching and assembling done in low-cost countries. The design process also added to the lead time. Hence, Benetton's lead time for making apparel was in the order of several months. Since Benetton had a selling cycle of six months and a lead time of several months (higher than six), Benetton had to forecast the demand for each stock keeping unit (SKU) and produce these SKUs in advance. It would typically find a mismatch

---

[16] Christopher, M. & Towill, D. (2002). Developing market specific supply chain strategies. *The International Journal of Logistics Management*, 13(1), 1–14.

of the apparel it had designed several months ago with the demand during the season. For some SKUs, Benetton would have stockouts as the SKU was in high demand, and it did not make a lot of units of that SKU. For other SKUs, Benetton found that it had a lot of excess inventories, which had to be heavily discounted (to the tune of 50–80%) at the end of the season. In response, Benetton designed an agile supply chain, where they would not dye the apparel in advance, but instead produce them in the natural colour of the fabrics at the beginning of the season. When the season would start, Benetton would dye a few test batches in different colours and launch them in the market. Colours that were not popular with customers would have fewer sales, and popular colours for test batches would sell out quickly. Benetton had acquired internal dyeing capabilities (they called this the "tinto in capo", or dyeing upon the garment strategy), it would then dye more apparel in the popular colours; as the process of dyeing was agile, it only took a few days. In this way, Benetton was able to match supply and demand much better, as batches of apparel that did not sell well were not replicated, and popular colours were made in larger quantities over the season.

The nanonized module concept that was elucidated in Chapter 3 is based on this principle of agile procurement. The provider can select vendors using the lean agile procurement process to begin with, following which, it has two choices. If the vendors have short lead times in which they can deliver components or complete sets of shared resources to the provider, the provider should ideally just design the first nanonized module and order the components required for this module only. When the utilization begins approaching 60–70% of the peak planned utilization based on the QoS guarantees, the provider can contract for the next nanonized module, thus planning the procurement of its resources in an agile manner. If the vendors have long lead times, the provider should reserve flexible capacity with the vendor based on its forecasts, and confirm the order for the resources by working backwards from the lead time to the point at which it intends to add the additional resources. This agile approach is demand-driven, and it ensures that the provider orders equipment as late as feasible and has a good cash flow.

Is it easy to transition from a traditional operational model to an agile model? What is the typical journey for a provider from the productization model to the XaaS offering? Deloitte identifies four stages in the evolution of a provider from product selling to a full-scale XaaS provider: crawl, walk, run and fly, with the complete evolution from the crawl to the fly stages taking a period of 3–5 years.[17] In the "crawl" stage, providers are experimenting with XaaS offerings, they typically have one or two servitized offerings with low revenues. The marketing models for as-a-service offerings are nascent and depend on existing customers adopting some of these offerings, with customers in limited locations. The priorities of the provider at the crawl stage are designing the strategy for the as-a-service offerings, assessing and expanding capabilities, planning operationally the delivery of the services, and securing internal resources. Internal processes at the provider are ad hoc and manual, limiting the ability to scale. When the provider has advanced to the "walk" stage, they have several customers and sales from the limited offerings, and their priorities are designing processes and technologies for automation. Hence, getting processes and technologies ready for scaling is the first win in the transformation process. The provider is ready to move to the "run" stage when the number of offerings has grown significantly, along with a higher proportion of sales from as-a-service offerings. The provider has specialized marketing strategies for as-a-service offerings that cover customers in expanded geographies. The provider's priorities in the run stage are experimenting with agile processes for renewing offerings, scaling systems and optimizing processes for scaling. Processes are well documented and mostly standardized with a high degree of automation for scaling. Finally, the provider takes the next step in the transformation process to the "fly" stage when it has adopted the XaaS mode for most of its offerings, its marketing methods are utilizing all channels with a global reach, its priorities are scaling and moving quickly to the next generation of offerings, and all processes are standardized and technologies are automated. The four stages of transformation show that it is not trivial to move from the productization model to the XaaS mode of offerings. In addition to business offerings, markets and geographical reach, providers also have

---

[17] Gill, J., Sharma, D., & Kwan, A., "Scaling up XaaS", *Deloitte Insights*, September 30, 2019, https://www2.deloitte.com/us/en/insights/focus/industry-4-0/anything-as-a-service-xaas-solutions-transformation.html, accessed June 20, 2020.

different priorities for execution at each stage. Processes and technologies also must evolve, the productization model involves a few offerings for the entire market, so manual processes and a lack of the use of standardized technology in the internal processes are acceptable. However, for scaling to a XaaS model, customer offerings must be nanonized. To deal with the varied needs of different customers, standardized processes with automated technologies for executing internal processes are a must.

In addition to working closely with vendors in the delivery of XaaS offerings, XaaS providers also have to work closely with channel partners like resellers. This is especially true in the world of IT offerings.[18] In the days of legacy systems where solutions where sold using the productization model, value-added resellers (VARs) helped technology providers connect with their customers. The provider's dependence on the reseller increased to the point where the resellers would act as the primary point of contact with the customer. The reseller would collate customer requirements, and source the solutions for the customer, taking up healthy profit margins from the providers. In the XaaS world, is there a role for channel partners like resellers? The research indeed finds that resellers have to play a role in the XaaS space as well, especially if providers do not have the capabilities to work directly with customers, and need the help of the distribution and customer proximity capabilities of the resellers. A survey by Alexander Group finds that providers are providing channel partners with 15% more revenues as they need the channel partners to develop an understanding of continually evolving customer requirements.[19] However, this extra spending comes with a catch: providers are spending more on a select set of resellers with a specific set of capabilities. Since XaaS offerings yield smaller revenues per sale owing to the payments being spread over time, lead generation is a very important capability of resellers. Hence, resellers who can provide a higher number of leads with higher scale are gaining in a winner-take-all reseller market. Second, resellers

---

[18] Deliver Infinite Opportunities with XaaS Offerings, Ingram Micro Cloud, https://www.ingrammicrocloud.com/sg/en/solutions-i-need-xaas/, accessed June 20, 2020.

[19] Ryan, S., "The Shifting Role of Channel Partners in a XaaS World, Alexander Group", https://www.alexandergroup.com/insights/the-shifting-role-of-channel-partners-in-a-xaas-world/, accessed June 20, 2020.

who can customize solutions for customers by integrating individual components from technology providers like managed service providers and systems integrators are winning more business. Third, resellers with servicing and training capabilities are in high demand, as vendors often do not have the scale for providing training and servicing. This phenomenon is not limited to IT solutions providers. Other service providers like ISA who offers refrigeration-as-a-service need local service providers to provide maintenance services for their offerings. Fourth, the XaaS offerings have made many solutions accessible to SMEs that were not affordable earlier. Resellers with networks to SMEs can provide an additional stream of revenue for technology providers.

We now highlight the actions that XaaS providers should take in a competitive environment.

4.3 COMPETITIVE ENVIRONMENT EFFECT ON XaaS

The degree of competition in the market has a significant effect on the XaaS offering for the following reasons. The as-a-service offering space does not lock in customers but gives customers the freedom of choice of trial of the service. The offering must provide value on a sustainable basis, or else customers are free to choose other providers if they are not satisfied with the service. In contrast, in the productization model, customers make a purchase with a large initial investment in the product at an early stage. If they find out later that the value of the product is not what they had expected, it is hard for them to switch to other offerings. While it is rational that any investment made should be regarded as a sunk cost and the customers should evaluate the value of their usage of the offering in the future, the behavioural research shows that decision-makers usually ignore the sunk cost fallacy. Hence, customers continue using assets for some time that they have purchased but are not happy with. On the other hand, in the XaaS mode, switching to other offerings is easier. The flexibility provided by as-a-service offerings is one of the key strengths of the as-a-service offering mode. However, this flexibility also comes at a cost, this is one of the main weaknesses of the XaaS mode of offering in a competitive environment.

In Chapter 3, we saw that the XaaS mode of offering is usually offered with the pay-as-you-go or pay-per-use pricing model, where the customer pays the provider for the resources used. The pay-per-use model discriminates perfectly on the frequency of usage, and partially on the utility-per-use, hence, it extracts customer value efficiently. In contrast, flat-fee pricing leaves a higher value on the table for customers. In competitive environments, however, customers choose the offerings that leave them higher surplus value. Hence, if two providers offer the same service to the customer, but one of them chooses subscription pricing and the other chooses pay-per-use pricing, the customer will adopt the pay-per-use pricing mode if the customer's usage frequency is low, and will adopt the subscription mode offering if his/her usage frequency is high. Hence, in a competitive environment, if there is no differentiation in the services offered, the provider offering the subscription mode has the high-value customers, and the higher profits. For example, if providers are offering media content that is primarily sourced externally, many providers can offer similar content, and the degree of differentiation is low. Netflix offers the subscription mode of pricing in this case, so that customers can access the content without having to worry about paying more for watching more, hence, high-frequency usage customers will adopt the Netflix offering.

The competitive environment forces providers to move from a pay-per-use mode to a subscription mode, and from a subscription mode to a flat-fee mode, as the flat-fee mode is the most robust in a competitive environment. What should XaaS providers then do in competitive environments? The answer is simple: the XaaS environment is ideal for providing differentiated services vis-à-vis competitors. XaaS offerings should be customized as much as possible to be differentiated to lower the intensity of competition. This tailoring of the provided services leads to a differentiated or "niche" strategy, where rather than competing on price with undifferentiated products, providers carve out their own niches for differentiating their offerings. In an environment of greater choice, customers choose providers based on the value of individual offerings to them. Hence, Disney offers its own content exclusively on its Disney + platform, while Netflix is following a strategy of developing and acquiring its own exclusive content. The acquisition of exclusive content enables Netflix and Disney to carve out their own niches, leading to a degree of differentiation in their offerings. Potentially, high-frequency usage customers can subscribe to both platforms, rather than having to choose one platform to access similar content.

In the IaaS set of offerings, the three largest providers are Amazon Web Services (AWS), Microsoft Azure and Google Cloud, each of them have their own core distinctive features.[20] AWS was the first mover in the IaaS space. It is the current market leader with a market share of 32.4% as of February 2020. Its key strength is the number of services with the quality of the services that have been honed over time. AWS offers a total of more than 175 services across computation, storage, analytics, tools and other applications. As the market leader, AWS also has the highest scale, along with the sheer breadth of offerings. Microsoft Azure has the advantage of the highest penetration of enterprise software offerings, leading to better long-term customer relationships. It had a market share of 17.6% as of February 2020 (Microsoft reports its cloud revenues across different categories, so the market share comparisons are not for the IaaS offerings of Azure alone). Azure has the strengths of complementarity and interoperability with enterprise software, and economies of scope across software and IaaS hardware offerings. Google Cloud has an edge in analytics with its deep expertize in machine learning, as well as its use of open source technologies like Kubernetes and the Istio service mesh. Google had a market share of 6% as of February 2020. The differentiation between the three providers has meant that each of them have carved out their own niches, and hence, they do not compete directly. In fact, many customers (especially the ones with large cloud spends) use more than one provider's offerings for their cloud services, showing that having a niche strategy enables customers to use multiple providers for different services. The carving of their own distinctive niches has led to each of the three providers charging on a per-second basis for most of their services (pay-per-use), at price points that are roughly similar to each other. Microsoft already

---

[20]Carey, S., "AWS vs Azure vs Google Cloud: What's the best cloud platform for enterprise?" ComputerWorld, January 23, 2020, https://www.computerworld.com/article/3429365/aws-vs-azure-vs-google-whats-the-best-cloud-platform-for-enterprise.html, accessed June 25, 2020.

offers their Office applications to customers on an annual subscription basis. Subscription pricing is useful in competition, and when it is hard to define usage metrics that are commonly understood by customers. It would be interesting in the future to see if any of the three providers also adds a subscription service to their current IaaS pay-per-use pricing for large enterprise customers, especially if IaaS offerings converge in terms of scope and quality of offerings.

The benefits of XaaS offerings as a cost reduction mechanism to the provider and for the environment using the circular economy are explained next.

4.4 BENEFITS OF CIRCULAR ECONOMY FOR XaaS

The benefits of the XaaS mode of offering in taking advantage of the circular offering are based on the twin features of the circular economy: legislation-driven and profitability-driven. The EU region has been the global leader in legislating on extended producer responsibilities for the acquisition and disposal of waste in different industries. Other regions have introduced similar legislation, too. The EU introduced the WEEE (Waste Electrical and Electronic Equipment) laws globally, where producers were made responsible for collecting a pre-specified fraction of the products that they had sold, and disposing them with minimal environmental impact.[21] When producers have to collect and dispose their own waste, they have to first collect used products that are sold to customers. They also must design systems for disassembly, sorting and reusing, and in some cases, disposing materials and components that cannot be reused. The XaaS mode of offerings reduces the complexity of complying with the laws by design, as the ownership of any supporting assets is transferred to the provider. The provider has access to the assets at the end of life of the asset, regardless of whether the resources are shared and are physically present at the provider's location, or whether the resources are

---

[21] European Commission, Environment, Additional tools Waste Electrical & Electronic Equipment, https://ec.europa.eu/environment/waste/weee/index_en.htm, accessed June 25, 2020.

dedicated and are at the customer's location. Hence, the cost of collection of used products is reduced dramatically. Second, the XaaS mode of offering is especially useful for services with assets of short lifecycles so that customers can transfer seamlessly from one generation of services to the next. The short lifecycle of the asset implies that providers in the XaaS mode will encourage vendors to produce in a way that is easy to disassemble and reuse, using principles of design-for-remanufacturing. The principles of design-for-remanufacturing are like the principles of design for quality and design for serviceability, which were reviewed in Chapter 2. Hence, the objectives of XaaS offerings are aligned better with the advantages of the circular economy that is driven by legislation.

While the move to the circular economy was driven initially be legislation, providers quickly realized that they could use the collected assets from the previous generation for their inherent economic value. Most asset designs retain some components from the previous generation, only modules that are driving new technology functionality or performance need to be changed. For non-IT products such as white goods and copiers, some components are durable, while others need replacement due to wear and tear. The same is true for assets like tyres, where the radial is durable, but the rubber casing and outer layer of the tyre need replacement by re-treading. Reusing the durable components and replacing the consumables and worn-out components adds economic value for the provider, the transfer of asset ownership to the provider is critical in this regard. Ahrend uses older furniture items as the base for the creation of new furniture, leading to lower waste disposal. By judiciously using materials from older designs, Ahrend can have substantive cost savings, which can help its profitability. Hence, cost savings are an important benefit of the XaaS mode of offerings if the provider uses the principles of the circular economy. An important aspect of the circular economy is the customer expectation set; many customers are environmentally conscious now and would like to see providers use sustainable methods of manufacturing and delivery. By adopting the XaaS mode of offerings, providers can send a strong signal of their commitment to the circular economy. They can encourage customers to avail of their offerings by using their activities relating to the circular economy as an important attribute for marketing. Finally, the circular economy has important benefits for the speed of offering maintenance services for the provider. While spare parts have to be ordered from vendors in the productization model, spare parts can be taken from used assets that have been replaced in the XaaS model, giving the provider an additional source for spare and replacement parts.

4.5 THE BROAD FENCES MODEL

We now present the BROAD FENCES model for the design, assessment and improvement of as-a-service offerings. First, the application of the BROAD FENCES model is meant to test the feasibility, profitability potential and the growth potential of the as-a-service offering. Hence, the tool should be used at different stages of the lifecycle of the XaaS offering. Second, the BROAD FENCES model offers a structured way of designing, evaluating and improving XaaS offerings, hence, the model will offer a standardized method. Third, the model can be used both with preliminary, anecdotal data as well as with structured, comprehensive data. If the model is applied in the design stage of XaaS offerings with preliminary, anecdotal data, it should be used as a scoring model with subjective scores assigned to different elements of the model. At the preliminary stage, the factors can also be scored using a subjective three-point assessment of Low, Medium and High, depending on the assessment of the firm's offering on that dimension. If on the other hand, the model is used with detailed, comprehensive data, the profitability and growth potential at different stages can be estimated. The BROAD FENCES model is intended to be a sequential model, as different factors have different degrees of influence on the XaaS offering at different stages. Hence, the model also helps to prioritize provider actions. The different factors in the BROAD FENCES model along with the accompanying questions that should be asked to design, evaluate and improve the service are described in what follows.

4.5.1 Budget Impact

The budget impact factor considers the impact of asset ownership transfer from the customer to the provider in the XaaS mode of offerings. It helps to design, evaluate and improve the XaaS offering from both the provider's and the customer's perspectives by ensuring that the advantages of the XaaS mode over the productization model are fully exploited. The business leader should analyze the efficacy of the XaaS mode of offerings compared to the productization mode first on the dimension of the costs of acquisition of the underlying core asset and complementary assets. For example, if the business leader is contemplating the offering of an enterprise software offering in the SaaS format, they should start by analyzing the cost of acquiring the software and the hardware requirements to support the software application's acquisition from the customer's perspective. Next, the business leader has to estimate the typical customer's cost of capital, cash flow and tax implications, the appreciation or depreciation of the core and complementary assets, costs of maintenance, insurance, installation to estimate the total cost of ownership (TCO) for the customer from the productization mode. At this preliminary stage, the leader then must estimate his/her own price range that the provider would charge for all the same services. The price range is important, as it enables the leader to get a ballpark figure for the feasible price set. The TCO would then need to be estimated for the as-a-service offering. There need not be a compulsion to have a lower TCO for the as-a-service offering compared to the productization mode, as XaaS offerings have other advantages like lower risk of capacity, payments and other risk factors. However, the TCO estimated for the as-a-service offering should not be much higher than the corresponding figure for the productization mode. After the financial comparisons have been analyzed, the leader should assess the benefits of moving from the capex mode of operation to the opex mode of operation for the customer. For example, the benefits of moving from the capex mode to the opex mode would include making the offering accessible to SMEs, which may not have been able to afford the high cost of the initial acquisition. Other benefits of the XaaS transfer of ownership are making consolidated payments every period for all aspects of the service, and the need for less internal staff.

The questions to be answered in the budget impact analysis phase are:

Are the underlying core and complementary assets expensive to acquire? Are asset values likely to appreciate or depreciate in the future? Do typical customers have access to sufficient own cash or debt to acquire the core and complementary assets? What are the cash flow and tax implications for the customer? What is the TCO of asset ownership for the customer?

What are the likely price ranges for our own offering in the XaaS mode? What is the duration of the customer's adoption of our offering? What is the TCO for the customer from our XaaS offering? What are the customer's other benefits from moving from a capex to an opex mode of operation?

What are the additional benefits of our XaaS offering to the customer?

The answers to these questions can enable the business leader to estimate the ease of acquiring new customers for the XaaS offering based on the initial budget outlay and the financial factors from the transfer of asset ownership.

4.5.2 Risk

The risk analysis of the productization mode is compared to the risk profile of the XaaS offering in gauging the customer's risk factors. The leader must assess the benefits of the XaaS mode of offering with regard to risk, as the risk analysis tends to be unidirectionally in favour of the XaaS offering mode. First, the leader must consider the estimation risks of the capacity of acquisition in the customer ownership mode against the XaaS mode. The estimation risk of capacity of acquisition is significant, as the customer may acquire more capacity than required if s/he acquires the assets, leading to waste of capital. It is also possible that the customer may acquire less capacity than required, leading to further acquisitions down the road, and lower economies of scale. In contrast, if the provider adds capacity for serving multiple customers using the nanonized module concept, the provider's risk of overestimation or underestimation is significantly lower from risk pooling effects. The risk of overrunning the budget of asset acquisition from the customer's perspective should also be considered, and weighed against the risk of mis-estimating payments from partaking of the XaaS offering (which is lower, as the customer typically pays for usage). Another source of risk is business risk from the potentially high lead time of asset acquisition of the customer. The leader should also estimate the effects of other risks like quality and reliability risk of asset acquisition, business cycle risk, and the switching costs and vendor lock-in in the asset ownership mode. While most of these risks are quantifiable with the value of risk (VAR) metric, as stated earlier, a simple three-point scale of low, medium or high can be used. The questions to be answered in the risk analysis are as follows:

What is the impact of risk of overestimation or underestimation of the capacity acquisition in the productization mode? How severe is the risk of budget overrun? Can the customer acquire assets quickly in the productization mode?

Are quality and reliability risk and business cycle risk important factors in the customer's consideration set in our business? Are there secondary markets that enable the customer to get some value if the acquired assets do not perform to the customer's expectations? Are the customer's switching costs high?

What are the customer's risks from our offering? Are there risks like mis-estimating the payment risk, or the inability to estimate the value from our offering? Should we offer the customer a free trial of our service? For how long?

The answers to these risk questions can provide an estimate of the stability of the productization mode, and if various risk assessments will motivate the customer to try the XaaS offering.

4.5.3 Obsolescence of Technology

While we label this factor by the term obsolescence of technology, we include all technology-related factors in this category; of course, the obsolescence of technology is an important facet of the role of technology in XaaS offerings for customer adoption. The analysis of technology issues like upgrading is conducted here from the customer's and the firm's perspectives. First, the leader should estimate the duration of the core and complementary technology lifecycles — the shorter the lifecycle, the stronger the case for customers adopting as-a-service offerings. The leader should also estimate if customers can predict easily which technology will be the dominant technology in the next generation, and if it will be compatible with the previous generation. If the next generation is compatible, the customer can upgrade from one generation to the next. If the next generation is based on a new technology, the customer must acquire a new set of core and complementary assets in the next generation. Next, the provider should assess if other technologies can be used to create value for the customer and the provider. For example, in the subscription model of Panera Bread and Burger King, both providers used an app to gather data on customer ordering patterns of food items with the coffee. With data analytics, they assessed customer usage patterns and shared information on promotions or other substitute food items that customers could order to personalize customer offerings. Technologies can also be used to add value to customers, for example, MAN and Michelin Solutions used technology to gather information on the use of vehicles. Using data analytics, they suggested best practices to customers for enhanced fuel efficiency and other objectives. Technology can also be used to create customer communities and for building long-term relationships with customers. The questions to be assessed in the obsolescence of technology category are as follows:

What are the durations of the core and complementary asset technology lifecycles? Is it easy to predict the dominant technology for the next generation of assets? Will the next generation represent an advancement of the current technology, or will it be based on a different technology?

How can we create value for the customer using technology in our offerings? How can we use technology to personalize our offerings to the customer? How can we use technology to create customer communities and a long-term relationship with the customer?

The answers to the questions in the Obsolescence of technology category provide important ideas for the provider in using technology to create value for customers and for themselves.

4.5.4 Agility

The need for agility exists throughout the design of XaaS offerings, their subsequent improvement, and for continuous innovation. While agility is an important enabler of as-a-service offerings, some activities needing long lead times that are beyond the control of the provider, such as procurement of some solutions components, need to be identified early. The leader must identify components of the service that can be changed in an agile fashion and plan a path of continuous innovation with iterative feedback from the customer. The provider must use the continuous feedback from the customer relationship to prioritize solutions components that are critical for customer acquisition and retention. The questions to be assessed in the agility analysis are as follows:

What are the solutions components that can be designed and refined in an agile fashion? Which attributes of customer utility can be enhanced in a modular fashion with the functionalities on those dimensions increased independently? What are the solutions components that have a long lead time of delivery and cannot be expedited currently?

Do we have the capabilities to gather customer feedback continuously? Can we categorize the utility elements of the customer feedback into high, medium and low value? What are the critical factors for acquiring new customers and retaining existing customers that we can add to the service, or improve in the current service?

The answers to the agility analysis questions enable the provider to attract new customers, retain existing customers and create a cycle of continuous innovation.

4.5.5 Deal Transaction Cost

The leader must estimate various elements of the inconvenience caused to customers in repeated transactions with the provider and aim to reduce them as far as possible. While a completely streamlined process would be difficult as that could endanger the security features of the provider, the leader has to strike a balance between making the services easily accessible in each transaction with the need for ensuring data and application security. The provider also has to make the pricing per use as transparent as possible to reduce the ticking meter effect (customers should not be thinking of whether they really need to access the service at this time and if the costs of access are justified at each time). The questions to be asked in the deal transaction cost analysis are as follows:

How can we make the service accessible as easily as possible to the customer each time, keeping the security features that we need in mind?

How can we take pay-per-use pricing off the customer's mind when using the solutions we provide?

4.5.6 Frequency of Usage

The frequency of usage estimation is a critical step of the model, as it is one of the primary strengths of the XaaS offering, and it can perfectly discriminate along the frequency of usage dimension. The leader must identify from market analysis if there are customer segments who would typically use the services frequently, and those who would use them infrequently. The infrequent users are the non-customers of the productization model who become customers in the XaaS mode. If possible, through simulations and pilot tests, it would be useful to estimate the range of the frequencies of usage of the heterogeneous customer segments. The provider should also have a rough-cut estimate of the potential market sizes for each of these customer segments. Next, an important part of this analysis is the seasonality of use, and analysis of the correlation of demand of the different customer classes. A high correlation of demand (equivalent to seasonality) would imply that the provider needs to plan for a high capacity for the core and complementary assets, as all customers use the services around the same time. As we saw in the Trringo example, farmers use tractors throughout the farming cycle, but they use tillers, disc harrows and reapers in a seasonal fashion. Similarly, for providers of tax consulting software in the as-a-service mode, the demand during the early months of the year is very high, as enterprises and individuals are preparing their tax statements for the previous year. The demand for tax consulting services is significantly lower in the second half of the year.

Hence, for assets with high seasonality, the provider either must acquire a large set of assets, or it must share assets across different locations with uncorrelated or negatively correlated demand. If customers have different patterns of usage from each other, and these patterns are uncorrelated or negatively correlated, the provider can plan for a lower capacity, as the customer usage patterns can be pooled. Finally, the provider must analyze how best to measure customer usage: in terms of time, or the actual usage of resources like processor execution units. The key questions to be asked in the analysis of the frequency of usage are as follows:

How does the frequency of usage differ across customers that will access our services? What are the personae of high-frequency and low-frequency users? Can we estimate the range over a period that typical customers in these high-frequency and low-frequency segments will use our services? Can we estimate the potential market sizes of high-frequency and low-frequency usage segments?

Will the usage of our services be seasonal? Will all or some segments of customers exhibit this seasonality? Do the different segments use our services at the same periods of time, or at different periods of time?

How should we measure the frequency of usage? Do we have the technology to measure the amount of time that customers used our assets? Do we have the technology to measure how much of the assets were utilized by the customer?

4.5.7 Expected Utility-per-use

The expected utility-per-use is the other component of customer utility that is a critical step of analyzing the profitability of the XaaS offering. Just as in the frequency of usage analysis, the leader has to analyze if the expected utility-per-use is high for some customer segments and low for others, and create personae for the high and low expected utility-per-use customers. This step should also estimate the potential market size in each of these segments. The analysis of the frequency of usage and expected utility-per-use should be combined to create market segments, and strategies for offering services and pricing. For example, if the market size of high-frequency usage customers with high expected utility-per-use is high, the provider can offer the services as a premium offering. If the largest market segment has a high frequency of usage and low expected utility-per-use, then the provider should also add a subscription pricing offering. If the largest market segment has a high expected utility-per-use but low frequency of usage, then pay-per-use pricing is optimal.

Next, the leader must estimate if the customer's expected utility-per-use is stable or diminishing over time. If the expected utility-per-use is stable, then the provider should ensure that at the very least, the pay-per-use price covers the operating expenses per customer with a healthy margin. Ideally, the provider should have completed the design of the nanonized module at this stage. The design of the nanonized module enables the provider to have a rough-cut comparison of the operating expenses and fixed costs of the nanonized module to estimate its profitability. At this stage, the provider should also assess the lifetime value of the customer. If the expected utility-per-use decreases rapidly over time, then the utility-per-use of the first instance should be higher than the operating expenses, and customers should be forecasted to use the service only once or twice. The provider should also analyze if the customer's frequency of usage and utility-per-use vary over time, leading to variable payment schedules on the part of the customer. Finally, the provider should check if there are standardized customer-oriented performance measures that mimic the usage of services, so that performance-based contracts with customer output-oriented metrics can be designed. The questions to be asked in the analysis of the expected utility-per-use are as follows:

How does the expected utility-per-use differ across customers? What are the personae of customers with high and low utility-per-use? What are the potential market sizes of these segments? Do we offer our services as a premium offering? Do we offer a subscription mode system of pricing or pay-per-use pricing? Is the utility-per-use stable or decreasing over time?

What are the expected operating and fixed costs of the nanonized module? Are the operating expenses for us lower than the lowest expected utility-per-use of customers that will adopt our services? Are the margins reasonable? What is the customer lifetime value (CLV)? Can we offer a standard performance-based contract to all our customers?

The analysis of the frequency of usage and expected utility-per-use along with the consideration of the deal transaction costs enable a rough-cut estimation of the profitability of the provider.

4.5.8 Niche

The analysis of whether the provider can create a differentiated niche for itself is related primarily to the expected competitive intensity of the market. If the provider expects to have a high market share in perpetuity, no further analysis is needed. However, if the market potential is significant, then the provider can expect competitive entry at a later stage. In a competitive market, the provider should ideate about how it can substantively differentiate its offerings. If substantive differentiation is not possible, the provider should analyze if it can price its offering in the subscription mode. The competitive analysis of the offering should answer the following questions:

What is the competitive intensity in the offering space (from both productization and XaaS offerings) now and in the future? In a competitive market, how can we substantively differentiate our offerings? If the services offered by competitors are converging to a dominant standardized set of offerings, can we price our offering in the subscription mode?

4.5.9 Complementarity

The complementarity analysis should check if the total utility of the different service elements can be combined to create greater value than the sum of the individual utilities. It should also check if there are economies of scope from sharing resources for offering the different services. For example, if voice and data are carried on the same cables, then telecom operators have economies of scope from offering two distinct services that share cost elements. The leader should then assess if the services should be offered as mixed bundles (where service elements are offered as a bundle, or as standalone services), or pure bundles (bundles only are offered). The provider should also check if significant integration efforts are needed to offer a seamless bundle, and if any interoperability issues need to be resolved across the different service components. The complementarity analysis should answer the following questions:

Will the customer get greater value from using the service elements together? Can we get substantial cost savings from economies of scope? Should we adopt a mixed bundling or pure bundling strategy?

Are there significant interoperability issues between our different services? How can we integrate our services better to resolve these interoperability issues?

4.5.10 Economies of Scale

Economies of scale arise from sharing resources and support services across different customers as much as possible. One of the major advantages of IT XaaS offerings is that there are economies of scale in resources, and sharing the same infrastructure among multiple firms lowers the cost of the provider compared to the sum of the acquisition costs of the users. The economies of scale analysis should estimate the fixed and variable costs of the nanonized module and compare that to the prices charged to customers using the nanonized module across the entire offering. The analysis should also consider savings from offering customer support, maintenance and insurance services, and the value of cost savings from the circular economy at scale. The provider should also assess the management of network congestion from activities at scale at the nanonized level, and the measures needed for ensuring data security. The questions to be answered in the analysis of the economies of scale are as follows:

Are there significant economies of scale from shared resources, shared maintenance, insurance and customer support, and from the circular economy? Does the fixed cost come down significantly as the number of nanonized modules increase?

How do we manage network congestion (limiting the total usage of nanonized modules to a given level of utilization)? How do we determine the QoS guarantees? What measures do we take in shared responsibility with customers for ensuring data and application security?

4.5.11 Solutions Approach and Customization

The solutions approach and customization have multiple components: the first analysis to be done relates to the interaction with customers. The analysis must include outreach to potential customers, the creation of market channels, gathering customer feedback and data and understanding customer priorities, use of relationship marketing, and utilizing existing customers to attract new customers. The second component is the set of capabilities for providing solutions: the ability to unbundle different service elements for customer choice, the ability to incorporate customer feedback into solutions, and creating solutions menus. The questions to be asked for the analysis of the solutions approach and customization are as follows:

How do we reach out to customers? Are our own marketing channels sufficient, or do we also cooperate with resellers?

What are the methods we use for gathering customer feedback and priorities? How can we use relationship marketing with customers for better retention? How can we use success stories with existing customers for attracting new customers?

Do we have a structured approach for incorporating customer priorities in our new solutions? Can we create menus of services (through bundling and unbundling) to give customers choices for their preferred solutions?

The BROAD FENCES model is constructed very imaginatively with the first letter of each factor in the order that the factors have been stated; B for budget impact, R for risk, O for obsolescence of technology, the reader has doubtless got the picture by now. However, there is a deeper significance to the order of the factors, which affects the order in which these factors should be considered. The budget impact is one of the primary factors for the transfer of asset ownership in XaaS offerings, and should be considered first to ask the question: should the offering adopt the XaaS mode? The risk factors and obsolescence of technology are other important factors in this feasibility consideration set. To outline the sequence of the recommended analysis of these factors, we first conduct the BROAD FENCES analysis of two sets of offerings: one in the IT offerings space, and the other in non-IT offerings. The contrast will elucidate why IT offerings have seen the as-a-service mode burgeon, and the challenges of offering non-IT offerings in the as-a-service mode. We will analyze the Alibaba Cloud offering and the WeWork space-as-a-service offering with the BROAD FENCES model. The WeWork services have already been described briefly in Chapter 1.

4.6 ANALYSIS OF XaaS OFFERINGS USING BROAD FENCES MODEL

We briefly describe the IaaS offering of Alibaba Cloud. The offering is similar to other IaaS offerings from top technology firms. Alibaba Cloud has the third largest global market share at 9.1%, and a market share of 28.2% in the APAC region.[22] The Alibaba Cloud offering, also known as Aliyun and christened as the Alibaba Cloud in August 2019, is quite similar to the IaaS offerings of AWS, Microsoft and Google.[23] The offering was launched in 2009, and the R&D and operations centres are located in Hangzhou, Beijing and Silicon Valley.[24] The Alibaba Cloud provided the infrastructure for supporting the first Single's Day Taobao shopping event in November 2011, and hosted 2.4 billion page views in 24 hours.[25] There is a big demand for colocation of data centres by many customers, and in 2019, Alibaba Cloud had data centres in 21 regions with 63 global availability zones, the global headquarters is registered in Singapore. It works with the entire gamut of private and public enterprises globally with a leadership position in China. It is the official Cloud Services Partner of the International Olympic Committee (IOC).[26]

The services offered also span a large range of cloud essentials including elastic computing, storage, networking and communication services, along with data processing services like artificial intelligence and machine learning, and data sensing services like IoT. Alibaba Cloud's services are bundled partially for business verticals like retailing, education, sports, media content and financial services. It also provides a range of functional and processing services like data security, enterprise IT governance, AI and data processing. In terms of pricing, Alibaba Cloud offers

---

[22] Businesswire, "Alibaba Named by Gartner as Third Biggest Global Provider for IaaS and First in Asia Pacific", April 27, 2020, https://www.businesswire.com/news/home/20200427005479/en/Alibaba-Named-by-Gartner-as-Third-Biggest-Global-Provider-for-IaaS-and-First-in-Asia-Pacific, accessed June 25, 2020.

[23] *Ibid.*

[24] Kharpal, A., "Cloud computing could be the 'next frontier' for Alibaba", *CNBC*, September 10, 2019, https://www.cnbc.com/2019/09/10/alibaba-cloud-business-may-follow-amazons-path-to-profitability.html#:~:text=Alibaba%20launched%20its%20cloud%20computing,year%2Don%2Dyear%20growth, accessed June 25, 2020.

[25] Zhang, J., "How Alibaba powered billions of transactions on Singles' Day with 'zero downtime'", South China Morning Post, November 20, 2019, https://www.scmp.com/tech/e-commerce/article/3038539/how-alibaba-powered-billions-transactions-singles-day-zero-downtime, accessed June 25, 2020.

[26] Wikipedia, Alibaba Cloud, https://en.wikipedia.org/wiki/Alibaba_Cloud, accessed June 25, 2020.

membership to their services on a monthly or annual basis, and the usage is priced on a pay-as-you-go basis.[27] Alibaba's main competitors in China are Huawei Cloud and Tencent Cloud, with a market share of 16% each. Alibaba also has the highest market share of cloud infrastructure services in China, with a market share of 41%.[28]

The budget impact of cloud computing services easily favours the XaaS offering. The diffusion of cloud computing services among large enterprises started many years ago and has picked up speed. Cloud services have been increasingly diffusing among SMEs as well, Gartner estimates that 60% of all businesses will be using the cloud in various capacities by 2022, which is twice the adoption ratio in 2018.[29] The pay-per-use pricing of cloud services can be estimated by usage and pricing calculators, which are offered by most cloud providers including Alibaba Cloud to customers to estimate their TCO. In addition to lowering the risk of adoption along all the dimensions like capacity estimation and budget overrun risk, cloud computing can be accessed and tested with free trials from Alibaba Cloud and other providers. Unlike the acquisition of own assets that requires detailed estimations of TCO and search costs for providers, cloud computing can be accessed quickly, and providers can use the cost estimates from the price calculators to compare with their current IT spend. Customers also do not need to estimate the duration of the lifecycle of their own assets, as for most of them, technology is not their forte, and any estimations will likely be faulty. Alibaba uses technologies like IoT and AI to provide data analytic services to their customers in business verticals. These technologies can use the data from hosting the customer's applications to provide deep insights into customer purchase and browsing patterns. The agility of Alibaba Cloud and other large cloud providers

---

[27] Alibaba, "Flexible Billing Options to Fit All Your Needs", Pricing, *Alibaba Cloud*, https://www.alibabacloud.com/pricing, accessed June 25, 2020.

[28] China Internet Watch, "China cloud computing market share; Alibaba's global share grew 54% in Q4", February 8, 2021, https://www.chinainternetwatch.com/30820/cloud-infrastructure-services/, accessed June 25, 2020.

[29] Costello, K. & Rimol, M., "Gartner Forecasts Worldwide Public Cloud Revenue to Grow 17% in 2020", Gartner, Nov 13, 2019, https://www.gartner.com/en/newsroom/press-releases/2019-11-13-gartner-forecasts-worldwide-public-cloud-revenue-to-grow-17-percent-in-2020, accessed June 29, 2020.

is fairly high, and the feedback that they get for services is generally from a mix of enterprises rather than being focused on large firms only.

The deal transaction costs (inconvenience costs of accessing the service) are negligible for cloud providers, in fact, they are often lower than if the customer acquires his/her own assets. This is because cloud providers have easy access for remote logins, while own assets will often have dedicated terminals installed on-site and lack the security features for enabling remote login from global locations. The frequency of usage estimation needs some guesswork initially, as the provider will have a learning curve from usage patterns across customers from different verticals. However, after the services have been offered for some time, the estimation is easier, as data about the customer's vertical and number of employees, along with key markets and revenues, can be used to estimate the initial frequency of usage. In their core China market, Alibaba Cloud can use the knowledge of the enterprise hardware investments, customers' web traffic and business model additionally to estimate the usage frequency. While Alibaba Cloud has a global footprint, their deep knowledge of the Chinese market is an additional advantage in this regard. Similarly, the expected utility-per-use of customers in different markets can be estimated, however, the expected utility-per-use has a different challenge. The utility that customers derive from each transaction is based on the second-choice option that customers have in each market. As far as the competitive intensity is borne out of the existence of all the large players, the estimation of the expected utility-per-use and the utility from the next choice is easier to estimate. However, customers in different markets have different lifetime values, different revenues per transaction, which leads to the need for price discrimination across different markets. Since data centres are typically collocated with the customer, the operational expenses of data centres may be different, even though the acquisition costs from global vendors may be the same. Alibaba Cloud must use a localized approach for estimating the expected utility-per-use, and at the same time, it cannot have a highly differentiated pricing structure across different locations. All cloud providers, including Alibaba Cloud price cloud services in local currencies, which enables them to have some degree of differentiation in pricing. However, this differentiation cannot be too large owing to arbitrage opportunities, and with the offering of global services, this differentiation opportunity will get narrower over time.

The competitive pressure on IaaS offerings is manageable as of now, as they offer the scope for significant differentiation based on customer requirements. The market for IaaS offerings is still growing rapidly, hence, providers will have a reasonably long growth phase before having to compete for market share. Large enterprises typically have multiple cloud infrastructure providers now, owing to the ability to mix and match preferred services. Similarly, the nature of the PaaS (platform-as-a-service) solution is customized, hence, it is hard for a dominant player to emerge in this space. The competitive pressures in the SaaS market seem to be the most intense, as the offerings have similar functionalities, and hence, are harder to differentiate. As of now, the competitive assessment of Alibaba Cloud yields a benign outcome to Alibaba Cloud, except for the core China market. Alibaba Cloud was the market leader by a distance, but Tencent's cloud offering was nascent, and Huawei Cloud was on the ascendance after a tepid start many years ago. However, the combination of the "niche" and "complementarity" analysis yield probably the biggest threat to Alibaba Cloud's dominance in China and Asia, and AWS's global dominance. Tencent has a much richer set of offerings in software (albeit in the B2C space, courtesy their gaming and communications origins), and Huawei has a regional and probably global front seat in the communications and networking space. Similarly, while AWS has the advantage of economies of scale, Microsoft is a global behemoth in enterprise software, and Google is the world's leader in the analytics space. The threat to AWS globally and Alibaba Cloud globally and in China comes from their newer competitors who bring years of software and communications and networking experience, along with deep expertize in complementary offerings. Amazon and Alibaba are global giants in retail, and hence, have a wealth of experience and complementary solutions in B2C outreach to customers. However, the real threat to their dominance of cloud services globally and in Asia, respectively, may come from this confluence of competitors with deeper software and communications knowledge. In terms of economies of scale, Alibaba Cloud is secure with a global dominance position, hence, today, their costs are well within control with the scale that they already have. Cloud computing may probably have the best economies of scale that are hard to match with non-IT offerings. In terms of the solutions approach and the customization, given the modular nature of the different cloud services like computing, storage and networking, offering bundles and providing customer choices is indeed easy. To summarize, the BROAD FENCES analysis of Alibaba Cloud (and the other IaaS providers) shows that the offerings are strong, likely to grow in the future, and competitive pressures will be limited owing to the sheer breadth of services. However, the threat comes from providers who have strong complementary solutions from the software, networking and communications, and analytics spaces.

While the IT offerings in the XaaS space have more demonstrable "wins" in their category, the non-IT offerings of the XaaS mode have also burgeoned in breadth, but with more varying success. We will analyze WeWork's space-as-a-service model here and identify if WeWork has a path to success in the future. The budget impact analysis of WeWork indeed makes sense for remote workers in the knowledge gig economy who want to access office space for a few days a month. Start-ups and entrepreneurs are usually strapped for cash; however, they do prefer to have office space where they can interact with clients, customers and investors. For these knowledge workers, the flexi-space options of WeWork indeed make financial sense, as they can pay for accessing office space on a pay-as-you-go basis. However, one of the success factors for IT XaaS offerings is the attraction of the as-a-service offering to large customers as well. Large marquee customers offer economies of scale in marketing and in providing services, as well as advertising value in being able to attract other customers. WeWork has managed to attract large customers like Microsoft, Standard Chartered, Li and Fung, PUMA and IBM in select locations.[30] However, the transition of office space expenses for large customers from a capex model to an opex model is not so clear. Typically, large customers use either a leasing model for their office space creation, or they acquire long-term leases for land and then build their

---

[30] Member Spotlight, WeWork, https://www.wework.com/ideas/tag/member-spotlight/page/2?utm_campaign=8438573415&utm_term=86795673115&utm_content=405352351140&utm_source=ads-google&utm_medium=cpc&gclsrc=aw.ds, accessed June 29, 2020.

own buildings for collocating their employees. When such customers need office space quickly without having to spend an arm and a leg on office space development, WeWork's offering is handy. For example, large customers typically use space service offerings from WeWork and other competitors when they need an office in a new city. However, the global or regional headquarters for such customers are usually designed by architects based on showcasing principles of the customer, hence, the scale needed by WeWork from large customers is not easy to acquire. Unlike IT XaaS offerings where the provider acquires assets at scale, WeWork's offerings are localized. Hence, WeWork typically acquires office space either by buying or leasing assets and then transforming them into co-working or dedicated office spaces. Large customers can lease office space from landlords and redesign spaces themselves for the long term, hence, cost savings for such customers from WeWork's offerings are not obvious. WeWork does have an advantage in terms of risk analysis, as customers can use spaces with short-term contracts. WeWork's offerings also add value from the technological perspective, as the app can bill customers by usage, and offer other value-added services. The agility from the customer's perspective is shown by the addition of WeWork's value-added services over time like the WeWork Services Store. The store offers localized discounts for customers for office needs, business tools and local fitness and food services.[31] The deal transaction costs for WeWork are fairly limited, while customers would need to travel to the local WeWork facility, commuting to the office is needed for customer designed office spaces as well.

The frequency of usage estimation is easy to do for customers who contract for dedicated office spaces. However, the estimation for pay-per-use customers can vary widely, as there is no basis for estimating repeat use frequency. The expected utility-per-use can be estimated from nanoizing competing office space rents on a monthly basis. The primary utility offering of WeWork is co-working spaces; however, WeWork can do more to develop the sense of community, e.g. business matchmaking services to increase the value proposition of co-working. Next, in terms of estimating profitability, WeWork did not grow their capacity using the nanonized

---

[31] WeWork, Services Store, https://store.wework.com/, accessed June 29, 2020.

module analysis. Rather, it grew capacity globally with the bet that the flexible co-working model would eventually be adopted. The financial model has been focused on growing revenue; WeWork is not the first firm to prioritize revenue growth over profitability in its early operations. The high costs of acquiring capacity and the lack of early acceptance has meant that WeWork has been unprofitable so far. Indeed, several analysts have pointed out that WeWork has been acquiring customers by pricing its services at a discount to the market in many cities. While penetration pricing does work for some categories of XaaS offerings, if WeWork chooses to price at a premium at a later stage, customers may baulk at using their services. WeWork also has a lot of common spaces for facilitating co-working, which implies that in cities where space is expensive, the common spaces offer utility to customers, but are expensive to provide. WeWork also does not have a clear value proposition that cannot be adopted by competitors, it does not have a clear barrier to entry for competition. Hence, if local landlords choose the fit-out model themselves and position themselves as competitors to WeWork, there is no core competence of WeWork that is difficult to emulate. Second, a number of financial organizations like Capital One are creating their own co-working and meeting spaces for customers.[32] Capital One is launching the Capital One café chain for use as a co-working space, WeWork will face more competition from cafes and other community building concepts in the future. WeWork does offer a number of complementary services like WeWork Labs. These services are designed to help entrepreneurs accelerate their businesses.[33] Perhaps the biggest difference between IT and non-IT XaaS offerings is the economies of scale. By default, WeWork's economies of scale are largely localized. Trying to have more customers use the same facilities has a visible effect in co-working spaces, which may dissuade customers from using WeWork's facilities in the future. Co-working spaces usually have a sweet spot in terms of the number of users; adding users adds value up to a point, adds to the expected utility-per-use of

---

[32] Capitalone, 9 Things You Can do at a Capital One Café, https://www.capitalone.com/learn-grow/money-management/explore-capital-one-cafes/, accessed June 29, 2020.

[33] WeWork Labs, Supporting Your Growth Wherever You Are, https://www.wework.com/en-GB/labs/, accessed June 29, 2020.

existing customers due to the community effect. Beyond the sweet spot, the impact of space congestion lowers the utility-per-use of existing customers, hence, WeWork's economic model must be aligned to the usage to have the optimal number of users at each location. Managing this trade-off between profits with congestion and the expected utility-per-use with optimal occupancy levels is hard. Finally, WeWork's solutions and customization approach of co-designing workspaces does provide flexibility in improving the customer's experience.

WeWork's space-as-a-service offering in the office market was first lauded and then pilloried in equal measure. However, in our humble opinion, it is too early to write WeWork's epitaph. WeWork should continue to focus on large customers, preferably early, during the development of office spaces. Commercial establishments like shopping malls typically design their offerings by acquiring an anchor tenant (typically a large retailer), the anchor tenant draws the primary footfalls into the mall. WeWork can utilize a similar concept, by identifying and advertising an anchor tenant, other users will gravitate to the location to interact with the anchor tenant. It should also price its services for profitability from the point of offering the service, as penetration pricing may not be easy for office real estate services offerings. It has grown its assets substantially and focused on revenue growth over the last decade, it may now be time to have joint objectives of revenue growth and profitability. Of course, the problems in corporate governance also played a role, which was one of the reasons for the withdrawal of the IPO offering.

A comparison of XaaS offerings in the IT and non-IT domains easily shows that the biggest advantages of IT XaaS offerings are the ease of offering complementary services and global economies of scale. In contrast, for non-IT XaaS offerings, economies of scale are only localized, hence, the need of analysis at the nanonized module level is critical. The higher economies of scale and scope achieved from shared resources and related offerings from IT services translates to lower fixed and variable costs. These cost savings can be shared with the customer by the provider, leading to optimized pricing for profitability and market growth. Offering complementary services and bundling is also harder for non-IT XaaS offerings but can be achieved with judicious planning and the use of agile processes.

4.7 VISUALIZING THE BROAD FENCES ANALYSIS: THE XaaS STAIRCASE

While the BROAD FENCES analysis comprehensively estimates the efficacy of XaaS offerings, it is important for the analysis to be conducted sequentially for refining the offering plan. The BROAD FENCES analysis has been structured to guide the firm's decision-making on introducing their offerings in an as-a-service mode. Based on our research, we find that the analysis of the factors differs in importance at various stages of the lifecycle. For the feasibility analysis of the offering, the leaders of the provider should consider the budget impact, risk, the obsolescence of technology and other technology factors, and if they can procure the assets in an agile fashion for the delivery. For the profitability analysis, the analysis of the deal transaction costs, the frequency of usage, the expected utility-per-use, and the ability to respond to customer feedback in an agile fashion are more important. In the growth phase, the analysis of whether the provider can create a niche, the analysis of competitive intensity, the complementarity and bundling potential of services, economies of scale, the solutions approach for continuous innovation, and the ability of the provider to deliver these services in an agile fashion are more important. We recognize that it is hard to divide the factors in a hard manner, for instance, economies of scale could also influence costs, leading to higher profitability from lower costs due to economies of scale. Hence, we recommend that the assessment of the factors should be holistic and iterative, with a focus on the specific factors that have a higher impact on the objective for that phase. Subsequent iterations will refine the plan for the as-a-service offerings and enable the provider to fine-tune the offering delivery.

Next, while the model provides several insights, the visual representation of the analysis is very important for guiding managerial action. We present the XaaS staircase as a tool that depicts the sequential nature of the actions recommended in each phase. The XaaS staircase should be depicted visually in a simple fashion, with an assessment of the merits of the offering on that dimension, along with the most important action to be taken to improve that metric further. Figures 4.1 and 4.2 present the XaaS staircase for the Alibaba Cloud and the WeWork offerings. The current

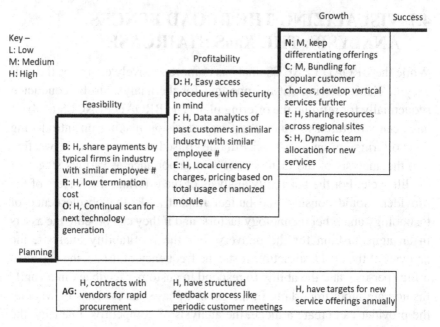

Figure 4.1:   XaaS Staircase for Alibaba Cloud

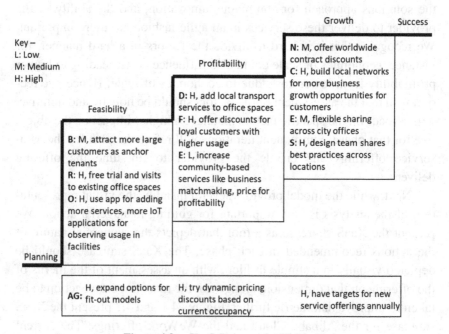

Figure 4.2:   XaaS Staircase for WeWork

scenarios are rated as Low (L), Medium (M) or High (H), to present a quick visual summary of the current efficacy of their offerings. Alibaba Cloud is one of the global leaders in the IaaS domain. It has a very good offering in terms of feasibility with a broad range of services offered to customers in the for-profit and not-for-profit spaces, as well as government entities. The actions that they can take in the feasibility analysis in the future include using past data to estimate actual spends for similar firms with a similar number of employees as potential customers. They offer a pricing calculator and free trial for potential customers already. The services are highly profitable; they should price in local currencies to offer some minimal degree of pricing differentiation in emerging economies.

To facilitate the growth strategy, the competitive niche and complementarity dimensions are their major concerns, as they do not have complementary software or networking offerings internally like Microsoft, Tencent or Huawei. They can focus on their core strengths in business verticals for carving out a niche in competitive markets and can possibly create licenses with firms like Salesforce for bundling complementary software services. The agility dimension is needed in all three phases of feasibility, profitability and growth; hence, the agility dimension is represented as a row below the main staircase, with agility actions recommended for all three phases.

Understandably, WeWork's XaaS staircase does not speak as glowingly of its offering as the offerings in the IaaS space, as while it is the market leader in the space-as-a-service offering, there are a number of dimensions on which it can do better. The biggest priority for WeWork should be attracting more large customers as anchor tenants in the feasibility space and estimating the frequency of usage better and the utility-per-use to price for profitability in steady state. They need to create more meaningful barriers to entry for competitors in the long run, one differentiating factor between WeWork and local competitors is WeWork's global footprint, they can use their global footprint to work with MNCs or expanding firms to offer global solutions. Similarly, for complementarity, WeWork should provide better business networking opportunities to its tenants, in addition to its services like WeWork Labs for entrepreneurs.

4.8 SUMMARY

This chapter presented the firm's perspective on launching XaaS offerings. The firm needs to have strong capabilities in marketing for reaching out to customers, and in procurement and execution for working with vendors. However, the capabilities needed for marketing and procurement for XaaS offerings is different from the corresponding capabilities for delivering products. First, in the productization model, depending on the durability and the lifecycle of the product, sales are typically made to the same customer with larger durations between purchases. In contrast, XaaS offerings provide the customer with the ability to use the service at their convenience at any point of time, necessitating repeated interactions with the customer. Unlike the customer journey for products which culminates in the purchase decision, the customer journey for XaaS offerings also has the customer decision to retain the service at every stage of usage. Given the repeated interactions, the revenue model and marketing model that the firm should ideally use are very different from those for products. First, the customer's acquisition represents a stream of revenues for the firm over time, rather than a one-time purchase decision. To estimate the value of the customer and compare the value to the customer's acquisition cost, we reviewed the customer lifetime value (CLV) model in this chapter. The CLV analysis requires the estimation of the usage frequency of the customer, the expected utility-per-use for each instance, the cost of accessing the potential customer and the rate of conversion of potential customers to using the service, the discounting factor and the churn rate. The customer's acquisition cost is the ratio of the cost of accessing each potential customer to the rate of conversion. The CLV is estimated first by estimating the discounted cash flows obtained from the customer over time, either from the price charged to the customer if there is no variable cost, or from the margin if there is a variable cost of serving the customer. These discounted cash flows are then summed up over the horizon, and the difference between the discounted cash flows and the customer's acquisition cost provides the CLV. The provider can also estimate the payback period for the customer by estimating the time it takes to break even on the customer acquisition cost. The churn rate can be used to estimate the lifetime of the average customer, which results in a reduction of the CLV compared to the case where customers are retained with certainty. If there are multiple customer segments with different characteristics, the provider can choose the segments of the customers it intends to serve, based on the payback period and the CLV.

The use of relationship marketing for XaaS offerings has three critical elements: first, the provider must create a community of users, rather than reaching out to users individually. Building a user community enables the provider to use existing customers for the acquisition of new customers and showcasing examples of the value of their services. Second, the provider must offer continued value to the customer beyond the service; the use of technology for the creation of sharing community experiences is a key element of relationship marketing. Building the user community enables the use of referrals, and viral marketing techniques are valuable in relationship marketing, as relationships add value by creating customer networks. Third, while product marketing refers to attributes such as durability and longevity, relationship marketing for services must highlight the customer experience features over the product attributes. Fourth, the roles of processes, people and physical evidence in the relationship marketing of services need a different set of capabilities. Processes must be standardized and automated as far as possible, as having a continuous conversation with customers cannot be achieved without standardized and automated processes of interaction. People skills needed include constant customer engagement, and the provider must use case studies to demonstrate physical evidence of customer wins to new customers.

In addition to reaching out to customers, XaaS providers also need a different set of capabilities for interacting with vendors and channel partners. First, resources must be procured as solutions using the lean agile procurement method. The lean agile procurement method requires the provider to broadly define outcomes, followed by discussions with multiple vendors about the potential solutions available. The provider then evaluates solutions, and eliminates vendors based on the fit with the outcomes. The process continues till the provider finalizes one vendor. After the vendor selection, the provider should also decide order quantities in an agile fashion, by first identifying the components with long lead times and those with short lead times. The components with long lead times need to have a flexible ordering process with the vendor, with some reserved capacity that will be used only if needed. For components with short lead times, the provider can order them based on the demand patterns observed. In terms of process maturity, Deloitte finds that firms making the transformation from the productization model to the XaaS model typically go through the "crawl, walk, run and fly" stages. The number of XaaS offerings, the revenues from these offerings and the regions where the services are marketed increase over time, and the marketing approaches get more service-focused. The priorities of the provider change from planning for XaaS offerings to fine-tuning the offerings over time. Finally, processes are standardized and automated over time. If the provider does not have capabilities for forming close ties with customers, providers should work with value-added resellers to market their XaaS offerings. The resellers should be able to generate customer leads in new regions, customize the solutions offered by the provider with other services, provide training and development services for customers, and reach out to smaller players like SMEs.

The chapter also presented the impact of competition and the circular economy on the provider's offerings. In a competitive environment, the provider should either use a differentiated or niche strategy, so that the competitive intensity in the market is lowered, or it should use subscription pricing if the services have evolved to be standardized across competitive offerings. For cloud computing services, large enterprise customers typically work with four or more providers, showing that differentiation is easier. In contrast, for non-IT offerings, the provider must make a concerted effort at differentiating its offerings. The advantages of the circular economy for XaaS offerings are driven by legislation and profitability. If the legislative environment for the offerings requires significant effort, the transfer of asset ownership to the provider makes for easy disposal of assets beyond their lifecycle. The provider can also extract economic value from re-manufacturing assets with durable components with a longer lifecycle, and from using spare parts from older assets for enhanced serviceability.[34]

---

[34] Savaskan, R. C., Bhattacharya, S., & Van Wassenhove, L. N. (2004). Closed-loop supply chain models with product remanufacturing. *Management science*, 50(2), 239–252.

B	udget impact		F	requency of usage
R	isk		E	xpected utility-per-use
O	bsolescence of technology		N	iche
A	gility		C	omplementarity
D	eal transaction costs		E	conomies of scale
			S	olutions approach and customization

Figure 4.3: Elements of the BROAD FENCES Model

To assess the feasibility, profitability and growth potential of their XaaS offerings, we recommend that providers use the BROAD FENCES model (see Figure 4.3). The analysis of the different factors in the BROAD FENCES model will enable providers to understand the advantages and disadvantages of the XaaS offering vis-à-vis productization offerings. It also enables providers to identify the actions that they need to take to improve the efficacy of their offerings. The factors in the BROAD FENCES model include the budget impact, which assesses the effect of the transfer of asset ownership from the customer to the provider. The risk assessment compares the risks of the estimation of capacity, vendor lock-in and switching costs, budget overrun, quality and reliability, asset acquisition lead time, and business cycles between the XaaS and productization offering modes. The obsolescence of technology evaluation considers the risk of the asset lifecycle being shorter, and the use of technology to create value-added services and personalize services for the customer. The agility analysis identifies the ability of the provider to expedite the design and launch of the offering, and the subsequent launches of new services and upgrades. The deal transaction cost assessment yields the hassle and inconvenience costs of repeated transactions. The frequency of usage estimation identifies seasonality effects, and customer heterogeneity in service usage over time. The analysis of the expected utility-per-use identifies customer heterogeneity in the derived utilities and provides a basis for pricing services in the pay-as-you-go mode. The analysis of the niche dimension enables the provider to plan its response to competitive entry, either in the form of differentiation, or its pricing mechanism. The complementarity assessment is useful to determine how to create added value from bundling service components. The analysis of the economies of scale helps to plan for growing the service and the advantage of reaching a larger market. Finally, the analysis of the solutions approach and customization can be used by the provider to assess if it can create continuous value for the customer.

The analysis of the BROAD FENCES model should be presented in the XaaS staircase, which is a tool for the visualization of the model results. The staircase should provide a subjective assessment of the efficacy of the provider's offerings on each dimension, along with the actions the provider can take to improve its efficacy. The staircase is designed to design and improve the feasibility, profitability and growth potential of the services, and the factors of the BROAD FENCES model are divided into these three categories. There is a need for agility in all the three categories, in addition, the feasibility phase involves the assessment of the budget impact, risk and obsolescence of technology. The profitability phase should assess the provider's offerings on the dimensions of deal transaction costs, frequency of usage and the expected utility-per-use in addition to the agility. Finally, the growth phase should assess the impact of competitive intensity, complementarity, economies of scale and the solutions approach of the provider. The analysis should be done iteratively to fine-tune the planned offering of the services.

Chapter 5

Organizing for XaaS

The ability of any provider to develop and deliver world class offerings in XaaS mode is influenced primarily by the structural ability of the provider's organization to consistently deliver value to customers, and its ability to capture part of that value. Structuring the organization to deliver value consistently using the XaaS mode of offerings requires a very different set of skills to the productization mode of delivery. There is a consistent finding in practice that the agile organization is the best structure to deliver consistent value; our own research is consistent with this viewpoint with some caveats. The agile organization has most of the characteristics that are needed for creating a successful and sustainable service-oriented organization. However, it needs some enhancements to move from a set of short-term goals to a model with goals for multiple horizons. To understand how the organization structure and systems for managing resources influence the success of XaaS offerings, we will start the chapter with a discussion of the goals of the organization structure and resource management systems. The discussion will help in understanding the efficacy of agile organizations in delivering XaaS offerings and identify the enhancements to the agile organization for sustainable competitive advantage.

5.1 OBJECTIVES AND PRINCIPLES OF ORGANIZATION DESIGN

What is the set of goals that the design of the organizational structure should be based on? The first point that we note is that the goals for organization design are not static; the environment that any firm operates in is changing constantly by default, and organization designs have to evolve over time to align with the changing environments.[1] The pace of change in different industry sectors dictates the fluidity of organization design — the faster the pace of change, the higher the fluidity of the ideal organization. The strategy of the organization is also a function of the pace of the change, and the method the organization uses to create value. The basis of creating value plays an important role in the design of the organization; in the early world of manufacturing, the basis of creating value was the cost structure of the organization, which depended on the availability of materials and equipment, the management of the flows of the materials, the cost of the labour and the scale of the demand. Over time, the locus of value creation moved to the management of information and the ability of the provider to match demand and supply flows and information seamlessly. The methods of information collection, processing and taking actionable decisions have meant that the organizational design has evolved based on the characteristics of these processes as well. For effective decision-making processes in organization design, the fluid nature of organizations implies the need to specify power structures for decision-making. Without the right control mechanisms, the decision-making process can get stalled. At the same time, while tight control of decision-making has its advantages in terms of accountability, micro-managing the decision-making process can result in hierarchical organizations with a lack of speed. Individuals with decision-making responsibilities need data and time to process the data to make decisions effectively, lowering the agility of the organization. The decisions to be made have to satisfy multiple stakeholders, like customers, investors and regulators. Hence, even with all the right information, decision-makers have to weigh the different objectives to decide on actions that balance the interests of different stakeholders. The different interests and the multiple ways to achieve the balanced objectives could be sources of conflict in the organization, and the organizational design has to identify mechanisms for resolving those conflicts.

---

[1] Daft, R. L. (2004). *Organization Theory and Design*. South-Western Pub, Cincinnati, Ohio.

Given the different objectives of organizational design, the design principles of organizations can be defined based on four dimensions: formalized structure, the need for employee specialization, the hierarchy of decision-making and the need for support activities. The formalized structure refers to the need for organizational charts, the division of employees into different departments or teams, and reporting structures (e.g., functional, matrix). Large organizations tend to have more formalized structures, whereas smaller organizations tend to exhibit low degrees of formalization. The need for employee specialization encapsulates the ability of the organization to clearly define the roles and responsibilities of individuals. High degrees of specialization imply that the employees perform narrow and pre-defined tasks, while low degrees of specialization imply that employees can be cross-trained or have multiple skills to perform a range of tasks. Assembly line workers tend to have a high degree of specialization, while work-cell workers have a lower degree of specialization. The hierarchy of decision-making is a function of the number of layers in the organizational chart; more hierarchical organizations have more layers, while flat organizations have a lower number of layers in the hierarchy. Finally, the need of support activities refers to the inclusion of non-core activities like administrative and IT support and R&D within business units, or the separation of these activities into separate support units.

5.1.1 Goals of Firm's Strategy

The goals and the strategy of the organization are defined with the frame of the organization in mind. Porter identified four basic strategies based on the portfolio of activities of the firm and the source of competitive advantage.[2] Firms with a standardized portfolio with few offerings and a competitive advantage from the low cost of their offerings have a strategy of focused cost leadership. In contrast, firms with a standardized portfolio of many offerings and that are focused on cost have a cost leadership strategy. Firms with a broad portfolio of offerings that are responsive to customers

[2] Allen, R.S. and Helms, M.M. (2006), "Linking strategic practices and organizational performance to Porter's generic strategies", *Business Process Management Journal*, Vol. 12 No. 4, pp. 433–454. https://doi.org/10.1108/14637150610678069

have a differentiation strategy, while firms with a narrow portfolio that are responsive to customers have a focused differentiation strategy. The differentiation strategy needs a solutions-shop capability set internally; the price and margin pressures in such strategies are relatively low. Customers are keen on responsiveness in these strategies, hence, being able to learn customer needs and deliver them as closely as possible to the requirements level is key to firm success. The effort of the firm is to grow its business by adding new customers, as differentiated or unique offerings do not have large scale. The firm's profitability is dictated by its ability to have more customers giving them small orders with large margins. In contrast, with the cost-leadership strategy, the firm is focused more on attaining scale with standardized offerings. The goal of the firm is to attain efficiency, eliminating waste in all its forms, and uses a tight control of all processes to achieve this efficiency and waste reduction. The breadth of the firm's portfolio (focus) is dictated by the firm's desire to serve a large set of customer segments or focusing on a narrow group of segments. Firms with a high degree of focus tend to have a very clear offering targeted to a specific group. For instance, as a family of different brands, Inditex has a broad portfolio, consisting of Zara, Massimo Dutti, Pull and Bear, Bershka, Stradivarius, Zara Home, Uterqüe and Oysho.[3] Each of these brands have a focused offering, for example, Zara is focused on all age groups, while Pull and Bear is focused on millennial fashion. Oysho targets middle-school and young university students, while Stradivarius and Uterqüe are high-end fashion targeted at young adults with a lower price sensitivity. A focused strategy enables the firm to design and develop offerings to customers with a clear set of values. For instance, while the entire airline industry is based on the hub and spoke network design, Southwest Airlines is among the few global airlines that has a point-to-point or spoke-to-spoke offering. The hub and spoke network offers the values of end-to-end service for customers with a focus on scale on the hub-to-hub flights, and a focus on connectivity for hub-to-spoke flights. However, early in its lifecycle, Southwest recognized one of the main

---

[3] Inditex, Who we are, https://www.inditex.com/about-us/who-we-are#:~:text=Inditex%20 is%20one%20of%20the,7%2C000%20stores%20in%2096%20markets, accessed July 5, 2020.

weaknesses of the hub and spoke model, which was the need for direct flights from some cities to others that were not large enough to qualify as hubs. Southwest offered flights in a regional network between cities that had a large enough volume to justify individual flights, but for which other airlines would need customers to fly two or more legs. The focus on identifying and creating the regional network enabled southwest to differentiate itself from the hub and spoke offerings of the competition.

5.1.2 Mapping of Strategic Goals to Organizational Structure

It is easy to see that there is a one-to-one mapping between the strategy of the firm, and the organization structure based on the four principles mentioned above. A low-cost strategy needs a highly formalized organizational structure with a high degree of stability. The need for efficiency precludes the option of experimentation, and the role of employees is highly specialized, to maximize utilization and minimize waste. Equipment and materials are procured to have no waste, and the role of people is to ensure a smooth functioning of the organization with no breakdowns (wasted time) in any parts of the process. Standard operating policies are clearly spelled out to all employees and for all processes, and tasks are defined to be repetitive and routine. The hierarchy of authority is rigid, with decision-making rules for quick action. The role of all supporting activities is to ensure the smooth functioning of the core operations of the firm and may be organized regionally (as in Southwest Airlines), or as standalone support units for the core activities. The extreme version of the organization structure for a focused low-cost strategy is the equivalent of the assembly line, where all employees have the goal of keeping the utilization as high as possible. While there is learning in the assembly line as well, the focus of learning by doing is to get a higher degree of quality and less defects by doing everything in a standardized fashion. The role of managers in the assembly line is to relentlessly eliminate all forms of variability or waste and ensure predictable outcomes. They also act as coaches and instructors to the team, with hands-on leadership on improving the output of the process. Processes in assembly lines are relatively stable — any degree of variability leads to continuous improvement projects to improve processes. In the limit, if the technology exists for the processes to be automated as far as possible, then robots could be used for manufacturing almost exclusively, replacing the need for human employees. Such organizational structures are referred to as mechanistic organizations, where the design emphasis is on making processes and people as mechanized as possible.

At the other extreme, a differentiation strategy needs the employees to be continuously experimenting and trying out new solutions to be responsive to customer needs. By default, a highly formalized structure will be antithetical to the need for experimentation, hence, the degree of formalization of the organization structure must be as low as possible. Given that solutions may not fit the tightly defined job description, the degree of specialization of employees must be low, hence, employees must be skilled in several domains. It may not be possible to have all the different skills needed in typical individuals, hence, the firm has to hire employees with diverse skills who can offer the complete repertoire of skillsets needed for cutting edge solutions. The fluid and flexible organizational structure must be complemented with flexible decision control systems. Hence, overarching hierarchical systems need to be replaced with relatively flat organizational decision-making structures. The control systems must empower employees to make many decisions at the lower levels, with higher level decisions on resource requirements and broad outcome planning being done by senior managers. Rather than the vertical communication and reporting structures enforced by hierarchical systems, there must be a stronger focus on horizontal communication across cross-functional lines. The employees must interact directly with customers for added responsiveness, and outcome-based performance review and reward systems must be designed for employee engagement. The role of support functions moves to ensuring outcomes at individual project levels are met, and the needs of projects must be matched, rather than trying to maximize the overall organizational output. This type of organization is called the organic organization in the literature, because of its adaptive ability.[4]

---

[4] Courtright, J. A., Fairhurst, G. T., & Rogers, L. E. (1989). Interaction patterns in organic and mechanistic system. *Academy of management journal*, 32(4), 773–802.

The systems and tasks in organic organizations are loosely defined, and the employees are highly skilled craftspeople who are adept in a variety of tasks. The employee training and engagement process is typically by apprenticeship and continuous upgrading, and performance is controlled by global professional standards, often accompanied by certifications from standards bodies. While change is hard to institute in the mechanistic organization, control and formalization are hard to institute in the organic organization. In the manufacturing context, the equivalent of the organic organization is labelled as the solutions shop or job shop. Job shops manufacture completely customized products, and machines are placed together by function, rather than having a linear flow that is common in the assembly line. For the ease of managing flow logic, each individual order is first analyzed for design requirements. The sequence of operations and the raw material needs are identified, and then materials flow from one machine area to the other. While the job shop has a lot of wasted time owing to the management of different flows, the flexibility from having different products being processed in different sequences at different machines makes the control of the process easier. In the services context, hospitals are organized as job shops, where patients are first diagnosed, and testing results are obtained. Based on the results of the tests, the patients are moved to different departments, and specialists in the different departments can then identify if the patient needs further treatment. Each subsequent process step is identified based on the outcomes of the previous step. We will now posit that the development of the XaaS offering needs characteristics of both mechanistic and organistic organizations.

5.1.3 Organizing for Mass Customization: Precursor for Agile Organizations

While agile organizations have been more successful in combining the mechanistic and organic approaches to have the best of both worlds, the early attempts to amalgamate the best characteristics of both approaches came from mass customization efforts. The principle of mass customization is simple: firms can define multiple products to have a common core, with the differentiation postponed to a later stage. For example, Dell configures and designs different products, but all of Dell's PC configurations can be assembled on a common core. Depending on the performance required by the customer, Dell inserts faster processors, RAM memories with more storage capacities, and other components that are needed for higher performance based on the customer order. Having the common core with postponement approach has resulted in the offering of increased variety for customers, hence, there is some degree of differentiation achieved. However, the core is manufactured in large quantities for the entire market. Hence, the firm can attain economies of scale with the core, leading to the principles of assembly lines (high formalization and specialization, hierarchical and tight control, support systems for maximizing capacity). Organizing for mass customization needed firms to have the best practices from both mechanistic and organic environments, as Toyota found out in their first attempts at mass customization.[5]

Toyota's processes and organization were optimized for continuous improvement in the mechanistic mould; it was the standard-bearer in being able to achieve cost and quality leadership. Toyota adopted a policy of mass customization in 1991 to take advantage of shared platforms and component commonality across its different vehicle classes. However, Toyota found that its organization and internal systems that were optimized for continuous improvement could not be effective in implementing mass customization initiatives. Its attempts at implementing mass customization resulted in production costs increasing and product proliferation, along with significantly higher levels of inventory at the raw materials, intermediate and finished goods levels. In response, Toyota slowed down its attempts at mass customization, and reduced the number of offerings in the finished product line by 20%. Why did Toyota's organization that was so adept at continuous improvement fail to deliver mass customization solutions? One reason is that continuous improvement processes target delivering a predictable outcome where the sequence of activities is known. The core design of the product is taken as a given, and subsequent improvements aim to improve on some functionality or production improvement. Such a mechanistic organization prefers to focus on routines.

---

[5] Pine, B. J., Victor, B., & Boynton, A. C. (1993). Making mass customization work. *Harvard business review*, 71(5), 108–111.

In contrast, mass customization requires an understanding of customer needs, followed by a dynamic network to be designed of teams that are operating autonomously that deliver components with specific functionalities. While each module or component provides functionalities that are delivered with routine tasks, they do not necessarily have the sequence of development for every offering. The combination of the different modules and the design of interfaces governing their interaction is based on changing customer needs. The change in customer needs must result in new capabilities acquisition for the firm. This capability acquisition is a dynamic and continuous process. The management of this dynamic and continuous process requires the dynamic network to combine product and process modules seamlessly to satisfy changing customer needs. The greater the heterogeneity of the modules, the greater is the need for diversity of employee skills to manage the customization to be offered. Toyota's system of continuous improvement did not enable it to have the requisite diversity of employee skills to satisfy the needs of disparate customers with mass customization. A second problem was the explosion of product offerings based on mass customization that Toyota's employees began designing. While it is easy to offer a variety using mass customization, the variety should be driven by customer needs, and not based on what functionalities are easy to combine and offer as a bundle. The goal of higher component commonality as an organizational objective for cutting costs was a third reason for Toyota's failure, as common components had higher functionalities than required for many products. While the costs of procurement and inventory were lowered, the resistance to adopt the common components among line managers meant that targets for cost and design sharing were not met.

The creation of the dynamic network needs the creation of innovation teams dynamically. The reader should note that the notion of dynamic, loosely connected teams in the world of mass customization is the precursor to the adoption of such teams for agile organizations. Some researchers have referred to this self-organizing dynamic team formation process as a holacracy.[6] However, the creation and member allocation of dynamic teams must be done carefully, as self-forming teams that do not communicate can create as many coordination issues as vertical hierarchy

---

[6]Wikipedia, "Holacracy", https://en.wikipedia.org/wiki/Holacracy, accessed July 5, 2020.

organizations that do not communicate horizontally. Toyota's experience was that its mass customization teams did not have rich vertical communication. This lack of communication led to a lack of sharing in the teams developing the features in the product, and the customer needs being postulated by marketing managers. Overall, the variety offered increased the cost without the concomitant increase in demand from higher customization.

An important element to execute the operations of the dynamic network of teams is the adoption of the design correspondence of product architectures and team designs. The responsibility for the creation and continual redesign of the dynamic network should be assigned to senior managers, and individual teams should have the authority to manage their own processes. Performance evaluation and reward systems must be outcome-driven, based on the value created by the mass customization teams. These dynamic processes that link modules to each other in final offerings must connect with each other as early as possible. Customers and vendor teams must be integrated in the development process. The cost of creating these linkages in the dynamic teams must be low, and the teams must adapt to rapidly changing connectivity seamlessly. The value of technologies to create this seamless integration of dynamic teams cannot be overstated. The automation of routine tasks enables teams to add value to non-routine tasks; technology can also be used to identify the modules that need a higher degree of interaction. These assessments can be useful in the design of communication patterns like meetings for information exchange between members of different teams. Shared information and knowledge systems can be used to update all team members of design changes from the last iteration, and subsequent changes that need to be done.

5.1.4 Team Formation, Communication Design and the Design Structure Matrix

How should dynamic team design and communication be aligned with the product architecture and the need to work closely together between the teams? There is a tool called the design structure matrix that enables designers of products to design modules and use the product architecture comprising of these modules to design communication patterns between teams.[7] The design structure matrix (DSM) is also known as the dependency structure matrix, and identifies the dependency of different activities of a project with other activities, or interactions of one component with another component. It was designed by Steward in the 1960s and was used to solve equations with dependencies on one another. The matrix shows the dependencies of project activities on one another, these dependencies can be circular or independent of each other. The analysis of the linkages in the dependencies can be used for designing component modules and the desired interaction patterns between design teams. Figure 5.1 shows a design matrix reported in Simpson and Simpson (2009).[8]

In the sample DSM shown in Figure 5.1, we assume that the product or service of interest has a total of seven components (labelled

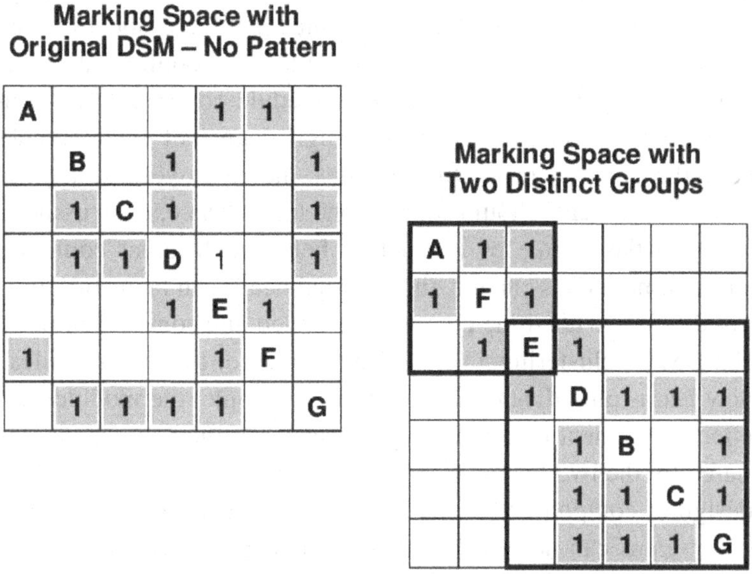
Marking Space with Original DSM – No Pattern
A 1 1
B 1 1
1 C 1 1
1 1 D 1 1
1 E 1
1 1 F
1 1 1 1 G
Marking Space with Two Distinct Groups
A 1 1
1 F 1
1 E 1
1 D 1 1 1
1 B 1
1 1 C 1
1 1 1 G

Figure 5.1: Design Structure Matrix (DSM) Example

---

[7] Eppinger, S. D. & Browning, T. R. (2012). *Design Structure Matrix Methods and Applications*. MIT Press, Cambridge, MA.

[8] Simpson, J. J. & Simpson, M. J. (2009). System of systems complexity identification and control. In 2009 IEEE International Conference on System of Systems Engineering (SoSE) (pp. 1–6). *IEEE*.

A through G), which can be equivalently thought of as activities in a project. The figure to the left is the basic DSM, which states all the interdependencies between the components. In the first row, there are two dependencies of component A, to components E and F, which can be interpreted as any change in component A's design will have a dependency on the design of components E and F. The direction of the dependence can be interchangeably defined, both conventions are used for DSMs. Similarly, component B's design influences the design of components D and G. The DSM can be used by clustering algorithms to create clusters of independent component groups, which have a high interdependence on each other, and not much dependence on other components. The figure on the right shows the clustered equivalent of the original DSM, where there is a high degree of interdependence between components A, F and E, and a high degree of interdependence between components E, D, B, C and G. This implies that the product or the service can be designed as two modules, with one module containing the components A, F and E, and the other module containing the components E, D, B, C and G. Given the high degree of interdependence between the components in the modules, the employees designing the clustered components should work in one team, hence, team assignment is based on the degree of interaction between different components. When customer needs change, the changed needs can be incorporated in a revised DSM, with some components added and some taken out. The revised DSM's clustering will yield the design of the new modules and the new teams on a dynamic basis. In the example, the modules have a common component (E), hence, any redesign of the component E must be shared by the two teams, which should interact frequently to finalize the design of component E. Once component E's design has been finalized, the teams can design the other components independently of one another. If component E's design can only be finalized late owing to customer need changes, then the teams should interact with each other frequently throughout the design process.

The implementation of this methodology in practice has been described by Sosa et al. (2007), for a large complex design project for Pratt and Whitney. Sosa *et al.* (2007) mapped the communication between design teams for the different components of the engine with the interactions between the components as in the DSM. They found that there was a one-to-one correspondence between the components interaction and the communication between the component design teams. However, they found that for many components that had repeated interactions, the corresponding teams did not meet multiple times. Mismatches between product component design needs and the communications of the corresponding design teams can lead to costly rework at a later stage.

5.1.5 XaaS and the Agile Organization

What are the organizational design characteristics of providers designing successful XaaS offerings? How do these characteristics influence the organizational structure? The operating environment of most XaaS providers is fast-paced, with underlying technologies that are provided by vendors having short product lifecycles. Owing to competitive pressures in the technology markets, technology vendors are introducing advancements at an increasing pace over time. Customers also adopt XaaS offerings as they want to have the benefits of fast-moving technology-based services without having to predict technology cycles. The plethora of base technologies has blurred traditional barriers to entry, leading to competitors using different resources to design offerings with similar functionality. Other stakeholders like regulators are moving more quickly with compliance measures to ensure fair competition and customer protection. The volume of information and the rate of information change are both getting faster, implying that rapid information acquisition and processing are key elements of provider success. Hence, XaaS offerings typically adopt the solutions provider approach with an agile organization, and the learning organization model fits the market and strategy dynamics.[9]

[9] Deloitte Insights, "Accelerating agility with XAAS", 2018, https://www2.deloitte.com/content/dam/insights/us/articles/4557_accelerating-agility-with-XaaS/DI_accelerating-agility_with-XaaS.pdf, accessed July 11, 2020.

However, the rapidly changing environment clashes with a need for cost control and the need for using standardized parts. XaaS providers ideally use standardized components as building blocks for offering solutions, rather than reinventing the wheel for designing solutions for each customer.[10] Second, XaaS offerings should ideally be nanonized on the dimensions of utility-per-use and the usage frequency, as well as the pricing. The nanonization of utility implies that providers must use a mix-and-match strategy to design their offerings, as developing solutions from scratch results in long lead times and an inability to keep pace with a fast-moving market. Adopting the mass customization approach, the provider can design standardized services that can be adopted on a standalone basis, or as a bundle, hence, mass customization works well for the nanonization of XaaS offerings. Providers can also offer a broader range of services to customers with the mass customization strategy, leading to increased revenues and the advantage of one-stop shopping for customers. Therefore, XaaS offerings indeed have mass customization as one of their core building blocks; many of the recommendations for organizing for mass customization carry over to the design of the XaaS organization as well. The transfer of asset ownership from the customer to the provider further enables the mass customization approach. The provider can combine their own assets to offer solutions, and not have to worry about distribution of mass customized products to the customer. The use of technology for coordinating mass customization activities is common to XaaS offerings as well. The one difference in approach is the need for agility in the XaaS offerings. While mass customization does not preclude the rapid revamp of product or service family offerings over time, the necessary conditions for adopting mass customization do not include the need for changing offerings to customers rapidly over time. Hence, agile organizations also necessarily incorporate the ability to change offerings quickly over time, leading to additional organization design needs to those for mass customization.

What are the characteristics of the agile organizational structure? McKinsey finds that one of the most important requirements of agile

---

[10] Gill, J., Sharma, D., & Kwan, A., "Scaling up XAAS", Deloitte Insights, https://www2.deloitte.com/content/dam/insights/us/articles/5197_tmt-xaas-transformation-execution/DI_TMT-XaaS-transformation.pdf, accessed July 11, 2020.

organizations is the need to balance stability and dynamism.[11] The reader will note that just like for the organizing of mass customization, the ability to move quickly to respond to market needs and customer requirement changes needs an element of dynamism for agile organizations. On the other hand, the ability to use standardized components to mix and match to provide solutions needs stability. The agile organization combines the needs for dynamism and stability by using the same methodology that organizing for mass customization recommends. Mass customized products have a common core that is standardized across different products. Specific customer-oriented solutions are designed and delivered in consonance with the common core to provide differentiation. Similarly, agile organizations should have a stable common core that moves slower than the industry clock speed. These common core elements support the dynamic capabilities needed by typical learning organizations. The differentiation obtained by mixing and matching elements of the common core enable the provider to act quickly to respond to customer needs.

The stable core of the agile organization is provided by the stable leadership of the organization. The leadership provides broad strategic direction, in terms of the services that should be added to the portfolio. The services to be added should be based on the understanding of customer needs in the future, along with the complementarity of these new services with the firm's current offerings. The stability offered by the leadership team and the strategic direction is complemented by a dynamic network of teams that is composed flexibly depending on the needs of the architecture of the offerings. The composition of the teams and the dynamic nature of the network can be designed using tools like the DSM. Changing customer requirements are reflected in the strategic direction, and the dynamic teams are structured based on the alignment of the teams' expertize with the architecture of the offerings. The objectives of the dynamic teams should be clearly stated with the teams being accountable for the delivery of the objectives. The accountability of the teams has to

---

[11] Aghina, W., De, S. A., Lackey, G., Lurie, M., & Murarka, M. (2018). The five trademarks of agile organizations (McKinsey Report). Online *verfügbar unter*, https://www.mckinsey.com/business-functions/organization/our-insights/the-five-trademarks-of-agile-organizations, *zuletzt geprüft am*, 20, 2019.

be coupled with the decision-making power and the ability to have horizontal coordination across teams. Without the transparency of each team's mandate, individuals are unable to determine the dependency of their objectives with those of other teams. It is important to be able to identify dependencies early, with the failure to do so creating the need for costly rework and delivery delays. The actual number of members in each team is allocated dynamically depending on the complexity of the project. However, the agile methodology requires that the team composition not get large, preferably, the size of the teams should have a limit. While the teams may be able to coordinate their own efforts, the creation of integration teams is an added measure that the agile organization can take for ensuring proper coordination of efforts. The teams should create their own alignment plans with the integration teams, with communication either being led or managed by the integration teams.

Adobe has adopted XaaS for almost all its offerings. More than 95% of Adobe's revenues today come from the as-a-service mode. Adobe has been a model case study of using an agile organization transformation to support its move from a productization mode to the as-a-service mode. It piloted its large-scale move to an agile organization with the development of Adobe Premiere Pro in 2008.[12] Prior to 2008, Adobe's Soundbooth team had used the agile framework and reported a high degree of satisfaction with the process. The objectives of the Premiere Pro pilot project were improved performance of the offerings, responsiveness to customer requirements, and enabling a healthier work schedule for its employees. The previous version of the Premiere offering was to make it compatible on the Mac platform of Apple; that project was executed using a stage-gate process. The pressures of shipping the product on time told on the health of many team members and resulted in quality issues and a lack of detailed customer testing. When the Premiere Pro team began using the agile process, some of the difficulties that arose were a lack of communication with remote team members, dividing the project into actionable sprints, and project structure mismatches with some teams that were using the Premiere Pro but using stage-gate processes. The team alleviated the

---

[12] Green, P. (2012). Adobe Premiere Pro Scrum adoption: How an Agile approach enabled success in a hyper-competitive landscape. In 2012 Agile Conference (pp. 172–178). IEEE.

remote team member communication problem by using Adobe Connect, which was Adobe's team communication tool. To tackle the problem of dividing the development process into manageable parts, the Premiere Pro team consulted with the Soundbooth team, who advised that the project could be delivered as a series of outcome-based functionality additions, rather than as a module building block approach. The problems of working with other teams using the stage-gate process was partially mitigated by the other teams designing the gates (milestones) more broadly. The pilot project was successful, and after the successful use of the agile methodology for other projects, the organization had a gradual transformation to an agile organization. The move to the agile organization enabled Adobe's transformation into a XaaS offering provider. Since Adobe had significant competition in design tools like InVision and dedicated solutions like Sketch, having the online cloud offering enabled customers to try Adobe products with lower risk. Updates and improvements were made on a continuous basis, while earlier Adobe sent CD-ROMS every two years for updates to customers. Initially, there were misgivings internally about the move to a XaaS mode of offerings and the management of the transition period. However, the Great Financial Recession of 2008–2009 enabled Adobe to make the transition to an agile organization by providing the motivation for change.

For the successful implementation of the agile organization, it is important for providers to have multi-skilled employees, who can perform different roles. Role mobility is indeed a key element of the agile organization. Salesforce has an established practice of assigning individuals to different teams on a regular basis. Marc Benioff had a high regard for this practice from his days at Oracle where he served in multiple roles.[13] Salesforce assigns senior managers to rotational roles in multiple capacities in sales, marketing, product development and business development strategy. This policy percolates to the middle management and development teams, as individuals who are exposed to responsibilities in different roles perform better in cross-functional teams and boundary-spanning design efforts. The

---

[13] Salesforce, "What You Need to Do to Become a Leader at Your Company", November 27, 2019, https://www.salesforce.com/ca/blog/2019/11/what-you-need-to-do-to-become-a-leader-at-your-company.html, accessed July 18, 2020.

senior leaders at Salesforce have a relentless focus on generating growth, which determined their strategic direction.[14] The senior leaders also engaged with all employees in sharing the firm's strategic direction, using platforms like Chatter.[15] Team leaders then self-organized teams by requesting individual members with different areas of expertize to join their team on a dynamic basis. The team composition was not limited to members with specific expertize in the areas needed for the team's objectives. Often, individuals without a directly identified domain of expertize that was relevant to the team were invited to be members. This enabled the team to have fresh pairs of eyes on the project, and someone to share ideas that were seemingly unrelated to the team's objectives. Salesforce also encourages senior managers to translate a 3-year vision to a 30-day execution plan, to help provide effective direction to teams. There is a conscious attempt to create a culture of tolerating failure, which gives rise to an increased degree of experimentation in team members. The development team and the operations team (DevOps) must be integrated in creating the solutions from the beginning of the development process. The integration of these teams helps to surface issues with the operations and maintenance of applications early in the development cycle.

5.1.6 Collaboration and Integrating External Partners with the Organization

RPX's IP services offerings using a subscription model also need a high degree of agility to understand customer requirements and respond to them. RPX has created multiple teams in three divisions for the purpose of enabling their IP subscription offering.[16] The direct sales division

---

[14] Forbes, Salesforce's Impressive Growth Continues, May 19, 2017, https://www.forbes.com/sites/greatspeculations/2017/05/19/salesforces-impressive-growth-continues/?sh=43a2dff47bb2, accessed July 18, 2020.

[15] Bridgepoint Consulting, 6 Easy ways Salesforce Chatter can Boost your Business, October 31, 2016, https://bridgepointconsulting.com/6-easy-ways-salesforce-chatter-can-boost-business/, accessed July 20, 2020.

[16] Lyang, "RPX Corporation: First Defense Against Patent Trolls", https://digital.hbs.edu/platform-rctom/submission/rpx-corporation-first-defense-against-patent-trolls/#, accessed July 20, 2020.

comprises a set of technically skilled individuals who have a consultative approach to sales with customers. The salespeople reach out to potential customers who have been involved in legal imbroglios over IP in the past with patent trolls, are currently facing litigation, or have other firms in the sector who are facing litigation. Using data from legal settlements in the past, the sales team members offer quantitative estimates of RPX's value from the subscription model to these potential customers. RPX also has teams working on the acquisition of patents that are of interest to their subscriber pool. It has dollar-based targets for patent acquisition, a division that comprises teams of legal, finance and technology domain experts, who evaluate the costs and benefits of acquisition of different patents. RPX has been acquiring patents for about $100M every year and has more than 10,000 patents in its IP set. The patent acquisition teams work closely with customers to find out the strategic directions of the customers in the future. Based on the strategic directions, RPX identifies patents that would be useful in providing subscribers with defensive capabilities in the future. For smaller potential customers who cannot afford the subscription plan, RPX offers insurance services for a smaller fee. Finally, RPX has multiple business development teams, who offer assessment and valuation services for large patent pools for customers and potential customers. They work together with a group of such customers and coordinate their efforts to jointly acquire the patent pool (the customers pay RPX a separate fee from the subscription). The value-added service of evaluation and coordination is now an added service of RPX. For all these service offerings, RPX dynamically changes the team composition to have the requisite expertize on the team to cater to the customer's needs.

The RPX example demonstrates the importance of integrating external partners in the provider's processes for developing the XaaS offerings. While the alignment and horizontal communication between internal teams that are composed dynamically is important, in our observations, providers are indeed cognizant of this factor. They have developed internal mechanisms for working towards these objectives, likc creating horizontal and vertical communication lines. However, the need for these teams to coordinate with external partners like vendors, customers and resellers is often overlooked. The need for aligning dynamic teams with external partners is harder to achieve, as external partners will have different goals and objectives, hence, defining common goals and incentives is a challenge. Next, vendors typically develop technologies for multiple customers, hence, having a shared product vision is hard, the ability to coordinate with multiple vendors is even more challenging. It is hard to ensure that even if partners' representatives are physically collocated with the provider's team members, they will communicate effectively with their own colleagues at their respective organizations in sharing the team's vision. The iterative nature of the agile process used by dynamic teams alleviates some of these issues by testing and restating the objectives of the team at every iteration. Finally, the organizational culture and the clock speed of operations of the partners may not be synchronized with that of the provider. The applied research literature has identified four critical steps for the management of collaboration in networks: managing central nodes in the network, increasing the connectivity of members with low numbers of connections over time, developing relationships between silos, and cross-boundary interactions.[17] In the context of fostering better collaborative relationships with external partners in the short run, the management of central nodes in the network is critical. About a third of the collaborative relationships formed are attributable to 3–5% of the people in the network, showing that critical resources for network collaboration develop organically over time. The provider must make a conscious effort to retain individuals with a high degree of connectivity and encourage collaborative loads to be shared with other individuals. If the specific role of the individual causes this node centrality, then the responsibilities of the role should be shared across individuals. Teams with multiple interdependencies would have a higher collaborative load, hence, project integration teams should share the collaborative effort for such teams. To ensure that the connectivity of members with low numbers of relationships currently increases over time, the provider must use a combination of informal and formal methods. Fostering informal relationships is often overlooked; creating a mentoring relationship with team members with high connectivity is one recommended action. The dynamic reassignment

---

[17] Crocker, A., Cross, R., & Gardner, H. (2018). How to make sure agile teams can work together. *Harvard Business Review*, May 15, 2018, Product H04BXH-PDF-ENG.

of such members into teams with high interdependencies with external partners can help develop these networks formally. Geographical and functional silos can be integrated better by quarterly or semi-annual forums or conferences, and employee rotations across different geographies can be useful in creating more connected networks with external partners across geographies. Having sharing sessions of best practices with external partners can also help in the integration of silos. Increasing the cross-boundary connectivity typically starts with the leadership of different organizations engaging with team members of the partner to engender the creation of informal relationships.

The physical environment of the teams is also an important factor in their efficacy. For teams working on core research ideas, the need for collaboration is more limited, hence, the physical environment should provide for creativity and personal space. In contrast, XaaS teams that are working on commercializing offerings have a need for a mix of collaboration space and private time to work on solutions. The research on the subject finds that to have the optimal results for commercializing offerings, teams need a "cave and commons" environment for optimal performance.[18] The genesis of the cave and commons approach was the policy of encouraging telecommuting at Yahoo, which was stopped by Marissa Mayer when she was CEO of Yahoo. The control of privacy of individuals when working in the office must be balanced with the needs for collaboration time. The ideal environment would be a combination where individuals have private spaces to work in (cave) for doing their own analyzes and developing their own ideas, and for performing routine tasks. The individuals should also have access to collaboration spaces as a team (commons), where they can meet at short notice, and discuss face-to-face the trade-offs across different elements of the offering, and make choices, or agree on further data needed for the analysis. While the value of the open environment is well understood for fostering collaboration, the research shows that individuals working alone have a higher degree of creativity than those who work solely in a group. Hence, the balance between team

---

[18] Thompson, L. (2013). Give workers the power to choose: cave or commons. *Harvard Business Review Blog Network*, March, 27.

interactions and individual time can be achieved by the cave and commons approach.

An important need for agile organizations is to shift the need for technology as an enabler for team performance to a central role for technology in every organizational activity to create value and quickly react to changing customer needs. The agile organization needs standardized processes as the core for routinizing tasks. The standardization can be achieved by a mix of standardizing operating procedures, and by partially automating processes as far as possible. For the delivery of the services, most offerings must be digitally enabled, for example, the automation of usage metering, payment and billing systems enables a seamless delivery to the customer. The transfer of best practices and the creation and sharing of knowledge management systems across different teams enables the diffusion of best technology practices in the organization. Using technology-based solutions like CAD/CAM and other software tools for presenting current designs and prototypes internally minimizes handover delays and costs internally, apart from providing a standardized interface for easy communication.

5.1.7 Enhancements to the Agile Organization for XaaS Offerings

While the agile organization fits well with the design and delivery of XaaS offerings, in practice, the agile organization is implemented with some lacunae. First, many leaders use the concept of R&D productivity in their decision-making on innovation investments. The R&D productivity is defined as the ratio of the growth in revenue for the current year to the R&D investments in the previous year.[19] While many firms have a higher degree of productivity using the agile methodology, these gains are not always obvious, as R&D investments tend to take a long time to fructify. The organizational leaders are justified in their desire to improve the R&D productivity with a quicker timeframe. However, the long lead time for

---

[19] Weisbach, R., "How I led 6 R&D groups through an agile transition", TechBeacon, https://techbeacon.com/app-dev-testing/how-i-led-6-rd-groups-through-agile-transition, accessed July 28, 2020.

observing the benefits of R&D investments depends on the lifecycle of the underlying technology. For example, early in the technology lifecycle, R&D investments help in growing the potential market and in gaining market share. However, while providers may see an increased market share, this may not result in increased revenues. If the provider is following a penetration pricing policy (pricing lower early in the lifecycle of the offering), then the benefits of R&D may not be immediately obvious. R&D investments may also have a longer lead time in many cases for the investment to generate returns. The ROI or R&D productivity is indeed a fair metric to measure the benefits of innovation when the lifecycle of the underlying technologies is maturing. The tendency to use R&D productivity, ROI and other such measures to estimate the efficacy of innovation in the development of XaaS offerings may introduce a short-term mentality in the provider's leaders, where the leaders look for immediate gains for any innovation investments.[20] For the long-term sustainability and profitable growth of the organization, leaders have to identify and invest in R&D opportunities for the short, medium and long term. Beyond the investments, leaders of XaaS organizations must institutionalize activities like the evaluation of customer needs, and the advancement of the technology landscape over the long term. The advancement of the technology landscape, evolution of technology standards, and the introduction of potentially disruptive technologies in the future are critical sources of competitive advantage if the provider is ready with scans of future technologies. On the other hand, if the provider does not continuously scan the horizon for new technologies, it risks being disrupted by the new technologies very quickly. This threat from new technology emergence is particularly valid for XaaS offerings, as customers can switch very quickly from one provider to another. The low switching costs of XaaS offerings make it imperative that the provider stay on top of technology developments on a continuous basis. While competing standards and technologies imply that most of the emerging technologies will not be

---

[20] Fehling, M., "Everything as a service: A closer look at the business model of the future", Siemens, July 11, 2019, https://blogs.sw.siemens.com/thought-leadership/2019/07/11/everything-as-a-service-a-closer-look-at-the-business-model-of-the-future/, accessed July 28, 2020.

successful, a careful evaluation of each of the opportunities will enable the provider to make adoption decisions. Often, hedging its bets by considering multiple technologies early in the process may also be a useful practice for the provider.

Emerging technologies have to be assessed based on their ability to enhance the current market or address a new market, by addressing customer pain points, or by providing enhanced customer value.[21] The vendor's ability to successfully commercialize the technology also has to be assessed, along with the promise of the technology in becoming the industry standard. Next the value of the technology should be assessed, along with business models and current offerings that can potentially be disrupted. For instance, the use of healthcare data from wearables and the sharing of this data on the cloud with healthcare providers can impact the business of diagnostics organizations in the healthcare sector. However, the degree of sharing can be limited by regulators due to privacy concerns. Hence, both the impact on healthcare players and the potential compliance measures introduced by regulators must be considered in the value analysis. Other sources of value may include lower costs and faster time to market. The potential adoption of the technology as an industry standard may lead to bandwagon effects with complementary services, hence, the network externalities and bandwagon effects must be considered as well. The provider also must assess its own capabilities to adopt and exploit the emerging technology. If all the assessments indicate that the technology holds promise for the provider, the provider must invest resources and plan a timeline to use the emerging technology in its services.

How should the innovation processes of providers be organized in the long run for XaaS offerings? The R&D process needs to account for the diverse needs of multiple customer segments, as different customer segments have different requirements. When the provider's offerings are adopted by customers in multiple countries, the country requirements can be diverse as well. While the customer requirements across countries may not be diverse for IT XaaS offerings, they are diverse indeed for other

---

[21] Govindarajan, V., Kopalle, P. K., & Danneels, E. (2011). The effects of mainstream and emerging customer orientations on radical and disruptive innovations. *Journal of Product Innovation Management*, 28(s1), 121–132.

offerings in the non-IT space. To cater to the needs of diverse customer segments, often located in different geographies, one option for the provider is to have R&D capabilities in multiple teams that are dedicated to markets. This approach to R&D is known as the local-for-local approach, where the innovation to satisfy customers' needs in local markets is conducted by local teams.[22] While this approach is indeed more successful in meeting the needs of local markets, it has three inherent drawbacks. First, the R&D horizon for teams in the local-for-local approach tends to be short-term, they are completely customer-driven in their understanding of innovation goals. While customers can share valuable feedback about services that they have been receiving, they find it difficult to imagine their needs in the long term. Local R&D teams also have resource constraints, as they rely on the revenues generated in the local market for funding innovation activities. This results in a lack of economies of scale. Third, when providers adopt the local-for-local approach to innovation, their offered services often "re-invent the wheel" in multiple markets, as local teams design similar solutions separately for common market problems. Apart from the higher costs of duplication of efforts, the local-for-local approach also inhibits the sharing of best-in-class innovations across multiple markets, leading to low spillovers.

On the other hand, most XaaS providers locate their innovation efforts at the headquarters for economies of scale, rapid communication with senior leaders, and for alignment of the innovation capabilities with the strategy of the firm. The approach of locating innovation capabilities at the headquarters also has the added advantage of being closer to the most loyal customer base, as providers would have a long term and loyal customer base closer to their home country. Hence, in the past, Alibaba Cloud's R&D centre was first opened in Hangzhou near Beijing. In the past, most companies — even those with a considerable international presence in terms of sales and manufacturing — carried out most of their R&D activity in their home countries. Conventional wisdom holds that strategy development and R&D had to be kept in close geographical proximity. Because strategic decisions are made primarily at corporate

---

[22] De Meyer, A. & Mizushima, A. (1989). Global R&D management. *R&D Management*, 19(2), 135–146.

headquarters, the rule of thumb adopted by many providers is that innovation facilities should be close to home. This approach is known as the centre-for-global approach, where one innovation centre conducts research globally for the provider. The centre-for-global approach has the advantages of economies of scale, as one innovation effort is conducted for the global needs of all customers. If customer requirements sensing in local markets can be done well and shared with the global centre, the global centre can roll out the innovation to other markets. The global innovation centre also predicts the requirements of customers in the long term better, as it is exposed to global trends. However, the centre-for-global approach has its own demerits. First, the centre-for-global innovation structure takes a one-size-fits-all approach for customer needs, and specific local market needs can be overlooked if the needs do not have a high degree of customer segment or local specificity. Second, the local units must be able to absorb and customize the innovation output of the global centre for local markets. The ability of local teams to absorb the innovation output and transfer technology successfully may be limited without local R&D capabilities. The ability to exploit and commercialize global innovation output may be limited for providers, as a lot of innovation knowledge is tacit — the ability to transfer tacit knowledge is limited without appropriate transfer mechanisms. Third, the speed of global rollout can be hampered from the lack of engagement with local teams.

The best approach, based on our experience, is a hybrid of the local-for-local and the centre-for-global approaches. The provider should have global centres-of-excellence in innovation in parts of the world where there is a localized domain of expertize. For instance, Microsoft has its R&D headquarters in Redmont in Washington. However, it also operates R&D centres around the world with locations in Canada in North America, China, India and Israel in Asia, Denmark, the United Kingdom, Ireland, Germany and Estonia in Europe, among other locations.[23] In addition to being connected in local markets and securing top talent in local markets,

---

[23] Microsoft Corporation, 2012 Annual Report, Research & Development, https://www. microsoft.com/investor/reports/ar12/financial-review/business-description/research-development/index.html#:~:text=While%20our%20main%20research%20and,Israel%2C%20and%20the%20United%20Kingdom, accessed July 29, 2020.

Microsoft has a long-term vision for its R&D centres. The global organization funds these innovation centres around the world to support them, and the mandate for these centres is to visualize customer needs in the future and identify solutions for the long term. However, in addition to the core research being done in the global centres, Microsoft also has R&D teams in business segments and at the country level. The role of the local R&D teams is to conduct applied research for specific business segments and locations and utilize solutions developed by the core research centres into business applications. The local and business R&D teams also coordinate localized solutions and leverage them globally. Microsoft also works with top academic institutions in its Microsoft Research initiative, to assess technology opportunities and trends in the future, and enhance the state of the art in computer science as a field.[24] The hybrid approach seeks to amalgamate the best of both the centre-for-global and local-for-local structures, by seeking to create a core research capability for the entire organization, and use the local teams for developing commercial applications.

5.1.8 Organizational Hierarchy for XaaS Offerings

The role of hierarchy in creating the right environment for XaaS providers is one of the most critical decisions to be made in the organizational structure. The hierarchy of the organization is influenced by the number of employees of the organization, the distribution by location of the employees, their profiles, the supporting infrastructure and technology, and leadership preferences.[25] The hierarchical structure's role is to clearly identify lines of reporting and communication, authority of decision-making, policy setting for roles and activities, and clearly defining individual responsibilities. The nature of leadership is clearly defined by the hierarchy, as are information flows for data gathering and decision-making. The two extremes of hierarchies in organizations are the pyramidal, or tall

---

[24] Microsoft, Collaborating with Institutions, https://www.microsoft.com/en-us/research/academic-programs/collaborating-with-institutions/, accessed August 1, 2020.

[25] Schwarz, G. M. (2002). Organizational hierarchy adaptation and information technology. *Information and Organization*, 12(3), 153–182.

structure, and flat organizations.[26] Pyramidal structures have several lay-ers between the senior leaders and the lower ranks, with clear role defini-tions and reporting structures. Organizations that have a pyramidal hierarchy have some advantages, e.g. transparent power structures and conflict resolution (by authority), and the clear incentives for better per-formance (promotion to the next level of the hierarchy). Specialized employees can acquire skills for rising in the hierarchy, and the belonging of individuals to localized units like departments enables a sense of stabil-ity. However, the structural advantages of role and decision-making clarity of hierarchical organizations are usually overshadowed by the increased bureaucracy of decision-making. The hierarchy typically introduces more checks and balances for routine decisions, which tends to slow down the decision-making process. Horizontal communication across teams is inhibited, especially if the hierarchy is organized by function. Individuals also make locally optimal decisions for the benefits of their department or silo, rather than the organization.[27]

In contrast, the creation of flat organizations is supported in the agile methodology, and several providers have reported a higher degree of suc-cess with flat organizational structures. Flat organizations have very few middle management layers, with a much higher scope for horizontal coor-dination and communication. The empowerment of individuals working in horizontal teams expedites decision-making, by delegating the author-ity and decision-making powers to autonomous teams. The team auton-omy increases agility, with no middle management layers to provide checks and balances. The senior leaders of the provider share the goals of the provider's offerings to the teams, and the teams identify pathways to achieve the goals in small, incremental steps that are aligned to the agile methodology. The process of composing teams is much more dynamic, with individuals self-organizing in teams to implement solutions in a phased fashion. While flat organizations are preferred for XaaS offerings,

---

[26] Denning, S. (2018). The age of agile: How smart companies are transforming the way work gets done. Amacom, New York.

[27] Satyendra, "Comparison between Hierarchical and Flat Organization Structures", *Ispatguru*, December 8, 2013, https://www.ispatguru.com/comparison-between-hierarchical-and-flat-organization-structures., accessed August 3, 2020.

they have their own drawbacks. First, individuals in flat organizations do not have a clear conflict resolution mechanism by a higher authority; leaders must design adequate resolution mechanisms. The lack of reporting structures may lead to the lack of visibility of individual performance, leading to a higher degree of ambiguity of expectations. Flat organizations typically have their own organically developed power structures that evolve from membership in a larger set of teams, or criticality of team assignment. Rewarding individuals and providing them with career growth opportunities is harder, along with the inability of individuals to develop specialized skills.

Our observations lead us to recommend relatively flat structures with some degree of middle management layers for XaaS providers. The organization of these structures should have teams that are focused on services outcomes, for example, computation, networking, and storage solutions would be ideal for organizing the relatively flat teams in IaaS providers. For coordinating the efforts of the teams within the groups focused on outcomes, one or two middle management layers would help in aiding the dynamic assignment of individuals with specific skillsets to solutions teams. While individuals within the groups should self-organize into teams with a clear role of their contribution to the outcome of the team's effort, the middle management can support the self-organizing and in identifying the team's outcomes. The team should be empowered to take decisions to achieve their outcomes. The role of the middle managers should also be to keep abreast of the latest technologies underlying the solutions, and enabling knowledge sharing and training opportunities for employees. In a fast-paced environment, as the provider scales the scope of the services, more groups would be added, reflecting the enhanced scope of offerings.

5.1.9 Performance Assessment and Reward Systems

When moving to a relatively flat organizational structure, the fairness and transparency of performance assessment and the design of reward systems are of paramount importance. In traditional hierarchical organizations, performance reviews are typically conducted annually, with the manager who is one level higher in the hierarchy typically conducting the review.[28] The manager would have a reporting relationship with the employee over the course of the year, and could provide meaningful feedback to the employee on his/her performance. The annual reviews would be collated by the Human Resources department, and a certain reward (in the form of a pay increment) would be awarded to each employee. This reward was usually assigned from a pool based on the firm's performance for that year, with some degree of normalization: individuals with a positive review from their superiors would receive higher rewards, while those with tepid reviews would get lower or no rewards.

When Adobe was transforming from a productization mode to the XaaS mode of offerings, it found that the fast-paced development and business environment of the XaaS mode was not supported by the annual performance review structure that was more suited to hierarchical organizations in stable environments.[29] Adobe decided to move away from the annual performance review process to a more dynamic performance assessment process. Adobe implemented a process that it called the "Check-in" — an interactive, continuous dialogue between individuals and the middle manager, where the performance and expectations of individuals were continuously assessed. The overall expectations of the individual were discussed and ideally documented at the beginning of the year, with on-going periodic meetings throughout the year for taking stock and reviewing the performance. While these interactions could be conducted as frequently as possible, a minimum period of quarterly feedback was prescribed. The Check-in process has created more efficiency in the performance review process and increased top employee retention. The performance assessment review and rewarding processes also must be

[28] Darino, L. Sieberer, M. Vos, A. & Williams, O. (2019). Performance management in agile organizations, McKinsey & Company, https://www.mckinsey.com/business-functions/organization/our-insights/performance-management-in-agile-organizations#, accessed August 5, 2020.

[29] Morris, D., "Death to the performance review: How Adobe reinvented performance management and transformed its business", *World of Work Journal* (Second Quarter), 2016, https://www.adobe.com/content/dam/acom/en/aboutadobe/pdfs/death-to-the-performance-review.pdf, accessed August 5, 2020.

synchronized with the resource allocation and planning processes. Providers typically use their planning processes to move from strategy to action plans, and for making hiring and resource acquisition decisions. However, the annual planning cycle may be extraordinarily long for XaaS providers, as resource requests are made with a much higher clock speed and dynamism. It is inherently hard for individuals in XaaS organizations to forecast their resource needs for the entire year. The dynamic assignment of individuals into teams requires a planning process that is more continuous as well, as critical activities can get stalled without the right resources. In our observations, the best-in-class providers have fluid planning processes as well, with a shorter planning cycle. Quarterly or semi-annual planning cycles replace the traditional annual planning cycles. This change in planning frequency gives the provider much needed flexibility in resource allocation.

The continuous performance assessment and rewarding system reflects other aspects of agile organizations, like the fast-paced additions in service offerings, and the dynamic assignment of individuals to teams. Individuals change teams and perform flexible roles in a network to offer more value to customers dynamically by rapidly refining offerings. Self-organizing teams are created and disbanded after their outcomes are achieved, with shared learning and increased connectivity across teams.[30] The performance in teams should lead to immediate feedback mechanisms, as working relationships are temporary in the dynamic network. There is frequent interaction with stakeholders, both internal and external. The continuous interaction helps teams create better solutions dynamically. The annual performance review system cannot capture these dynamic interactions, as changing roles and goals of individuals on an annual basis cannot provide an accurate snapshot of the employee's contributions. The continuous assessment and feedback mechanism enable the clock speed of the performance assessment and reward process to match the dynamically changing roles and contributions of individuals in XaaS providers. The reward processes should incentivize teams to come

---

[30] Shein, E., "XaaS: Making the shift to services-oriented IT", CIO, March 25, 2019, https://www.cio.com/article/3373841/xaas-making-the-shift-to-services-oriented-it.html, accessed August 10, 2020.

up with the best ideas and percolate these ideas throughout the organization. The traditional reward processes that were concomitant with annual performance reviews rewarded individuals on a normalized basis, with the rewards typically divided into normalized tranches. High-performing individuals got larger rewards with other individuals getting proportional rewards based on their review assessment on a continuum. However, the normalizing of rewards was based on the assumption that individuals' contributions were normally distributed. In contrast, the research on individual performance in teams finds that the contributions of individuals in organizations are not normally distributed.[31] Rather, the performance of individuals is governed by the Power Law distribution, with a small number of individuals who are hyper performers, a majority of individuals with reasonably good contributions, and a small number of individuals who do not perform to expectations. Hence, the variation of contributions from individuals is wider than predicted by the normal distribution, with the contributions of hyper performers often being the driving force behind the organization. Unlike the normal distribution where the mean is also the median, for the Power Law distribution, the median is below the mean. A much smaller proportion of performers have an average above the mean, implying that hyper performers significantly outperform their colleagues significantly. The performance assessment and reward system must capture the value add of the high performers on a continuous basis, and reward them for their contributions. The annual performance review with the graded reward system does not fit the XaaS organization, hence, the move to a continuous review with a reward system that is contribution-based is needed for the retention of top talent. The firms that perform well in the space of XaaS offerings treasure their top performers, and make every effort to retain them, including providing incentives to other individuals to attain the higher achievement status of top performers. We fully understand and agree that hyper performer status is neither static nor is it unchangeable, with the right support and incentive structures, the hyper performer status should indeed be achievable by a wider swathe of

---

[31] Aguinis, H. & O'Boyle Jr, E. (2014). Star performers in twenty-first century organizations. *Personnel Psychology*, 67(2), 313–350.

individuals. The continuous review and skewed reward system to top performers is not meant to be a deal-breaker for the good but not excellent performers. Rather, it seeks to provide incentives that are outcome-based to prove the worth of their contributions to all individuals. The focus of the continuous assessment and outcome-based reward system should be on coaching and providing support facilities to all individuals, albeit with the recognition of top performers on a continuous basis.

5.1.10 Tasks and Processes for XaaS Offerings

We hope the reader sees a pattern across the recommended organizational structure for providers of XaaS offerings: we recommend a hybrid of the best practices for learning organizations and focused organizations. Providers of XaaS offerings need to incorporate the best of both worlds in their organizations structure: they need the flexibility to offer multiple solutions, and they need standardized offerings to be able to mix and match to provide this flexibility. The exploitation of this dichotomy carries over into the organization of tasks and processes as well internally. Tasks and processes can be classified from routine on one extreme to creative on the other extreme.[32] The characteristics of routine tasks are easy to enumerate: the identity of these tasks is repetitive in nature, with a very high degree of standardization, indeed, the usage of completely standardized operating procedures is highly recommended for routine tasks. On the other hand, creative tasks are non-repetitive in nature, with a high degree of interdependence on other tasks, and inherently require more time to complete. While processes in XaaS organizations need to deliver customized solutions that require a threshold of creative input, delivering them from scratch does not enable any economies of scale. While innovation is a must for XaaS offering organizations, even innovative tasks can be separated into creative tasks and routine tasks. The distinction between routine and creative tasks is identifiable from the degree of predictability of the task. Creating engineering drawings, writing software code when

---

[32] Bradler, C., Neckermann, S., & Warnke, A. J. (2014). Rewards and performance: A comparison across a creative and a routine task. *Academy of Management*, 1, 14335.

the requirements for the software code are known are examples of routine tasks in the process of innovation.[33] The processes for executing these tasks are standardized at a high level, and very specific examples may need a higher degree of creativity for executing them, such examples are the exception rather than the norm. In contrast, identifying the deliverables and the concept of the service, identifying task interdependencies and, subsequently, identifying good service architecture candidates are examples of tasks needing higher creativity. These tasks need significant problem-solving and evaluation skills of different candidate solutions; hence, these tasks need different processes.

Our recommendation is that when defining the service concept and the service architecture, the teams need a higher degree of creativity, and they need to spend more time on these tasks than scheduled. These problem-solving and architecture-defining activities need a buffer for the management of time, and excess resources allocated in some cases. The team should adopt a rapid iteration and experimentation approach to these problem-solving tasks, by using processes like design thinking. Processes like design thinking use standardized approaches to creativity, with rapid interaction between stakeholders, and brainstorming and rapid testing for solutions. The teams can interact in an agile fashion with customers, vendors, and other external stakeholders, and define and prioritize the list of attributes needed for the service. After brainstorming for multiple solutions approaches, rapid prototyping techniques should be used for creating proofs of concept. These proofs of concept can be tested with customers, and the design thinking process can be used iteratively. The teams should also define standardized protocols for facilitating interaction and communication between the different stakeholders. Organizations often have key concepts and processes defined internally, these concepts and processes should be shared with stakeholders to make the communication as standardized as possible. The exchange of information should be as seamless as possible. In our experience, a lack of standardized protocols of sharing information often results in needless rework at a later stage. When the concept and the service architecture are defined, the teams should move

---

[33] Khurana, A. (2006). Strategies for global R&D. *Research Technology Management*, 49(2), 48–57.

more quickly with standardized approaches to the delivery of the requirements. The resources allocated at these stages should be in line with the actual forecasted requirements, as standardized, routine tasks without a high degree of variability can be executed with a high degree of certainty. Finally, the learning aspect of tasks is critically important. Certain solutions that are found in creative task execution can be standardized for the future if the tasks are repeated in future projects. In such cases, knowledge management systems that share the best practices and experiences of the team in creating the solution can enable rapid execution of these tasks in the future.

5.1.11 Segregation of Product and Service Organizations

When providers transform themselves from a productization mode to a XaaS mode of offerings, they often face an organizational confusion from their dual missions. IBM used to be a behemoth in the field of mainframe computing, but it integrated PC products as well in its portfolio when the global shift in computing resources from mainframe to minicomputers threatened its existence. IBM's experience is not unique; providers pivot their offerings and business models in response to changing customer requirements. However, IBM's core strength was always its innovation capabilities and its ability to compete in high-margin businesses. The computing business was getting rapidly commoditized, and consequentially, IBM began moving from a productization model to a solutions and services provider model in the 1990s. This shift was achieved from a mix of internal organic transformation and inorganic growth. However, it also had a legacy business of memory devices, printers and PCs, many of these businesses had been pioneered by IBM in the past. IBM had to divest off their product businesses to focus on the new core service offerings, hence, IBM sold their PC business to Lenovo, and other businesses to other firms, to focus on their new service offerings with high value add and high margins.[34] The implications for organizational culture and mission were

---

[34] Spooner, J. G., "IBM sells PC group to Lenovo", *Cnet*, December 8, 2004, https://www.cnet.com/news/ibm-sells-pc-group-to-lenovo/#:~:text=IBM%20sells%20its%20PC%20group,hand%20in%20the%20PC%20business., accessed Aug 15, 2020.

far-reaching; IBM went back to their core capability of using their innovation capacity for providing solutions. Recently, IBM again announced that it was spinning off its infrastructure services business in its global technology services (GTS) division into a separate standalone unit.[35]

Rolls-Royce went through a similar transformation process when it moved from the productization mode to a XaaS mode for the offering of its aircraft engines. First, it introduced a "power by the hour" scheme, where participating airlines paid for engine maintenance services based on the hours of flight of the engines, over the long run. Airlines would buy their assets (aeroplanes) with the engines from Boeing or Airbus, and then they had a choice of availing of Rolls-Royce's power-by-the-hour scheme, as engine maintenance is the most significant part of preventive maintenance of aeroplanes. After the introduction of the power-by-the-hour scheme, Rolls-Royce introduced its "total care" services, where new engines were equipped with IoT sensors for collecting information on the operational data of engines. A whole slew of sensors collected and sent data on the temperatures, air pressure, vibrations and other parameters to Rolls-Royce's database facilities. Rolls-Royce analyzed this collected data from a total of 54,000 engines, and from its analysis, it gleaned valuable insights about the maintenance schedule of its engines.[36] The smart analytics program enabled Rolls-Royce to predict engine performance, and anticipate the need for replacing components, potential field damage, which it incorporated in its preventive maintenance routine. While Rolls-Royce had extensive data analytics capabilities earlier, its focus on designing engines did not enable it to capitalize on service-oriented data. As a result, Rolls-Royce established Control and Data Services Ltd., as a subsidiary to the main organization, the responsibilities for data analytics for services were housed within this new organization. By using the smart

---

[35] King, C., "Why IBM is Spinning Off its 'NewCo' Global Infrastructure Business", *eWeek*, October 14, 2020, https://www.eweek.com/it-management/why-ibm-spinning-off-its-newco-global-infrastructure-business, accessed August 15, 2020.

[36] Rolls-Royce, "Rolls-Royce combines businesses to bring new benefits to engine life management", June 30, 2014, https://www.rolls-royce.com/media/press-releases/2014/300614-engine-life-management.aspx, accessed August 15, 2020.

analytics program, Rolls-Royce improved the efficiency and effectiveness of its maintenance services, leading to better after sales performance.

General Electric (GE) had a similar experience with selling its products in its capital-intensive energy, infrastructure and aviation-oriented divisions. The products had a high cost of acquisition, and many customers baulked at acquiring GE's products, owing to the massive upfront capital outlay involved. In response, GE set up a financial services unit (GE Capital), to enable the acquisition of its products in an as-a-services mode.[37] GE Capital offered financial solutions in the form of services for the use of GE's products. All three examples (IBM, Rolls-Royce and GE) showcase the difficulty of pursuing multiple missions within the same organization. The productization mode needs a different mindset with a focus on a longer-term horizon and stability with standardized offerings. In contrast, service-oriented organizations need an agile mindset, and a mix of short-term reactivity with long-term proactivity. Given the inherent dichotomy between the two types of missions, providers are advised to have separate organizations that deliver the two types of offerings if both types are offered in steady state. In contrast, if the provider is transitioning from a productization mode to a XaaS mode, then the provider can evolve all parts of the organization to being aligned to service offerings using the "crawl, walk, run, fly" modes described in Chapter 4. The different sets of requirements of dealing with partners like customers, vendors and other stakeholders, as well as the different set of internal capabilities needed make the integration of both types of businesses within the same organization difficult. Separating the organizations to align with the type of offering enables the provider to operate with distinct mindsets and cultures within different units that are aligned to the type of offering.

5.2 SUMMARY

The goals of organizational design are manifold — the organizational design and structure must enable the provider to have organizational

---

[37] Ashkenas, R. N., DeMonaco, L. J., & Francis, S. C. (1998). Making the deal real: how GE Capital integrates acquisitions. *Harvard Business Review*, 76(1), 165–170.

capabilities to deliver customer value in the present and in the future. The organization design must be attuned to the pace of change of the industry sector — stable industry sectors with durable goods and a slow pace of change need a unique set of capabilities. In contrast, industry sectors that have a fast pace of change need a flexible structure to be able to respond to continuously advancing technologies and changing customer requirements.[38] Organizations are living entities that need to evolve and keep pace with the external environment. The organization's design also must be aligned with the basis of creating value for customers. If the provider is serving price-conscious customers, then the basis of value creation is the cost of the provider. If the customers are primarily seeking a high performance or a large set of functionalities and features from the offered services, then the basis of value creation is the ability of the provider to match the customer's needs. The two extremes of value creation (cost competitiveness and solutions provider approach) represent the two extreme strategies that the provider can adopt. A focused strategy enables the provider to have a set of standardized offerings, and the provider's focus is on standardizing its processes to drive quality, economies of scale and a lower cost. In contrast, a differentiation strategy is adopted by the provider when it wants to create solutions for customers that match customer needs as closely as possible. In addition to the basis of value creation, the breadth of the provider's portfolio also influences its strategy and organizational design. A broader portfolio leads to more opportunities to match diverse customer preferences with specific offerings. The design of the organization also must account for control mechanisms and decision-making processes within the organization. Providers with clearly defined control mechanisms have a higher degree of stability, while providers with more loosely defined control mechanisms have a higher degree of fluidity. The organizational design also must account for multiple stakeholder interests, and the competitive intensity. In general, providers that create value based on cost operate in stable external environments and have a

---

[38] Krishnan, V. & Bhattacharya, S. (2002). Technology selection and commitment in new product development: The role of uncertainty and design flexibility. *Management Science*, 48(3), 313–327.

focused strategy. The breadth of the portfolio is typically low, and the provider's internal management efforts are to maintain the stability of the process. The organization typically has clear mechanisms of control and decision-making, and the organization operates in a regulatory environment that is stable. Such organizations are typically organized by function, and the goals of each function are clear. In contrast, providers that create value based on matching customer preferences operate in dynamic environments and have a differentiation strategy. The breadth of the portfolio is typically larger, and the provider's management efforts are dedicated to increasing the agility of the process. The organization has fluid mechanisms of control and decision-making. It typically tries to balance multiple stakeholder interests, and regulatory regimes are more fluid. Such organizations are known as learning organizations. The goal of individuals in learning organizations is to be nimble and flexible, to adapt to changing environments as rapidly as possible.

Providers that offer their services in a XaaS mode have both extreme sets of objectives as part of their goals. Customers who partake of such offerings need solutions to enhance their own utilities, they also need low costs in many cases. SMEs are an important market segment for XaaS offerings, who cannot afford high prices for services. Hence, XaaS providers need characteristics of both learning and functional organizations embedded in them, to match the dual needs of providing solutions at a low cost. The principles of organizing for mass customization offer a starting point for the organizational design of XaaS providers. Mass customization offerings are designed to have a common core for all the product offerings, with the customized components being added on at the last minute. For instance, smart phones offer the ability to have basic calling and messaging features, and customers can customize the use of smart phones by adding apps on an as-needed basis to customize the phone to their requirements. Organizations that offer mass customized products should ideally have an organizational structure that can develop a standardized set of solutions. The stability needed by the organization is provided by the common core, the part of the organization that creates the common core focuses on value on the basis of maximizing component commonality and reducing the need for multiple component inventories to reduce costs. For adding the customized components, the provider needs a network of dynamic teams with changing composition depending on the needs of the customers. Individuals are allocated to teams dynamically depending on their skillsets and ability to contribute to the customized solution. Such teams need to interact closely with customers to elicit their needs, and then self-organize rapidly into teams to be able to deliver the customized functionality and features desired by customers.

To define the team composition and team interaction needs for mass customized products, there is a well-known tool called the design structure matrix (DSM). The DSM adopts a two-step process for identifying team assignment and interaction needs. First, the team that uses the DSM methodology defines all the activities and the required interdependence of those activities in the design structure matrix. Following the activity and interdependence elicitation, the team should then cluster the activities so that interactions within the cluster are maximized, and interactions with other activities outside the cluster are minimized. The clusters then are grouped together, and all components associated with the activities within each cluster are defined as a module. In this fashion, the DSM can be used to first identify the architecture of the product or the service. Design team assignments are based on a one-to-one correspondence basis between individual teams and clusters or modules. The modular architecture helps identify the team composition in this manner. The interdependencies between these modules need communication mechanisms to be developed between the teams designing these modules, the alignment matrix is a useful tool to map the quality of design team interaction with the product architecture. When predicted team interactions are missing, the causes could range from the benign (the design of those modules did not change from the previous generation), to the more worrisome causes of missed interactions by design teams. The costs of missed interactions are typically borne based on the point where design flaws caused by the missing interactions are identified. In extreme cases, they can lead to significant rework, increased costs and delays in new service launches.

Agile organizations build on the structure of organizations offering mass customized products and are very close to the requirements of organizations with XaaS offerings. Agile organizations are suitable for dealing with a rapid pace of change in supporting technologies and customer requirements. They need a mix of stability and dynamism to be able to respond to customer requirements quickly and at a low cost. Ideally, XaaS providers should have a common core of leadership, who share changes in their strategy frequently within the organization, along with sharing the provider's direction in the future. They should also have a common core of services that are standardized and delivered at scale and can be mixed and matched for creating customized offerings. For identifying customer requirements, and for identifying new customized components to be developed for customers, XaaS providers should have a dynamic network of teams who self-organize themselves. These teams should typically consist of a small size so that coordination and communication can be meaningfully achieved. The teams should ensure that all stakeholders like customers and vendors are engaged in the customization process. The teams should also use technology solutions like CAD/CAM tools as much as possible to ensure a common language for communicating the design of the customized components. Finally, agile organizations have a need for constant collaborative environments with the need for quiet time for individuals to be able to execute some tasks by themselves. The "cave and commons" approach that combines individual working spaces with shared spaces for collaboration is recommended for facilitating the mixed objectives of collaboration and quiet time.

While the agile organizational structure has many benefits for XaaS providers, one shortcoming of the agile organizational structure is the short-term mentality that comes from being led by customer requirements. Customers can share adequate feedback about their experiences with current offerings and express their needs for gaps in the offerings to be filled. However, being customer-driven often leads to the inability of the provider to think of what customer needs would be on a long-term horizon. The provider needs to have capabilities of scanning technologies in the long run that could be potentially disruptive for several objectives. Ideally, the provider should prepare for absorbing these technologies in their own offerings as early as possible. To develop capabilities for a long-term vision of how the provider's services should evolve, the organizational structure of the provider's innovation organization is key. Many providers have organized their innovation capabilities based on customer segments or countries of operation. This approach is known as the local-for-local approach, and providers using this approach recognize market requirement shifts well in the short term. However, the local-for-local approach to innovation often reinvents the wheel, does not have economies of scale, and innovations developed for one segment are not transferred to other customers. Other providers have innovation capabilities organized globally usually in the home country, or in locations where world class capabilities exist for that innovation. These providers usually adopt a one-size-fits-all approach to their offerings, which may be suitable for some XaaS offerings, but will not be able to cater to specific customer segments or localized needs. The best practice for organizing innovation capabilities in the long run is to have a mix of capabilities: core research should indeed be done in one global location for economies of scale. However, teams catering to specific segments and localized teams should have their own innovation capabilities to apply the solutions designed by the global research organization specifically for target segment or local needs.

The hierarchy of the organization for a focused strategy is ideally a pyramidal or tall structure, as the clear control of decision-making is enforced by the hierarchy. In contrast, the differentiated strategy with the learning organization is more highly enabled with a flat structure, with a more fluid control of decision-making. While agile organizations typically recommend flat structures, XaaS organizations are better served with relatively flat organizations with a couple of middle management layers. The role of the middle management layers is to coordinate the activities of self-organizing teams, and to enable learning and training of employees. Middle management layers also serve to enrich horizontal communication by facilitating project integration. The lack of multiple layers of middle managers also needs performance assessment and reward systems to be redesigned. Traditionally, employees' performance was reviewed, and incentives were awarded on an annual basis. However, with the rapid clock speed of dynamic teams in the agile organization, the annual resource acquisition and evaluation processes are not suitable any more, as they are not synchronized with the pace of contributions of dynamic teams. The performance review and reward systems should be more continuous for XaaS providers. Ideally, expectations should be shared frequently with employees, and the feedback process should be more continuous, to synchronize with the faster pace of changing assignments. The frequency of feedback should be at least quarterly, and the planning processes should be conducted quarterly as well. Employee contributions were assessed on a continuum and incentives awarded were in pre-defined tranches in the traditional annual performance review and reward systems. The basis of designing reward systems in pre-defined tranches was the assumption of normalized contribution of different employees. However, in fast-paced environments, the contributions of top performers are much higher compared to those of average performers, hence, significantly higher incentives should be awarded to top performers to retain them, as their retention has a significant impact on the future performance of the provider.

Tasks and processes in XaaS organizations can be classified on a continuum of routine to creative tasks. Routine tasks have a high degree of repetition and predictability, while creative tasks are more unique and unpredictable. The provider should use design-thinking like processes to create standard operating procedures for creative tasks as well and assign a larger set of resources with time buffers for creative tasks. Creative tasks are typically required at the front end of the innovation process for acquiring customer feedback, generating concepts and designing the service architecture. Once the above tasks have been done, the implementation of the solutions should use standardized routines as far as possible, including using solutions from previous designs. Solutions that are designed in creative tasks should be standardized over time if those tasks are repeated in other projects, and knowledge management systems should be used for disseminating best practices and solutions from creative tasks within the organization. Finally, when the provider is transitioning from a productization to an as-a-service mode of offerings, it should keep the product and service organizations separated, as the two types of organizations have different goals and practices.

Chapter 6

People Skills for XaaS

6.1 INTRODUCTION

Organizational strategy, structure and processes play important roles in being able to deliver XaaS solutions effectively. However, the execution of the solutions boils down to the abilities of the people within the organization. They need to respond to rapidly changing technologies by being able to work with each other in self-organizing teams, and rapidly respond to customer preferences by working in an agile manner. They need to focus on the value created for the customer, and work with vendors and other network partners to co-create value in a collaborative environment. People must be motivated by an ingrained attitude of service orientation that develops relationships with customers for the long term, rather than having a short-term mentality of convincing customers to adopt their offerings once. Delivering XaaS offerings needs the matching of provider capabilities with customer preferences. The resulting long-term relationship should ideally create loyalty in the customer, and a sustainable core competence in the provider. The effective delivery of XaaS solutions also needs a diverse set of people skills. Employees must deliver creative solutions to customers at a fast pace by using standardized modules. Hence, teams need both creative constituents, as well as individuals with the ability to standardize tasks and modules effectively and quickly. Leaders must be able to develop the skills of the employees and make them effective contributors. They also need to be cognizant of the need to deliver superior organizational performance to customers and other stakeholders.

In addition to the need for specific leadership skills and styles to enable organizational agility, leaders also need effective change management skills to manage the transformation from the productization to the XaaS mode of offerings. It is challenging for individual employees and leaders to embody all the skillsets needed to deliver XaaS offerings. Hence, teams must be constituted at all levels with diverse skillsets represented at the team level. The composition of teams and the assignment of individuals to teams must take into consideration the need for teams to have these diverse skills. At a higher level, the hiring process should be tailored to have a mix of individuals with different skillsets to enable the organization to deliver on XaaS solutions effectively.

The switch from the productization mode to the service mindset needs a mindset shift from a discrete value-adding process to a continuous value-adding process, and a focus on the intangible value-added from the services and interaction components. The mindset shift from value creation and one-time interaction to the model of value co-creation needs an upskilling of the organization for effective delivery. We have identified several core skills for value delivery and leadership in XaaS organizations. This chapter will focus on the enumeration of the desired skills along with processes for their acquisition and assessment. For the acquisition and assessment of these skills, based on our observations in the industry, we recommend a gamification process. Games have been found to enhance learning-by-doing and are typically more effective than sharing a set of principles to be followed in all actions. An important skillset that is needed for delivering XaaS solutions effectively is the ability to think creatively. In this chapter, we outline the process and drivers of engendering creative thinking first. Creative thinking is needed in understanding customer preferences, creating the service architecture for the offering, and in identifying solutions using the mix-and-match approach with standardized components as far as possible. The ability to standardize tasks is also a key required skill. We provide some guidelines on proven methods for standardizing tasks. Putting together standardized modules with new modules and assessing the performance of the system needs an understanding of the interdependence of different elements of the system. Hence, we provide a brief description of the systems thinking skills needed for creating XaaS solutions in this chapter.

One of the requirements of being able to work in an agile fashion for creating solutions is the need for self-organizing teams to be created dynamically in a network. This dynamic creation of teams and the self or assisted assignment of individuals makes the ability of being able to work in a team critical. Hence, we also share key skills needed for effective teamwork and methods to develop and assess these skills in this chapter, along with some best practices for enhancing role mobility. Finally, leaders must be attuned to the needs of their employees first so that they can effectively deliver solutions. The organization's performance must be subordinated to the need for developing employee capabilities in XaaS organizations. We outline the key skills leaders need for developing a servant leadership mindset, along with change management skills for coaching the organization in the transformation to the XaaS mode. All these different skills are needed for the organizational culture to be effectively tuned to the XaaS offering. We conclude the chapter by linking the different skillsets needed to create an effective culture for XaaS organizations.

6.2 CREATIVE THINKING SKILLSET

The need for creativity for developing XaaS solutions arises for a variety of reasons. Customer interaction processes can be designed in different ways, depending on the novelty of the solution and the customer's behavioural patterns. Some customers may be able to express what they need more clearly; others may provide generic feedback. The ability to elicit customer requirements, process the feedback, and the design of solutions need creative thinking skillsets. In designing the solution, employees will need to design the concept and the service architecture for which there are multiple possible solutions. Employees should ideally be able to generate multiple candidate concepts and architectures, which require creative skills. Does creative thinking come naturally or can be the result of nurturing or training? The research shows that creative thinking skillsets are a mix of nature and nurture, there is some element of both involved.[1]

---

[1] Feist, G. J. (2010). The function of personality in creativity: The nature and nurture of the creative personality. In J. C. Kaufman & R. J. Sternberg (Eds.), The Cambridge handbook

Creative thinking derives from processing information based on what the individual already knows, and reassembling this knowledge so as to have a divergent set of ideas. Neuroscientists have found that individuals who express artistic creativity have a special feature of the brain that is different from other individuals.[2] The two hemispheres of the brain are connected by a set of fibres called the corpus callosum. Artistic individuals have a robust connectivity of the two hemispheres via the corpus callosum, resulting in an enhanced connectivity. The brains of creative individuals also have each hemisphere of the brain developing independently. This relatively independent development of the brain hemispheres with the higher connectivity results in the ability of the brains of artistic individuals to enhance divergent thinking skills needed for creativity. Creativity arises from a mix of divergent thinking and creating associations of new information with existing knowledge. The ability to reassemble information differently is based on the connectivity of different areas of the brain. These denser connections are a function of the genetic makeup of the individual, showing that there indeed is a link between genetics and creativity.

Divergent thinking can broadly be defined as the ability to develop ideas in different directions compared to the norm.[3] The brain of individuals exhibiting divergent thinking generates ideas that are different from common expectations, resulting in thinking out of the box. Measuring the divergent thinking of an individual involves the ability of the individual to generate many different ideas about a topic in a short-time interval. The process of divergent thinking requires the individual to disaggregate a topic into component parts to gain insights, and then assemble ideas from the insights together to form solutions. Divergent thinkers can move away

---

of creativity (pp. 113–130). Cambridge University Press. https://doi.org/10.1017/CBO9780511763205.009

[2] Christopher, B. (2017). Highly creative people have well-connected brain hemispheres, *Psychology Today*, February 21, 2017, https://www.psychologytoday.com/sg/blog/the-athletes-way/201702/highly-creative-people-have-well-connected-brain-hemispheres, accessed August 18, 2020.

[3] Acar, S. & Runco, M. A. (2012). Creative abilities: Divergent thinking. In *Handbook of Organizational Creativity* (pp. 115–139). Academic Press. Cambridge, MA.

from constraints of situations and norms. They can generate ideas spontaneously in a random fashion. The ability of associating from one field of thought to another is higher in such individuals, enabling them to move quickly from one idea to the next. Such thinkers also have a higher degree of risk-seeking behaviour, are non-conformists and exhibit greater propensities to challenge the status quo. On the other hand, convergent thinking results in ideas that are practical, can be implemented easily, and will have wide acceptability as the correct solution to a problem. Children below the age of five exhibit divergent thinking to a much larger extent compared to adults, showing that imaginative thinking is correlated with divergent thinking. The ability of adults to imagine concepts is tempered by their life experiences, while children can imagine concepts that are out of the box more easily, as they are not encumbered with many experiences. The results of risk-taking behaviour correlates strongly with divergent thinking. Children below the age of five are much more likely to exhibit risk-seeking behaviour. In contrast, most adults exhibit risk-averse behaviour. The ability to take risks is an important element of divergent thinking.

Can divergent thinking be nurtured? Can individuals who are not lucky enough to have a high degree of creativity genetically be taught to think out of the box? Indeed, creativity can be nurtured as well. There are five essential skills needed for an individuals' creativity to be developed.[4] As mentioned earlier, the ability to associate ideas from seemingly different fields and assimilating them to create unique solutions is an important skill for creativity. Individuals typically associate concepts with experiences from their own lives, a higher degree of experiences enables individuals to make more connections with concepts. The number of connections is positively correlated with creativity, as more connections lead to more diverse ideas. While individuals may have limited experiences, teams with diverse individuals will have a larger set of experiences. Hence, if teams operate in an integrated fashion, they can build on each other's connections to have a larger degree of associativity, leading to

---

[4]Dyer, J., Gregersen, H., & Christensen, C. M. (2019). *Innovator's DNA, Updated, with a New Preface: Mastering the Five Skills of Disruptive Innovators*. Harvard Business Press. 'Boston, MA.

higher team creativity. XaaS teams should ideally include individuals with different backgrounds. One reason that Salesforce encourages job rotations for individuals is to ensure that they develop a larger and more diverse set of experiences. The second skill needed for enhancing creativity is the ability to question conventional wisdom. Individuals should constantly question established practices in their organization. Standardized routines and processes tend to become established practices if they worked successfully a certain number of times. However, there could be better ways of implementing those routines at lower costs and at higher speeds. Individuals who question such practices often lead the way to different business models. Marc Benioff saw the success of eBay and Amazon by creating selling platforms on the Internet, and asked the question: why is software always distributed by sharing individual copies of CD ROMs rather than on the Internet? The third skill needed for nurturing creativity is observation. A well-known tenet of anthropology is the need to observe the behaviour of participants rather than eliciting responses from questions. Observing how customers use a solution can help providers improve their offerings by analyzing customer pain points. For example, the pay-per-use method of payment leads to a higher deal transaction cost if customers must pay for each use at the end of the transaction. Observing customer behaviour when they are required to pay every time for laundry facilities enabled WeLive to design a monthly billing and payment system, rather than using coin-operated laundry facilities that were cumbersome to use. The fourth skill needed for engendering creativity is the propensity to experiment when looking for solutions. The ability to try several solutions and fail early and often is an important part of creativity. 3M has a culture of celebrating failures, as failed experiments provide learning tools for designing better products and services. Facebook's virtual gifts shop and Honesty Box were failed experiments. However, the failures enabled Facebook to design interactivity better between users. The fifth skill that is critical for creativity is networking. Networking with individuals from different fields, attending conferences that are from different fields, provides individuals with ideas that are beyond their traditional competency set. Earlier, steam irons were known to bunch up owing to friction between the surface of the iron and the fabric. Engineers at Calor, which developed steam irons, networked with the developers of non-stick cookware at

Tefal, and shared the issue of creating a steam iron with a smoother gliding movement over fabric. The Tefal developers responded that in their non-stick cookware business, they coated the surface of the cookware with resins to reduce the surface friction of food with the cooking utensil. Calor's engineers then used resins to coat the ironing surface of the steam iron to enable the flow of the steam iron over fabric to be smoother, leading to the development of the Ultraglide steam iron.

There are several exercises that can be used for nurturing creativity in individuals. While these exercises are meant to assess the ability of individuals in regard to divergent thinking, many of these exercises are also used for stimulating creative thinking. For nurturing creativity, we need to start by measuring creativity. One such exercise for measuring creativity is the "Thirty Circles" challenge.[5] This challenge tests the ability of individuals to draw as many circular objects as possible that are from different domains in a period of 3 min. Individuals should be given a sheet with 30 empty circles on it. A template is shown in Figure 6.1.

Examples of circular objects could be a basketball, oranges and bottle tops. After the individual has completed drawing as many objects as possible, the evaluation of the attempt at the challenge should assess the number of completed circles. Most individuals do not complete more than 20 objects. The diversity of ideas should also be tested. Ideally, the objects should be from different areas like balls, fruits and celestial objects like the Sun and Moon. The Thirty Circles exercise tests the individual's ability to quickly generate many different ideas, as well as generate ideas from different fields.

IDEO also has developed a framework for skillsets to be developed for creative thinking. They are classified into learning roles, organizing roles and building roles.[6] Individuals can fulfil any one or a subset of these roles in making the organization more creative. The learning roles enable a continuous upgrading of individuals' skillsets. The first of the three learning roles is the anthropologist's skillset, which focuses on observations in the field, and developing the observation skillset needed for

---

[5] Kelley, T. K. & Kelley, T. (2013). *Three Creativity Challenges from IDEO's Leaders.* Harvard Business Review, November 8.

[6] Kelley, T. (2005). The ten faces of innovation: IDEO's strategies for beating the devil's advocate & driving creativity throughout your organization. Crown Business, New York.

30 CIRCLES TEST

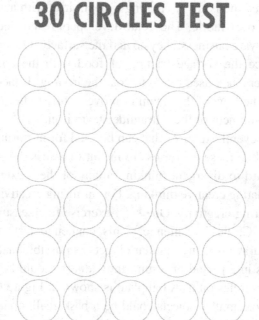

Figure 6.1:   Template for the Thirty Circles Challenge

creativity. Individuals should learn how to observe customers using services and experiences and reframe problems from the customers' perspective. Developing these skills enable individuals to hone an open approach to problem solving and developing empathy and an eye for detail. The second learning role is that of the experimenter. Hence, learning this role enables individuals to hone their experimentation skillset for divergent thinking. Individuals who refine their experimentation skills focus on the innovation process and take risks to generate multiple solutions. The third role is that of the cross-pollinator, which develops the associativity skillset for divergent thinking. Individuals should broaden their horizons and experiences, and use solution triggers from different fields. Next, the organizing roles are intended to develop skillsets for screening ideas and moving the best ideas forward in the organization. The first of the three organizing roles is the hurdler's skillset. This skillset enables individuals to tackle problems in teams effectively. Individuals with the hurdler's skillset are questioning in nature, and do not ascribe to the notion that feasible solutions do not exist for any problem. Next, the collaborator's skillset is about enhancing teamwork, and ensuring the contribution of the team is greater than the sum of contributions of the individuals in the team. Individuals with the collaborator's skillset are effective in forming teams quickly and identifying the potential roles of individuals with a coaching style. Finally, the acquisition of the director's skillset enables individuals to form a strategy from the goals and motivates team members to execute the strategy to achieve those goals. The final set of skills are the building roles. Individuals aspiring to acquiring the skillset for building roles can execute solutions creatively for the organization by building on the learning and organizing skillsets acquired by teams. The first of the building roles is that of the experience architect. An individual who has these skills can create better customer experiences. This skillset enables the team to use innovative methods to create a better customer experience even with the same set of services. The set designer role makes the working experience of other individuals more fun, by making the organization's environment livelier and vibrant. The storyteller's skillset helps in motivating team members by using multimedia methods to create inspirational messages. Finally, the caregiver's skillset enables individuals to understand the pain points of customers and colleagues and enables the team to develop human-centred solutions.

6.3 SKILLS FOR STANDARDIZATION OF TASKS

While creative thinking is needed for providing customers with innovative solutions, the ability to deliver creative solutions with some new and some standard components, and the ability to standardize tasks for designing those components is a vaunted skill for delivering XaaS offerings. Standardizing tasks and processes for XaaS offerings enables the firm to move quickly to meet changing customer requirements at low cost with reliably designed services. The standardization of processes and tasks follows the well-known six-sigma methodology, which eliminates as many sources of variability and errors as possible.[7] The six-sigma methodology optimizes processes to be standardized, so that the output of the process has a high quality with very low deviations from acceptable ranges. The methodology is data-driven, with quantitative methods that identify the value-added of every part of the process. Non-value-added activities are eliminated or redesigned to retain only those parts of the activity that add value to the core product or service. In this aspect, the six-sigma methodology is similar to business process reengineering.[8] While the reengineering methodology needs the process owner to start with a clean slate, the six-sigma methodology typically starts with the analysis of existing processes. The six-sigma methodology identifies the root causes of variability, and then helps process owners to make the process robust by eliminating or mitigating the effect of all random causes of variability. The methodology is implemented in organizations by Green Belt or Black Belt holders who are trained in the methodology and have varying degrees of experience with standardizing processes. The process has five basic steps: define, measure, analyze, improve and control.[9] The definition step defines the process to be standardized, and lists the objectives of the six-sigma implementation. The measure step identifies the objective's metrics that are verifiable, followed by the analysis of the factors that influence the process. The improvement step suggests means for creating standardized operating procedures for lowering the variability of that process. This is followed by the control step, which ensures that the improvement steps will be adhered to strictly by designing failsafe methods.

The implementation of the six-sigma methodology needs participants to be well-trained in statistical skills. The quality improvement processes also need deep domain expertise, as six-sigma specialists need to work hands-on and understand the different steps of the process. Hence, unlike many methods that are implemented by external consultants, the

---

[7] Arnheiter, E.D. and Maleyeff, J. (2005), "The integration of lean management and Six Sigma", The TQM Magazine, Vol. 17 No. 1, pp. 5–18. https://doi.org/10.1108/09544780510573020.

[8] Shin, N. and Jemella, D.F. (2002), "Business process reengineering and performance improvement: The case of Chase Manhattan Bank", *Business Process Management Journal*, Vol. 8 No. 4, pp. 351–363. https://doi.org/10.1108/14637150210435008.

[9] DMAIC, ASQ, The Define, Measure, Analyze, Improve, Control (DMAIC) Process, https://asq.org/quality-resources/dmaic, accessed September 1, 2020.

application of the six-sigma methodology needs domain experts within the organization to be trained as Green or Black Belts. While the six-sigma methodology is rooted in product and services improvement, there are similar approaches like Initiate, Diagnose, Establish, Act, Learn (IDEAL) that have been adapted for standardizing software development processes.[10]

At the meta-level, senior leaders need the skill of identifying end-to-end processes that impact the highest number of customers and prioritize the parts of the process and the process owners which should be standardized with a high priority. The standardization of tasks is closely aligned to the standardization of solution components. Providers following the mix-and-match offering of standardized modules can have a higher degree of standardization. Process owners should have monitoring and evaluation skills, to be able to pick the tasks that will have the highest impact in cost and time for Green or Black Belt intervention, and then be able to guide the process to completion. In addition to statistical skills, Green and Black Belts also need process analysis skills like knowledge of the Theory of Constraints methodology to be able to measure the impact of their intervention. Finally, soft skills like communication and inter-personal skills are needed for the implementers, as the six-sigma approach is only successful if XaaS team members can be convinced of the value of the standardized operating procedures.

There are several games that show the value of standardized processes for eliminating process variability and for robust operation. The paper airplane exercise is probably the most famous. Teams are given different designs of paper airplanes, and asked to measure the distance they travel before they hit the ground after they are launched. The teams are then asked to identify the design that has the most robust performance. Some of the designs have a high degree of variability, with a high distance travelled on some launches, and small distances travelled on other launches. Often, the design with the lowest variability does not have a high distance of travel on average, indicating that robust performance may lead to trade-offs with average performance of processes. A second game that makes

---

[10]McFeeley, B. (1996). *IDEAL: A User's Guide for Software Process Improvement*. Carnegie-Mellon Univ Pittsburgh PA Software Engineering Inst.

users familiar with the six-sigma concept is the catapult game. The purpose of the game is to show that depending on different settings like the angle of launch and the pulling force, objects that are launched from the catapult travel variable distances. The settings that exercise more control have less variability, while those that exercise less control have a higher degree of variability.

6.4 SYSTEMS THINKING

The creation of solutions in the XaaS mode needs to focus on solving customer problems and enhancing customer value. As noted earlier, the creation of these solutions needs the integration of different components to work together in a holistic system. However, individual components of the solution are not independent in XaaS solutions, they usually have a high degree of interdependence. For example, customers may have a mix of some legacy software applications, some recent solutions developed by external providers, and the storage and networking requirements for these applications may be shared resources. For the seamless operation of the system, the interdependent applications need to have interoperability, with human input added to the mix. The need for systems thinking skills within organizations designing XaaS offerings is important, as the developed solutions should be holistic, and delivered with interconnected components.[11] XaaS offerings are typically designed iteratively, with the management of the core services at the heart of the offering. The systemic performance is a function of the integration of the individual components into an integrative whole, and the analysis of the integrative whole as a function of the interaction of the components is the basic premise of systems thinking. A systems thinking approach enables designers of XaaS solutions to understand the links between the various subsystems and components, and enhance the performance of the system as a function of the linkages.[12] The primary skill needed to develop a systems thinking

---

[11] Kim, D. H. (1999). *Introduction to Systems Thinking* (Vol. 16). Waltham, MA: Pegasus Communications.

[12] Ben, L. (2020). Systems, Thinking, https://searchcio.techtarget.com/definition/systems-thinking, accessed July 17, 2021.

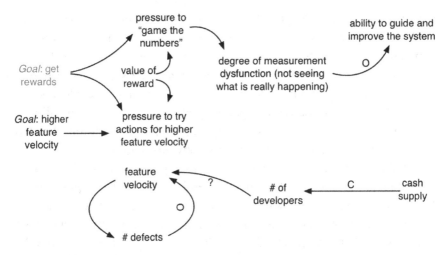

Figure 6.2:   Systems Dynamics Mapping of Software Development Process

Source: From https://less.works/less/principles/systems-thinking.

approach is the analysis of interdependence of different components of a system. Specifically, systems thinking models the dynamics generated by systems using open-loop and closed-loop relationships, and uses diagrammatic approaches for the visual presentation of the systems dynamics.[13] Typically, simulation is the preferred tool to analyze the impact of the dynamics.

Figure 6.2 shows a partial diagram of a system's interactions in the software development process of an organization.[14] The analysis started with the mapping of the lower loop, depicting the relationship between the feature velocity of the software development process and the number of bugs or defects. A high feature velocity implies a more attractive application with more features. However, increasing the feature velocity increases the number of bugs as more code leads to more defects, and a higher number of bugs in turn reduces the feature velocity, as time is consumed in debugging the application. This leaves less time for coders to have a

---

[13] Teaching About Systems, Modeling a System: Making Connections, https://lsintspl3.wgbh.org/en-us/lesson/syslit-il-pdsystems/6, accessed September 2, 2020.

[14] LeSS Framework, Systems Thinking, https://less.works/less/principles/systems-thinking, accessed September 2, 2020.

high feature velocity (depicted by "O", or opposite effect). The systems analysis approach also enables the testing of unknown interactions by simulation, for example, the effect of the number of coders on the feature velocity can be tested. Adding developers when the staffing size is thin helps in increasing feature velocity, but adding too many developers can reduce the feature velocity owing to integration needs. The availability of cash supply (internal resources) can be modelled as a constraint (denoted by "C") on the number of developers for obvious reasons.

In the upper part of the diagram, the twin goals of increasing feature velocity and the promise of financial incentives for the development team lead to actions to try and increase the feature velocity. However, since the feature velocity is directly linked to the number of developers (unknown relationship) that are constrained by the cash supply, the team may be influenced to try and increase the measures of feature velocity. This "gaming" of the measures has been observed in several behavioural studies, which show that when measures are imperfectly linked to final outcomes, actions to influence measures may be detrimental to outcomes. The increased motivation for added feature velocity and the desire to influence the measure of the feature velocity is dependent on the actual size of the reward or financial incentives. A higher motivation to make the measure of feature velocity higher is detrimental to system performance and leads to a higher degree of dysfunction (influencing of measures that are not related to outcomes). The degree of dysfunction is negatively correlated (labelled by an opposite relationship, or "O") to the ability to optimize system performance by guiding and improving the development of the system.

While the example in the source is more detailed, the above partial description of the system illustrates the value of systems thinking. The design of incentives and financial rewards for feature velocity and the cash supply are management decisions, while the other variables are state variables of the system. By using simulation and varying the impacts of the various relationships, management can identify robust ranges for cash supply and financial incentives that improve the system performance. Some of the relationships can be characterized by past data. For example, the relationship between the number of developers and the feature velocity can be tested using past data. The analysis can show if there is a curvilinear relationship with an inverted "U" shape between the feature velocity and the number of developers. The advantage of using simulation is that systems can be checked for robustness of performance, and parts of the system that are susceptible to high variability can be identified. If some relationship causes a high degree of impact on system performance, the variables connected in those relationships must be managed very closely.

At the meta-level, systems thinking models can be analyzed using some simple rules of thumb. These best practices are broadly intuitive.[15] They provide important guidelines for the management of real systems. First, the actual value of the parameters (numbers) should be interpreted in ranges, and if the system output is particularly sensitive to some parameters, those parameters must be held in a tightly controlled range in practice. Managers can identify the parameters that cause the system performance to fluctuate with a high variability, and monitor those parameters closely in practice.[16] Next, the management controlled resources and flows within the system influence the outcome, and the simulation results can yield how resources and variables at each stage change with different simulation settings. The analysis of resources and flows can yield insights into the management of the system during operations, and broad guidelines for resource allocation and flow management can be inferred. The management of variables in loops is one of the critical elements of systems thinking.[17] A negative loop implies that the detrimental effects within the loop are multiplicative, and if the performance of the variables in the negative loop starts degrading, those variables have to be managed with a high priority. In an unstable system, negative loops can cause systems to stop functioning if not managed well. On the other hand, positive loops imply that the beneficial impact of the variables in the loop are

---

[15]Leyla, A. (2017). Tools for systems thinkers: The 6 fundamental concepts of systems thinking. *Medium*, September 8, 2017, https://medium.com/disruptive-design/tools-for-systems-thinkers-the-6-fundamental-concepts-of-systems-thinking-379cdac3dc6a, accessed September 2, 2020.

[16]Anderson, V. & Johnson, L. (1997). *Systems Thinking Basics* (pp. 1–14). Cambridge, MA: Pegasus Communications.

[17]Forrester, J. W. (1994). System dynamics, systems thinking, and soft OR. *System Dynamics Review*, 10(2–3), 245–256.

multiplicative. Hence, the management of variables in those loops should be prioritized as well, as the positive effects of variable increases in such loops are complementary and build on one another. The flow of information in the system is another important factor to be managed. If some information flow is highly correlated with the system performance, then the management should act to make that information flow as visually as possible. Finally, the goals of the system and the alignment of the measures of those goals are key to the management of the system. The systems thinking approach can identify if the goals, measures and incentives align with each other.

In the context of XaaS offerings, systems thinking can be used effectively both in the design stage for new services, and in analyzing how different components of the system perform in practice. The analysis of the performance of the system is easier if components are completely modular, and not interdependent on each other. However, in most physical and software systems, interdependencies exist between the different components. In the case of Infrastructure as a Service (IaaS) offerings, individual components like computing, storage and networking resources interact with one another in the delivery of the system. Hence, checking the impact of load factors on different components with different demand patterns can be useful in identifying system performance. Taking these factors into account at the design stage can help providers in designing the nanonized module well, by balancing the capacities of different components in the nanonized module robustly. Systems thinking can also be used to check the impact of cybersecurity attacks targeted at one part of the system on the performance of other resources.

Using systems thinking models can enable individuals in XaaS teams to hone several skills. The first skill is the ability to incorporate dynamic thinking into the design and operational process. Dynamic thinking skills imbibe the ability to understand interactions of people and components in systems over time, the deduction of the causes of the resulting behaviours, and the ability to exploit these behavioural changes. Complex interactions between systems lead to significantly different behaviours compared to causal relationships or two-way relationships. Systems thinking enables individuals to think of the bigger picture, rather than focusing on individual components and people. A systems approach enables individuals to also learn structured thinking skills, where they understand how individual elements combine to produce a systemic output. The ability to plot individual elements of the system in a systems diagram inculcates the ability to consider all components and interactions, along with structured visual representation and analytic methods. The ability to consider features and functionalities in a continuum rather than thinking only of discrete impacts of components and their performance is another skill that is enhanced by systems thinking. Overall, the analysis of systems by first identifying component level effects on performance with their interdependencies and then integrating different behavioural issues in systems thinking models enables individuals to holistically assess systemic performance. The analysis leads to insights about management levers that can be used to influence operational systems performance.

How should the ability of individuals and teams to think systemically be tested? There are several exercises that test the systems thinking ability which can be gamified and used easily. Peter Skillman designed an exercise called the Marshmallow challenge at IDEO, which has been tried with individuals of different ages, from senior leaders to school children.[18] Individuals or teams are given twenty sticks of spaghetti, one meter of masking tape, a standard-sized marshmallow, and a meter of thin rope or string. Using these items, they are tasked with creating as tall a self-standing structure as possible within 20 min, with the marshmallow at the top of the structure. While Skillman has used the game for showing the benefits of getting straight to the design by trying different ideas and the benefit of agility, the exercise is a very useful way of illustrating the benefit of systems thinking. Most individuals and teams start by building a tall structure and then adding the marshmallow at the top towards the very end when they are running out of time. The tacit thinking is that the marshmallow is very light and will not cause the system to destabilize. It so turns out that adding the marshmallow to most systems makes them unstable and causes the structure to fall. The teams that make stable structures and build a structure of reasonable height understand that the core feasibility implies having the marshmallow at the top. Hence, they start

---

[18] Peter Skillman Design, http://www.peterskillmandesign.com/spaghetti-tower-design-challenge, accessed September 5, 2020.

experimenting with stable structures with the marshmallow at the top to begin with. Following that, they make efforts to increase the height of the structure, showing that the sequence of efforts in creating the system is key to the successful completion of the marshmallow challenge. The seemingly simple challenge enables individuals to understand the interaction of different components must be tested with developing a minimally feasible structure first. The performance of the system can be improved later by adding spaghetti sticks in different configurations to increase the height of the structure.

6.5 TEAMWORK SKILLS FOR XaaS

To manage offerings in the XaaS mode, the need for self-organizing teams to have an optimal collaboration within the team is well-documented. However, the challenges for effective teamwork in the XaaS space are manifold. First, the pace of change of technologies is very high. There is a need for constant engagement with customers, and often, the lack of physical collocation of teams implies that virtual collaboration is needed for effective teamwork. The high pace of technology change implies that teams may not have adequate time to have a human connect with each other, which is one of the requirements for effective teamwork. Second, the technological interface enables continuous communication with the customer, implying customer feedback is continuous, and the relationship with the customer is ongoing. The teams must continuously monitor customer usage of the services, and iteratively improve existing assets and services, while continuously designing new services. Third, the lack of physical collocation implies that teams must use technology for collaboration; and share individual progress on tasks with each other, as tasks have a high degree of interdependence. Developing the right skills in individuals for effectively contributing to teams is an important skillset for successful XaaS offerings. The assessment of skills, sharing feedback on team contributions, and building the right team environment are also key elements of successful teamwork. There are several instruments that have been developed for assessing the capabilities of individuals for working in teams. While some of these instruments rely on self-reporting, the team member evaluation form at the end of a project is a mechanism that is frequently used as a method of 360-degree feedback. It is important for these feedback exercises to be constructive. Often, the exercise leads to a feeling of victimization and recrimination. There are some popular team building exercises like the scavenger hunt and the egg drop exercise, these exercises add value for building cohesion in collocated teams.

Belbin's framework of the nine roles needed for effective teamwork is still relevant in the fast-paced XaaS context. The nine roles are divided into three categories: action-oriented roles, people-oriented roles and cerebral or thinking roles.[19] Belbin has identified the skills needed for each role, and a set of allowable weaknesses — the characteristics of individuals who have these skills, but exhibit some negative behaviours in enabling effective team performance. Just as in the IDEO 10-faced approach to skills, teams do not need individuals that span all skills, as each individual can contribute more than one role to the team. In the set of action-oriented skills, there are three sets of skills that are needed for effective teamwork. The first set of skills needed are those of shapers of the team — individuals with shaping skills drive tasks with a clear sense of what needs to be done. Shapers are dynamic, they are driven and enterprising, but they may have a pushy personality, and may provoke other team members. The second action-oriented role is the implementer, these individuals have similar skills to shapers. They get actions implemented, and their primary strengths are their discipline and efficiency. However, implementers may be rigid and inflexible in personality, leading to a low responsiveness to change. Finally, individuals with the completer-finisher skills are effective systems integrators who complete and integrate tasks and projects. The attributes of completer-finishers are that they are methodical, identify errors and stick to a deadline. These individuals may be prone to worry and prefer finishing tasks themselves. In the set of people-oriented roles, Belbin identified three personae: the coordinator, the team worker and the resource investigator. The coordinator typically performs the leadership role and manages the group member's interactions with each other. Individuals with coordinating skills

---

[19] Belbin, The Nine Belbin Team Roles, https://www.belbin.com/about/belbin-team-roles/, accessed September 5, 2020.

are typically pragmatic, confident and enable adherence to the goals of the team, along with making quick decisions. However, coordinators may not do their fair share of the tasks, rather, they focus on getting the best efforts out of others. The team worker helps in building personal relationships and a rapport between team members and facilitating a healthy working environment. They are usually empathetic, and avoid confrontation, though they may be indecisive under pressure. Finally, the resource investigator acts as the external liaison for the team. Individuals with these skills are well-connected with a wide network, and they enable the team to get external support. These individuals are gregarious and enthusiastic and add value in the early process, but they may lose interest when the team is focused on individual tasks. The last set of skills are cerebral skills — individuals with these skills are classified into the plant, monitor-evaluator and specialist roles. The plant is the ideator of the team and creates imaginative solutions to complex problems. The plant thinks out of the box and may have ideas that are difficult to implement. The monitor-evaluator is the ideal partner of the plant. Individuals with these skills are good at screening ideas and making decisions for moving forward. They are open, strategic and have good filtration skills, however, they are process-oriented and uninspiring. Finally, specialists have expert domain knowledge on certain fields, and can support teams in their area of specialization. Individuals with specialist skills are conscientious and motivated, but they are very focused on details and have a narrow skillset.

The Belbin set of roles in a team is indeed an effective starting point for composing teams that develop and deliver XaaS offerings. Teams that deliver solutions in the XaaS mode need creativity, effective collaboration and the ability of rapid implementation. Hence, Belbin's roles differentiation is aligned with XaaS team composition. In addition, XaaS teams also need to use technology effectively, especially when they are not collocated with each other. The use of applications like Slack, Microsoft Teams, Zoom and other collaboration applications, along with storage sharing like Dropbox and Google Drive, is de jure for globally distributed teams.[20]

---

[20] Karan, M. (2019). Slack and zoom have proven that the future of work is agile. *Forbes*, October 22, 2019, https://www.forbes.com/sites/karanmehandru/2019/10/22/

The team members need to be skilled in the use of collaboration technologies, including tools like CAD/CAM if the teams perform design activities. Many of these applications are often necessary for collocated teams as well, as these tools can share design updates for interdependent tasks in real time. In addition to technology interfacing, virtual teams must be actively managed to ensure their performance levels meet expectations. Beyond the use of technology for enhancing collaboration, another necessary component is the creation of a cohesive collaboration environment. The development of trust in the team is necessary and having face-to-face communication opportunities is an important enabler of trust. Extensive research on the topic of communication in virtual teams shows that technology-enhanced communication can augment face-to-face communication, but cannot replace it.[21] A lot of information exchange in innovative activities is tacit or implicit, and hallway communications convey more tacit information than purely formal exchanges that are supported by technology. Ideally, virtual teams should have some opportunities for face-to-face meetings at the start of the team effort (achievable if the team effort takes at least a few months). If the planned timeline for the team's delivery is very short, then a virtual meeting will suffice. Additional face-to-face meeting opportunities during the team's collaboration like monthly meetings, and an integration meeting, would be useful in sharing tacit knowledge. If meetings must be supported by technology, having a tighter control of the meeting is more important, as individuals may be joining the meeting from different time zones. Some obvious practices like sharing attendee names and agendas before the meeting, and displaying attendee names during the meeting, along with giving all individual members some airtime, go a long way in building trust. After virtual meetings, summarizing the decisions taken in the meeting along with the planned agenda for next steps is a good practice for deciding on the project plan going forward. Overall, virtual teams need more structure in interaction and dynamic planning of tasks. While agile teams are designed to offer

[21] Allen, T. J. (2007). Architecture and communication among product development engineers. *California Management Review*, 49(2), 23–41.

more flexibility, the lack of collocation implies that some degree of structure needs to be imposed on the interactions as the team's time together is constrained, and hence, valuable.

6.6 ROLE MOBILITY FOR XaaS ORGANIZATIONS

A number of firms (with offerings from both the productization mode and the XaaS mode) have a policy of rotating high potential senior managers through different functions, business units and locations.[22] While this policy is certainly laudable, it has its own set of caveats. When rotating employees, it is generally recommended that the employee experience one change at a time to be able to absorb the impact of that change.[23] For instance, if the manager is being rotated into a new country, it is advisable that s/he keeps their role in the same department and business unit in the new country. Second, the skills to be imbibed in the new role should be for a clearly defined goal. For instance, rotating functions helps develop cross-functional skills and for being able to perform multiple roles in a team, while rotating business units enables the manager to learn the ropes for a corporate general management role. Role mobility should have verifiable goals for each individual, and should be results focused, with a set of time-bound objectives. While it is important for the organization to be clear about the goals of role mobility, these goals should also be communicated clearly to the manager whose role is being rotated. A personalized approach to role mobility is indeed ideal. However, most organizations do not have the number of qualified HR personnel and leaders who can follow the individuals' learning closely. At the site level, self-organizing teams offer one solution, as individuals can take up assignments in

---

[22] Chau, T., Maurer, F., & Melnik, G. (2003). Knowledge sharing: Agile methods vs. tayloristic methods. In *WET ICE 2003. Proceedings. Twelfth IEEE International Workshops on Enabling Technologies: Infrastructure for Collaborative Enterprises*, IEEE, 2003, pp. 302–307.

[23] Nalbantian, H. R. & Guzzo, R. A. (2009). Making mobility matter. *Harvard Business Review*, 87(3), 76–84.

different teams to advance their own learning. But the number of learning opportunities within the individual's domain is limited. Within the younger demographic, there is an expectation that their careers will be managed in a personalized manner by the organization, while they focus on contributing their efforts to the team's objectives. It is important for organizations to enable smart mobility solutions internally that enable individuals to learn different roles to contribute to the organizational agility. These smart mobility solutions must cater to both individual and organizational objectives.

As the technology clockspeed gets shorter and customer preferences change rapidly, there may be a tendency for managers to be allocated to roles for much shorter periods of time. While the approach is required as managers desire faster learning curves and career development opportunities, this approach may be counter-productive at times.[24] If managers are rotated very quickly, they may not have sufficient time and information processing bandwidth to be able to learn the skills for the new role, and may not be able to contribute significantly. It is true that the learning curve is steepest towards the earlier part of any new assignment, however, a certain gestation period is needed for the assimilation of different information sets and for the processing of the information. Very rapid changes in roles affect the performance of the individual, and the performance of the organization suffers as a result. The recommended minimum time in the new role is dependent on the ability to make a contribution that can be judged clearly. This time can vary from a few weeks to a couple of years.

While the policy of rotating high-potential managers makes sense from the perspective of developing talent for XaaS roles, it is important not to limit role mobility to individuals who have been judged to have a higher performance than expected only. In the XaaS organization, all team members have important roles to fulfil, it would be beneficial to find if some individuals can contribute more to certain roles compared to other roles. In other words, in addition to rewarding talent and developing a learning orientation, role mobility also enables individuals to find the right

---

[24] Onyeka, N. (2020). Why talent mobility is important for the workforce. *HRSG*, April 1, 2020, https://resources.hrsg.ca/blog/why-talent-mobility-is-important-for-the-workforce, accessed September 20, 2020.

fit for their skills. Delivering XaaS offerings needs a higher versatility of skillsets, and role mobility can develop that versatility, as well as offer individuals multiple opportunities to contribute to different roles. Engendering creativity also has a greater need for team diversity. Individuals can often contribute significantly by performing roles that were not in their core set of skills earlier. Having a lack of in-depth knowledge can be useful in asking basic questions about processes and tasks that are typically not questioned by others who are accustomed to those roles and processes. The role mobility policies of Salesforce showcase one set of best practices in role mobility management, where individuals are advised to seek multiple learning opportunities for career development. The human resources team acts as a facilitator for individuals in enabling the desired role mobility opportunities for them.

6.7   THE SKILLS NEEDED OF XaaS LEADERS

Leaders of organizations offering their services in the XaaS mode need a different mindset and skillset compared to leaders who lead product-based organizations. The primary difference between the leadership needs of the two kinds of organizations is the degree of customer centricity: both kinds of firms need to consider the customer first. However, the leader of the product organization keeps the customer front and centre by understanding customer needs, segmenting them based on those needs, and designing products to closely match the needs of customer segments. Given the fixed costs of designing, developing and launching multiple stock-keeping units, the product variety is limited by default, the typical firm can only introduce a select number of new products. In contrast, with the XaaS approach of introducing offerings, understanding the needs of multiple customer journeys and experiences, and supporting and empowering employees to provide these experiences is key.[25] The leader needs a skillset to identify the direction of the organization, guide colleagues on the values to achieve this direction, and motivate employees to deliver a

---

[25]Van Dierendonck, D. (2011). Servant leadership: A review and synthesis. *Journal of Management*, 37(4), 1228–1261.

superior customer experience. The role of the leader in the XaaS organization is primarily to serve the employees' needs so that they have all the tools they need to have the optimal services portfolio at any point of time. Hence, for leading XaaS organizations, we believe that the leader's skill-set must closely align with the persona of the servant leader.

Robert Greenleaf coined the servant leader term 50 years ago, where he posited the different style of the servant leader compared to other styles of leadership.[26] Apart from the common skills of having a vision, awareness and foresight that are common to other leadership styles as well, the primary role of the servant leader is to serve employees within the organization. Servant leaders use persuasive power over authority and focus on employee support and empowerment. They focus on the values of the organization and on the well-being of others rather than self and develop and nurture people in the organization to contribute to its success. While the performance of the organization is important, the servant leader believes that ensuring the well-being of employees and the absorption of the right values will influence the organizational performance in the right direction. Hence, while servant leaders share their vision for the organization, they view the organization's ability to fulfil that vision and improve performance as a two-step outcome. Their own actions are oriented towards serving, developing and empowering employees; with the right values and tools, the employees achieve the desired outcomes. The power structure of such organizations is an inverted pyramid, where rather than the employees serving the leader, the leader's purpose is to serve the employees.[27] At the team level, the servant leader focuses on enabling team members to achieve their full potential, and creating an environment where every member is motivated to do his or her best for the team's objectives. Delivering value consistently to the customer needs a high degree of individual and team creativity, and the servant leader enables team members to have the freedom to express that creativity. The higher

---

[26] Greenleaf, R. K. (1998). *The Power of Servant-Leadership: Essays.* Berrett-Koehler Publishers, Oakland, California.

[27] Tyler, H. (2018). Servant leadership and the inverted pyramid. *Trig*, May 12, 2018, https://www.trig.com/tangents/leadership-and-the-inverted-pyramid, accessed September 20, 2020.

degree of uncertainty in customer expectations for typical XaaS offerings makes the servant leadership style more appropriate. In a stable environment, a structured and optimized plan must be adhered to, and directional leadership is more suitable to ensure the adherence of employees to the plan. In contrast, in highly uncertain environments with changing preferences, supporting technologies and market conditions like competition, the servant leadership style enables a higher degree of flexibility for the organization. Teams function with a higher degree of autonomy and have a higher degree of trust in the leadership when working with servant leaders. They do not need to focus on their own needs and growth potential if that trust has been established, as they understand that the leader will safeguard their own individual interests.

Marc Benioff has been credited extensively in the software industry as a leader who possesses the servant leadership style.[28] At the Dreamforce conferences, Benioff shared Salesforce's product updates, as well as internal management policy initiatives, along with the goals of these initiatives. He was one of the first global business leaders to act to improve gender-based pay inequity, and he introduced the role of the Chief Equality Officer at Salesforce.[29] The role of the Chief Equality Officer at Salesforce is to create an inclusive recruiting policy, an environment conducive to the participation of diverse communities, and the ethical and humane use of technology to drive social change. The value of equality is embedded in many of Salesforce's other management initiatives as well, including the pay parity policy for similar roles for all types of diverse communities. For employee development, Salesforce has a policy of extensive rotation for job learning, and a culture of entrepreneurship that is ingrained in all employees. Compared to the industry's average figures, a larger number of leaders have emerged as successful entrepreneurs after leaving Salesforce, and they credit the learning and development that they

---

[28] Graham, W. (2018). 4 Leadership Strategies Marc Benioff Swears By, Inc., June 18, 2018, https://www.inc.com/graham-winfrey/marc-benioff-salesforce-ceo-leadership-lessons-facebook.html, accessed September 20, 2020.

[29] Abhinav, M. Salesforce appoints Tony Prophet as first Chief Equality Officer, *Techseen*, https://techseen.com/tony-prophet-chief-equality-officer-salesforce/, accessed September 20, 2020.

received at Salesforce for their success. Salesforce also has a policy of new recruits having an orientation at the location that they work in, followed by doing volunteer work on the first day they join Salesforce. This policy has been enacted to align themselves with the service mindset of the firm. The firm's stated mission is about building trust with employees and customers, as it believes that the eventual performance targets will be achieved if trust exists in all stakeholders.

Leaders also need requisite skills to shift the organization's mindset from the productization to the XaaS mode at the outset of the transformation when delivering XaaS offerings. Changing the organization from a productization mode to the XaaS mode has been introduced in Chapter 5 with the "crawl, walk, run, fly" sequence of incremental changes to be made in the organization. While phased change is indeed more structured and feasible for larger organizations, XaaS leaders need to use a number of change management skills to manage the impact of change in organizational mindset effectively.[30] Of all the skills recommended in change management playbooks, probably, none is more popular and effective than the ability to identify the "low-hanging fruit" as the first candidate for implementing the change. Leaders know the importance of starting with a quick win for getting buy-in from different constituents, and the ability to learn the potential pitfalls from the change within a controlled environment. Project managers are familiar with the superiority of the well-executed lower scope plan over the badly executed ambitious plan. The principle of first picking the low-hanging fruit is in consonance with the phased approach to change, it helps in creating and maintaining organizational momentum for the set of changes.

While picking the low-hanging fruit is effective in initiating the implementation of change, an important skill at the outset of the move to the XaaS mode is the ability to tell the story of why the change is needed. There can be several ways for sharing the driver for making the change and motivating the organization. Leaders can point to the rapid change of technology and the need to be more agile to keep ahead of the curve. The

---

[30] Adrian, H., Cloud First Strategy: How do you manage change in XaaS?, https://adrianhollister.com/2015/08/24/how-to-manage-change-in-an-xaas-it-model/, accessed September 20, 2020.

positive way of telling the story would be the value that the organization can add to the customer by moving to the XaaS mode of offering. While the phenomenon of human resistance to change is well known, the need to add value to the primary stakeholders of the organization acts as a powerful motivating tool. The research finds that using added value for the customer is one of the best storytelling approaches for the motivation for change. Employees are more willing to accept change when it is customer-driven, as they understand the alignment between the need for customer value and their own interests. Ideally, if the storytelling can be supported by data about customer preferences or a pilot project, that would increase the trust internally about the need for change. The incentives for the change must be aligned as well. While leaders often motivate employees well for the initial buy-in, they do not focus as much on the alignment of employee incentives with the change. Employees fear change for good reasons: they do not know the outcome for their own individual interests at the end of the change. To move to the XaaS mode of offering, there is a need to remove middle management layers to flatten the organization and make decision-making agile. If the middle management layers are not clear about the outcome for them at the end of the change process, they can obstruct and derail the change by not participating in the efforts at best, or may actively seek to insert a spanner in the works at worst. The leaders must plan for the impact of the change and share the outcomes for individuals at the end of the change process. If certain individuals must be made redundant, it is better to do so earlier in the process rather than later. However, such actions can cause demoralization in the rest of the organization. To retain people with domain expertise and the right degree of personal flexibility, leaders must share their vision for individuals at the end of the change process and equip them with the skills needed to make the shift.

Finally, the leaders should be ready for absorbing the impact of the change in the organization resulting from the move to the XaaS mode. The hockey stick effect is a well-known effect in change management. All changes cause disruption within the organization. While changes that were ill-conceived to begin with will lead to a detrimental effect on performance in the short term and in the longer term, changes that are for the better also lead to short-term degradation in performance. Any change needs some time for the system to absorb the impact of the change, learn the tools for facilitating the change, and reorganize processes to work effectively after the change. During the transition learning period, the performance of the system dips, as people learn new tools and processes are redesigned and retooled. After the impact of the change has been internalized, the system's performance picks up again, and the organization is ready to work in the new paradigm. This short-term dip followed by the long-term improvement in performance is known as the hockey stick effect in change management. Leaders should communicate that the change may not yield immediate results always (this is why picking the low-hanging fruit early is important for creating some trust), and the organization will stay on the path for the long haul.

6.8 RELATING PEOPLE SKILLS TO ORGANIZATIONAL CULTURE

How do the people skills recommended for employees and leaders of XaaS organizations combine to enable an organizational culture aligned to the nature of XaaS offerings? The organizational culture can be regarded as the norms guiding the behaviour of different entities in the organization and is a characteristic of the organization's DNA. Schein proposed an organizational culture model with three distinct layers from an external observer's viewpoint.[31] At the top layer, Schein's model starts with the most visible sign of the organization to the external observer. This layer is referred to as the artifacts layer, and includes such visible signs as the organization chart, the organizational structure, process maps, and behavioural patterns such as customs and rituals. The vision and mission statements, physical infrastructure of the organization, and dressing and behavioural codes are also visible elements of organizational culture. Hence, the existence of flat organizations with a few middle management layers, a relatively open office space, vision and mission statements that highlight customer centricity are some examples of the expected artifacts

---

[31] Schein, E. H. (1990). Organizational culture. *American Psychological Association*, 45(2), 109.

of XaaS organizations. The ability to use changing technologies to deliver new services to satisfy dynamic customer preferences would also be a part of the artifacts. The rituals of the organization are exemplified by the stories that internal people communicate, for example, Salesforce employees communicate the open environment and the freedom to experiment as some of their model behaviours. The next element of the organizational culture is the set of values that are stated by members as part of the DNA of their organization. The values should be shared across different members of the organization, it may often be the case that senior leaders espouse one set of values as their shared values. However, other organizational members would state a different set of values, the common set of values that would be espoused by most members would be a part of the second layer. Again, based on the servant leadership example of Salesforce, the values of empowerment, equality and diversity would be highly rated internally at XaaS organizations. The third level of the organizational culture is the subconscious element of the firm, which Schein called the tacit assumptions of the firm's organizational culture. Organizational members find these elements to be hard to identify and clearly articulate, but several behaviours are motivated by these subconscious elements. The differences between the three layers of the organizational culture can explain the misalignment of actual behaviours with professed values. For example, while collaboration and accountability may be two professed values of the organization, members may be unwilling to help each other on tasks, as they believe that the primary person assigned the task should perform it as s/he was accountable for the task. A clearly aligned organizational culture would be easy for new employees to imbibe, assimilate and adjust their behaviours to. On the other hand, a culture that was misaligned at different levels would require a significant amount of time to internalize for new members, increasing the time to be meaningfully productive for them.

Based on the three layers of organizational culture, changing the firm's culture is obviously a daunting task as it needs changes to be made at many different levels. While changing the organization's visible aspects of culture is easier (physical elements are tangible, changes can be designed, measured and monitored), changing the subconscious elements of the culture is harder. The subconscious cultural aspects of the organization outlive people, processes, products and services, and are highly resistant to change. Changing the artifacts can indeed be the first step in making the organization change its culture in the desired direction. For instance, when a firm moves from the productization model to the XaaS mode, it needs to change its culture from understanding customer needs during R&D to a culture where it has a long-term relationship with the customer, and is continuously responsive to customer needs.[32] Rather than having a culture of getting the product's design right before the launch, the firm needs to have a culture that encourages trial and error, and learning how to improve solutions based on the trials.

Schein believed that organizations develop cultures as a function of external as well as internal forces. The external forces create the need for adaptation of the organizational culture, and the internal forces create the need for the right amount of integration of different components of the organization. The skilling of different needs at adequate levels is particularly important for teams developing XaaS solutions, owing to the mixed need of external adaptation and internal integration. For example, a XaaS team with several individuals with coordination skills, and not enough members with action-oriented skills, will create an environment of resentment at the tacit level. The few action-oriented members will feel that they are performing most of the tasks, while the coordinators are not pulling their weight in the team. As another example, the team's objective may be to create a relatively incremental innovation with mostly standardized components. The presence of several individuals with creative skills and not many individuals with the ability to perform standardized tasks creates a mismatch of roles with available skills, leading to misalignment between the first two and the third layers. Matching the staffing needs of the organization to the market requirements and the solutions profiles with the

---

[32] Bruce, S. 2020). Everything-as-a-service (XaaS) has disrupted the traditional IT procurement model, opening the doors to more revenue streams for original equipment manufacturers (OEMs). *Technative*, October 5, 2020, https://technative.io/how-oems-can-rethink-their-culture-and-skill-sets-to-achieve-high-impact-xaas/, accessed September 20, 2020.

team's skillsets is an important factor in creating a sustainable and healthy organizational culture.

When Adobe was making a shift from the productization model to the XaaS mode about a decade ago, it had to make a conscious effort to incorporate a service culture into the organization. To create an integrated culture with the customer as part of the organizational DNA, Adobe combined the customer experience team, which focused on customer and technical support, with the human resources team.[33] The human resources team was initially known as the employee experience team. After the combination, the group was known as the customer and employee experience group. Adobe made this conscious change to communicate internally that it was as focused on the customer experience with the new as a service offering mode as it was on employee experience. When they made this shift, Adobe had their human resources team visit customer support centres and listen in on customer calls. The content of the calls enabled the HR team to understand customer pain points better and impress the need for more responsive offerings on the rest of the organization. Several callers also expressed satisfaction with the firm's offerings. Since Adobe sold their products previously through channel partners in the productization mode, there was a lack of relationship building and, consequently, a lack of empathy for the customer. Combining the customer support and employee teams started the process of customer centricity at Adobe, with the newly forged relationships enabling a more direct integration of customer needs awareness in Adobe's culture. Integrating customer feedback through the installation of small call centres at the development sites enabled all employees to be able to interact with customers. Customer issues were also shared internally through knowledge sharing systems on the firm's Intranet sites. Further, designers interacted with other employees on new products and services in meetings called "experience-athons", where employees could test new products as customers and share their feedback with the designers. In addition to the policies and measures for better customer integration, incentives were provided to employees for

---

[33] Will, B. (2018). Melding the employee/customer experiences at adobe. *Human Resource Executive*, July 30, 2018, https://hrexecutive.com/how-to-achieve-true-employee-satisfaction-like-adobe/, accessed September 20, 2020.

participating in customer experience improvement programs. The changes resulted in more engaged employees, as the satisfaction from hearing about positive experiences from the customer directly created a more aligned incentive for employees.

6.9 SUMMARY

To deliver consistently successful XaaS offerings, providers need to have the requisite skillsets within individual employees, within teams and within leaders. At the individual level, employees delivering XaaS offerings need a mix of creative skills, skills for the standardization of tasks, and the ability to execute systems thinking to develop holistic solutions. At the personal level, they need to have the ability to switch roles in an agile fashion.

While creative skills are acquired genetically, they can also be nurtured. The ability to think creatively is a function of the divergent thinking capability of individuals. Divergent thinking is defined as the individual's ability to ideate along different chains of thought to generate multiple ideas. Divergent thinking is usually negatively correlated with age, and positively correlated with risk-seeking profiles. Divergent thinking can be augmented by developing the skills of associativity, questioning, observation, experimentation and networking. Creative skills can be developed and assessed by many tools, e.g., the Thirty Circles challenge. At the level of the team, a diverse set of creative skills needs to be embodied in the different individuals of the team, so that the team can execute the XaaS offering successfully. These skills are divided into three classes: learning roles, organizing roles and building roles. Each of these three categories needs a different set of skills, and teams need individuals to have a combination of these kinds of skills.

In addition to creative skills, teams executing XaaS offerings also need individuals who have the skills to standardize tasks, as the ability to design standardized modules to deliver creative solutions enables XaaS providers to scale effectively. The standardization of tasks needs individuals who can execute the six-sigma methodology of continuous improvement. In each cycle, the team eliminates sources of variability and non-value-added activities by following the DMAIC approach. The DMAIC approach (define, measure, analyze, improve, control) is the building block of the continuous improvement cycle for standardizing tasks. Software processes can be standardized using a similar approach known as the IDEAL cycle (Initiate, Diagnose, Establish, Act, Learn). There are several exercises like the paper airplane game that can be used to enhance the skillset for the standardization of tasks. Finally, the integration of different modules and the ability to assess the performance of integrated systems needs a set of systems thinking skills for XaaS teams. The ability to analyze the interdependence of component systems enables XaaS teams to design the system holistically. The tool needed for systems thinking is simulation; it enables the team to identify system parts that need to be designed more robustly. Systems thinking skills can be augmented with games like the marshmallow exercise. At the individual level, individuals must be able to perform multiple roles. They should be able to define their goals for learning from each role clearly, personalize the goals for themselves, and should have sufficient time to learn their roles. Teams delivering XaaS solutions also need skills to be able to collaborate effectively. The Belbin nine-role framework with action-oriented, people-oriented and thinking or cerebral skills need to be embodied within the individuals of the team.

The leader of the XaaS organization should have the requisite skills for a style of leadership known as servant leadership. XaaS organizations must be highly agile and customer centric. Hence, rather than being directive, the leader of the XaaS organization should be able to guide his or her colleagues towards the goals of the organization. The leader should serve their needs in being able to acquire capabilities and tools to execute on serving customer needs in an agile fashion. The leader should also have change management skills in the transformation of the organization to providing XaaS solutions. Finally, the people within the XaaS organization should be able to align themselves to the artifacts, set of values and the tacit elements of the organization to create a coherent organizational culture.

Chapter 7

Analysis of XaaS Models
for Product Assets

The offering of the use of product assets in the XaaS mode has developed over the years to encompass the use of various products. The use of products in the as-a-service mode is an emerging niche that enables customers to use the product assets in a flexible use mode. It also has the corresponding benefits of outsourcing servicing and other peripheral services to the provider, giving customers the option of one-stop shopping. The origins of using the XaaS mode for product offerings began with time-sharing and rental systems in recent times and has now grown to the providing of sharing systems with an asset-light model. In this chapter, we will showcase some examples of using the XaaS mode of offering product assets, which do not involve core IT assets (examples in the IT domain like IaaS and SaaS will be showcased in Chapter 8). The case studies come from diverse industries such as battery-as-a-service (Epiroc and NIO), PCs-as-a-service (Dell), aircraft engines-as-a-service (Rolls-Royce), equipment-as-a-service (TAFE), homes-as-a-service (Ziroom) and design-as-a-service (ARM Holdings). We will analyze these product offerings in the XaaS domain by using the BROAD FENCES model, and then summarize the analysis of each case study using the XaaS Staircase.

7.1 BATTERY-AS-A-SERVICE (EPIROC AND NIO)

Epiroc, a manufacturer of materials for railroad construction and operation, was founded in 1873 in Stockholm (as a division of Atlas). In 2018, Epiroc was separated from its parent, Atlas Copco, and was listed as a standalone firm. Epiroc specialized in the development, manufacturing and marketing of drilling and mining equipment for use in surface as well as underground mining. For its operations supporting mining businesses, Epiroc launched electric vehicles in 2016, which could run on efficient batteries, also built by the company. Epiroc aimed to offer a complete fleet of battery-operated electric equipment versions for underground mining equipment by 2025.[1]

Electric vehicles are an alternative to diesel-powered machines and provide several advantages in the mining sector. The use of batteries eliminates emissions and improves the working environment for operating personnel. Battery-operated machines also boost productivity and result in enhanced safety in addition to reducing emissions. An additional advantage is that these machines can lower total cost of operations, because of the elimination of fuel costs and the implementation of costly ventilation systems to handle emissions. Battery-powered electric vehicles also require less service and maintenance; however, the greatest advantage they offer is that they minimize the environmental footprint. Battery-powered electric vehicles also provide greater efficiency and can improve on-ramp haulage productivity by almost 10%. The electric hydraulic functions of the equipment can provide on-demand power using batteries — without dirty air emissions, excessive heat, or noise that diesel-run machines emitted. Battery-powered equipment also reduce ventilation needs, cooling requirements and decreased risk of fire associated with diesel and heat. Batteries also allow for more efficient energy consumption and improved operations at high altitudes.

---

[1] Epiroc, About Epiroc, History, https://www.epirocgroup.com/en/about-epiroc/ history#:~:text=History%20milestones,a%20stand%2Dalone%20listed%20company, accessed September 30, 2020.

However, batteries used for machines also have a significant number of disadvantages. Batteries used for mining vehicles are bulky and cumbersome and are hard to transfer from one machine to another. For example, a mine truck battery weighs 42 metric tonnes. It also requires regular servicing to ensure smooth operation. From the perspective of mining operators, one of the biggest disadvantages is the rapid degradation of battery life from frequent charging and infrequent servicing. Moreover, battery-operated electric machines have almost double the manufacturing cost of comparable diesel models. To solve these problems, Epiroc offered a solution which could enable miners to avail of the usage of electric mining equipment without the initial high cost and inconvenience of training their teams to service, maintain and transfer bulky batteries. When Epiroc introduced batteries-as-a-service (BaaS) in 2018, it enabled the initial capital investments on electric equipment to be significantly reduced. The operational costs of battery-operated machines were lower than those of comparable diesel-operated machines, but companies are wary of the high capital costs. Offering the BaaS mode helped remove the inhibitions of clients imposed by capital costs, by reducing the price of the machines owing to the cost of the battery not being included in the initial capital outlay.[2]

The offering of the BaaS mode also mitigated the risks of owning batteries while extending the benefits of electrical power to customers. With the BaaS mode, Epiroc took over the entire responsibility of maintaining the batteries, including certification, maintenance, and technology upgrades. The batteries also had the flexibility of being used for equipment that were not built by Epiroc as well. Epiroc has also introduced the Internet of Things (IoT) technology in its machines which allows the firm to monitor the performance of the products offsite. Using IoT, the BaaS team can keep track of the battery performance and replace batteries when required. The service team also ensures that a battery has the required capacity for a selected application. When an equipment sale was made, clients were provided with a battery plan, which helped them pay only for

---

[2]Epiroc, Mining Equipment, Newsroom, Epiroc charges forward with Batteries as a Service, July 14, 2020, https://www.epiroc.com/en-jo/newsroom/2020/epiroc-charges-forward-with-batteries-as-a-service, accessed September 30, 2020.

the service provided, making running costs for the machines predictable. The battery plan was defined based on the operation needs of the customer. To create a battery plan that suited the needs of operation, Epiroc worked directly with the customer to create a custom plan. Battery lifespan was guaranteed, and the battery status was monitored to enable predictive maintenance with reduced downtime. If a customer wanted to increase or decrease their capacity, the plan could be adjusted, and the service was tailored accordingly. With BaaS, the functionality effectiveness of the batteries was always guaranteed.[3]

The BaaS model was also tied to Epiroc's ongoing sustainability commitment, wherein the company would remove old batteries from a mining site and replace them with new battery packs. A circular business model approach was used for the offering, implying that Epiroc would have cost savings from being able to use durable parts discarded batteries. The older batteries were used for secondary applications and then recycled. Additionally, the recycling process also ensured that clients would always have batteries based on the latest technology for greater efficiency. The objective of the BaaS mode was to allow smaller mining houses avail the benefits of using electric equipment and gain a larger market share for Epiroc. Bigger mining houses have the financial means to buy all products, but for the smaller and mid-sized customers, the investment could be a challenge. Reducing the cost of the equipment by removing the battery costs could enable such companies to make the capital expenditure more readily.

In the customer electric vehicle (EV) domain, NIO introduced the offering of its EVs with the battery provided as a service, rather than as an integrated feature of its vehicle offering. Unlike fuel energy systems for fossil fuel driven cars, the battery in the electric vehicle is a modular component. The electric batteries can be changed from one vehicle to another, and hence, the charging of the battery can be done offline. When the next generation of batteries is introduced, if the core elements of the design like battery dimensions and interfaces are kept constant, then customers can just upgrade to the next generation by adopting the battery-as-a-service mode, along with an annual subscription, or pay-per-use mode. NIO

---

[3] Ibid.

proposed to lower the price of the battery by 70,000 RMB if customers choose the BaaS offering, with monthly subscription prices starting from 980 RMB for a 70kWh pack. Additionally, NIO also offered the Worry-Free service plan for a monthly guarantee fee of 80 RMB. The BaaS was offered by Weineng Battery Asset Company, which was a joint venture of NIO with other partners. The coverage of the BaaS scheme was offered on a nationwide scheme in China with a total of 143 service centres, where customers could just drive up to the service centre, replace their older batteries with charged packs and drive away. Regulatory authorities in China supported the BaaS mode by offering subsidies on EVs priced over 300,000 RMB if they had battery exchanging ability.[4]

7.1.1 Batteries-as-a-Service (BaaS) Analysis

Feasibility: The budget impact factor for the offering in the BaaS mode is genuinely salient, as machinery and vehicles based on batteries are indeed more expensive compared to machinery and vehicles that operate on fossil fuels. Since the capital outlay for electric machines is higher, any reduction in cost from the use of the as-a-service mode can significantly impact the adoption decision by the customer. The BaaS mode can be complemented by offering the entire machine or the vehicle in the as-a-service mode. If the entire machine or vehicle is offered in the XaaS mode, then the capital outlay is significantly lower. However, some customers may prefer buying the machine or the vehicle up front, and use only the BaaS mode, as the TCO from the direct acquisition of the underlying asset may be lower. In such instances, offering only the battery in the as-a-service mode may still have a significant impact on the customer's adoption decision. The initial cost of the battery is a high component of the overall product cost for electric machines and vehicles. For instance, NIO sells EVs for a price range of a few hundred thousand RMB. At this pricing level, offering the battery in the as-a-service mode reduces the initial capital outlay by 70,000 RMB or higher, leading to a reduction of about 25% of the initial capital outlay. Second, one of the characteristics of

---

[4]Nio, Nio Launches Battery as a Service, News, August 20, 2020, https://www.nio.com/news/nio-launches-battery-service, accessed September 30, 2020.

rechargeable batteries is the correlation of the battery lifetime with the right amount of maintenance, the number of times the battery is charged, and the extent to which it is charged. If batteries are always charged to the full capacity, then the battery lifetime is lower. The battery lifetime is enhanced by charging it to close to full capacity, but not completely to full capacity. If the provider charges the battery or supervises the battery operations, then the provider can manage the servicing and charging of the battery pack, leading to an enhanced lifetime.

From the risk perspective, the customer is exposed to the battery lifetime, quality and reliability risks if s/he undertakes the servicing of the battery. By transferring the ownership of the battery to the provider, the customer has a lower risk from the quality and lifetime issues of the battery, and the usage risk. If the battery is offered with the pay-per-use mode of pricing, then the customer typically pays depending on the number of times the battery needs to be charged. If the battery is offered using the subscription mode as is the case with Epiroc and NIO's offerings, the customer does not have the risk of overestimating or underestimating payments, as the payments will be based on a predictable scale. While there is no capacity risk in terms of the number of vehicles needed for Epiroc's customers, and NIO's customers will use only one battery pack at a time, the risk of overrunning the budget is zero for the customers of both firms. The provider maintains and services the batteries, hence, there is no lead time of acquisition in the BaaS mode. The potential obsolescence of technology and the upgrading of battery technology are compatible with the BaaS mode, as the provider can switch the batteries to the technology of the next generation when they become available seamlessly. The use of IoT technology by Epiroc is also beneficial to the customer, as maintenance issues can be flagged, and preventive maintenance can be conducted on an as-needed basis. For agility, Epiroc and NIO can use data analytics from the customer's usage of their batteries to provide better solutions to the customer in an agile manner. For instance, if NIO's customers are using batteries with a smaller capacity and they need to charge the batteries frequently, or swap them frequently, NIO can suggest that customers use batteries with a higher capacity based on their usage data. This will reduce the range anxiety of the customer, i.e., the anxiety of running out of battery charge on a long trip. While batteries are simple components that provide only one solution (energy) and are modular so that bundling does not have any additional utility, providers can enable customers to acquire the right battery based on their usage data.

Profitability: The deal transaction costs are non-negative for the customer in the BaaS mode, but they can be controlled as the batteries are replaced by the provider when the battery lifetime is over. NIO's customers have to go to the nearest customer service centre (there are 143 service centres in China currently) to replace their batteries. As NIO's sales increase and more customers enter NIO's BaaS base, NIO will have an incentive to expand their service centre network, leading to lower deal transaction costs. Hence, for services like the BaaS, the deal transaction costs improve with economies of scale. Epiroc's customers will have their batteries replaced on-site, leading to zero deal transaction costs. High-frequency usage customers will find NIO's subscription model suitable for their needs, as they typically have higher degradation of battery life owing to driving their EVs for longer distances. The ability to swap their batteries when needed gives them the ability to drive for longer distances and have the safety net of the replaced battery at the end of life. Infrequent drivers of the EVs may not find NIO's offering attractive, NIO may consider introducing a pay-per-swap scheme for infrequent buyers at a later stage. Epiroc's customers pay based on their usage of the service (pay-per-use), so Epiroc has the ability to extract customer utility more efficiently by discriminating on the frequency of usage dimension. Since the capital outlay effect is more pronounced for small and medium firms, Epiroc's customers who are large mining firms may likely utilize the BaaS option only, leading to a graded payment schedule for Epiroc from such customers. Smaller customers may adopt the entire machine or vehicle as a service, Epiroc has to price its offerings carefully for such customers to ensure its profitability. The expected utility-per-use will be typically correlated with the frequency of usage for the larger customers of Epiroc, and for NIO's customer base, and the expected utility-per-use is stable over time. Epiroc is pricing its services with the pay-per-use model. Given that large customers are B2B customers with a long relationship, Epiroc does not need to introduce a subscription model that will lead to a higher surplus for such customers. NIO can however introduce a pay-per-swap model of pricing for customers with a high expected utility-per-use, but low usage frequency. Given that pricing needs to be profitable, the pay-per-service payment model of Epiroc and the subscription price of NIO (payback period of six years for NIO with a price reduction of 70,000 RMB and 980 monthly subscription charge) need to result in profitability for both firms.

Growth: The analysis of competition is important for both providers. Since Epiroc operates in a B2B environment for niche customers (mining opera-tors) with specific solutions and uses battery technology, it has a niche compared to most other machinery providers in the mining sector who use fossil fuel-based solutions. On the other hand, NIO operates in a competi-tive market with Tesla and BYD being the market leaders. Since custom-ers choose the vehicle first and then the battery offering mode, the BaaS offering of NIO operates in a niche environment. However, there is an opportunity for the EV manufacturers to help develop the EV market by creating a shared BaaS offering. Why did petrol and diesel cars grow to be dominant the world over? The associated infrastructure like the highway network, the global pump facility network that can be used by customers of all manufacturers were key in developing the automotive ecosystem. If the EV manufacturers could have a common battery architecture, then potentially, all battery swapping stations of different manufacturers could recharge batteries of competitors as well, leading to economies of scale. The battery technology of individual manufacturers could still be differen-tiated, so that the stations could only swap like-for-like batteries based on the manufacturer. This collaboration of EV manufacturers and the joint adoption of the BaaS model could help lower the barriers to entry for EVs as the dominant mode of vehicular transportation. Batteries are typically standalone modules, so the ability to offer complementary services for manufacturers like Epiroc and NIO is minimal, however, they can still offer servicing and technology solutions. The benefits of economies of scale are huge for NIO, as they can add more service stations with a higher degree of adoption, and both firms benefit from circular economy advan-tages from economies of scale. The ability to offer solutions is based on the need for market mediators: while Epiroc has a direct relationship with the customer, NIO decided to set up a joint venture with other players like

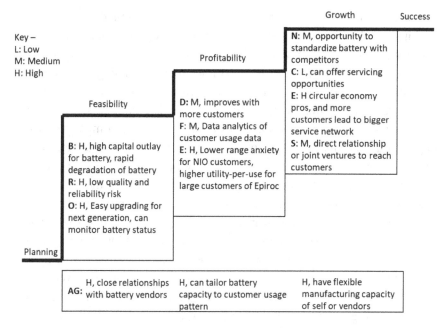

Figure 7.1: XaaS Staircase for Batteries-as-a-Service

CATL, a battery manufacturer, for their BaaS offering. Epiroc can indeed use relationship marketing for offering targeted services, while NIO has to offer the BaaS to its customers when they acquire the EV.

The BROAD FENCES analysis and the XaaS staircase (Figure 7.1) of the batteries-as-a-service mode reveal that the services have a high value for customers. The only challenge for the BaaS offering is the lack of bundling opportunities of services for complementarity owing to the modular nature of batteries. The BaaS model offers several positives for customers, and if the provider can design a profitable model, then the model can be expected to grow reasonably well, and add value to the core product that the battery provides energy for.

7.2 PCS-AS-A-SERVICE (DELL)

Dell is indeed a well-known organization and traces its origins to being an assembler of personal computers built from stock components. Its founder, Michael Dell, was the youngest CEO of a Fortune 500 company, and it used the direct sales channel instead of selling to individuals and households due to very low profit margins. However, by 1996, its Internet site began to gain traction in the customer market, leading to a boom in the sale of Dell computers. Customers were willing to pay a premium to buy powerful computers with multiple features that required less technical support and that were customized to their needs. The company quickly captured a high market share to become the largest PC manufacturer. A part of its success was attributed to its low operating costs compared to competitors and its high-quality products. However, as the PC market matured and competitors began improving their manufacturing operations, Dell's price differentiation weakened, and sales started to dwindle. The company's obsession with direct sales did not help much either, as the percentage of online buyers saturated. Dell's revenue growth was muted at the turn of the millennium, and it began looking for new avenues to boost its business. Subsequently, the firm expanded into non-PC segments such as storage, services and servers, which provided some additional revenue sources. In 2017, Dell launched its PC-as-a-Service (PCaaS) solution which combined client devices, software and deployment services along with security and support services for a monthly subscription price. The objective of the PCaaS offering was to reduce the cost of managing hardware for a PC's lifecycle, free up IT resources and allow them to focus on more value-added activities and projects.[5]

The approach to PC lifecycle management in most organizations was manually intensive with very little leeway for employees to choose a device of their choice. Procurement of PCs was mostly done by procurement departments which worked in silos with little communication with other departments (like IT management and application deployment and IT asset recovery and retirement) involved in the lifecycle. The amount of time that IT departments in organizations spent on allocating PC's to staff, maintaining and upgrading the devices and eventually retiring devices was substantial and involved a complex web of decision-making which did not drive much value. Moreover, employees often did not get a device that

---

[5] Britannica, The Editors of Encyclopaedia. "Dell Inc." *Encyclopedia Britannica*, May11, 2020, https://www.britannica.com/topic/Dell-Inc, accessed September 30, 2020.

was well-suited to their job function, as the process suffered from a one-size-fits all approach, that did not take individual employee needs into consideration. To alleviate these problems, the Dell PCaaS solution had a wide target segment consisting of small businesses and large and medium enterprises. The solution included Dell's latest PC technology, lifecycle services like deployment, support and asset return and exclusive Dell tools to troubleshoot and resolve system issues quickly and efficiently. The solution was packaged for a subscription fee that enabled client firms to predict costs of device deployment for employees and track total costs in a periodical manner.

The packages were offered to suit different client needs and allowed clients to tailor the technology that they needed to implement for their orders, depending on individual employee needs and requirements. Employees could choose to pick powerful workstations or ultra-light laptops, large monitors or other accessories. All business packages came with the Dell Client Command Suite, which was enabled to manage client devices. The packages were bundled for small businesses and larger enterprises separately. The package for small businesses catered to organizations needing less than three hundred units, and larger enterprise packages were offered to businesses needing more than three hundred units. The solutions included fully customizable laptops, desktops and workstations, factory installed software options, service support, asset recovery and optional deployment and financing options for PCs. Financing options were flexible and offered for a 3 or 4-year term with the option to extend or shorten or upgrade mid-term. Companies could further enhance their packages by choosing to supplement them with latest security software protection to secure the devices. This option included software options from the Dell Technologies Security Software Portfolio as well as VMware Workspace One.

A suite of deployment services, which came along with the PCaaS subscription, allowed firms to deploy PCs in a faster and more efficient manner. Fully configured systems could be used right out of the box. For those firms that preferred on-site installation, Dell also provided the option of a client installation service, for a single installation project of 25 systems or less. Service support for devices was provided through a range of options, again creating flexibility for the client firm to choose the kind of services they want for the devices provided. Support services were automated to detect issues in the devices and quickly resolve them to prevent further issues. The service support was further enhanced through a 24×7 expert hardware and software support service, and a next-business-day on-site service support for coverage of accidents. Asset recovery in most organizations was the process of taking back a device from an employee once the stipulated time of giving the device to an employee was completed, and he/she was due for getting a new device. Through the PCaaS offering, Dell helped organizations manage their asset recovery, arrange pickup, sanitize the data and transition to a new technology. For large orders, Dell also offered additional incentives. For an order that exceeded 300 systems, the service appointed a Services Delivery Manager (SDM) who would act as the single point of contact for the client firm throughout the PC lifecycle. The SDM facilitated smooth deployment and enhanced support and management throughout the asset lifecycle, further offloading the planning headache on part of the client firm's IT management team. The PCaaS or the device-as-a-service (DaaS) market is highly competitive, with several other firms having entered the arena, including firms like HP, Avaya, Bizbang and Lenovo. CompuCom offered the DaaS suite of services for Apple devices. The global PCaaS market is expected to grow at a 54.9% CAGR from 2019 to 2024. North America is anticipated to be the early adopter, followed by the European and Asia-Pacific regions.[6]

7.2.1 PC-as-a-Service (PCaaS) Analysis

Feasibility: There is a one-to-one correspondence of the need for PCs and the number of white-collar employees at most organizations, with some organizations providing two devices (a desktop and a laptop) for more senior employees. One of the biggest benefits of the PCaaS offering is that

---

[6]GlobeNewswire, PC-as-a-Service (PCaaS) Market Report 2019: World Market to Register a CAGR of 54.9%, Research and Markets, November 15, 2019, https://www.globenewswire.com/news-release/2019/11/15/1947885/0/en/PC-as-a-Service-PCaaS-Market-Report-2019-World-Market-to-Register-a-CAGR-of-54-9.html, accessed October 2, 2020.

the entire organization will adopt the provider's devices, hence, the signing of one PCaaS contract guarantees the usage of a large number of devices. However, this feature of the PCaaS offering is also detrimental. For example, some employees may prefer Apple's devices, and the employer may not get the benefits of the PCaaS offering if they have to retain some internal staff for managing device procurement and deployment for such employees. From the client's perspective, the client will need to estimate the TCO of the two approaches (procuring PCs for its employees itself, versus using a PCaaS provider). From the client's perspective, the budget impact of the PCaaS suite of offerings may not be high, as PCs typically need replacement at most organizations with a clock speed of one and a half years to four years, depending on the nature of the organization. Employees of technology organizations typically get their devices replaced with a higher frequency. The maximum limit of four years is based on the complete obsolescence of the older generations of PCs that cannot keep pace with the higher hardware and supporting software needs of new applications. While the move of the devices from the capital expenses mode to the operating expenses mode is indeed useful, the cost of most modern day PCs is not high enough to make a significant dent in the procurement budget of the organization. The capacity risk is also not a significant factor, owing to the one-to-one correspondence between the number of employees and the number of devices needed, nor do quality and reliability risk impact the decision to adopt the PCaaS mode. The predictive capabilities of the PCaaS offering can allow customer IT teams to plan their budget in advance and manage their cash flow more effectively. While the obsolescence of technology risk has some impact, the impact is not high, as the PC industry is a mature market, and the development of new processors drives the obsolescence of devices. The clock speed of development of new processors is about a year to eighteen months with a reasonably tight standard deviation, hence, the obsolescence of technology is not an influential factor in the adoption of the PCaaS model. The usage of other technology factors like IoT for monitoring usage is also minimal, as the usage of PCs for office use is fairly standard.

The key offering of the PCaaS mode is the extent of flexibility for customers, more efficient utilization of time and costs savings through bundling of different services (deployment, support and asset recovery) that is the value generated by such a subscription offering. The agility factor for the client is indeed important, and the use of agile methods by Dell for offering this flexibility to the customer is the core value of the PCaaS offering. A critical advantage of the flexibility of Dell's PCaaS offering to enterprise IT teams is the ability to choose the exact devices and software that are best suited to their organizational needs. They can either choose to configure the devices themselves or transfer this duty to service providers like Dell. They can also either opt for remote management services to help employees fix issues remotely or choose to ask the service provider to do the fixes on-site. Freeing up scarce IT resources of the customer is another key advantage. Tasks like everyday IT support for devices or asset recovery can use up a lot of a firm's resources. A PCaaS proposition allows customers to offload such tedious tasks to the service provider, freeing up their internal IT resources to then do more value-add activities like focussing on business transformation goals.

Profitability: The effect of deal transaction costs for the PCaaS offerings is minimal, as employees use devices in a similar manner whether the devices are offered in the productization mode or the XaaS mode. Similarly, the role of the PCaaS offering in being able to discriminate on the frequency of usage, and the ability to enhance the expected utility-per-use by offering multiple services on the core PC asset is also minimal. Unlike the offering of enterprise computing services like the IaaS and the PaaS, where computing resource usage can be charged based on the degree of usage, the pricing of the PCaaS offering does not depend on the usage of the PC. The IaaS and PaaS offerings charge customers based on usage as these resources are shared across multiple customers, however, PCs are allocated typically to individuals, there is no congestion effect from shared resources. The optimal pricing scheme is indeed the subscription pricing scheme, as the PCaaS mode helps mitigate cost spillage by bundling devices, software and services into a single package offer. This enables enterprise managers to better control device costs, and the subscription-based solution also has ripple advantages like increased predictability of electronic device procurement. More predictable device procurement can help IT departments predict the long-term cost of purchasing decisions.

Growth: Creating a niche in the PCaaS market is hard as the market is very competitive. The PC industry is a mature industry with standardized offerings across customers. Most top PC manufacturers offer the PCaaS or the DaaS options, there are other players like Biz Bang with a competence in device management in the competing set of firms. Creating a niche for Dell is hard, the services are complementary to the products, and the core competence of Dell is the ability to offer devices of its own brand. The offering of complementary services like deployment, support, management, recovery and retirement is indeed the core value of the PCaaS offering, hence, the PCaaS offering scores highly on the complementary dimension of the BROAD FENCES model. There are indeed benefits from the economies of scale with the PCaaS offering, as collecting older devices is easier for Dell as it also manages the recovery and retirement of older devices. Hence, it can use the circular economy to extract value of older devices. Since different enterprises have different time horizons for using devices, Dell can potentially use devices from some enterprises in fast-paced technology industries for serving other organizations with PC needs that are not avant-garde. The economies of scale allow customer IT teams to scale procurement based on demand. The offering of the solutions model allows Dell to understand customer needs better, and using their one-to-one relationship management, Dell can tailor solutions for larger customers. With more and more companies switching to the cloud for data management, PCaaS can also help extend the power of cloud to configure devices and implement required settings and applications by remote access.

The analysis of the PCaaS offering (Figure 7.2) shows that it offers value by bundling multiple services like procurement, deployment, management, recovery and retirement throughout the lifecycle of the core asset. From the cost perspective, it is important for the client that the TCO of the PCaaS offering is comparable to the TCO of own procurement, as PCs are a commodity. The PCaaS approach also enables predictable cash flows and frees up expensive IT resources of organizations. While it does offer another stream of revenue for a mature industry, the offering is not as compelling as for some other product assets. The growth rates of the service are high as the offering is in a nascent stage. If providers can offer more compelling reasons for customers to adopt the service, the PCaaS

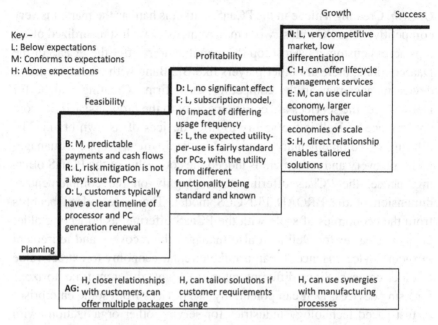

Figure 7.2:   XaaS Staircase for PCs-as-a-Service

business can compete with the selling of PCs for more substantial market shares. However, the offering does not create new markets or reach out to non-customers, it offers the prospect of added value offerings to the existing customer base.

7.3 ENGINES-AS-A-SERVICE (ROLLS-ROYCE)

In the early days, the aircraft turbofan engine market was dominated by General Electric and Pratt & Whitney; Rolls-Royce only had a share of 8% in 1987. By 2007, Rolls-Royce had become the second largest engine maker, and the number one supplier for large turbofan engines in the market. In the late 1990s, Rolls-Royce launched its first Trent turbofan which was built to cater to the needs of large airplanes like the twin jet Airbus A330 and Boeing 777. The Trent turbofan was an advancement in technology, which was engrained in the design, materials and manufacturing process of the engine, offering an improvement in fuel efficiency and engine durability. Advances in technology and improvements in internal cooling of the machines meant they could sustain much higher temperatures than before. Another key feature of a later model of the Trent was the introduction of the swept fan, which required fewer blades and significantly increased the damage resistance and durability of the engines. However, such improvements also meant a dip in the demand for spare parts and the replacement of damaged components. Coincidentally, the demand for spare parts and replacement components contributed to a significant part of the revenue earned by manufacturing companies like Rolls-Royce. Profit margins on spares were estimated to be seven times higher than that of new engines, albeit on lower revenue bases. This conundrum presented a challenging dilemma for the manufacturers, as increasing the reliability of the engine design resulted in a lower revenue from repair, spare parts and services. Rolls-Royce tried to cope with this challenge by introducing an innovative strategy for its service business, and a new business model for charging for its services.[7]

The first step in this change process was the transformation from being a "product-centric" organization to being a "customer-centric" organization. The objective of the service-centricity was to create more value from its installed engine base. The business model to create value relied on offering spare parts as in the past, however, Rolls-Royce also added maintenance services that were innovative and distinct from traditional maintenance, repair, and operations services. The new business model was based on engine guarantees and fixed price contracts. OEMs in airlines industry provided limited maintenance, repair operations (MRO) services, and most services were catered to by in-house engineering departments of major airlines or through contracts with independent MRO providers. Rolls-Royce took a two-pronged approach to attain its "customer centric" vision. First, it tried to establish a strong MRO services wing to expand its repair and overhaul business. The second approach was to design solutions using these MRO services to extract more value from its installed base. For the first strategy, Rolls-Royce

---

[7] Rolls-Royce, About, Our History, https://www.rolls-royce.com/about/our-history. aspx#:~:text=Rolls%2DRoyce%20grew%20from%20the,sold%20quality%20cars%20 in%20London, accessed October 2, 2020.

assimilated and reorganized its repair and overhaul operations within the organizations across its key geographical markets. Next, it acquired infrastructure facilities for repair and overhaul operations across the globe, growing from 6 sites to 16 sites in a span of over 8 years.

For its second strategy, Rolls-Royce introduced an integrated solution which was initially marketed as "power-by-the-hour". The solution was packaged as a contract that typically ascertained Rolls-Royce as the sole service provider and charged a fixed price for each hour that the engine was in the air. For a flat hourly rate per engine, the service handled installations, check-ups, maintenance and decommissioning. The service offered several benefits for the airlines. For starters, it improved the ready-for-use engine availability rate to 80%, compared to the prior 70% figure. Second, airlines were not stressed with the uncertainty of unpredictable breakdowns and repair costs any more. Unexpected engine failures were expensive for airlines and the costs of these failures were enormous, shooting up to millions in engine replacement costs, lost flight revenue, rescheduled flights and other costs. Third, an improved level of service and increase in ready-for-use engine availability provided additional flying time at the same cost. Moreover, as charges were by-the-hour, overall service costs were lower. In a few years, the ready-for-use engine availability increased further to 85%, while the time between engine removals had risen from 700 hours to over 900 hours, with engine removal rate falling to 15%. The power-by-the-hour scheme had aligned incentives between Rolls-Royce and its customers (airlines) tightly, resulting in Rolls-Royce investing in better engine performance, and a higher engine availability for the airlines. For airlines, power-by-the-hour meant a high degree of predictability of availability of engines and their performance, as well as saved time that they could spend focussing on their core business of flying passengers.

From Rolls-Royce's perspective, it made sense for it to service its own engines, as it could create economies of scale and build increased expertise from research in detecting failure points. The research could provide insights in implementing preventive maintenance procedures and improving the performance of the engines. However, the primary benefit was the cost control benefit for airlines, along with aligned incentives for improved service. A contract service agreement based on repairing engines as and when needed provided little incentive to a service provider to reduce the costs of maintenance. The "power-by-the-hour" scheme allowed airlines to service their engines for better operation in a cost-conscious way.

Although Rolls-Royce had started the service for the US Navy, it quickly realized the potential of the offering and extended it to civil airlines under the label of "Total Care". Total Care was provided in the form of various packages depending on the need of the airline. For the defence and corporate sectors, Rolls-Royce introduced similar packages called "Mission Care" and "Corporate Care". The packages were integrated with a decision support system, that allowed the firm to coordinate data from the aircraft, engine and overhaul shops and was backed with logistics support and engineering knowledge. A centralized operating centre maintained the engines on a real-time basis with the help of telemetry data.

The "power-by-the-hour" offering resulted in increased revenue and market share for Rolls-Royce. The company saw increased revenue from its services wing in the subsequent year, and by 2011, the revenue from services had become the major contributor, amounting to more than half (53.4%) of the total revenues. The Rolls-Royce engine-as-a-service created a ripple effect in the market, and competitors soon followed the same path. Both General Electric and Pratt and Whitney soon started offering maintenance agreements based on the number of operating hours alongside conventional repair and overhaul, creating a major shift in how the services market in the turbofan engine segment operated.

7.3.1 Engines-as-a-Service Analysis

Profitability: The baseline comparison of the power-by-the-hour scheme should be conducted with the older mechanism in the airline sector of the MRO services being provided by the airline, or the subcontracted organization of the airline. We shall refer to the baseline scheme of services offered by the airline or its subcontractor as the external provider scheme. While the power-by-the-hour scheme is a performance-based contract, where the payments made by the customer airlines are based on the number of hours, the payments in the external provider scheme were based on a time-and-materials contract. In that scheme, the airline or its subcontractor charged the airline based on the costs of the spare parts, labour and margin. The shift of the locus of servicing as provided by the power-by-the-hour scheme is based on the relative reliabilities of the mechanical and electrical/electronic components of the aeroplane. While mechanical components have a much higher need for servicing, and the engines are the primary mechanical components with wear and tear, electrical and electronic components have a much higher degree of reliability. Hence, the need for maintenance and servicing of aeroplanes derives primarily from the need of maintenance of the core asset of the engines. The manufacturer of the engines has invested in the design and development of the engines and has a better knowledge of the processes of engine maintenance. Hence, the shift from the external MRO providers and internal engineering divisions to the engine manufacturers as the services provider makes better sense. The engine manufacturer also has access to better data, better access to technologies like IoT that it has installed in the engines and has the scale to offer its maintenance services to all airlines. The budget impact of the providing of the engine maintenance services favours Rolls-Royce and other engine manufacturers. The TCO for the airline from having the engines serviced by Rolls-Royce is lower than the TCO from having the engines serviced by the MRO providers like the airline's own engineering department or subcontractors. The lower TCO derives from the above-mentioned reasons like better access to data, the incentive alignment leading to more investments in technologies like IoT, and the better knowledge base of causes of engine damage. The power-by-the-hour scheme also mitigates quality and reliability risk for the airline, owing to the incentive alignment of the higher quality and reliability from engine design leading to lower costs for engine manufacturers. Second, the capacity of the internal engineering teams of airlines must be scaled depending on the number of operational aeroplanes. If the servicing is done by Rolls-Royce, the capacity risk is mitigated. The obsolescence of technology factor is not high, as engines based on newer technologies are installed by plane manufacturers like Boeing and Airbus, and hence, engines with new technologies are available equivalently if the services are provided by the engine manufacturer or the external provider. However, the impact of technology investments from the engine manufacturer are higher if the engine manufacturer provides the services. The agility of the services are based on the ability to collect data to provide better services, react to the data by analyzing it and improving services processes, and being able to scale the use of the data by using it for multiple customers. The agility advantages of the engine manufacturer offering the MRO services are higher compared to the case when the external MRO provider offers the services. While both the engine manufacturer and the external MRO provider have continuous contact with the engines when they offer MRO services, the engine manufacturer has a higher capability to use the contact and influence maintenance processes to improve the services.

Profitability: The deal transaction costs for the airline customers are lower when the engine manufacturer provides the MRO services, as they can do better predictive maintenance based on their higher capability of predicting failures. Hence, the airline loses less time owing to grounded planes with the engine manufacturer as the provider. From the customer airline's perspective, the gains from an increased frequency of usage that stem from a lower breakdown rate are indeed shared with Rolls-Royce in the power-by-the-hour scheme. If the planes can fly for more hours, the revenues for Rolls-Royce from the services component are higher. In contrast, the external MRO provider is not incentivized for a higher frequency of usage by the airline if the services are offered by a subcontractor. Subcontractors are incentivized by time-and-materials contracts, hence, the more repairs they perform, the higher are their revenues. Internal engineering departments of the airlines also have aligned incentives to keep the planes flying for as many hours as possible, but they do not have the same degree of expertise as the engine manufacturers. The expected utility-per-use of the airline is the same regardless of who performs the servicing if the servicing is of the same quality. However, if the engine manufacturer can use its knowledge to save fuel consumption for the airline, and optimize the aircraft's performance in other ways, the expected utility-per-use for the airline is also higher from having the engine manufacturer perform the service.

Growth: While the aircraft engine maintenance market is competitive, the main competitors for the engine manufacturer are the internal engineering department of the airline, and external MRO providers. Rolls-Royce and other engine manufacturers have carved niches by offering performance-based contracts like the power-by-the-hour scheme, whereas internal maintenance and the external provider services are driven by keeping the costs down for the airline. The scope for offering complementary services is limited for Rolls-Royce and other engine manufacturers, as they maintain and service only the engines. In contrast, external MRO providers and internal engineering departments service the entire aircraft, hence, their scope for offering complementary services is higher. The economies of scale for engine manufacturers are easily higher compared to other providers, as they can use parts from one engine that has been repaired earlier in other engines, giving manufacturers the benefits of the circular economy. Having more customer airlines also makes it easier to justify the costs of building additional MRO sites closer to customer locations, hence, there are reasonable benefits of scaling for Rolls-Royce. Finally, the close relationship with the customer airline enables Rolls-Royce to understand the maintenance needs of aircraft based on the number of flown hours and the planned schedule, so that Rolls-Royce can use this knowledge to optimize its own schedules for preventive maintenance, along with maximizing the ready-for-use availability of its engines. However, this benefit also extends to external MRO providers and internal engineering departments.

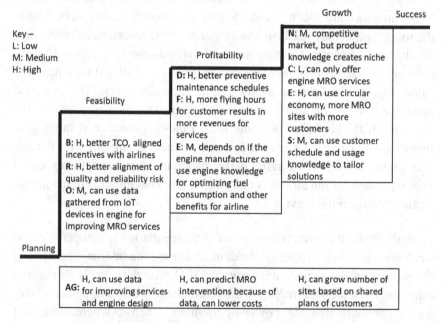

Figure 7.3:   XaaS Staircase for Aircraft Engines-as-a-Service

The BROAD FENCES analysis and the XaaS staircase (Figure 7.3) show the advantage of the power-by-the-hour scheme of aircraft engine manufacturers offering MRO services in the XaaS mode. The engine manufacturers have a genuine advantage of using performance-based contracts for aligning incentives with customer airlines. The aligned incentives between airlines and providers are the primary reason for the ubiquity of this business model in the MRO services domain for aircraft engines.

7.4 AGRICULTURAL EQUIPMENT AS-A-SERVICE (TAFE)

Established in 1960 in Chennai, India, TAFE was the world's third largest tractor manufacturer with an annual sale of over 150,000 tractors. The organization was one of the leading exporters of tractors from India with a turnover of more than $1.24 billion. The firm manufactured a range of tractors under four brands — Massey Ferguson, TAFE, Eicher, and agricultural equipment brand Industrija Mašina i Traktora (IMT). TAFE also made several other agricultural equipment like powervators, disc ploughs, harvesters, planters and power harrows. TAFE products were known for their quality and dependability and were supplied to over 100 countries across the globe.[8]

JFarm was established as a separate unit of TAFE in 1964. The objective of JFarm was to empower farmers with advanced farm technologies for increased farm productivity. Over the years, JFarm launched many initiatives to enable sustainable agriculture through technological innovation in farming. The purpose was to develop solutions that were suitable for local farming conditions and then educating farmers about these technologies. Examples of such initiatives involved local weather forecast for farmers, sharing latest market prices of crops and agriculture-related news and advisory with farmers. In 2017, JFarm launched an equipment-as-a-service pay-as-you-use initiative to provide farmers easy access to farm mechanization solutions through rental of tractors and farm equipment.

---

[8] TAFE, TAFE History, https://www.tafe.com/corporate/tafe-history.php, accessed October 2, 2020.

The service was particularly targeted towards small and marginal farmers who constituted 85% of land holdings in India. Small farmers had limited income, which was seasonal. Most of such farmers could not afford purchasing a tractor and other mechanized solutions for farming. As they continued to use age old techniques of farming, the productivity of their farms was low. To address the pain points of small and medium farmers, JFarm designed an equipment-as-a-service offering which could offer farmers the option of using tractors and other farming equipment to improve their farm's agricultural productivity. JFarm formed partnerships with agents — tractor and equipment suppliers in rural areas to establish Custom Hiring Centres (CHCs) to implement the rental model. Farmers could search for available rental options in their locality through a mobile app. The JFarm App created a hub from where farmers could gain access to specialized equipment. The intention of the services was to extend its offering to smallholders with added services including modern farm practices, technical know-how, high-yielding crop varieties, crop protection advice and other such training and knowledge to the farmers through a simple mobile app.[9]

The JFarm equipment-as-a-service offering enabled a direct interaction between CHCs and farmers to facilitate a fair and transparent rental process. The proximity to the customer ensured that CHCs delivered the equipment in a timely manner, increasing dependability. Farmers could directly negotiate with the CHCs on the number of hours they needed to rent the equipment and the frequency of rental, depending on the needs of the individual farmer. The service also created employment for the rural population, enabling farmer entrepreneurs who could afford to invest in such equipment to run it as a side business. A low per hour rental plan motivated farmers to plan the usage of the machinery more efficiently. Moreover, in case of any breakdown, the CHC could provide servicing of the tractor and other equipment and replacement services if required. The JFarm equipment service was initially pilot tested in one state before being rolled out to other states in the country. In a span of two years, JFarm was able to reach out to over 85,000 farmers across 10 states in the country. The JFarm approach had helped in two ways. It had provided

---

[9]TAFE, JFarm, https://www.tafe.com/jfarm.php, accessed October 2, 2020.

farmers an affordable way to access farm mechanization and fostered digital empowerment among the farmers. It had also helped create a new breed of rural entrepreneurs and significant job opportunities and employment for the rural population. JFarm also provided flexibility of services to farmers, they had the flexibility of choosing a long-term or short-term hire, depending on their needs. JFarm let smallholders share the equipment across farms for both short-term and long-term hires, enabling farmers to take advantage of the sharing economy. For instance, JFarm had enabled mechanisms for peer-to-peer (farmer-to-farmer) lending of tractors, enabling a higher adoption from shared economy savings. Farmers could also choose the make and model of the tractor and the attachments they needed for their agricultural activities. Moreover, farmers were not required to build an expensive shed to store the tractor and machinery and keep it secure from burglary. JFarm gave farmers the flexibility of upgrading to a newer or more efficient model at no additional cost, and the choice of trying various equipment to figure out what worked best for their farms. This also meant that a farmer could always operate a regularly maintained and tested piece of farm machinery. Additionally, after a few years of using the as-a-service model, farmers had the opportunity to learn more about different makes and models of equipment and identify the ones that suited their requirements the best. This enabled a faster and more accurate purchasing decision when the time came for the farmer to consider buying agricultural equipment. Although a simple model in itself, it was the pairing of the rental service with maintenance and servicing, free delivery at the farm and a useful app to tie that all in, that really made the TAFE equipment-as-a-service a meaningful innovation. During the COVID-19 pandemic, many farmers faced a shortage of labour, TAFE enabled farmers to access the equipment services for free as a CSR initiative.

7.4.1 Equipment-as-a-Service Analysis

Feasibility: The biggest issue for customer adoption of agricultural equipment in developing countries is the budget impact factor. The budget impact of offering agricultural equipment as a service is the difference that converts non-customers into customers. Most smallholders in India cannot afford to buy agricultural equipment. Before the as-a-service model was offered, there were a few community initiatives that enabled smallholder cooperatives to purchase agricultural equipment as a group. However, these initiatives were not successful, as power and group dynamics came into play in the process of fair usage practices. Many smallholders complained that they did not get the benefit of the equipment to the extent that they contributed to the cost. The as-a-service offering enables a fair distribution system to various smallholders, alleviating incentive alignment and free-riding issues that are inherent in joint asset acquisition. Hence, the conversion of capital expenses to operating expenses was a big incentive for smallholders to access mechanized farming solutions. The as-a-service usage of equipment also creates a healthy cash flow for farmers, which was a big issue for them. The bulk of the farmer's revenues accrues during the harvest season. With a limited cash flow during the rest of the year, a rental plan was more feasible than a regular monthly instalment plan. While the capacity risk was not relevant, the risk of overrunning the budget with the maintenance needs for tractors and other equipment was high. Smallholders typically have a tight budget, and they only consider the costs of acquisition when purchasing new equipment, without considering maintenance and other associated costs. Having a predictable payment schedule for the short term was much easier than having to compare the TCO from the as-a-service and acquisition options. For farmers who could afford tractors, the obsolescence of older tractors was a major concern. Having invested once in a tractor, farmers chose to defer replacing them with newer models, so that they could extract value from their investment. That meant that they were often stuck with an outdated model for many years, affecting their farm's productivity. The as-a-service offering alleviated the obsolescence of technology problem for these farmers. The as-a-service model also enables the agility afforded by crop rotation for smallholders. Different kinds of crops need different kinds of agricultural equipment, for example, potato harvesters are designed differently from beans harvesters. If farmers bought one kind of equipment, they tended to stick to growing crops that the equipment was meant for. The as-a-service model enables smallholders to increase the land fertility by rotating crops, by using different equipment as there is no lock-in effect induced by purchasing a specific type of equipment. From TAFE's perspective, it can buy multiple farm equipment, and share them across service centres, and can then shift the equipment around based on the crop growing plans of farmers in different locations.

Profitability: The deal transaction costs for the smallholders are low to negligible for two reasons: all transactions with JFarm are conducted through the app, with payment upon delivery. Second, the equipment is delivered to the farmer's doorstep, hence, the farmer does not have to undergo any inconvenience from picking up the equipment at a centralized location. The frequency of usage was a big factor that inhibited the purchase of the equipment apart from the tractor. While tractors are useful for farming and haulage purposes throughout the agricultural process, tillers, planters and harvesters are used for very specific periods during the agricultural process and are idle otherwise. As mentioned for the Trringo example in Chapter 1, the as-a-service model enables farmers to avail of the services of the other equipment apart from the tractor, which they could not afford to do until now. However, from TAFE's perspective, they must think of ingenious ways to enable the utilization of the other equipment to be more stable throughout the year. The expected utility-per-use depends on the size of the holdings of the smallholder, the ability to share the equipment locally enables the expected utility-per-use to be significant. With similar land properties, the expected utility-per-use is similar across homogeneous smallholders per unit land, enabling a sustainable pay-per-use pricing approach.

Growth: The degree of competition for the equipment-as-a-service model is non-existent as of now. Trringo and TAFE are the two biggest providers of agricultural equipment-as-a-service, they operate in a duopolistic environment where the two providers offer their services to similar regional markets. However, the degree of penetration of these services is low, as both providers began offering the as-a-service model within the last three years. The potential of growth for both providers is very large in the range of millions, and the total number of adopting farmers for the services of both providers is barely in the range of a few hundred thousand. Both providers offer a range of complementary services to the tractor, like tillers, planters, harrows and harvesters, the scope of complementary services is high. Additional complementary services like modern agricultural technology knowhow, rainfall and local weather forecasts, current and forecasted market prices for different kinds of crops in spot and future markets are also offered by these players. Integrating the different services into specific solutions for the smallholders may be needed, as offering each of these individual elements may not offer a lot of value to smallholders, who do not possess the skills to determine the value of the bundled service. While the economies of scale are partially enhanced by peer-to-peer sharing, since all the equipment is tied to the CHCs, there is a limited ability on the part of TAFE to take advantage of economies of scale. As the region served by each CHC gets larger, there is a lot of time and resources wasted in travelling to the customer's location for delivering the equipment to farmers located further away from the CHC. Hence, improving the ability to benefit from economies of scale by some regionalized sharing mechanisms of equipment would be useful for providers like TAFE and Trringo. While maintenance services are included in the package, having a total solutions approach where the providers consult with the farmers on the crops to be grown, methods of farming to be used and other advisory services would increase the utility of the farmers further.

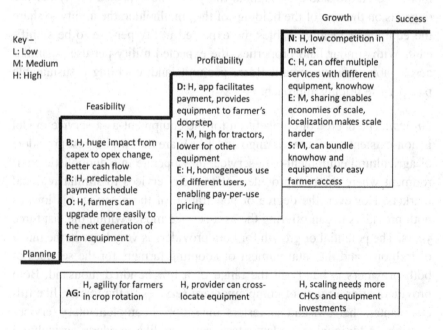

Figure 7.4:   XaaS Staircase for Agricultural Equipment-as-a-Service

The analysis and the XaaS staircase (Figure 7.4) of the agricultural equipment market shows that the scope for growing the equipment-as-a-service business for smallholders is high. The providers have several factors like the budget impact, risk, technology obsolescence and agility that make the potential market for this set of services much larger than the current market. The key to being able to grow the equipment-as-a-service set of offerings depends on the ability to induce economies of scale in the offering. If the providers can design mechanisms to increase the economies of scale, then the degree of mechanized farming practices in developing countries can grow exponentially.

7.5 HOUSING-AS-A-SERVICE (ZIROOM)

Ziroom is a Chinese real estate firm and was founded in 2011 with the vision of providing housing as a service to the millennial population in China. Ziroom delivered its home-as-a-service offering to its market segment of young and mobile professionals using a mobile app. The service was timely since China was seeing a booming real estate market, socioeconomic changes and a new breed of urban millennials who preferred mobility and renting over purchasing a property. A forecast by financial firm Orient Securities Co. had estimated that the housing-as-a-service market in China would reach $664 billion by 2030, which is about half of all home sales executed in 2017.[10] Ziroom was unlike other real estate companies in the region in that it provides rental homes to its customers through an app. By 2019, the Ziroom portal had extended its services to more than 3 million tenants across cities like Beijing, Shanghai, Shenzhen, Hangzhou, Nanjing, Guangzhou, Chengdu, Tianjin and Wuhan. With a database of more than 500,000 properties, the portal managed every aspect of the rental property market. Ziroom was coined from the Chinese word "zi ru", which meant 'carefree', and had a clear philosophy that it presented to its customers — providing hassle-free property rentals with complementary services to make rental living enjoyable. After creating a

---

[10] Ang, T., "Why Chinese millennials are choosing the rental lifestyle", *China Economic Review*, August 8, 2018, https://chinaeconomicreview.com/why-chinese-millennials-are-choosing-the-rental-lifestyle/, accessed September 18, 2020.

profile on the app, "Ziroomers," became part of an active online community where property seekers could chat, share stories and reviews and choose to attend offline property events. The strong social online community that Ziroom represented was a bonus for millennial customers.[11]

Ziroom offered customers various rental offers through its host of services categorized by the property type — ZR Friendly home, ZR Apartment, ZR Mansion, ZR Hostel, ZR Home Stay, ZR Selected, Zinn and Ziroom stay. All properties available for rental in the platform were verified as genuine and were fully furnished and renovated in a sleek modern style by Ziroom. A host of other services like cleaning, professional maintenance and moving were also provided via the app for customers to choose during the rental period. Ziroom also eliminated time-taking and stressful aspects of the property search process like negotiation of rental period or contract and the whole process could be managed online. Property seekers could choose to pay on a yearly, quarterly or monthly basis, making it attractive even for short-term rental customers. The platform also provided a 100% money-back guarantee within three days of signing the contract if the customer was not satisfied with the property for any reason. Millennials were mobile-centric and were accustomed to using their phones for everyday needs like food delivery, shopping, commuting and frequently used online-payment services such as Alipay and WeChat Pay. The Ziroom app was built to have similar aesthetics to such apps where users could browse through a directory of refurbished rental properties, arrange viewings and settle online transactions to finalize a deal in a hassle-free manner. Ziroom customers could also opt for additional services that could help them lead a carefree urban lifestyle while the provider took care of all the property maintenance and cleaning needs. Customers could choose a "Friendly Home" or a "Full House" — the two core rental options that allowed Ziroom to distinguish itself from pure rental models, which offer a "bare-bones" apartment for lease. Customers also had the option of selecting home furnishings, and cleaning and trash-collection services. The platform also provided the

---

[11] E-House, Ziroom:Winning in China's Housing Rental Services Market, March 2018, http://d1c25a6gwz7q5e.cloudfront.net/reports/2018-05-22-Ziroom-E-house-English.pdf, accessed September 18, 2020.

option of co-living spaces in apartment blocks, where tenants had access to shared social spaces like lounges, cafes, gym facilities. Such apartment blocks were typically located in convenient locations with easy access to restaurants and supermarkets.[12]

Ziroom also presented an attractive offering for property owners by removing the inconveniences faced by owners in renting their property. Ziroom provided them access to hassle-free rental contract arrangements and good maintenance of their properties while they were let out, and charged a small fee from the property owners, which was typically a percentage of the rent. Moreover, any complaints, repair requirements and payments were all handled by the app, so owners could enjoy rental income without having to worry about the responsibilities that come with property rental. Moreover, Ziroom guaranteed the rental output and promised 15 days' worth of rent monthly in the event of a property lying vacant.

Ziroom had become a part of China's e-commerce bandwagon at a time when the property rental segment in the country was seeing a surge due to an overheated property sector. Average house prices in cities like Beijing, Shenzhen and Shanghai were estimated to be 40 times higher than the per capita annual income of the population in those cities. In Chinese society, the purchase of a property was traditionally associated with social status, personal success, and was a prerequisite for marriage and starting a family. However, the social and economic dimensions of a rapidly changing population demographic had made the attractiveness of a property less captivating as more and more youngsters are starting to look for an experience-based lifestyle. For such customers, the HaaS offerings provided them the flexibility of changing jobs, moving to different cities, and more disposable income. To fix the imbalance in housing prices, the government had begun rolling out incentives to make renting an attractive option. Protection measures to curb unwarranted rent increases and evictions, tax deductions and release of pension funds to pay for rents were some of the measures implemented to make renting attractive. Rental companies were also incentivized to trade publicly, making it attractive for rental business to expand their horizons. Ziroom's services

---

[12] *Ibid.*

helped support the cooling measures that the government had put in place to control the rise of property prices in major cities.

7.5.1 Housing-as-a-Service Analysis

Feasibility: Housing is by far the biggest ticket item that most customers will spend their earnings on in their lives. We have reviewed the office space offering of WeWork earlier in Chapter 4. While the good old-fashioned renting model by individual landlords predates most as-a-service offerings, Ziroom goes beyond the standard rental offering. For those readers who have rented properties before, the quirks of individual landlords will bring smiles on some faces, and frowns on others. Renting properties through a platform standardizes the rental offering and makes the customer's expectations easier to match. While WeWork has a mixed model of property acquisition (it buys some properties and leases others), Ziroom acts as a platform where customers can acquire a standardized set of services provided by Ziroom. Hence, the platform aspect of Ziroom's offering is similar to the leasing of properties by WeWork, the risk of the property not getting leased exists for Ziroom as well, since Ziroom has some guaranteed rental income for owners of unoccupied properties. From the customer's perspective, the budget impact is indeed very significant, as property prices in most large cities in China are beyond the reach of the middle class, white collar workers. After paying the down payment, cash flow issues of mortgaging the property using a longer-term horizon may result in similar cash flows as rentals. However, making the down payment of 10–20% of the price of the property may not be an obviously easy step for many customers. The risk factors favour the mobility offered by the housing-as-a-service option, and the obsolescence of technology factor corresponds to the risk of asset depreciation for home ownership. Given China's rapid urbanization, it may be a long time before property prices start decreasing in the larger cities. Hence, the risk of asset depreciation in the ownership option is not high, but given the transaction costs associated with home ownership, the risks of losing more money if the customer does not stay in the city for a long time are reasonably high. While customers can avoid fluctuating mortgage payments in the home ownership option by paying higher mortgages based on fixed interest rates, such fixed rates are also offered for limited time horizons. The agility of customers is higher with the housing-as-a-service option, and the availability of monthly and annual leases also enables agile reactions for Ziroom and the property owners. Renting their second or third properties gives property owners the ability to generate income from their secondary properties and wait for prices to increase even further until they contemplate selling these properties. Property owners who want the flexibility of being able to sell their properties in the near future can offer them for relatively short-term leases. Hence, the agility of the housing-as-a-service offering is uniformly higher compared to the home ownership option.

Profitability: The deal transactions costs are minimized by Ziroom using the app, as all transactions can be executed at the customer's fingertips. Hence, Ziroom performs well on the transaction cost dimension. The frequency of usage is indeed an aspect that needs careful management by Ziroom. Offering short-term leases to customers and a rental income guarantee to property owners exposes Ziroom to potentially unprofitable transactions. Ziroom needs to ensure that the property locations, the condition and facilities of the building and the neighbourhood meet minimal standards for rapid rental utilization. The expected utility-per-use and the rental price can be determined from historical data of rental prices in the neighbourhood for similar properties. At a higher level, Ziroom should operate in cities where the proportion of mobile millennials is high, as a lack of potential customer base can result in a lack of profits.

Growth: While individual landlords do pose a competitive threat to Ziroom, Ziroom's wider range of services and the standardization of services enable Ziroom to have a competitive advantage over individual property owners. Ziroom's two biggest competitors are Danke and QK365, Ziroom manages more properties than these next two biggest competitors combined. However, if the housing-as-a-service market picks up steam, Ziroom can expect to have competitors entering the space, including real estate developers who offer properties as serviced apartments. Ziroom has a wide slate of complementary services like the use of laundry, gym, social gathering spaces and get-togethers, and cleaning services, that enable it to provide value-added services to customers. The scope of bundling other services like tickets to local attractions and events, and club memberships, is high, enabling it to offer more revenue-generating services. The benefit of economies of scale at the city-wide level are higher for Ziroom than individual landlords, as cleaning contracts with cleaning agencies, furnishing contracts and circular economies from home furnishings, offer cost savings opportunities at scale. While many of these savings need some degree of localization within the city to be effective, the potential for economies of scale of residential properties is higher for Ziroom, compared to the potential of economies of scale for WeWork in the office-as-a-space business. Individual residential property owners usually have one or two smaller properties that make it harder for them to compete on economies of scale. In contrast, commercial developers and commercial property owners are larger, making it easier for them to have similar economies of scale as WeWork. Finally, the ability of Ziroom to offer customer solutions is moderate, as they have a standardized suite of services for customers. While they can follow the customers' choice of services from the app and provide more suggestions for customers, individualized contacts with customers are difficult, hence the app provides Ziroom with the ability to provide customers with a moderately wide suite of solutions.

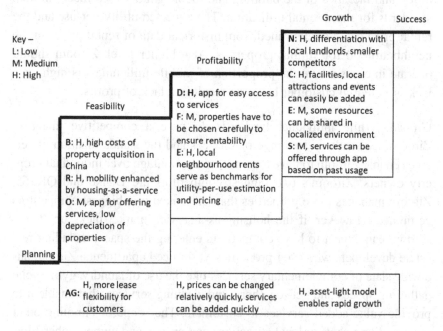

Figure 7.5:   XaaS Staircase for Housing-as-a-Service

The analysis of the housing-as-a-service offering of Ziroom (Figure 7.5) yields the conclusion that the service is still growing rapidly and can be expanded for some more time. The model does need careful management to be profitable, the asset-light model enables growth potential and agility. However, Ziroom should not expand to second-tier cities with a small proportion of mobile millennials, and should choose properties carefully, ensuring that the chosen properties are in attractive locations and can be priced reasonably for rentals.

7.6 DESIGN-AS-A-SERVICE (ARM HOLDINGS)

ARM started its journey in 1990 with a team of 12 co-founders and had grown to become a leader in semiconductor Intellectual Property (IP) development. At the heart of ARM's offering was its microprocessor architecture and its IP licensing business model, paired alongside strategic partnerships with semiconductor and original equipment manufacturing (OEM) firms. ARM had also developed an ecosystem of partner organizations, which helped accelerate the adoption of its IP. ARM was spun off from its parent company Acorn, the first Acorn RISC Machine (ARM) processor was designed in 1985 based on the principles of Reduced Instruction Set Computer (RISC). RISC processing was adapted by Acorn to build processors that could perform at a higher speed for their computers and still offer the right level of cost. ARM was developed by Acorn for its newer generation of computers and was fabricated by VLSI Technology Inc., a developer of chips that acted as a foundry (manufacturer) for custom-designed chips.[13]

In November 1990, ARM Ltd., a joint venture between Acorn, VLSI Technology Inc. and Apple Inc. (Apple), was spun off from Acorn as a separate entity. The founding team at ARM set out on an ambitious goal of producing 100 million chips by the year 2000. At the start, their focus was on building processors for applications where ultra-low power consumption, high performance and low costs were the base criteria. By that

---

[13] Howard Thomas & Lipika Bhattacharya, ARM Holdings: IP Licensing to Internet of Things, HBR.org, July 18, 2019, https://store.hbr.org/product/arm-holdings-ip-licensing-to-internet-of-things/SMU526, accessed February 2, 2020.

time, the ARM processor had been embedded in 13,000 chips and sold to three end-user clients.

ARM's foundation was laid on a partnership business model, where the firm partnered with fabricators and original equipment manufacturers (OEM) to licence its processor IP. The ARM processor was licensed to semiconductor companies and OEMs for a license fee, and then royalties were charged on the silicon production volume. This effectively incentivized ARM to help its licensee partner get to high-volume shipments as quickly as possible. The license fee payments were made before the licensor got to sell the chips, with a third paid up front, a third on handover of the design database and a third when working ARM samples were manufactured by the licensor. Some of the primary market segments initially targeted were mobile phones, personal and portable computers, digital watches, and embedded control used in customer and automotive electronics. ARM appointed a dedicated sales and technical marketing representative for each market segment. Working closely with key partner OEMs and semiconductor companies helped ARM resources gain broad technical experience in addition to sales knowledge. However, transferring technology across different organizations positioned at various points along the value chain was challenging. Developing a reusable IP was several times the cost of developing the same functionality to be used as a one-off. The engineers at ARM worked closely with the various technical teams in partner companies to ensure that their design was seamlessly incorporated in the final product.

The team at ARM also concentrated on growing the company's core competence, which was the ability to create, own, market, and sell IP. The idea was to build a long-term relationship with clients (both semiconductor partners and key OEMs in chosen market segments) and make ARM the standard in the microprocessor industry. OEM partners were chosen carefully, as ARM's objective was to grow with the partners in the market.[14]

As part of its licensing strategy, ARM decided to license its core as is, and licensee companies (semiconductor manufacturing companies) were not allowed to make changes to the architectural design (the layout of the

---

[14] *Ibid.*

core could however be modified to port it to different manufacturing processes). ARM required the licensees to perform a specific set of tests before they could sell the chips and use them commercially. These aspects of the ARM licensing model were beneficial from the revenue recognition perspective as well. Notably, the delivery and validation of the design represented stages that matched with the accounting principles of revenue recognition. The standard architecture reduced the risk for OEMs when choosing the architecture and thus was a benefit to the semiconductor partner as well.[15]

The initial processor licenses were offered with very limited modification rights. This ensured that the ARM technology was the same across different semiconductor partners. Also, customizing designs was significantly more expensive and the company had limited resources. As ARM grew, it was able to offer a more expansive set of IP rights and develop better ways of ensuring architectural compliance — however, such rights would typically be offered to a smaller subset of preferred partners. As the company grew, it began developing IP products with different price points.

One limiting feature of the IP licensing business model was the time it took to generate revenue — it could take years from the time a license was signed until the royalties started to kick in. As the ARM architecture became more and more widely licensed, ARM put a lot of effort into building a partnership ecosystem of fabricators, OEM's, circuit design tool producers and third-party suppliers of software libraries (for graphics, sensors and networking). A "relational" approach to building technology in association with partners allowed ARM to create an environment of uninterrupted value creation for the customer, and lock in customers to its technology. The processor market was segmented based on application areas, level of processing power, and the specific requirement of the actual chips designed and developed by semiconductor companies. To become the standard of the processor industry, ARM's model had enabled customers to modularize the system design, as its flexible architecture allowed clients to make elements of its processor design reusable and adaptable.

---

[15] *Ibid.*

Over time, ARM was able to capture a 90% share in the mobile market and showed no signs of slowing down. The companies that used ARM technology in their chips had also started to use ARM processors in chips for their other markets. That led ARM to invest both in new technology that could be used in powerful applications, and applications that needed much smaller processors, such as the tiny microcontrollers that could enable IoT. In 2014, ARM shifted its focus to create processor chips for IoT products. By then, it had sold 7.9 billion units of ARM Core processor designs. By 2017, its sales numbers had grown to 21.3 billion units. Creating a monopoly through its unique IP Licensing-based service model, ARM had illustrated that niche services and ecosystems could work hand in hand as long as the service provider was able to build its service as a trademark that could be adopted and scaled easily by clients.

7.6.1 Design-as-a-Service Analysis

Feasibility: The base case for comparing ARM's design-as-a-service mode of offering is the complete manufactured processor offering models of competitors such as Intel and NXP semiconductor. ARM's model is different, as it just offers the design of the processor. In its early days, ARM offered standard designs that could not be altered. Today, it offers designs that can be customized to the needs of individual application providers like mobile phone and tablet designers and manufacturers. The processor design-as-a-service offering is also complemented by the offering of the designs of other kinds of semiconductor products beyond processors, as well as software design tools for chips. The budget impact for ARM's customers is not a significant factor in the adoption of ARM's design-as-a-service offering. ARM's customers need physical processors for enabling and controlling all functionalities of the phone, tablet or other appliances like smart TVs. They can acquire these processors either as a complete unit from firms such Intel and Qualcomm, or they can acquire the design from ARM, and then after customizing the design of the processor, ARM designs are typically executed by manufacturers such as AMD, NXP and Broadcom. These finished processors are embedded in the final phones, tablets, and other appliances. If customers acquire processors from firms like Qualcomm, they pay one price for the entire processor (including the design). On the other hand, if they acquire processor designs from ARM, they pay ARM royalties for the design for each product sold and sometimes a fixed fee, and then a fee for each manufactured processor to the manufacturer. While there may be a case for double marginalization increasing the final price of processors designed by ARM, ODMs like Qualcomm may also have a high margin. Depending on the point of time when the royalties are paid to ARM (on sale of the final product, or on sale of the processor to the manufacturer), the risk of ARM's design-as-a-service is lower or comparable to that of the base case processor selling model. There are no significant differences in the risk of capacities and budgets, hence, the risk impact of the design-as-a-service is low. The obsolescence of technology factor impact is also low, as the lead time of manufacturing for ARM's designs would be comparable to that of the processor selling model. The agility that ARM's customizable design affords to customers, along with the scope of selling solutions, is the differentiating factor of ARM's offering. ARM's unique value proposition is the ability that customers must use ARM's customizable design options to optimize the processor design for the product. The customer can design the processor in a way that is aligned with the applications and the other needs of the manufacturer's final product, leading to better processor designs than standardized processors. By designing their processors to be customizable, ARM is also able to offer its designs to more customers and for more applications, hence, the agility factors are a big advantage for ARM's model.

Profitability: There are no deal transaction costs for the customer. They do have to customize the processor's design for each application, but they can choose to use the standard options on ARM's designs. The frequency of usage is directly the volume of the chips in the final products sold by the customer. The royalty model enables ARM to discriminate perfectly on the frequency of usage. The expected utility-per-use is the royalty value of the individual processor, which can be estimated by ARM based on the value of its designs in terms of the customer's willingness-to-pay for customized designs. The value of the customized design should be higher than the value of standard processor designs.

Growth: ARM faces competition from firms such as Ichor and Synopsys for their design-as-a-service model, and from design and manufacturing ODMs such as Intel and Qualcomm. However, ARM's leadership position for applications such as mobile phones and tablets shows that its unique customizable designs have given it a niche position today. However, this niche position may be challenged in individual markets and as a business model in the future if the margins from manufacturing processors get pressurized further. ARM performs well on the complementarity dimension, as it sells other chips beyond processors as well as software tools. It can bundle these offerings for providing added value to customers. Since ARM only incurs costs on its design effort for processors, as the volumes of processors increase, ARM has significantly higher profits from scale after the initial royalties have enabled it to break even. Hence, ARM performs well on economies of scale. The ability to provide solutions with customizable designs for ARM is very high. ARM needs to work closely with customers to design the core of the processor, hence, it scores well on the solutions dimension.

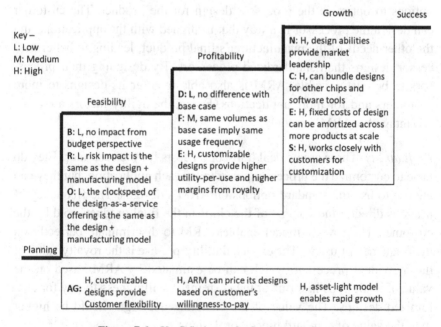

Figure 7.6   XaaS Staircase for Design-as-a-Service

The XaaS Staircase (Figure 7.6) shows that the primary value of ARM's design-as-a-service offering is the agility offered to the customer by the customizable design of ARM's chips. This enables ARM to have an advantage in offering solutions to the customer, as well as the potential for offering complementary services. The scalability of ARM's model is very high as it is not limited by capacity constraints, hence, ARM's growth potential is excellent. However, it can only continue growing until it has the edge in customizable designs. It is conceivable in the near future that other firms will acquire capabilities like ARM's, and the increased competition may challenge ARM's dominant position in the market.

7.7 SUMMARY

In conventional wisdom, the most common reasons for choosing renting over selling are the budget impact and the risk impact. The transfer of ownership of the core product asset ameliorates the budget impact for XaaS offerings, as the transfer from capital expenses to operating expenses makes the payments smaller and more predictable. As can be seen from the NIO BaaS offering and the TAFE equipment-as-a-service offering, the availability of the XaaS option enables customers to avail of the product asset's use. The budget impact of XaaS solutions is indeed critical in being able to reach customers at the base of the pyramid (BoP) in B2C markets, and SMEs in B2B markets. The budget impact of XaaS solutions enables the conversion of previous non-customers like BoP denizens and SMEs to customers. While this reduction is more substantial if the entire product is offered as a service, the battery-as-a-service example shows that even if expensive components are offered as a service, the budget impact plays a meaningful role in customer adoption. For expensive items like homes, the housing-as-a-service offering enables customers to avail of housing for smaller monthly payments. Cash flows work in a similar way as the initial cash outlay, as even if customers can get loans for the initial outlay, the cash flow advantages favour the XaaS solution, as can be seen in the case of the equipment-as-a-service offering of TAFE, or the Ziroom housing-as-a-service offering. While the TCO of the XaaS option is often larger than the TCO of the asset acquisition model, the TAFE example shows that if customers use the service infrequently, then the TCO of the

XaaS solution may be lower. The budget impact may not always be an important factor (as in the PCaaS, engines-as-a-service or EaaS, and design-as-a-service examples). For short lifecycle products like PCs, the initial cash outlay is equivalent to less than two years of subscription fees as the lifetime of a PC is about 2 years. However, the cash flows and predictable payment schedules still make the budget impact salient when there is no substantial initial payment effect.

The risk impact almost always favours the XaaS mode if subscriptions do not have termination fees and the service can be availed for short periods, as demonstrated in the Ziroom housing-as-a-service case. Performance-based contracts align the interests of the client and the provider as demonstrated in the Rolls-Royce case. The alignment of incentives could potentially be even better if Rolls-Royce could work with Boeing and Airbus to offer the entire engine (not just the maintenance of the engine) as a service to airlines. Boeing and Airbus could then offer the option to airlines to pay for the acquisition of the aeroplane without the engine and pay for the engine-as-a-service to Rolls-Royce, GE or Pratt and Whitney. While the idea sounds far-fetched, the BaaS idea for customer products had also sounded far-fetched until it was implemented by NIO. The Rolls-Royce case also demonstrates the benefit of capacity risk, as internal engineering departments of airlines may have to be scaled based on the number of operational aeroplanes. The quality and reliability risk of the product asset are alleviated in the XaaS mode since the provider maintains the product asset (as can be seen in the Epiroc, Nio, Rolls-Royce, TAFE and Ziroom cases). The steady stream of payments in the XaaS mode also mitigates the budget overrun risk. The obsolescence of technology risk is high for products with long lifecycles like batteries and agricultural equipment. The XaaS mode enables customers to mitigate this risk by switching to the next generation of the technology with a low switching cost. The use of technology for maintaining assets (Rolls-Royce) and interacting with customers (TAFE and Ziroom) shows the benefits of technology for enabling interactions with the product and the customer. XaaS solutions like design-as-a-service enable customers to change their offering quickly in the B2B context and enable customers like farmers to rotate their crops easily in the B2C context. Hence, the offered customer agility enhances the adoption of XaaS offerings. The provider can assemble services in an agile manner as well to satisfy customers (customizable designs by ARM, cleaning and gym offerings by Ziroom, enhanced repair services by Rolls-Royce) to enhance adoption. The XaaS mode enables the provider to lower costs (using data analytics for failure prediction to lower servicing costs by Rolls-Royce) and provide better customer solutions (aligning equipment to farmer needs by TAFE, aligning battery power to customer driving patterns by NIO) to increase profitability. Finally, provider agility is important to be able to generate growth (bundling software tools with processor design by ARM). For XaaS offerings in the B2C space, a higher scale lowers the deal transaction costs. For example, with more scale, NIO and TAFE will be able to have more service centre coverage regionally, enabling customers to exchange batteries at the service centres more easily for NIO, and reducing the time of delivery of equipment for TAFE. The higher coverage by service centres lowers the travel time for the customer, and correspondingly, the inconvenience factor for the customer each time they use the provider's service. In the B2B context, if the customer has dedicated product assets (Epiroc and Dell), then the deal transaction costs are lower. The use of technology (TAFE and Ziroom) can also lower the deal transaction costs.

The frequency of usage discrimination can be achieved in several ways by XaaS providers. For instance, the design-as-a-service offering of ARM uses royalty contracts rather than fixed fees only, enabling ARM to benefit from their design being used in a larger number of processors. Similarly, the power-by-the-hour offering of Rolls-Royce enables Rolls-Royce to benefit from more flying hours of the airline. The frequency of usage may differ by period owing to seasonality (TAFE). The provider must design methods to maximize the utilization of product assets in the case of seasonal demand. The expected utility-per-use can be used to determine the customer willingness-to-pay and practice value-based pricing for XaaS offerings. The ARM, Ziroom, Epiroc and NIO cases show that the pricing of the service can be done based on the value provided by the service each time. For services where the utility docs not vary over time and the utility-per-use is standardized (as in the PCaaS case), the subscription pricing model can be used. If the use of the product can be measured accurately, the pricing can be offered on a pay-per-use basis (associated offerings of Ziroom like cleaning services). The design of the nanonized module for products is also done locally, for instance, the nanonized module for NIO and TAFE is the service centre. NIO must decide how many batteries to hold and the number of charging stations at the service centre, while TAFE must decide the equipment mix it holds at each service centre. The nanonized module for Epiroc, Dell and Rolls-Royce is the individual customer, the nanonized module for Ziroom is a certain locality within a city, while the nanonized module for ARM is the entire market. The larger the market served by the nanonized module, the higher the economies of scale, as economies of scale are achievable at the nanonized module level.

The impact of competition in XaaS offerings can be mitigated by differentiating services (the battery-as-a-service offering of NIO is unique), or by a market leadership position. However, over time, the need for differentiation is paramount. In growing markets, this differentiation can be achieved by serving different geographies (TAFE and Trringo). In stable markets, this differentiation can be achieved by bundling multiple service components together (design of different components by ARM, bundling of localized lifestyle options by Ziroom). If differentiation is hard to achieve, then the subscription model of pricing is useful in competitive markets (as in the PCaaS offering of Dell). The growth of the industry can often be impacted by solutions that influence the interoperability of components across competitive products. For instance, one reason that the EV market has grown more slowly is the inability of EVs to be charged instantaneously like cars powered by fossil fuels such as petrol and diesel. If NIO can cooperate with other EV manufacturers in China and design a common battery architecture, then customers can drive to any manufacturer's service station and exchange their discharged battery for a charged battery for a fee. This would dramatically lower the time required for charging. The standardized battery-as-a-service offering can help expedite the growth of the EV industry by standardizing battery designs in this fashion. If the battery design is a core competence, the EV manufacturers can still cooperate by making the batteries of different manufacturers exchangeable at any service centre. While the exchange will only be for like-for-like batteries, the expanded service centre exchange footprint will increase the adoption of the battery-as-a-service offering and alleviate the range anxiety problem. This could also make the market for battery manufacturers more attractive, and the EV manufacturers could then focus on the design and assembly of other components besides the battery.

The complementarity of services is useful for achieving rapid growth, as the utility of the bundled group of services is higher than the sum of the individual utilities (Dell, Ziroom). If internal IT staff are still needed for managing the procurement, deployment and retirement of PCs, then Dell's services do not add that much value to the customer. Having the complete suite of services makes having internal staff for these processes redundant, and the PCaaS offering adds more value to the customer. The economies of scale for IT offerings are hard to match for product asset offerings, as IT services can be offered over the Internet, leading to better economies of scale, to a larger pool of customers. In contrast, the economies of scale of XaaS offerings with product assets are limited as the economies are only local in nature. The sharing economy for customers that has been designed by TAFE is one best practice that can be used for XaaS offerings with product assets. Another best practice is the use of the circular economy for achieving economies of scale — the Epiroc, NIO, Dell, Rolls-Royce and TAFE cases exemplify the use of the circular economy. The circular economy collects components or completely used products and refurbishes them to provide services to new or older customers. Providers of as-a-service offerings with product assets must carefully manage and design their services to benefit from maximum economies of scale. This is probably the critical reason that service offerings with product assets have not grown as quickly in the non-IT domain as they have in the IT space. Finally, the offering of total customer solutions by Dell, TAFE, Ziroom and ARM exemplify the value added of XaaS offerings compared to added services for sold products. The solutions approach should identify customer pain points and offer solutions to ideally address all the customers' pain points.

Chapter 8

Analysis of XaaS Models
for IT Assets

The popular press refers to XaaS offerings synonymously with cloud computing applications like the IaaS, PaaS and SaaS offerings. The cloud computing applications framework refers to the offering of computing resources like software resources and computing and network applications on the Internet. The speed of accessing the Internet has enabled providers to offer on-demand services on the Internet primarily to businesses, and infrequently to customers in the B2C space. Some of the earliest examples of cloud computing are the Salesforce CRM offering in 1999 for software, and the offering by Amazon Web Services of its Elastic Compute Cloud (EC2) services in 2006.[1] Most of these services are offered by data centres to a multiple set of users. These data centres may be located across multiple locations. Cloud solutions used by a single user are referred to as private or enterprise clouds, while solutions that serve multiple locations are known as public clouds. The rate of growth of cloud computing has been much faster compared to the growth of XaaS offerings with non-IT product assets owing primarily to economies of scale. We have previewed the three categories of IaaS (infrastructure-as-a-service), PaaS (platform-as-a-service), and the SaaS (software-as-a-service) models in Chapter 1. In this chapter, we review some IT XaaS offerings with case studies on

---

[1] Amazon, "Announcing Amazon Elastic Compute Cloud (Amazon EC2) — beta", https://aws.amazon.com/about-aws/whats-new/2006/08/24/announcing-amazon-elastic-compute-cloud-amazon-ec2---beta/, accessed October 5, 2020.

Blockchain-as-a-Service (Tencent), Disaster Recovery-as-a-Service (Bluelock), Unified Communications-as-a-Service (DingTalk), Visual Search-as-a-Service (ViSenze), Platform-as-a-Service (OpenShift) and Workplace-as-a-Service (Atos).

8.1 BLOCKCHAIN-AS-A-SERVICE (TENCENT)

The Tencent Blockchain as a Service (TBaaS) offering was launched in 2017. It was built on the Tencent Cloud and enabled customers to construct their own IT infrastructure and blockchain service in a flexible, open cloud platform. Tencent Holdings Ltd (Tencent) was a global multinational conglomerate holding company established in Shenzen, China, in 1998. Tencent's foray into blockchain technology had begun since the launch of its internally developed business framework — TrustSQL (a B2B blockchain supermarket), which was like Ant Financial's Blockchain-as-a-Service (BaaS) platform. The platform comprised an efficient mixture of public and private cloud technologies. It also offered reliable storage capabilities that boasted of advanced cryptographic algorithms, user privacy and confidentiality, with continually changing encrypted transaction background information. A secure key management system and high security threat detection capabilities were also part of the offering. The platform's customers included major banks and insurance companies in China (examples include Bank of China, Bank of Communications Limited and the People's Insurance Company of China). It offered three different engines to fulfil varied customer needs. The Hyperledger Fabric engine provided high-performance and scalable enterprise-level blockchain network service. The FISCO BCOS engine provided an open source, safe, controllable, stable and easy-to-use underlying blockchain interface. The TrustSQL engine provided a scenario-based convenient and easy-to-use blockchain platform.[2]

All three engines were billed to customers monthly with usage-based pricing. For example, access to the FISCO BCOS engine and TrustSQL

---

[2] Higgins, S., "Chinese internet conglomerate Tencent is building a suite of blockchain services, detailing the plans in a new white paper", *Coindesk*, April 25, 2017, https://www.coindesk.com/internet-giant-tencent-blockchain-platform, accessed October 10, 2020.

market (both services shared the same price plan) were charged at $1,000 per node per month. Hyperledger Fabric was charged from about $400 to $2,000 per node per month, depending on the different node configurations based on customer requirements. The Tencent cloud blockchain platform was positioned as an external service for organizations to improve their technical capabilities. Based on this positioning, the service offered three primary attributes. First, the platform provided a one-stop blockchain service that could interact with multiple blockchains. Second, Tencent tried to work with customers and partners to build solutions that could be used as benchmark to promote the use of blockchain technology. Third, it tried to actively promote the building of blockchain communities and ecosystems to foster the adoption of the technology. The company tried to build close relationships with blockchain communities like Hyperledger, the Golden Chain Alliance and ICT.

At the TBaaS level, Tencent had tried to improve the functionality of the platform in multiple iterations over time. Interoperability was at the heart of the platform; it supported many platforms including Hyperledger Fabric, Tencent TrustSQL and FISCO BCOS. The TBaaS platform also supported additional features like financial-grade security, security algorithms and integration with authoritative certification authorities (CA). As a pioneer in blockchain technology, Tencent tried to drive blockchain adoption by trying to find use cases and implementations in more business areas. By 2020, the platform had been successfully used in business scenarios in banking, insurance, securities, mutual funds, government affairs and medical fields.

A typical blockchain project used a few key technical features. The first was the smart contract, which was the carrier of the business logic. The second was the consensus mechanism, which was the key to achieving business consensus and data consensus in distributed commerce and required targeted design. The third was trusted identity, which identified a user's identity through key technology and authoritative CA, and facilitated the signing of a multi-party agreement and electronic contract with judicial effect in the blockchain. TBaaS worked synchronously with Tencent Cloud to allow customers to build secure interoperable platforms. Depositing money was by far the largest application area of the Tencent blockchain. Tencent Cloud provided a complete set of trusted deposit and verification capabilities, which customers could use to build their own deposit and certification platform. In addition, Tencent also offered its own solutions in supply chain finance, data exchange and sharing. The blockchain technology had caught everyone's fancy, and the market had many players offering blockchain solutions. As of 2020, there were as many as 20 companies that offered blockchain solutions and services. The main competitors of TBaaS were Baidu XuperChain, Alibaba AntChain, and JD Chain. Baidu XuperChain used artificial intelligence to analyze copyright infringement allegations and had reduced the time to a judgement from three months to one week. TBaaS served both large enterprises as well as major banks in China in assisting them in their digital transformation. The firm also served SMEs by helping them improve their credit financing and information management capabilities.

Although the blockchain market was still in its infancy, blockchain solutions offered many advantages. TBaaS used blockchain technology to link corporate procurement, production, and sales activities, thereby balancing the amount of time suppliers spent on production and supply activities. Furthermore, the blockchain technology enabled the traceability and tracking of the supply of components, which helped save time, and enhanced quality assurance. Producers could conduct on-demand production and implement dynamic adjustments according to the market conditions based on information from blockchain nodes. In other words, the introduction of blockchain could enable "smart manufacturing". Manufacturers could also provide an intelligent (smart) sales and service platform by uploading production data to the blockchain in real time. Deploying blockchains in the cloud provided a flexible infrastructure that could potentially reduce the cost of integration, deployment and operations of multiplatform solutions for companies. However, many organizations were sceptical of the technology, and apprehensive of associated data risks and regulatory requirements essential to run blockchain systems within an enterprise.

8.1.1 Blockchain-as-a-Service Analysis

General: The blockchain technology has been promising to revolutionize payment, exchange, security and verification applications since its inception. As the name suggests, each block of new transaction data is added in an encrypted fashion as a block to the earlier chain of recorded transactions with a time certification, hence, the data is not alterable. As a result, blockchain technology enables the verification of transactions and an unalterable record of transaction history without needing the involvement of third parties like banks for transaction verification and enabling. Depending on the rules of the blockchain, the transactions data need to be verified by a majority or by all members of the blockchain. The total set of transactions (ledger) is distributed across multiple nodes of the blockchain, hence, the distributed set of transactions enhances security. However, despite all the advantages of the blockchain technology, its adoption has been slow and tedious. There have been many sporadic adopters of the technology across multiple sectors like financial services, manufacturing and supply chain management, and healthcare. However, some key challenges have inhibited the large-scale adoption and diffusion of the technology. The first of the challenges is the speed of the processing of transactions owing to the needs of verification. Blockchain transactions take a lot of time for transactions processing, e.g. the copyright infringement analysis time of Baidu XuperChain is one week. While it is shorter than the corresponding manual process time, the time for processing financial transactions on traditional financial messaging and exchange systems like SWIFT is much shorter than the corresponding time for blockchains. Hence, blockchain technology is not commercially viable yet for large applications.

Feasibility: The budget impact of blockchain technology favours the adoption of the service version of the technology, as the costs of acquiring commercial blockchain technology internally is much higher. Even at the cost of a few thousand dollars a month, the number of small enterprises that have adopted the technology is still quite small. However, medium and large-sized enterprises have a number of advantages from adopting the technology. Beyond the budget impact, the analysis of the risk factors favours the as-a-service mode of the technology. Customers may be able to assess the number of transactions using traditional means with some degree of certainty. However, the adoption of blockchain-as-a-service alleviates the risk of an unpredictable number of transactions. Tencent's subscription model enables the cost of adopting the technology to be predictable, leading to a controlled risk pertaining to the number of transactions. One of the biggest disadvantages of the blockchain technology is the hitherto lack of interoperability between different blockchain standards and systems. There are many providers of blockchain technology adhering to different standards and systems. Until a dominant standard emerges for the technology, the interoperability of multiple systems will cause the diffusion of the technology to be slow. Tencent's blockchain-as-a-service offers a higher degree of inter-operability compared to the offerings of many other systems, hence, the obsolescence of technology risk favours the adoption of the Tencent service. From the perspective of customer agility, the three platforms of Tencent enable customers to use the services for multiple applications, enabling customer agility. Tencent also offers its own cloud services and can use its cloud infrastructure to offer the services at a lower cost and for scaling the services. Hence, the agility of Tencent in being able to use internal assets to add services on the platform when needed is high, leading to more profitable and scalable blockchain services.

Profitability: The deal transaction costs of using the blockchain-as-a-service from Tencent are miniscule, as the services are offered off the Tencent cloud, hence, customers can access the services remotely. The global access ensures that deal transaction costs do not lead to any inconvenience for customers, hence, the expected utility-per-use for customers is not diminished by using the service online. The frequency of customer usage and the expected utility-per-use do need careful management from Tencent's perspective for the service to be profitable. Offering blockchain services is extremely energy-intensive, blockchain applications burn a lot of electricity in the decryption processes, hence, the cost of offering blockchain services can be high. Tencent offers its services using a subscription model via the cloud. If some customers use the service a lot, their applications consume a lot of electricity, increasing Tencent's costs. Hence, the subscription model may cause a problem for Tencent if the service is availed of primarily by large customers who process several transactions on Tencent's platforms. At the early stage of the offering, Tencent's goal is to attract more customers to its platforms, thereby increasing the viral network effect of adoption. Hence, in the early stages, the subscription model makes more sense, as it enables customers to try out the service for a relatively low risk. Once the number of adopters of Tencent's blockchain services is above a critical number, Tencent may want to consider other pricing schemes. For example, Tencent may be able to ensure a higher degree of profitability if it adopts a mixed payment scheme of a subscription model that offers a certain threshold number of transactions that can be processed for free. Any additional transactions after the threshold can be charged at a nominal fee, enabling Tencent to ensure the profitability of its blockchain services.

Growth: The competitive environment for Tencent's blockchain services is highly intense in China, there are several competitors like Baidu, Alibaba and JD. While Tencent and Baidu have their roots in software, Alibaba and JD have their roots in e-commerce. Hence, Tencent and Baidu may have an advantage at this stage in the competitive environment, owing to their software competencies. However, Alibaba and JD will have their own advantages in the retail vertical owing to their deep e-commerce experience. Given the slow diffusion of the blockchain application globally owing to the interoperability issues across different sets of standards, one approach that the top four providers in China could take is to adopt one uniform standard. The uniform standard in China could lead to solving the interoperability issues locally, leading to all transactions in China being processed on uniform standards, and a higher degree of adoption of blockchain services in China. The providers could also try to maximize the interoperability with other standards (as they do currently). Next, Tencent also offers a number of complementary solutions to the blockchain service like AI and IoT solutions. Tencent can offer the AI solutions bundled with their blockchain offering, leading to more value for customers from the complementary bundle of services. The software competencies of Tencent can be leveraged to bundle more cloud solutions with the blockchain. The bundling strategy could be a way to scale Tencent's cloud offerings more generally, and the blockchain application specifically. The economies of scale from the cloud offering provide Tencent an easy way to grow their services more quickly. The economies of scale from software solutions are large, this is one of the reasons that software offerings in the XaaS mode have been successful. While the high variable cost of blockchain transaction processing due to electricity consumption lowers the scalability of blockchain applications, having the common platforms on the cloud gives Tencent high economies of scale. Finally, Tencent's three platforms offer the customer base with a number of solutions,

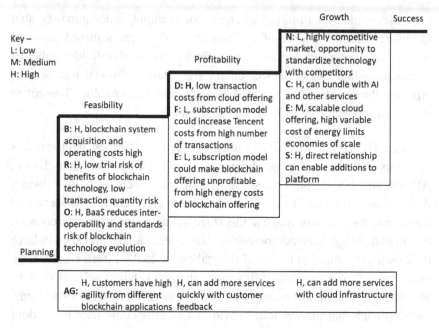

Figure 8.1: XaaS Staircase for Blockchain-as-a-Service

the cloud offering enables Tencent to have a close relationship with its larger customers. Tencent can use this relationship to keep adding services for its blockchain customers, as the offering is still in a nascent stage.

The BROAD FENCES model analysis and the XaaS Staircase for Tencent's blockchain-as-a-service (Figure 8.1) shows that the blockchain offering of Tencent is attractive to customers vis-à-vis the acquisition model of blockchain technology. However, the factors affecting block-chain technology adoption in general could act as potential inhibitors for this service. Tencent can consider more nuanced pricing schemes and working with competitors in China to adopt a uniform standard as potential measures to grow the blockchain service suite profitably.

8.2 DISASTER RECOVERY-AS-A-SERVICE (BLUELOCK)

Bluelock was founded in 2006 and offered disaster recovery services to clients. In 2018, the firm was acquired by InterVision, which was a computer-aided design (CAD) consulting service provider originally. By 2008, InterVision had pivoted its business into data centre and corporate IT networking computing and storage services. Bluelock's key offering was a service-oriented approach called Recovery Assurance, which enabled it to provide expert disaster recovery advice and co-manage clients' recovery processes. The company offered its services based on a service contract and pricing was determined based on several factors that were influenced by the client's needs. Bluelock assigned a dedicated recovery account manager expert to each client. The Bluelock team became an extension of the internal IT department of the client and worked closely to implement a tailored solution. The firm had streamlined this interaction process by introducing an expert onboarding process, playbook creation, targeted testing processes, and extensive service level agreements (SLAs). The Bluelock disaster recovery-as-a-service (DRaaS) was aimed mainly at mid-sized organizations, who were cost conscious and could not afford expensive recovery software solutions. The services varied based on the size of the network, storage and virtual machine sizes, and were offered through its trademark recovery assurance methodology, which had 100% test success. Rollback options for managed services could vary from Run (recovery time objective (RTO) in the order of minutes), Ready (RTO in a few hours) to Restore (RTO in the order of many hours to a couple of days). The recovery time objective (RTO) was a service level objective that defined the time it took to achieve a desired operational capability after a disaster had occurred.[3]

DRaaS solutions like those offered by Bluelock had several advantages. They offered customers with an alternative to purchasing software licenses for backup and recovery which could be resource-intensive and expensive to implement for a smaller organization. Moreover, DRaaS was more extensive than other disaster recovery services like Backup-as-a -Service (BaaS) and Recovery-as-a-Service (RaaS) and had the capability of rapidly recovering data in the event of a disaster. Hence, DRaaS enabled the restoration of normal operations after a disaster at a quicker pace.

---

[3] Bluelock, Case Study, Bluelock Disaster Recovery-as-a-Service Solution Slashes Disaster Recovery Costs in Half for Financial Services Company, 2014, https://www.bluelock.com/wp-content/uploads/2016/02/Bluelock_FinanceCaseStudy_DRaaS.pdf, accessed February 5, 2020.

Gartner had predicted that the DRaaS market, which was estimated at $2.4 billion in 2018, would grow to $3.7 billion by 2021.[4] As DRaaS solutions were often offered over the cloud, customers also benefitted from significant savings in hardware and software licensing fees and consumption of operational resources. DRaaS solutions involved the replication and hosting of servers and their data in cloud servers that enabled lower downtimes in the event of an unexpected interruption. A replication process involved duplication of data from a production environment and posed a few challenges. Since most organizations did not have fully virtualized infrastructure, the replication methodology required the capability of transmitting data from both virtualized and non-virtualized (physical) servers.

The Bluelock DRaaS model offered services in three categories — managed services, professional services and self-services. Managed services were best-suited for clients who had large IT teams with heavy involvement in strategic operations of the business. Managed services helped overburdened IT teams to deliver more by completely outsourcing the recovery process to Bluelock. Fully managed DRaaS was popular as it offered customers guaranteed recovery for low, predictable costs. Bluelock's service and support team designed various combinations of managed services based on client requests. Managed services also offered cloud strategy optimization techniques to handle day-to-day management tasks such as firewalls, load balancing, monitoring, antivirus, OS patching and networking. Professional services offered clients with assistance in the planning, implementation, testing and management of disaster recovery processes. Bluelock primarily managed the recovery infrastructure and data replication and served as the client's advisor. Because this model did not offer a recovery SLA, it was less expensive than managed services. The third option available was self-service, which offered clients a quick, cost-effective alternative for implementing disaster recovery procedures. Self-service customers relied on their internal IT services team to cover most procedures of the disaster recovery process. Self-service DRaaS was in many ways like an on-premises DR solution; however, the

---

[4] Panetta, K., "Gartner Research and Advice for Disaster Recovery", https://www.gartner.com/smarterwithgartner/gartner-research-and-advice-for-disaster-recovery/, accessed October 20, 2020.

administration of the underlying infrastructure of the cloud server where the backup was maintained was provided by Bluelock. One of the key features of Bluelock's services was the recovery playbook. It provided users with a detailed outline of all recovery objectives, restoration steps, configuration details of systems and networks, authorization hierarchies, roles and responsibilities of teams (client team and Bluelock team) and recovery instructions. The playbook also included contact information of both the client and the assigned Bluelock team for user support. Another feature was the onboarding & training guide, which trained users through the process of implementing Bluelock solutions. After the training, a recovery test was scheduled within 30 days.

An example of Bluelock's services was the recovery process it implemented for Siemens.[5] eMeter was a 200-employee unit of Siemens that produced software for electric, natural gas and water utility management systems and had contracted with Bluelock's cloud data centre services to store the recovery copies of its system. As part of the Bluelock service agreement, virtualized copies of first-tier production systems of eMeter were created and stored in Bluelock's data centre. In the event of a disaster, the sleeping virtual machines would become active and restore client servers to the last known point of data integrity. In this particular event, an eMeter customer in India mishandled Siemens' effort to install an energy management system. eMeter immediately approached Bluelock for help, and within three hours' time, the backup copy of the server in Bluelock's cloud centre was activated and the data feed was restored. A task of such volume could have taken four to five business days for clients like eMeter to recover using off-the-shelf disaster recovery products. However, with Bluelock's services, such recoveries could be expedited because of Bluelock's expertise in dealing with disasters.

8.2.1 Disaster Recovery-as-a-Service Analysis

General: The DRaaS suite of services offers risk management services for clients. In disaster studies, it has been observed that organizations suffered

---

[5] Gish, M., "How Siemens eMeter Implemented a Hybrid Cloud Solution", April 16, 2014, https://www.bluelock.com/blog/how-siemens-emeter-implemented-a-hybrid-cloud-solution/, accessed October 20, 2020.

catastrophic data loss in some form or the other. Those who experienced major data losses never got back to normal operations in 43% of the cases, while in 51% of the cases, organizations were paralyzed for over two years. Only 6% of organizations were able to survive long term without significant after-effects in such scenarios. If firms experience data outages for more than 10 days, they are unlikely to recover financially. Almost 80% of global IT organizations have experienced at least one outage or system failure in the last few years. Therefore, adopting a DR plan is a key necessity for organizations. Customers do have the option of implementing their own on-premises DRaaS solutions, however, DRaaS is a specialized service that is difficult to replicate internally for most organizations.

Feasibility: The budget impact of DRaaS solutions is akin to the effect of buying insurance; higher protection levels also require paying higher premiums. If the customer wants to have the same level of risk management expertise in its own internal teams, it will have a higher cost than if it outsources the service to an expert like Bluelock. Disaster recovery is also not a core competence that most organizations strive for in the long run. Hence, outsourcing such services is driven by the lack of internal expertise, coupled with the fact that this expertise can be obtained externally at a lower cost. The risk factors are dominated by the quality and reliability risk being significantly lower if the service is outsourced, rather than if it is acquired in-house. DRaaS providers have a better idea of the internal capacity needed for managing the risk from unforeseen events. Customers can avail of the self-services mode from providers like Bluelock, who can advise them of the internal manpower needed to supplement Bluelock's services. Hence, the risk impact factor favours the adoption of the external DRaaS solutions strongly. The obsolescence of technology factor is also in favour of the adoption of the DRaaS offerings, as retraining internal teams periodically for disaster management is expensive. Any on-premises system will eventually be hard-pressed to keep pace with more ingenuous methods of cyberattacks that evolve over time. In contrast, providers of DRaaS solutions continuously upgrade their recovery solutions to cope with the evolving nature of cyberattacks. Providers like Bluelock are also exposed to disasters from multiple customers, who face outages on a continuous basis, and hence, have a wider set of experiences that enhances their learning capabilities. This continuous learning enables DRaaS providers to upgrade their skills to deal with outages that are caused by natural and human sources. Using the services of DRaaS providers enables customers to get trained by Bluelock's representatives periodically on the new methods they need to learn if they use the professional or self-services suites. Hence, customers gain insights continually on dealing with disasters, and they can identify unforeseen events quickly and work with Bluelock for quick resolutions of the effects of the event. Hence, the customer agility from using the DRaaS offerings is enhanced. If the customer chooses the managed services suite, it can completely outsource the recovery process to the provider and focus on its own strategic issues that need IT support. Bluelock's SLAs that guarantee recovery within a couple of days after the event from the Restore RTO enable customer agility in recovering from disasters. From Bluelock's perspective, it uses its knowledge gained from every recovery experience to upgrade its standard operating procedures based on the nature of the event. Hence, the expert system-like learning process enables Bluelock to design if-then rules for every scenario, giving it a higher degree of agility in responding to disasters. The scalability of the agility is also supported by using standard procedures that can be automated for multiple customers, hence, the DRaaS offering scores well on agility in the feasibility, profitability and growth phases.

Profitability: Since Bluelock's offerings are typically offered on the cloud, the deal transaction costs for the services are negligible. The low transaction costs can be ascertained from the "Run" SLA offered by Bluelock, in which the RTO is guaranteed to be a matter of minutes. From the customer's perspective, Bluelock charges an additional payment based on the infrastructure used and replication charges if a disaster occurs. These charges are incurred beyond the original subscription charges that are based on the level of integrated services and the chosen SLAs by the customer. Hence, if the customer has several disasters in a given period of time, it may need to pay an additional amount to the provider for the recovery charges. If the customer's installed cybersecurity systems are weak and it is prone to repeated cyberattacks, then the charges paid to the DRaaS provider may be correspondingly high. The substitutability between the investments in cybersecurity and disaster recovery is a good opportunity for Bluelock to offer security and recover services in a complementary bundle. If the customer chooses to use the bundle, Bluelock can eliminate the additional payments for the recovery process, as the customer is also subscribing to its security offering. The expected utility-per-use is geared towards extracting the customer's willingness-to-pay efficiently, as the DRaaS solutions are offered at three tiered levels: managed, professional and self. The customer can choose its level of investment in the external recovery process and its own investments, based on its tolerance of downtime if an unforeseen event occurs. Hence, the DRaaS suite of services discriminate well on the frequency of usage, and price the services corresponding to the customer's expected utility-per-use that determines its willingness-to-pay.

Growth: Given the high cost of systemic failure and the potentially high downtime, DRaaS solutions are offered by several competitors, including Unitrends, Zerto and INAP. While each of the competitors have their own proprietary solutions for disaster recovery, the technology underpinnings of the different methods are derived from a common set of principles. Hence, there is a competitive pressure on pricing services, leading to a fragmented market for DRaaS providers, with no clearly dominant player in the market. Given the high degree of competition, the ability of the provider to bundle complementary services can give it an edge in encouraging adoption of its services in the growth phase. Intervision offers a wide range of services in the data centre space with IaaS, storage services, communications and data analytics services in addition to its resiliency services like DRaaS and security solutions. The ability to mix and match service bundles has enabled Intervision to create a wide range of solutions for customers, one of the reasons for Intervision acquiring Bluelock was to enhance its range of solutions. Since all InterVision's offerings can be offered on the cloud, and the services can also be designed to have a mix of on-premises solutions. Intervision has high economies of scale and scope from its offerings. The range of solutions and the close contact with customers who adopt its solutions has enabled Intervision to grow the range of its solutions sustainably.

The analysis of the DRaaS suite of services shows that from the customer's perspective, adopting recovery services externally indeed has a high degree of attractiveness. The model is profitable, however, the highly competitive intensity pressures prices. The ability to offer complementary

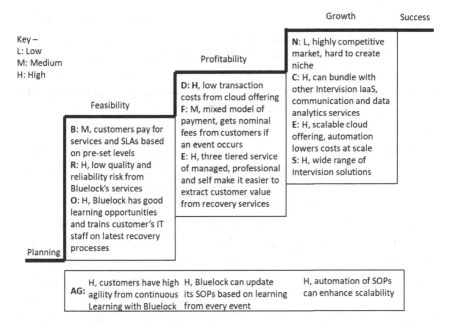

Figure 8.2:   XaaS Staircase for Disaster Recovery-as-a-Service

services and bundle the DRaaS offerings with other services as a solution will be a key factor for successful adoption, profitability and growth of recovery services.

8.3 UNIFIED COMMUNICATIONS-AS-A-SERVICE (DINGTALK)

DingTalk was launched in 2015 as part of Alibaba Group's efforts to compete with its archrival Tencent's popular messaging platform WeChat.[6] Over time, the application underwent several modifications to emerge as one of China's leading enterprise communication and collaboration platforms. The platform's main functionality was called "DING" — it allowed employees to send messages and voice call reminders to colleagues and

---

[6] Zhao Lei, "DingTalk: The Fight To Become The Gateway To A Trillion RMB Market", *tmtpost*, December 22, 2015, https://www.tmtpost.com/1490901.html, accessed October 28, 2020.

collaborating teams. Fundamentally, DingTalk was different from WeChat in that it did not have to send messages immediately to receivers, but at a pre-specified time. DingTalk was similar in functionality to Slack, which provides chat-based and direct messaging functions, and was available as a free tool for enterprise users. The first commercial version of the application — DingTalk 1.0 — was released with the slogan "The Communication Tool for Next-Gen Teams". The core offering was to position the app as a new offering to fill the gap between personalized chatting and meeting needs of users at work — creating a "DingTalk work circle". DingTalk 1.0 included many additional functions like free calling, conference call and an enterprise phone book. Within four months of the release of the first version, DingTalk 2.0 was released in May 2015. The platform's slogan was changed to "DingTalk, a work style", and many additional functions like email, smart on boarding administrator (OA) and shared storage were added. The OA function allowed users to request for leave, seek permission on tasks, broadcast announcements and monitor daily reports and logged work hours. The shared storage enabled users to access files through multiple devices, synchronize files and share documents with colleagues conveniently and efficiently. In October 2015, DingTalk integrated three simplified functions to the platform which were developed in collaboration with RedCircle (a SaaS marketing product built by Chinese company Hecom). The three functions — data analysis, visit plans and customer information were added to the platform as plugins. With the addition of these functions, DingTalk could also provide basic mobile marketing management services. Over time, Alibaba collaborated with other providers like Sensor Tower to add market intelligence and project management applications to the service. With the help of Sensor Tower's added features, users could share the progress of an assigned task with other colleagues and groups, enabling the monitoring of the progress of the task until its completion.[7]

The pricing structure of DingTalk's basic services was an organizational subscription fee, regardless of the number of employees of the organization using the platform. Customers could choose free basic functions usage only, or fixed price usage (applicable for enterprises). The free

---

[7] *Ibid.*

plan included features like 100 GB free storage and 1,000 minutes of free calls. Additional functions like video conferencing were charged on a metered basis annually, e.g., video conferencing was charged at the rate of $6,000 up to 500,000 minutes, and storage was charged at $1,400 up to 1TB annually. Today, DingTalk offers both B2B and B2C offerings and has been designed for both enterprise and individual users. It provides software bundles for human resources management, video conferencing and support for online education. It also offers hardware support for smart office management, attendance-taking equipment, and cloud printing machines. In addition, it also has packaged solutions like "digi-campus" for universities, "digi-hospital" for hospitals, "digi-retailing" for retailers, and "digi-government" for government workers.

Over the years, DingTalk has added new features to its platform, including commuting services by Uber for employees (since discontinued), discounts for users when using Xiaomi music, Tmall supermarket and Taobao Koubei food takeaway. The objective was to act as a platform gateway and bring in more users from other platforms onto its platform by creating forced conversions. The aggregator of apps model was similar to the WeChat model. By March 2020, DingTalk had amassed a customer base of over 300 million users and 15 million enterprises. Although, DingTalk had originally been designed with the small enterprise in mind, it was widely adopted by large enterprises as well including educational institutions. In 2018, DingTalk launched its English version in Malaysia, which was its first foray outside China. A key advantage of the DingTalk platform was the scalability of its cloud infrastructure. DingTalk could also support 11 languages in its instant messaging function. It had the added bonus of natural language processing features which supported translations in real time. These features had been developed by Alibaba's DMO Academy — the group's global research unit.

One of the success stories of DingTalk was its use by a customer who was a training provider in the IT industry. Being a training provider, the customer dealt with multiple parties from different locations to ensure that the training interventions could be implemented as scheduled. Effective communication was an essential enabler for the customer; in the past, employees used several forms of communication including WhatsApp and email, however, tracking events and tasks remained a challenge. With

DingTalk, the customer could prioritize and track tasks efficiently, and DingTalk's applications allowed the customer to implement paperless approvals, reducing the waiting time for approvals across multiple offices and locations. Approvals for claims, purchase requests and last-minute orders were also simplified and easier to handle. Additionally, DingTalk features like off-site attendance allowed managers to manage flexi-hours of salespersons easily.

However, DingTalk's wide acceptance in the Chinese enterprise market encouraged other firms to develop their own solutions, as the features in the services could be easily replicated by competitors. Many competitors launched similar platforms — Tencent launched the "WeChat Work" platform, ByteDance introduced the "Lark" set of services, and Huawei Co. offered the "Welink" suite. In a crowded market with so many communications services offerings, DingTalk had obviously taken the lead due to its early market entry. Its ties to Alibaba had ensured that it could continue to upgrade its offerings with features targeting evolving customer needs due to the readymade technology support to design new features and functionalities on its platform.

8.3.1 Unified Communications-as-a-Service Analysis

General: The Unified Communications-as-a-Service (UCaaS) offering, in which many different communication methods are jointly offered on one platform, has enabled enterprise communications to be integrated seamlessly. Hence, the primary dimension of the BROAD FENCES model that the UCaaS suite of services outperforms on is the complementarity of utilities offered by independent communication technologies. These UCaaS platforms have enabled team collaboration efforts to be taken to the next level. These platforms are cloud-based offerings and can be accessed through any device by users. Hosting the application on the cloud also takes away the need for constant reinstallation of advanced versions. The added security from the cloud-based provider securitizing all team communications is an added value offering of the UCaaS offerings. The simplified communications are complemented by simplified billing procedures, as the customer pays one bill every cycle for accessing the platform. The core value offer of these services is the ability to use functions on one platform to address all team communications needs, thereby taking away the need for interoperability of different technologies. Apart from the reduced need for hardware and better access owing to the cloud offering, the added collaboration functionality offered by advanced technologies provides added value beyond the one-stop shop proposition for collaboration. From the customer's perspective, it provides a simplified platform for communicating with other stakeholders beyond their own organization. For example, customers and vendors who have to be involved in the tasks of the team can be integrated into specific team groups on the UCaaS platform, and information on other aspects of the organization does not have to be shared. Global accessibility to the UCaaS platform is another utility-adding feature, as remote teams can coordinate their efforts on the platform. Features that share team availability make it easier to coordinate meetings across remote team members. The reliability of the provider depends on the reliability of its cloud. Alibaba is one of the top four global cloud service providers, hence, the reliability of its cloud services is high.

The pioneer in the UCaaS offering space was Slack, which began as an instant messaging service for enterprises, and then added more features for enhanced communications over time. From operating in a start-up mode in 2013 to its leadership position today for SMEs, Slack has grown exponentially through the judicious offering of new services for enhanced communications. It still has among the best features for sharing software code and integrating communications across business functions, but its dominance is being challenged by competitors like Microsoft Teams and Zoom. Like Slack, the enterprise niche had helped Ding stand apart from its competitors — this had enabled the platform to provide offerings that were different from regular social networking apps. Clearly demarcating its functions and features had enabled the platform to be distinctive in its enterprise offerings.

Feasibility: As DingTalk was a free tool for users, with a reasonable subscription fee for the enterprise, it had become an instant hit with small and mid-sized companies who could not afford expensive enterprise management software. The cost of accessing the DingTalk platform does not depend on the number of employees accessing the platform. Hence, the budget impact of the UCaaS offerings on DingTalk is high, the high budget impact has enabled DingTalk to diffuse quickly as the chosen UCaaS platform for Chinese enterprises. If the enterprise had to acquire its own communication technologies like the email system and videoconferencing system, the cost would have been higher compared to the bundled subscription fee charged for all services in the UCaaS mode. The risk impact is also substantial, as security risk, reliability risk and the budget overrun risk are well-managed by the adoption of the subscription-based UCaaS solutions. The obsolescence of technology risk strongly favours the as-a-service model, as any on-premises communications system will have to be used for longer periods of time to justify the initial cash outlay. In contrast, Alibaba can upgrade DingTalk features with added utilities from new technologies as they appear, owing to their higher economies of scale. The agility offered to customers from the UCaaS suite of services is high, as after the initial learning phase, customers can use added features that are developed with similar interfaces to the existing features easily. From Alibaba's perspective, since the technologies are modular, they can add interfaces between technologies to perform seamlessly with each other, increasing the complementarity in utility from the technologies. Since the core integrated technologies are standardized and have standardized interfaces, the agility in the growth phase is also high.

Profitability: The deal transaction costs are high in the initial phase owing to the learning curve but are negligible after the learning has been absorbed by customers. It is hard for the provider to discriminate based on the frequency of usage and utility-per-use, as metered pricing will lower the adoption of the services. The high intensity of competition in the UCaaS space where basic functions are offered for free, and high-end feature use is charged with a subscription model by almost all providers, also makes it harder to use metered pricing. Hence, the performance of the UCaaS solutions on the dimensions of frequency of usage and the expected utility-per-use is moderate.

Growth: The space of UCaaS offerings is very competitive globally and in China, as integrating communications technologies to work seamlessly with each other is easy to replicate. Hence, the ability to create a niche in the UCaaS space is low. The primary value offered by the as-a-service offering of team collaboration tools is the complementarity benefit from the ability to integrate the use of multiple technologies seamlessly. To improve the complementarity further, providers can increase the degree of interoperability of the UCaaS suite with other services. Microsoft Teams and Google Meet have been enhanced by the ability to share files that are created with Microsoft Office and G-suite tools. Other UCaaS providers also endeavour to create this complementarity with other services like the IaaS solutions. The economies of scale are also enhanced using these services, as the services are offered using the cloud, hence, UCaaS solutions are highly scalable using cloud infrastructure. While it is hard to tailor the needs of individual organizations into UCaaS offerings as the technologies are typically standardized, if there is a large set of customers requesting a certain utility, providers can integrate those utilities easily to create a holistic offering.

The analysis and the XaaS Staircase of the unified communications-as-a-service offering show that the UCaaS solutions offer extensive

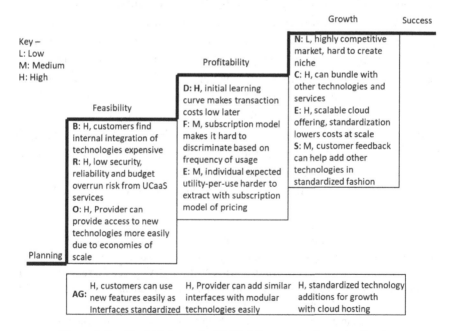

Figure 8.3: XaaS Staircase for Unified Communications-as-a-Service

customer value and will be the dominant mode of offering team collaboration solutions. However, the high competitive intensity and easy replicability of UCaaS solutions make it hard to extract a lot of value for the provider, and the profitability and growth prospects will need a constant upgrading of the services in the solutions suite.

8.4 VISUAL SEARCH-AS-A-SERVICE (VISENZE)

ViSenze was founded in 2012 in Singapore and aimed to solve real-world problems through the innovative application of AI-based technology. Originating from research conducted by the National University of Singapore-Tsinghua Extreme Search Centre (NExT), ViSenze was established with the vision of revolutionizing the way web users searched for products online — using images rather than text. The firm's visual recognition and search technology was developed to process and interpret visual content (images and videos) to provide users with useful information and enable purchase decision-making. As the adage goes, a picture is worth a thousand words. Studies had shown that 90% of the information transmitted to the human brain is visual.[8] Studies also showed that visual information is processed 60,000 times faster than text.[9] Visual search technology based on image recognition algorithms was touted as one of the most exciting trends in e-commerce. However, technological limitations and security features of platforms had throttled the ability of visual search in enhancing e-commerce, particularly via mobile apps. Companies like Google and Zappos had made visual search viable more than a decade ago, but mobile e-commerce applications had transformed the application of visual search. The widespread commercialization and adoption of visual search in mobile e-commerce platforms had created a competitive edge for

---

[8] Shift, "Studies Confirm the Power of Visuals to Engage Your Audience in eLearning", https://www.shiftelearning.com/blog/bid/350326/studies-confirm-the-power-of-visuals-in-elearning#:~:text=According%20to%20the%20Visual%20Teaching%20Alliance%3A&text=90%25%20of%20information%20transmitted%20to,are%20linked%20to%20the%20retina, accessed October 28, 2020.

[9] Eisenberg, E., "Humans Process Visual Data Better", September 15, 2014, https://www.t-sciences.com/news/humans-process-visual-data-better, accessed September 20, 2020.

retailers. E-commerce retailers had introduced solutions that incorporated visual search for improved customer experience, engagement and capturing impulse purchases. Visual search had been implemented in numerous retail sectors including apparel and accessories, home improvement and decor, electronics and toys, as well as daily need items like groceries.[10]

The ViSenze platform was offered to clients as a software-as-a-service (SaaS) platform with a pay-per-use pricing model. The pricing was based on the volume of usage of API (application programming interface) calls that an e-commerce website made to the platform. ViSenze's pricing tiers were created to cater to various clients, based on the volume of user searches and volume of images indexed. For some applications, the platform required a one-time customization to suit the specific requirements of the client. In these instances, the company charged a one-time customization fee on top of the usage price. ViSenze image recognition technology comprised three distinct solutions — a search and recognition API, an inference-based recommendation engine, and a fully automated cloud-based image indexing and analysis system. The image search API enabled shoppers to take a picture of an item in-store and search for it online. The recommendation engine provided shoppers with intelligent product recommendations that were aligned to the customer search process. An automated product tagging API also allowed users to identify and tag a product for improved search experience. The solutions worked in tandem with product recommendation algorithms that had expanded from simply showing the most popular products in-store. ViSenze's solutions also enabled customers to display products based on their affinity with similar shoppers with similar behaviours, and showed personalized recommendations based on each shopper's past behaviour.

The ViSenze search API provided accurate, reliable and scalable image search, with end points that allowed e-commerce platform developers to index their images and perform image searches efficiently. The search feature included a software development kit (SDK), which accommodated various languages, such that the API could be easily integrated

---

[10]Chokshi, S. & Bhattacharya, L., "Transforming the vision of retail with AI: Visenze", Hr. org, November 2, 2020, https://store.hbr.org/product/transforming-the-vision-of-retail-with-ai-visenze/SMU894, accessed February 20, 2020.

into the client's web and mobile applications. The solution could detect the primary object in the uploaded image and search it against the image database. Alternatively, the user could specify a bounding box as an API request parameter to search for the bounded object. Multiple product search solutions allowed detecting multiple objects in the uploaded image, and search for corresponding similar images in the image database. The API response then returned the search results for each detected object. The recognition API could be used to detect individual products/objects in images, find their detailed fashion attributes/styles, and predict the image's quality. The API could be easily integrated with the client's in-house product catalogue management system. The image recognition tool could uncover every layer of a fashion image. Fashion attribute recognition parameters could analyze images and extrapolate the fashion attributes within it. Fashion trend and occasion recognition parameters allowed identification of fashion elements and trends in images. A key feature of the ViSenze solution was the 'You may also Like' feature, which showcased recommended products on the product detail page. The client could apply custom recommendation rules for each application based on the customer demographic or other metadata such as brand, price and colour. The algorithm then created a similarity score and ranked products in order of the score. This solution offered an opportunity for the client to promote more products based on visual similarity and other relevant recommendation rules. Moreover, if a requested product was out of stock, the feature could help the platform convert the search into a sale by providing the customer with similar alternative products. This feature worked in a similar way to the in-store experience, where a customer could ask the retail assistant to find a specific product, say a similar dress in a different colour. By training machines, ViSenze was able to replicate that offline experience in an online setting.

ViSenze had used a three-pronged approach to ensure that its API-based SaaS was scalable and delivered highly engaging experiences to end customers. First, the company provided scalable infrastructure to support the indexing and processing of billions of images without sacrificing performance and with minimal pre-processing. Second, the speed of its search engine enabled results to be generated in 100 to 200 milliseconds for search based on an existing database item, and up to one second for search based on a newly uploaded image. The engine's ability to search and find matching and similar results was evaluated at an above 90% satisfaction rate by customers. Finally, the firm also provided support services for built failovers combined with professional services to ensure reliability and availability of service. The company used high-quality training data for enhanced accuracy and continuous improvement of its recognition models. Additionally, speed improvements and search refinement processes were implemented regularly. Also, new APIs were developed and launched to provide users with additional functionality. After their success in the apparel market, ViSenze's key question was if its solutions for retail customers could be beneficial in other markets. While they had tested some solutions in other markets, the tests had yet to be conducted on a larger scale.

8.4.1 Visual Search-as-a-Service Analysis

General: The ViSenze solution suite of AI services is part of a broad category of AI-as-a-service solutions that have been commercialized by providers in different industry sectors. A number of these solutions are in the space of retail, competitor examples include NetraDyne, ReadSense and Levatas. The offering of visual search-as-a-service (VSaaS) is being used by many retailers to provide an optimal customer experience, by moving away from textual and keyword search to more informative methods of search. ViSenze conducted a study of more than a thousand individuals in the Gen Z and millennial demographic and found that more than 62% of the respondents said that visual search capabilities were the most exciting new technology on the horizon. Customers can use their phones to take pictures from billboards, television ads and other sources, and upload the picture to an app. The app can help them find that exact item or similar items in e-commerce sites. The service supports the search process for customers for apparel products, toys and other product categories that can be identified visually and have a simple visual attribute space defining the category. Shopping for apparel, toys and other goods had a significant brand effect in the past, the visual search utility enables lesser known brands to compete on an even keel based on the visual appeal of their products. The use of AI approaches for pattern recognition can identify the same product and similar products, that functionality of AI and adaptive learning algorithms has been known for many years. However, the ability to create personae of individuals based on their searches, and the concomitant ability to predict the likes in similar categories by mapping individual preferences has taken the application of AI services in retail to the next level.

The specialized skills and knowledge of AI algorithms needed to develop such specialized services for visual search are hard to acquire internally for retailers if they have limited product assortments. While small and specialized firms like ViSenze can be acquired by large retailers, the core competence of ViSenze is enhanced by training their algorithms with large and diverse datasets. It is well known that adaptive learning algorithms of AI and machine learning make better predictions as a function of the training data available. The more diverse and larger the training datasets, the better the predictive power of the AI algorithms. If large retailers were to acquire specialized technology firms like ViSenze, they might find that working with one firm's data would provide limited learning and training opportunities for the algorithms. This would result in limiting the predictive power of the algorithms, hence, availing of the offerings of ViSenze in the as-a-service mode may add more value for customers than trying to acquire the provider. Hence, the quality of services would be higher if ViSenze (and other competitors) stayed independent and worked with many customers with diverse offerings.

Feasibility: Since ViSenze charges customers on a pay-per-use basis and visual search has a much higher chance of resulting in a sale compared to text or keyword search, the budget impact of availing of Visenze's services is moderate to high. The risk factor impact of using VSaaS is high, as retailers can correlate the outcome of the visual search process with the eventual buying behaviour of customers. Hence, the testing of the value of the AI service is easy to do, and retailers can try the services of multiple providers together, eventually adopting the services of the provider with the highest search to sale conversions. Search techniques deploying AI and machine learning tools evolve quickly, hence, the adoption of the as-a-service mode enables the retailer to stay nimble and try other providers to test the efficacy of their services. The customer agility from using the VSaaS mode is enhanced as the customer can use the services of multiple providers for different product categories, based on the efficacy of their solutions. Customers can also change the provider easily with the pay-per-use mode, as there is no subscription period that locks them in. The provider can experiment with different underlying algorithms for the prediction and recommendation engines and can refine the search process continuously with new results being added to the learning datasets. This creates a cycle of continuous improvement for the provider's core services. For scaling the offering of its services, ViSenze uses AWS and Google cloud infrastructure, enabling it to scale its services in an agile fashion.

Profitability: The deal transaction costs for the use of ViSenze's services are negligible, as the service is automated. However, the pay-per-use mechanism does result in the ticking meter effect for the customer, as every search process does not result in a sale for the customer, hence, the deal transaction costs are moderate. The pay-per-use mechanism of payment enables ViSenze to discriminate perfectly on the frequency of usage dimension of customer utility, leading to a high impact on the frequency of usage dimension. While the expected utility-per-use from the customer's perspective is the margin it makes from the eventual sale of its product, ViSenze can only charge a fraction of the margin from the customer. Hence, the price-per-use is standardized based on the API calls made to the platform. ViSenze cannot discriminate based on the value of the expected utility-per-use or the margin, it charges a standard price-per-use for high-margin and low-margin product sales alike, leading to a moderate performance on the expected utility-per-use dimension.

Growth: The market for AI applications-as-a-service is highly competitive, with small and large providers offering specialized services to customers. However, the sheer range of products that can be sold on e-commerce sites does leave the potential for carving out a niche for smaller providers in specific product categories. Therefore, the performance of the VSaaS solutions in the competition or niche category is moderate. While larger firms offering VSaaS can bundle their services with other complementary services, specialized providers like ViSenze with targeted portfolios do not have the ability to offer complementary services with their AI solutions. The scalability of the services is enabled by offering their services on the cloud, hence, ViSenze indeed has high

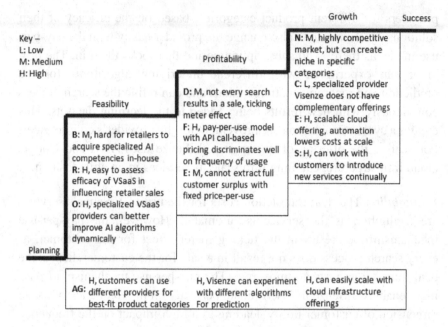

Key –
L: Low
M: Medium
H: High

Planning

Feasibility

B: M, hard for retailers to acquire specialized AI competencies in-house
R: H, easy to assess efficacy of VSaaS in influencing retailer sales
O: H, specialized VSaaS providers can better improve AI algorithms dynamically

Profitability

D: M, not every search results in a sale, ticking meter effect
F: H, pay-per-use model with API call-based pricing discriminates well on frequency of usage
E: M, cannot extract full customer surplus with fixed price-per-use

Growth

N: M, highly competitive market, but can create niche in specific categories
C: L, specialized provider Visenze does not have complementary offerings
E: H, scalable cloud offering, automation lowers costs at scale
S: H, can work with customers to introduce new services continually

Success

AG:
H, customers can use different providers for best-fit product categories
H, Visenze can experiment with different algorithms For prediction
H, can easily scale with cloud infrastructure offerings

Figure 8.4:   Visual Search-as-a-Service

economies of scale. ViSenze does work closely with retailers to understand the theme behind the product offerings of the retailer. This enables ViSenze to understand customer requirements and tailor solutions in the VSaaS space to customer needs over time, hence, the solutions impact of ViSenze's offering is high.

The XaaS Staircase of ViSenze's VSaaS offering is depicted in Figure 8.4. The analysis and the staircase show that ViSenze does have its strengths in every phase: feasibility, profitability and growth. However, it needs to create a competitive niche in which it offers best-in-class services globally to have a sustained profit stream, and it can use its capabilities to develop and offer complementary services to customers to sustain its growth in the long run.

8.5 WORKPLACE-AS-A-SERVICE (ATOS)

Atos was a global leader in digital transformation services with over 110,000 employees in 73 countries worldwide, and was headquartered in

Bezons, France.[11] It was the leading European firm in cloud, cybersecurity and high-performance computing solutions. It offered end-to-end vertical solutions, smart data platforms and infrastructure solutions. In late 2019, the firm launched a workplace-as-a-service solution in partnership with Google Cloud to provide enterprise customers with a way of enhancing the employee workplace experience, through greater choice for users and a boost to productivity. As part of its service partnership, Atos provided an integrated and secure package, which incorporated the supply and support of Google Chromebook (electronic devices), Atos Circuit (enterprise cloud-based communication and collaboration platform) software, and Google's G Suite (a suite of cloud computing, productivity and collaboration tools and software) product. The package was supported with setup, migration and management services. The combination of G Suite and Chromebooks enhanced user experiences, providing consistency of usage across all devices and apps, enabling increased workforce productivity and engagement. Security and compliance features were built-in into the package in accordance to the 'zero trust' security framework, which entailed stringent ID verification procedures to prevent data breaches. The workplace-as-a-service combined three elements: device, collaboration services and success management. Chromebooks were laptops, detachables and tablets powered by Google's Chrome operating system, and were fully managed in the cloud. Collaboration services comprised the GSuite and Atos Circuit. GSuite was a host of applications consisting of tools to connect, create, access and control data for the workplace environment. The Circuit was a communication and collaboration platform, which was like the UCaaS suite of services. The Success Management comprised services by Atos to deliver a personalized user-centric workplace experience. A one-time fee was charged for the initial project services to implement G Suite, Circuit and Chromebooks into an organization's IT setup. The rest of the service was charged as a monthly subscription and covered workplace success management. Subscription fees were charged on a per user basis. The workplace management focused on the user experience of the workplace while keeping the data secure according to the client's security policies.

---

[11] Wikipedia, Atos, https://en.wikipedia.org/wiki/Atos, accessed November 1, 2020.

Key Performance Indicators were implemented to measure the performance of the experience level agreements (XLAs).[12]

The project approach for implementing the workplace-as-a-service was divided into three main phases. In the first phase, work streams were introduced to enable technical configuration, change management, support management and aligning the service with the business. The second phase catered to deploying the workplace and data migration activities. The last phase was the ongoing workplace experience, which started with the deployment of the G Suite. A focussed approach was taken to improve employee workplace experience, which used a workplace transformation and management contract based on the XLA agreements. Both human and technical metrics were used to perform regular assessments. A transition score was calculated to measure user experience during the transition to G Suite. The score was based on users' perception of the implementation and real-time data from support tickets, migration errors, training attendance and communication statistics. Other metrics like adoption score and effectivity scores were also used to measure the adoption level of the tools. User perception data were collected through polls, while an effectivity score was measured using queried polls combined with data from the platform. Reports of the metrics were collected monthly, and learnings from the reports were assimilated into the system in a data-driven change approach.

The workplace-as-a-service provided several advantages to Atos as well as its clients. For clients, the service suite improved productivity through smart, simple and consistent apps installed on every device. It also allowed devices to have built-in security and compliance features, to enable a zero-breach-of-trust security framework. The innovative contract model created a sense of commitment and enabled user responses to be measured with respect to the agreed upon XLAs. Additionally, it allowed an organization to switch to 100% cloud making the workplace more agile, and the easy utilization of the Google Cloud platform for technologies as Search. For Atos, the service created an extra source of income that was recurring and could be scaled easily without the need for additional resources. Atos's workplace-as-a-service offering has been highly lauded

---

[12] *Ibid.*

since its launch in 2019. Gartner rated the Atos digital workplace as a market Leader in its Magic Quadrant for Managed Workplace Services for Europe as well as North America.

8.5.1 Workplace-as-a-Service Analysis

General: The reader will recognize that the workplace-as-a-service (WaaS) offering combines separate attributes of XaaS services that have been discussed in this book. It has elements of the PCaaS or device-as-a-service (DaaS) offering, in that the devices will be provided by Google and Atos for all employees of the firm. Hence, the subscription fee is charged based on the number of employees or users in the customer firm, to recover the cost of devices by the provider. It incorporates the collaboration and communication platform, which is Google's offering in the UCaaS space. The third suite of services in the WaaS offering — success management — is a customer support service, and is offered at three levels. The Foundation level offers the services of a chatbot to the customer's employees and can answer queries on the first two offerings (device management and the communication platform). The service also offers a callback feature at a specific time for providing support services online. The Advanced level of services offers contact with a service desk. The Enterprise level of customer support offers the service desk services, in addition to a smart locker in the customer's physical office location. The smart locker enables the employees of the customer to exchange a damaged device for a new one.

The digital workplace is a must for large organizations today. While most firms continue to have a physical workplace, the Covid-19 aftermath has shown the importance of a digitally connected workplace. While digital workplaces have the benefits of increased connectivity for large organizations that enable better digital collaboration in addition to the benefits of co-location, they offer SMEs the ability to operate without a physical workplace. The Atos WaaS offering adds to the device and collaboration services by offering the ability to measure employee engagement periodically and encouraging the use of technology for increased productivity. However, digital workplaces also have negatives like lower interpersonal communication, a resistance to the digitization of the workplace, and a lack of human interaction leading to lower communication effectiveness using technology. The lack of human interaction also leads to less connectivity with customers and vendors, leading to more mechanistic interactions and a lack of skills in understanding customer needs. The workplace-as-a-service offering should create tools for enhanced social interaction between employees to build this connectivity, and the customer should organize social events with physical interaction.

Feasibility: The budget impact and the risk impact factors are a combination of the device-as-a-service and the UCaaS offerings. The budget impact of the WaaS offering is moderate, as the devices are offered on a subscription basis that is akin to the rental of the devices, and since devices have short product lifecycles, the budget savings from the device-as-a-service mode are not high. However, since the integrated WaaS offering can make the need for physical office space redundant for SMEs, there could be a significant budget impact for SMEs if they adopt the WaaS suite. The communications and collaboration tools in the WaaS offerings enable the use of collaboration tools at a lower cost than the customer would be able to acquire internally. However, the risk of lock-in for devices is also high, as customers will be tied to the devices offered by the provider, and some employees who prefer to use other devices will not be able to avail of their choice. Hence, the risk impact factor has a low effect on the adoption of the WaaS offering. The obsolescence of technology factor has a moderate impact favouring the adoption of the WaaS mode, as the devices can be replaced and the collaboration tools available will evolve at a pace that is similar to the rest of the industry. The agility of customers with the WaaS offering is enhanced although at moderate levels, as the customer can upgrade devices regularly, and access advances in communication tools. Atos can offer different devices at suitable price points in collaboration with Google and can upgrade the collaboration tools with new technologies periodically. The agility needs to support Atos's scaling is also at moderate levels, as devices can be acquired from Google and collaboration tools can be upgraded easily on the cloud.

Profitability: Since devices and collaboration tools can be used without a significant effect of deal transaction costs in both the acquisition and as-a-service modes, the deal transaction costs have a low impact on the profitability of the WaaS offering. The frequency of usage cannot be discriminated perfectly by Atos either on the devices or on the collaboration tools, as the subscription fees are based on the number of users. The pricing mechanism of the subscription model can benefit from a higher number of employees though. It is interesting to note that both the PCaaS provider reviewed in this book (Dell) and the UCaaS provider (DingTalk) use a subscription mode pricing model. The combination of the two services bundled with customer support services also uses a similar subscription model that is based on the number of users (though DingTalk's model does not charge for basic services on the number of users). The expected utility-per-use cannot be extracted fully by the provider using the subscription model, hence, the performance of the WaaS mode is moderate on the expected utility-per-use.

Growth: The competitive space for digital workplace services is crowded with players like IBM, HPE, Accenture and HCL offering similar services along with other players. The standardization of devices and collaboration tools technologies implies that it is hard to carve a niche in the WaaS space. The complementarity between devices and collaboration tools being designed by Google is the primary value offering of the WaaS mode by Atos, along with the bundling of these services with Atos's cloud security offerings. The economies of scale are moderate owing to the physical devices not being as scalable as the collaboration tools. However, the digital workplace service suite can be enhanced depending on customer requirements with other standardized services from the wide suites of Atos and Google, leading to the performance of the WaaS offering being high on the solutions impact.

The XaaS Staircase for the workplace-as-a-service offering (Figure 8.5) coupled with the BROAD FENCES analysis shows that the offering's primary value is the ability to outsource all digital workplace needs to an external provider. The benefit of complementarity from availing of the device-as-a-service and the unified communications-as-a-service offerings must be weighed against the cost of locking in to one provider. Employees may desire to have a choice of devices as devices offer personalized utility for employees as well. However, the WaaS offering is growing fast, the COVID-19 pandemic has accelerated the move towards

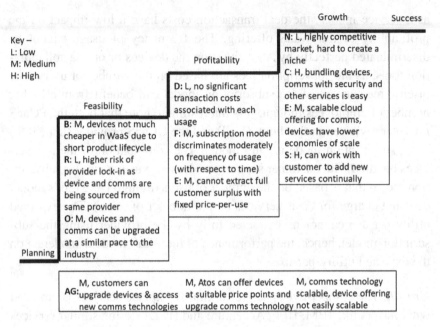

Figure 8.5:   XaaS Staircase for Workplace-as-a-Service

enhanced digital services for most customers. In a survey conducted in the Asia-Pacific region in 2020, IDC found that over half of all organizations would increase their spending on the acquisition of digital workplace services for their employees within the next one year. This shows that the digital workplace is here to stay after the pandemic as well, and providers that offer more value can be industry leaders for an enhanced or new style of working in an enterprise.

8.6 PLATFORM-AS-A-SERVICE (OPENSHIFT)

OpenShift was Red Hat's platform-as-a-service (PaaS) offering, which became an open source technology in 2012. The platform resulted from Red Hat's acquisition of Makara — a firm with a proprietary PaaS platform based on Linux containers. Red Hat Inc. was an American multinational software company which offered open source products to enterprises. It was founded in 1993 and became a subsidiary of IBM in 2019. Red Hat had started its journey as a catalogue business selling Linux and Unix software accessories. The OpenShift container platform was Red Hat's on-premises private PaaS product built around core application containers on the Linux core operating system. The Docker application containers used OS-level virtualization to deliver software in packages (containers). A container was a standard unit of software that packages code and related dependencies to allow an application to run quickly and reliably in an interoperable environment. A Docker container was a standalone executable package of software that is supported on Red Hat Enterprise Linux.[13]

The OpenShift Enterprise PaaS offering was an extended version of the online OpenShift PaaS, which had a subscription pricing model that organizations could install in their own data centres or on other dedicated hardware. The OpenShift platform leveraged many technologies in enterprise Linux to enable applications to be run in a multi-tenant environment securely, and in a predictable manner. OpenShift enterprise was also based on an extensible architecture, which allowed for the integration of a broad ecosystem of middleware and tools. Many PaaS environments were like hosted services and delivered web-based APIs with a set of programming interfaces to a specified host application. PaaS offered services that enabled developers to write, run and manage applications without the need to handle the operating system and other infrastructure. The Red Hat OpenShift PaaS made application deployment even less cumbersome — the ease of use was like that of an application pushing code into repository. The OpenShift PaaS offering provided auto-scaling, self-service and monitoring tools, which allowed the developer to create applications with familiar tools, languages and frameworks. The platform supported many programming languages and frameworks, allowing the developer the flexibility of choosing the language that they were most comfortable with to develop their applications.

Architecturally, the only constraint of developing applications on the OpenShift PaaS was the operating system — Red Hat enterprise Linux. To facilitate a choice of language for the developers, OpenShift offered

---

[13] Jagielski, J., "Announcing OpenShift Origin — The Open Source Platform as a Service (PaaS)", OpenShift Blog, April 30, 2012, https://web.archive.org/web/20160513212018/ https://blog.openshift.com/announcing-openshift-origin-the-open-source-platform-as-a-service-paas/, accessed November 1, 2020.

cartridges for different programming languages. In addition, the platform also supported popular development tools like Apache Maven — a software project management tool, which allowed developers to build, report and document projects from a central model. The availability of multiple consumption options of the OpenShift PaaS — such as OpenShift Online and OpenShift Enterprise with dedicated offerings — provided customers with choices to adopt PaaS as appropriate for their environment. The OpenShift platform also offered value in terms of facilitating timely and flexible delivery of usable applications and services across heterogeneous IT environments. Moreover, developing applications on the OpenShift platform required fewer testing and production servers. Since the platform supported containerization, micro-services and multitenancy, it drove down infrastructure costs and enabled cost-effective scaling even as the applications expanded.[14]

From the customer's perspective, the OpenShift platform enabled developers to bring applications to market fast. Besides, OpenShift also increased the quality of the applications as it facilitated more environments where they could be tested, meaning that developers could perform various stages of testing from development, QA and UAT all in one place. This not only enabled the development process to be executed in an agile fashion, but also made the applications less prone to error. Deployment and consecutive releases were also simpler to execute because of the one-platform offering. An International Data Corporation (IDC) report had noted that applications developed on OpenShift required an average of 19% less staff time for day-to-day management of applications.[15]

Applying patches also became a simpler process as organizations could implement fixes without causing disruptions to the existing application usage. Additionally, release automation, smoother application support across diverse IT environments, and improved application configurations were additional advantages from the platform. With a common platform for developing applications across their IT ecosystems, customer

---

[14] Shipley, G. & Dumpleton, G., "OpenShift for Developers", O'Reilly, 2016, pp. 19–71.

[15] Katarki, T., "Red Hat OpenShift 4.6 Is Now Available", OpenShift Blog, October 27, 2020, https://www.openshift.com/blog/red-hat-openshift-4.6-is-now-available, accessed November 1, 2020.

organizations could use OpenShift to reduce inefficiencies that arose from using different tools and approaches for different types of applications. In many organizations, PaaS offerings were also used as standardization tools as they allow all applications to be uniform with similar development workflows and increased consistency. Standardization was critical as more organizations adopted agile development models to build a rapid, iterative approach to developing applications and systems. A high-security operating system like enterprise Linux further added to this value by providing an environment which could withstand security threats and help deploy highly secure applications, which were also interoperable and could link with other applications without compromising data.

8.6.1 Platform-as-a-Service Analysis

General: The platform-as-a-service offering has seen rapid growth over the last few years, owing to the advantages it offers firms in creating applications with a pay-per-resources-used mechanism. The use of the platform enables the customer to develop and create their own applications in a secure environment, with standardized tools. In addition to the physical infrastructure that is provided by the IaaS offering, PaaS offerings also provide software tools like operating systems, along with user libraries and tools for applications development and deployment. In addition to the software tools, most PaaS offerings also offer simple interfaces to the customer to enhance the ability to learn and use the platform, and other software applications like analytics for improved development. For customers who need to create customized applications for their own clients, the PaaS offering provides a standardized interface for the development of different applications, easy testing and deployment processes and, concomitantly, lower costs if used effectively. The lower costs results from using standardized tools, eliminating the need for low-level code, not needing to set up and maintain the core stack, and the lower downtime from a provider maintaining the platform with standard penalty clauses to ensure the availability of the platform. Having a set of standardized tools and libraries for the development of applications results in a shorter time of application development, and the ability to react faster to customer needs. Hence, the

PaaS offering enables the customer to develop applications with standard-ized tools in an agile fashion, leading in lower time-to-market, and the ability to provide upgrades on a continuous basis when new tools are added on the platform. Along with the benefits of lower costs and faster develop-ment time, the ability to scale the business with the economies of scale afforded by the platform is an added asset from the customer's perspective. Since most PaaS providers charge for resources used, the customer has the ability to scale its business effectively, and vice versa, pay less if the busi-ness does not increase in volumes based on the planned timeline.

Feasibility: From the customer's perspective, the ability to pay-per-resources-used represents a high budget impact factor, as the customer can use the platform for its infrastructure and tools needs. The budget impact factor is further enhanced for SMEs who need access to a diverse set of tools, as the on-premises solution for acquiring and maintaining a diverse set of tools would be prohibitively expensive. SMEs and start-ups also need to pivot multiple times, as the average entrepreneur needs to pivot the offering and the business model multiple times in their lifetime. The in-house acquisition of tools would be expensive and pose a high risk to the customer, as the customer may need to pivot to new offerings over time. Hence, the accessing of tools on the platform mitigates the customer's risk substantially, as the customer can move to using new tools available on the platform when it changes its offerings. By using the pay-for-resources model, the customer protects itself from the cost of pivoting multiple times and uses its scarce resources more efficiently. This ability to support the development of changed applications quickly leads to a high risk impact factor that enables the adoption of the PaaS offering. However, the PaaS model also suffers from some shortcomings, chief among them is the risk of vendor lock-in. By using the tools, utilities and libraries of the provider, the customer's development team has the risk of getting used to the ser-vices of the provider over the long run. This increases the switching costs for the customer if it wants to move to a different offering from a different provider, or if it wants to move to an own operating model at a later stage. While the PaaS provider should ideally be able to keep pace with changes in the technology over time owing to its larger scale, the customer runs the risk that the provider's offerings of tools and libraries are not getting updated at the pace of the market. The customer may also have some teething issues when integrating its existing systems on the platform, owing to the lack of interoperability of the platform with its legacy systems. Red Hat's OpenShift platform is reputed and has access to the large resources of Red Hat. Hence, while the risk of the offering not being able to keep pace with the market is minimal, the risk of vendor lock-in with any PaaS offering remains real. The proliferation of middleware components and tools has led to PaaS providers creating pre-integrated suites of these tools, and the standardization of these suites across providers would reduce the risk of vendor lock-in. However, the state of the art has mostly provided specific suites of tools, and the offerings are not close to being standardized across providers. This problem is exacerbated if the customer wants to use multiple vendors for PaaS offerings. Hence, currently, most customers use a single PaaS provider to satisfy their development needs. From the customer's perspective, the agility offered by the standardized middleware tools is high, as the customer can lower both its costs and development time by using the PaaS offering. Hence, the customer's agility is enhanced, leading to an assessment of high agility for the feasibility analysis. From the provider's perspective, if some tools are being requested by several customers, the provider can create this middleware easily with its standardized interfaces. Hence, the agility analysis for profitability yields a high grade. The use of the platform for satisfying hardware and software tools needs has a high degree of agility, as the provider can acquire hardware as and when it observes the utilization of its assets increasing. The addition of software tools on the platform in the growth phase is also easy, as providers can market the offering to customers in domains where they have many pre-integrated tools.

Profitability: As with other XaaS offerings in the IT domain, the deal transaction costs of the PaaS offering are low. Customers can access the services online from any place globally with a few keystrokes, hence, the PaaS offering scores well on the deal transaction costs dimension. The frequency of usage can be discriminated perfectly using the pay-per-resources-used model, hence, the PaaS offering scores high on the frequency of usage dimension. The expected utility-per-use can be estimated and charged based on the type of firm accessing the service, and the nanonized price can be set differently for different tools and infrastructure offerings. Hence, the ability to charge differentiated prices for access to different tools enables the PaaS model to score high on the expected utility-per-use dimension.

Growth: While there are a large number of providers in the PaaS domain, with the usual suspects like Amazon AWS, Microsoft Azure, Google and IBM leading the pack, the suite of services are not as standardized as the IaaS solutions. The offering of customizable tools and middleware enables providers to furnish some degree of differentiation in their services, leading to a moderate score for Red Hat's OpenShift offering on the competitiveness dimension. The degree of complementarity between the hardware and software tools, and between the software tools themselves, enables a greater ability on the part of the provider for adding value from bundling different utilities. Hence, the PaaS solutions score high on the complementarity factor. The use of the platform also enables economies of scale from Red Hat's perspective, as the platform is hosted on the cloud, leading to higher economies of scale. Finally, the PaaS approach enables the provider to develop new infrastructure and middleware

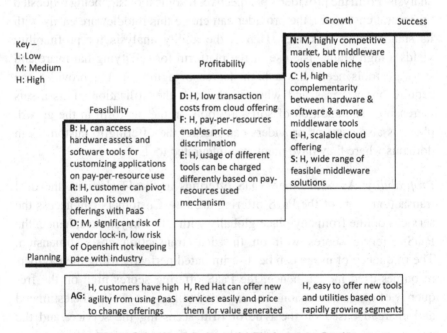

Figure 8.6:   XaaS Staircase for Platform-as-a-Service

offerings easily based on customer feedback and offer them on the cloud, leading to high performance on the solutions aspect.

Figure 8.6 exhibits the XaaS Staircase for OpenShift's PaaS offering.

The analysis of the PaaS service shows its strengths and comparatively few weaknesses. The offering does well from the customer's perspective by creating value in the form of lower costs, lower time-to-market, and high economies of scale. From the provider's perspective, the model enables the provider to offer hardware assets and an intermediate layer of software tools for customers to develop their own applications. The two potential weaknesses in the form of vendor lock-in and high degree of competition are mitigated by the ability of the provider to potentially create niches in specific industries, and a move in the future towards possible standardization of the interfaces of the middleware tools. Like the basic IaaS and SaaS models, the PaaS model has been going from strength to strength. The ability to enable customization for the customer with standardized tools has driven the growth of the PaaS suite of services.

8.7 SUMMARY

The XaaS Staircases of the six case studies presented in this chapter reveal the reasons for the popularity of the IT-enabled XaaS offerings. The SaaS market alone has been valued at $135B in 2018, and is expected to grow at a CAGR of 13.1% till 2022, showing that the distribution of software products using the as-a-service model is getting increasingly popular.[16] The markets for other types of IT-enabled XaaS offerings are also growing at a fast clip; indeed the growth of different IT-enabled services in the as-a-service mode has been the dominant story of the world of as-a-service offerings. The reasons for the explosive growth of XaaS models in the IT sector are manifold. First, the budget factor is uniformly moderate to high

---

[16] Research and Markets, "Global Software as a Service (SaaS) Market Report 2020: Market was Valued at $134.44 Bn in 2018 and is Expected to Grow to $220.21 Bn at a CAGR of 13.1% through 2022", December 6, 2019, https://www.prnewswire.com/news-releases/global-software-as-a-service-saas-market-report-2020-market-was-valued-at-134-44-bn-in-2018-and-is-expected-to-grow-to-220-21-bn-at-a-cagr-of-13-1-through-2022-300970629.html, accessed November 10, 2020.

for all IT XaaS offerings, showing that the budget indeed has a big impact on the growth of IT-enabled XaaS offerings. The budget impact is influenced by multiple factors: the ability to pay based on usage or a subscription fee, the ability to manage the cash flow better, and the ability to have a higher functionality and access to expertise compared to in-house development. The buying or developing of specialized software like blockchain services (Tencent), disaster recovery (Bluelock), AI analysis (ViSenze) and development platforms (OpenShift) in-house can be considered as an on-premises solution. However, the ability to test the suitability of the software is limited and poses a high risk for the customer. Relatively less complex services like the unified communications (DingTalk) and the digital workplace (Atos) can be built in-house, as these services need the integration of different off-the-shelf technologies. However, the advantage of having a seamless bundle of communication and workplace services represents an advantage for the customer. While the development of in-house modules is hard, the buying of these modules from external vendors is a challenge as well, as the customer may find it hard to assess the match between the products of the external vendors to the needs of their organization. Next, having access to the services with a subscription model (Tencent, DingTalk, Atos), a pay-per-use or pay-per-resource model (ViSenze, OpenShift) or a mixed payment model (Bluelock) makes it easier for customers to manage their initial cash outlay and cash flow. The phased payments every period are easier to manage than high upfront investments. The impact is also substantial in managing the cash flow, and the change from capital expenses to operating expenses makes the value of the services transparent.

The risk factor for most of the models works in favour of the XaaS model. The budget overrun risk is managed tightly with the subscription model (Tencent, Dingtalk, Atos), as the payments are made with a predictable schedule. The budget overrun risk for the pay-per-use or pay-per-resource models (ViSenze and OpenShift) are managed by the ability to predict the usage required based on testing the use of the services, and the estimation of payments given by the provider. While the budget overrun risk is high for disaster recovery services (Bluelock), the risk is offset by the cost of not having access to the services, as these services work as insurance against system downtime for the customer. The quality, security and reliability risk are uniformly lower for the customer from outsourcing these services, as the provider has specialized skills, which are difficult to replicate in-house. The ability to align the value of the service with customer outcomes is high for some XaaS offerings, as the customer can observe the correlation between the service outcome and the impact on revenue, as exemplified in ViSenze. The use of IT-enabled XaaS offerings also enables customers to access more tools and utilities required with the subscription model (OpenShift). However, the risk of vendor lock-in is high for many of these services, especially when employees get used to the operation of these services internally (Atos, OpenShift).

The obsolescence of technology factor is clearly in favour of the IT-enabled XaaS offering in all the cases. The basic advantage of using the XaaS model from the customer's perspective is the ability to keep pace with state-of-the-art technology, without having to search for the best available technology continuously (Tencent, Bluelock, DingTalk, ViSenze, Atos, OpenShift). The ability to upgrade continuously also has the added advantage of not having to incur the cost of procurement of the latest systems, which enhances the budget impact factor. Since technologies in the IT sector are highly fluid, customers may have to change the entire system in case of technology disruption if they adopt the on-premises approach. In contrast, the adoption of the XaaS offering enables customers to move seamlessly to the next generation if the basic technology is upgraded or move to the new technology with some switching costs if the basic technology is disrupted. In specific cases such as disaster recovery (Bluelock), the providers can keep pace with new methods of cyberattack, and continuously learn from the cyberattacks on multiple customers. Similarly, AI algorithms that have been trained with data from multiple customers will provide access to a larger set of customer insights (ViSenze). Since most technologies are designed today in a modular fashion, upgrading technologies is easy for the provider. Tencent can add new systems based on different standards on the platform, DingTalk can incorporate other communications technologies with its standard interface, and Atos and OpenShift can add more collaboration tools and design and utility tools easily to their service suites. The growth of commercially viable blockchain technology has been slow due to the processing time, energy requirements and the lack of interoperability between different systems and standards. However, technology improvements over time and the advent of a dominant standard should hasten the adoption of blockchain technology as a service.

The three aspects of agility (customer agility for feasibility, firm agility for profitability and growth) are enhanced by a moderate to high degree by IT-enabled XaaS offerings. From the customer's perspective, the customer's agility is enhanced by the Tencent's three different blockchain applications. The customer's ability to learn about the latest security attacks and security features from Bluelock, and the use of standard interfaces by DingTalk, Atos and OpenShift enhances the customer's agility. The customer's agility is also enhanced by the ability to use multiple providers for different purposes to gain more insights about their own customers (ViSenze). The profitability of the firm is enhanced by the firm's agility in the XaaS offering mode, as using standard interfaces (Tencent, DingTalk, Atos, OpenShift) and procedures enables providers to lower their own costs. The profitability is further enhanced by the learning and upgrading of processes from every customer interaction (Bluelock and ViSenze). In all the cases, the agility for growth is enhanced by offering the services on the cloud, as the cloud offering implies enhanced economies of scale. Atos's agility to respond to customer requirements is limited by using devices from Google. However, since the device design and operating platforms from Google can cater to all applications, the disadvantages of limited agility can be compensated by the wide set of Google's offerings.

The deal transaction costs in the IT-enabled XaaS offerings are low in general (except for ViSenze), as all the offerings are cloud-based. ViSenze's customers may experience the ticking meter effect, as not all transactions with ViSenze result in sales. Since the accessing transactions for cloud-based applications are primarily done with identification with one or two factors like a password and an instantaneously generated code, the accessing transaction costs are low. While customers may need some time to familiarize themselves with the applications, the use of the services in steady state does not incur any additional transaction costs. Hence, the deal transaction costs have a high impact on the profitability of XaaS offerings. The discrimination of the frequency of usage for profitability is high when providers use the pay-per-use or pay-per-resource-used charging methodology (ViSenze, OpenShift), as customers' utility is extracted more efficiently. However, while ViSenze charges a standard price-per-use from all customers, OpenShift can customize the charge per use based on the tools used, giving it a more granular pricing mechanism. The impact of the expected utility-per-use is therefore higher for OpenShift, and moderate for ViSenze. The use of the subscription model (Tencent, DingTalk, Atos) does not discriminate well on the frequency of usage, hence, customers with a larger usage frequency will have a greater surplus from using these services. While the variable cost of DingTalk and Atos's service offerings are not high, the high unit variable cost of the Tencent blockchain implies that Tencent may need to add a usage-based pricing charge when it has acquired a reasonable number of customers. The expected utility-per-use is also not efficiently extracted by the subscription pricing mechanism; however, the market share is higher from subscription pricing in a competitive environment. In terms of the impact of the frequency of usage, expected utility-per-use and pricing, Bluelock's mixed model is the most efficient. Bluelock offers its services at three levels: professional, managed and self, hence, it extracts the expected utility-per-use efficiently. The frequency of usage is also extracted well with the charge for each recovery. The subscription model for accessing the basic service ensures that customers can insure themselves against disasters, leading to a high market share.

The competitive intensity is high for all IT-enabled XaaS offerings, explaining the proliferation and growth of the business model. This leads to a limited ability to create a niche, and a low to moderate impact on the competitive intensity dimension in all cases. The services of Bluelock, DingTalk and Atos use standardized hardware and software, making it hard to create a niche in these domains. The lack of unified standards gives Tencent the ability to create a niche by using its brand and proprietary technology. Similarly, ViSenze's specialized services can enable it to create a niche in specialized retail categories, and OpenShift's customizable middleware, tools and utilities can help it create a niche for customers developing applications in certain categories. However, as the technologies mature and get mainstream acceptance, the inevitable creation of dominant standards will help with market adoption and concomitantly make the competitive intensity higher.

The complementarity factor is used well by almost all providers in the IT domain with the exception of ViSenze. Tencent also offers AI and IoT solutions in the Industry 4.0 space, while Intervision (Bluelock's parent company) offers a range of services including IaaS, storage, communications and data analytics. Alibaba (DingTalk's parent company) offers IaaS and other cloud solutions, while Atos offers security applications in addition to bundling devices and communications tools in its WaaS offering. Red Hat (OpenShift's parent organization) is the largest provider of open source solutions in the world. Hence, the larger organizations in our case studies can use complementarity effectively to create customer solutions with a bundling strategy. ViSenze is a specialized provider of AI analytical insights, and it may be able to grow its own service suite over time. The economies of scale are uniformly high for all our case studies, as all the offerings are provided on the cloud. The high economies of scale enable the growth of XaaS offerings on the cloud and is one of the main drivers of the rapid expansion of XaaS offerings in the IT domain. Finally, the providers can provide customized solutions uniformly for their customers as their offerings are on the cloud. The usage data coupled with periodic interactions with customers enable the providers to gather insights on the potential enhancements of their offerings. The cloud-based delivery model enables the providers to develop and enhance their suite of offerings leading to a higher growth potential.

Chapter 9

XaaS Offerings with Unbundled Services

The bundling of utility from multiple sources is one of the founding principles of all enterprises. Without the ability to bundle different elements of utility, the notion of the firm would not have existed. Customers would have to acquire individual components from multiple vendors and integrate these components themselves. The firm provides value to customers by integrating or bundling components into a product or service, thereby alleviating the need for customers to carry out this integration. However, the degree of bundling or integration performed by firms changes over time. The Ford Model-T was manufactured in a completely integrated manner, with Ford making basic components like nuts, bolts and crankshafts internally, then assembling them together to make the Model-T. Over time, Ford and other auto manufacturers found that evolving technologies makes it difficult to have a core competence on every aspect of automotive manufacturing. Large suppliers who specialized in designing and manufacturing specific components had a higher level of expertize on those components, and manufacturers outsourced the component design and manufacturing to these suppliers. A similar decomposition of the OEM's activities happened in the PC industry as well, with suppliers like Intel and Microsoft acquiring expertize in the design and manufacturing of hardware and software components, respectively. The OEM was left with the tasks of designing the system architecture, or the set of rules by which different components would interact with each other. The OEM also assembled the components together into the final product and branded and marketed the product. The tiered supply chain emerged to create fragmented roles for different players in the industry, with each player having specific expertize in specific activities and components. This fragmentation or decomposition of activities is also beneficial for service offerings. Services are offered as… well services, hence, the usage over time has already been unbundled, and customers can choose the time that they want to avail of the services. Bundled services imply that customers do not have the choice of specific elements of the service but must avail of the entire service. The unbundling of services into its constituent components enables the nanonization of the XaaS offering. Customers can choose the components that provide them utility and discard the components that do not offer them utility. Bundled services are akin to the choice of main courses that are served with side dishes; in contrast, unbundled services are like standalone items being served as à la carte items, with customers choosing the items that they want.

One of the primary advantages of unbundling services is the ability to convert non-customers to customers owing to the budget impact. As an example, in the music industry, this unbundling of services has resulted in the move from selling CDs with many songs from either one band or based on a certain theme, to the offering of singles as a service. When music collections were sold on CDs, many customers baulked at the idea of buying the entire CD as they only wanted one song from the collection. However, the cost of burning the music content onto a CD, packaging and mailing the content to the customer incurred a certain amount of costs for every CD. Music album providers included a lot of content onto a CD and sold them at a higher price to convince the customer that buying the CD gave them some surplus, as they were getting a lot of content on one CD. While some customers bought the CD, other customers did not see the value proposition of acquiring the entire CD for listening to one or two desired songs. The offering of music singles as a service converted these non-customers to customers, resulting in an increased number of potential customers. While the provider may lose some revenue from not being able to sell the bundled content at the higher price, the provider can compensate for the lost revenue by pricing the desired services by the customer at a higher level. In this chapter, we review some unbundled services with case studies on unbundled airline services (AirAsia), unbundled media content (HBO), unbundled music (iTunes), unbundled communications services (WhatsApp) and unbundled audiology services (Wake Forest Baptist Health).

9.1 UNBUNDLING OF AIRLINE SERVICES (AIRASIA)

AirAsia was the first airline to adopt the long-haul Low-Cost Carrier (LCC) model. However, it wasn't the first airline to adopt the LCC model, the first LCC carrier was Pacific Southwest Airlines. The concept had been popularized more than half a century ago by American airliner Southwest Airlines who flew its fleet on a set of four simple principles. Firstly, Southwest operated the same make of aircraft to keep down engineering and maintenance costs. Second, it tried to keep down overhead costs as much as possible. Third, it minimized wasted time by having the objective of preparing the aircraft for the next flight as soon as possible. Fourthly, they dumped the hitherto popular loyalty and air miles schemes. The notion was simple — provide fuss-free travel to destinations in more convenient timeslots, with on-time arrivals, and at the lowest possible fare while ensuring that passengers were comfortable and enjoyed their journey. Very quickly, the LCC concept became a success, and started being adopted by airliners who wanted to capture the nascent budget market.[1]

Southeast Asia was one of the last regions to embrace the LCC phenomenon, with AirAsia leading the bandwagon and adopting the model in 2002. A key to the LCC operation was the unbundling of services provided by the airlines. The reason for the success of LCC had primarily been low fares, and unbundling allowed airliners to lower the fare by offering services that formed part of regular air travel as separate services. The key to delivering low fare was to reduce costs, and unbundling allowed airliners to reduce the cost of the fare by removing ancillary services. AirAsia relied on a similar strategy as Southwest to deliver low fares — focus on getting passengers from point A to point B. All other services were considered extra, and customers could avail them for a

---

[1] AirAsia, What LLC, https://ir.airasia.com/what_lcc.html, accessed November 12, 2020.

small extra fee. There were a few services which were considered basic that the airliner removed from its air ticket offering. The first were the food, beverage and meal services, which were rendered as optional. The airlines had noted that some passengers did not like to eat during their travel. They preferred to rest during a flight; others preferred to have their meals before the flight. However, for those passengers who wanted to have meals in the flight, meals could be purchased in the flight for an affordable fee. The second service was assigned seating, which was usually offered for free by full-service airlines three days before the flight. Some guests wanted to change their pre-assigned seats, and they could do so by paying a small fee to choose a seat of their liking. Third, the airlines charged for baggage, and passengers were only allowed to carry small baggage cases for no charge at the basic ticket price. Fourth, the airlines eliminated baggage insurance for baggage delay from the basic fare.

To implement the unbundled services more efficiently, the airlines created fare choices based on the services customers were willing to pay for. It offered four kinds of packages for customers to choose from — Low Fare, Value Pack, Premium Flex, Premium Flatbed. The low fare package was the most basic and excluded all additional services other than allowing cabin baggage. The value pack was a package that included additional services like baggage allowance, standard seat selection, a meal, and insurance for baggage delay. The premium flex and Premium flatbed packages offered additional services like dedicated check in, and quick baggage transport. Passengers could either choose to buy the additional services inclusive packages or buy the low fare ticket and buy the additional services based on their need. Each service was available as an add-on for a small price. AirAsia's low-cost strategy led to an increase in frequencies and a 60% cut in headline fares for many of its domestic services in Malaysia. With the unbundled fare approach, the airline was able to offer customers overall lower fares. Its highest fares were 20% below those offered by its close competitor Malaysian Airlines. With 43% of the local market share, AirAsia was the market leader in Malaysia, and predominantly sold unbundled fares to most customers.

To support its LCC business model, the company had implemented several strategic organizational initiatives like a flat management structure and laying the groundwork for incorporating employee feedback into its day-to-day operations. Employee feedback was encouraged through informal get-togethers. Moreover, employees were given 5% of the company's equity to ensure that there was a feeling of belonging. Over time, AirAsia's key objective was to provide add-on services to its customers to the best of its ability. As a low-cost structure was key to the success of providing unbundled services, it tried to keep its expenditures to the bare minimum by eliminating dependencies that could add to the cost. Towards this end, the company had sought to reduce its dependency on agents to sell tickets and set up an online reservation system. The aim was to dramatically reduce the split between commission bearing travel agency sales and direct sales via the Internet and call centre. Internet sales formed the bulk of ticket sales and accounted for 85% of the bookings. Sales offices were limited and only established if the company was confident that the volume of sales generated from the office was worth the costs. For locations where customers had limited access to the Internet, the company relied on travel agents.

The second strategy implemented to support unbundled low-price airfares was to maximize aircraft utilization. This meant that the aircrafts in the fleet had to be flying as much as possible. It also meant that airplanes would have to spend less time in airports, and the processes of cleaning and readying an aircraft for its next flight had to be optimized. AirAsia's turnaround time was 25 minutes, compared to the standard one-hour time used by a full-service carrier on the ground. The utilization of an aircraft was 12 hours per day, which was about 17% higher than that of full-service airlines. The third strategy was to streamline operations by using a single type of aircraft for most of its flights. Pilots, flight attendants, engineers, mechanics and operations personnel had expertize in a single type of aircraft, meaning any problems with the aircraft or flight could be fixed quickly, and staff were not required to be trained in different aircrafts, reducing overall operational costs. Additionally, the flights offered a single class of seating, further reducing costs of readying flight attendants to cater to different seat classes. Having the same type of aircraft and a single seat class also enabled the airlines to introduce standard operating procedures to ensure the same level of competence among all staff — driving uniformity of service throughout the company.[2]

---

[2] Wikipedia, AirAsia, https://en.wikipedia.org/wiki/AirAsia, accessed November 12, 2020.

However, an unbundled ticket was not the only solution that AirAsia offered, as often, LCCs were not associated with the concept of a great travel experience. AirAsia used a brand building approach to cater to this challenge and convert customers who had a negative view of low-fare flying. It started selling items like caps, watches, T-shirts to create brand awareness, and established an online retail store to further expand its brand. It also began offering hotel booking facilities on its website to provide customers with a one-stop shop for their travel needs. Overall, AirAsia's pioneering approach to offer unbundled airline services in Southeast Asia had made it a market leader. Asia was well known for having price-conscious customers, and amidst a changing trend in air travel where point-to-point travel had overshadowed the hub-and-spoke model, AirAsia offered a unique flying experience in Asia. The hub-and-spoke model used by full-service airlines had led to large airports becoming more crowded with an increase in the number of flights, and the point-to-point model offered customers a different value proposition. The unbundled approach had stemmed from a simple concept — while price provided revenue, other elements attributed to costs. AirAsia had taken this concept to the next level and converted it into an à la carte meal where additional dishes could be easily ordered by customers, providing them with more choice.

9.1.1 Unbundling of Airline Services Analysis

General: The aviation industry has expanded at a rapid pace in the last few decades fuelled by the growth of LCCs.[3] For many years, barriers existed in many countries to the offering of LCC services driven primarily by regulatory barriers owing to security resulting in a monopoly for national carriers. The lack of airport infrastructure and a high capital intensity of operating in the airline sector were additional barriers to entry in the airline sector. However, the move to an increased open environment for competition was supported by the rise of bilateral and multilateral trade agreements, the harmonization of laws governing aviation regionally, and the liberalization of local economies. The low-cost business model has

---

[3]Wensveen, J. G. & Leick, R. (2009). The long-haul low-cost carrier: A unique business model. *Journal of Air Transport Management*, 15(3), 127–133.

enabled the LCCs to carve out a niche in the airline sector, by focusing on cost optimization and the point-to-point service model as their core sources of competitive advantage. Governments recognize the role played by LCCs in supporting travel and tourism, and most local governments have created additional terminals at large airports or smaller airports that are dedicated to LCCs. In the era of full-service airlines dominated by national carriers, the drive for efficiency was minimal, with many airlines operating with losses that were subsidized by national governments. The liberalization of the aviation sector has had the added benefit of forcing full-service airlines to streamline their operations for increased productivity and efficiency. The other elements of the LCC model like streamlined sales processes, reduced need for employees and optimized turnaround and asset acquisition models have kept LCCs ahead of the game in being able to offer customer value. For the analysis of unbundled airline services, we will use the corresponding full-service offering as the benchmark.

Feasibility: From the customer's perspective, the budget impact is the primary reason for choosing the LCC, hence, the budget impact is high. LCCs attract customers who are travelling for personal reasons primarily, though their adoption for business travel for short haul flights is on the rise. The price consciousness of customers, especially in developing countries in Asia, is high, hence, the lower cost of flying is a big plus for such customers. The ability to pick different levels of services (e.g., small, medium, and large amounts of baggage) is a big plus for customers, as they do not need to pay for more than what they need for baggage service. The risk impact factor does not make a substantial difference to the choice of the LCC, as customers pre-pay for the ticket and choose their services up front, hence, they can compare the prices of the LCC with the full-service airline. The obsolescence of technology factor is not relevant, neither are other technology factors, as the technologies for budget airlines and full-service airlines for booking and for the offering of the service are similar. From the customer's perspective, the agility offered by the budget airlines is not a significant factor in their choice of the budget airline, as full-service airlines also offer the ability to book and cancel at the last minute. However, customers can indeed pick and choose the services they want. From AirAsia's profitability perspective, the point-to-point service offers the ability to add flights quickly as the plane assets can be switched from one route to the other, depending on the demand of the routes. From the perspective of growth, the hub-and-spoke model of full-service airlines is indeed better than budget airlines' point-to-point model, as hub-to-spoke flights typically need smaller planes, and the ability to serve a larger network with the hub-and-spoke model is higher.

Profitability: The deal transaction cost impact is low for the adoption of LCCs, as they typically do not have frequent flyer or customer loyalty programs. Hence, the full-service airlines perform better on the deal transaction cost impact dimension. The frequency of usage of LCCs is not higher than that of full-service airlines, as tickets for full-service airlines are also sold on a per-flight basis, and there is no impact of consolidation of multiple flight tickets. Hence, the impact of the performance of LCCs on the frequency of usage factor is low. However, the expected-utility-per-use factor impact is high for LCCs, as the prices are nanonized based on the utility-per-use for each offering from the service. Hence, the ability to price based on the utilities of the choices of the customer makes the expected utility-per-use an important dimension in ensuring the profitability of the LCC.

Growth: While the competition for both full-service airlines and LCCs is intense, the competitive intensity of LCCs is a little lower. The niche offering for LCCs is given by the point-to-point routes taken by the LCCs. Full-service airlines have networks that serve a lot of cities as spokes and a few cities as hubs, but they have fewer point-to-point flights, primarily between hubs and hubs with some spokes. On the other hand, LCCs have a few routes that they operate on, and their unique selling point is the direct flight offered, resulting in a shorter sojourn time. Beyond the specific routes served by LCCs, there is no other way of creating a niche. The complementarity dimension does not offer any specific advantages to either full-service airlines or LCCs, as the degree of complementarity between the individual services is limited. Hence, LCCs score low on the complementarity dimension. The economies of scale are better for full-service airlines, as adding a spoke to the network enables the full-service airlines access to the complete network of destinations. On the other hand, LCCs do not perform well on the economies of scale dimension, as there are hardly any economies of scale and economies of scope for them. Their costs are dependent on the number of flights between routes, and adding more routes results in very minimal cost saving or cost sharing opportunities. Hence, LCCs do not perform well on the economies of scale dimension vis-à-vis full-service airlines. On the dimension of providing solutions, LCCs indeed perform well as by unbundling services and enabling customer choice on individual elements of the service, the LCC can allow customers perfect discrimination mechanisms of choice. On the other hand, full-service airlines do not offer the solutions approach, instead, they offer a one-size-fits-all approach. Hence, LCCs score highly on the solutions offering dimension.

From the analysis of the unbundled services model of LCCs (Figure 9.1), it is easy to see that the value proposition of unbundling services by LCCs in the airline sector is their ability to fly point-to-point at minimal cost. When the services are unbundled, each service must be optimized in terms of cost and pricing, so that the standalone service is profitable. This results in a focus on every aspect of the service, ensuring that value-adding

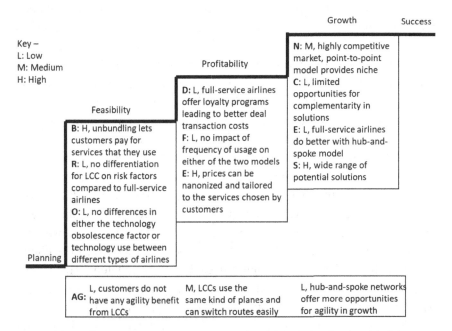

Figure 9.1: XaaS Staircase for Unbundled LCC Airline Services Model

activities are retained, and any non-value add activity is discarded. While LCCs have a structural advantage in their point-to-point model, if other airlines replicate services between the same points, the LCC model is susceptible to competitive pressures.

9.2 UNBUNDLING OF MEDIA AND ENTERTAINMENT SERVICES (HBO)

Home Box Office (HBO) was launched in 1972 by Warner Media and is one of the largest media and entertainment conglomerates in the world today. As its name implies, the channel's business model had been the broadcasting of uncut and commercial-free movies to its subscribers for a fee. HBO had several firsts in the media and entertainment industry: in 1975, it became the first American channel to deliver its programming through satellite. Though HBO was a staple for many years on the cable TV programming circuit, the winds of disruption challenged its business model at the turn of the millennium. Taking advantage of the proliferation of the Internet and higher bandwidth and speeds, content providers with streaming services like Netflix reached out to customers directly with a subscription model. Cable TV content providers began responding with XaaS offerings of their own; in 2010, HBO released an Internet streaming service called HBO Go. HBO Go was the successor of HBO on Broadband — a service which allowed users to download content to computers at no extra charge. However, the rights of accessing HBO on Broadband were only offered to digital cable customers. On the other hand, HBO Go was accessible only on personal computers via the online HBO website initially. In 2011, the service was expanded and made available on smartphones and tablets. In 2015, HBO launched HBO Now as an over-the-top (OTT) subscription to HBO cable subscribers. However, unlike other services provided by HBO, HBO Now was not marketed through the cable services provider but directly to the client, which is like Netflix. Like other streaming video content, HBO Now allowed subscribers to use video services through the Internet directly. The unbundling of the HBO streaming services meant that the company could now target a broader customer base for its streaming services rather than just focusing on cable subscribers and television network provider subscribers.[4]

In 2019, HBO launched its OTP streaming services suite called HBO Max. Under the HBO Max brand, HBO offered several services as standalone unbundled offers under different subgroups. In addition to HBO Max and HBO streaming service, HBO also offered OTP streaming on Apple TV channels, Amazon video channels and the Roku channel. It also offered Internet protocol television services on AT&T TV, Hulu TV and YouTube TV. However, HBO had not moved its entire suite of services online. It continued to operate with a mixed model and offered satellite and cable TV content through its traditional TV subscription packages. The unbundled services allowed HBO to create new customer segments without cannibalizing existing revenue streams. The streaming services were for customers who either did not have existing cable subscriptions or preferred to access content online. The unbundling and the online streaming services had also served to expand HBO's customer base. While HBO cable subscribers were limited to the U.S. market, web-based online streaming services had allowed HBO to expand its customer base globally on a much larger scale. Even in the U.S., there were only roughly 30 million pay-TV subscribers, and there were 80 million homes that do not subscribe to HBO. The streaming services allowed the company to target this customer group for its OTT offerings.

Rather than being an innovation strategy, unbundling services was more of a competitive strategy for HBO. It was a defensive move to keep as many customers loyal to its services as possible, and target those who wanted to switch to online streaming providers because of convenience. The intention was to keep customers glued to HBO by providing them with an alternate solution without the need for a switch. HBO had always marketed its services with the television subscriber in mind and had offered its services mostly through third-party distribution partners. However, in Northern Europe, it had started selling direct to the customer, with a video-on-demand function called HBO Nordic. By 2019, HBO Nordic had acquired about 380,000 subscribers in Denmark, Finland, Norway and

---

[4]Amandou Diallo, "HBO Unbundled: What It Means for Cord-Cutters", *Forbes*, October 16, 2014, https://www.forbes.com/sites/amadoudiallo/2014/10/16/hbo-unbundled-what-it-means-for-cord-cutters/?sh=2f9979e765d7, accessed November 12, 2020.

Sweden, establishing a substantial user base. The HBO Nordic offering had been a pilot for offering direct services to the customer, and proved to HBO that it was feasible to venture on its own and provide its services directly to customers instead of offering content through partnerships. However, selling standalone services also means that HBO will have to bear the infrastructure and marketing costs of its services. In the past, while HBO did not use traditional distributors for the purpose of offering its content, it partnered with multichannel video programming distributors to offer these services. HBO had long-standing partnerships with multichannel video programming distributors (MVPDs) like Comcast, Verizon and Time Warner Cable for its existing services. Entering a distribution partnership implied the sharing of revenue with distributors. Initially, HBO had intended to use the same partners for its OTP streaming services, as this would enable the company to avoid the transaction costs of acquiring new distribution partners. However, unbundled services from HBO were provided at similar rates to its cable TV subscriptions — which were significantly higher than the monthly subscription rates of video-on-demand streaming service providers like Netflix and Hulu. Pricing was likely a strategic consideration, as the move towards OTT streaming was a defensive move on HBO's part. The intention was to provide customers with an alternate access choice and not to incentivize them to cancel their existing cable subscriptions. Setting a lower price for unbundled services could potentially cannibalize current revenue streams and irritate long-time distribution partners. The bundling of channels had worked for HBO in the past as it allowed the services to meet the myriad tastes of varied segments and tap into the customer's willingness to pay. However, with the advent of streaming OTP services like Netflix, this willingness to pay had reduced by quite a bit, forcing HBO to offer unbundled services that enabled customers to pick the content that matches their tastes closely.

9.2.1 Unbundling of Media and Entertainment Services Analysis

General: The unbundling of media content (OTT model) that was previously bundled in a cable TV package has a clear set of advantages and disadvantages. The advantages of the bundled cable TV package are obvious: from the customer's perspective, members of households with different tastes and watching habits can watch individual channels at different points of time in the day on a common device. Bundles are typically created with tailored content for different age groups and interests. Content creators provide content in specific genres, and the distributor offers the ability to get the base content at the base price, with premium content offered at a premium. Pre-packaged content also enabled the revenue model to be enhanced with advertising revenue beyond the subscription fee. The entry of streaming providers like Netflix disrupted this bundled model of offerings. While Netflix could also offer content for diverse age groups and interests, it had the added benefit of content being offered on demand for a flat fee, which was in contrast to the on-demand model of cable operators who used pay-per-use pricing. The Netflix offering forced Disney, HBO, CBS and other content providers to offer their own content independently on the Internet with subscriptions by using the OTT model. The primary problem of the unbundling of media and entertainment content are the higher deal transaction costs: households with members of different age groups and varied interests will need multiple subscriptions from content providers. Subscribing to multiple providers' offerings increases customers' monthly payments to be comparable to the cable TV bills of old, and it requires customers to keep track of multiple subscriptions and billing statements. The fragmentation of the market also makes it harder for content providers to achieve economies of scale as it is harder to reach an entire set of customers with cable TV package subscriptions as in the days of yore. Content providers offer streaming services independently of distributors in the OTT model, leading to the need for own marketing and distribution capabilities. Beyond the marketing and distribution provided by the cable TV package provider, content providers also must provide customer service in the OTT model. It also requires customers to manage multiple apps, and keeping track of new content on each app. The cable TV model had the advantage of one-stop shopping, the new model with a requirement for multiple subscriptions makes the deal transaction costs for customers high. The unbundling of services also makes competition much more intense, even though content providers may not be offering the same kind of content to customers. The unbundling of services has made the competition for the share of the customer's wallet more intense, as customers must choose the kind of content they want to access. However, it also enables providers to create more distinct niches in terms of provided content.

Feasibility: The advantages of the unbundling of media and entertainment content are significant in their own way, which is what made Netflix popular in the first place. Households with one or two members do not have to subscribe to the entire base set of channels along with premium content if the content they watch is limited in breadth. Hence, the budget impact factor of unbundling services is indeed high, as customers pay only for the specific content that they watch, and do not have to pay for all the other channels that they do not watch. Since almost all the content providers use a subscription model and do not use a pay-per-use model, the ability to predict the total monthly payment is also good. However, this predictability of payment feature is also present in the cable TV model, hence, the risk impact factor of unbundling media and entertainment content is low. From the content provider's perspective, the capacity risk is mitigated for both models (cable TV and OTT). In the earlier cable TV model, cable TV service providers built the capacity for broadcasting stations; for OTT services, the number of servers is based on the number of subscribers. The technology obsolescence risk is indeed lower for the OTT model, as customers can access content on multiple devices including tablets and phones. The cable TV model uses an older technology. Any advancement in device technology will be compatible with the streaming offering. Data analytics for customer watching behaviour in the cable TV services model were offered by ratings agencies like Nielsen. In contrast, data on customer watching behaviour in the OTT model are easier to access and analytics are easier to conduct, owing to the servers being owned by the content provider. From the customer's perspective, switching out of the subscription in the OTT model is easier, as the contract period specified is typically lower than that of cable TV service providers. Hence, the OTT model has a high obsolescence of technology factor. The agility offered by the OTT model from the customer's perspective in the feasibility analysis has a moderate advantage over the cable TV service model. This moderate advantage is since customers can potentially access niche content in the OTT offering that is not available on curated cable TV subscription packages. The agility for the provider in the profitability analysis also has a moderate benefit, as the customer adoption of the OTT offering is more sensitive to new content versus the cable TV services offering. Customers choosing the bundled cable TV services will assess the utility of the entire suite of channels in the cable TV offering, of which the new content of the provider is only a small part. In contrast, any new content on the provider's own platform in the OTT model can directly influence new subscriptions and pricing changes. The advantage of agility in the growth potential analysis is also moderate, as there is no revenue to be shared with the cable TV services provider, the increased revenues from growth accrue directly to the provider.

Profitability: While the deal transaction costs for the OTT model are high, the frequency of usage does not have an impact on either model, as couch potatoes who watch entertainment content all day do not have additional payments to make in the subscription model. However, the expected utility-per-use indeed favours the OTT model, as customers pay for very specific content that they watch, and the subscription price can be tailored to the expected utility-per-use.

Growth: The competitive intensity in the OTT market is indeed high, while content can be created for niche segments, the competition for the wallet share is intense. The complementarity of the OTT model is obviously lower than the bundled cable TV package, as the bundled model offers the provider with the ability to offer more content breadth compared to the OTT model for content providers. The economies of scale factor has positives and negatives for both models. Content providers can access more customers easily with the cable TV bundling model, as their content is offered to every customer either in the base price, or as a premium offering. In contrast, the OTT model enables economies of scale by offering the content on the cloud. Finally, designing solutions for the cable TV service model is easier as diverse content providers can be added to the package more easily. In contrast, the solutions offered in the OTT are typically narrow and created in specific genres. Figure 9.2 exhibits the XaaS Staircase for unbundled media content providers.

The XaaS staircase for the unbundling of media and entertainment content (Figure 9.2) shows that while the model has its advantages in reaching price sensitive customers, it imposes a cognitive burden on customers when

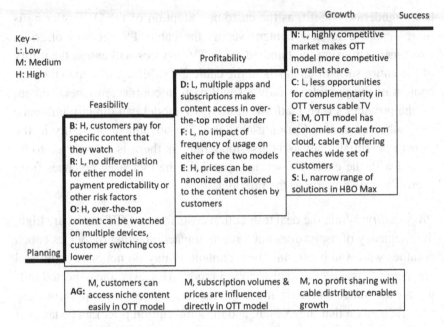

Figure 9.2:   XaaS Staircase for Unbundled Media and Entertainment Content Model

the range of offerings in the industry is very high. The cognitive burden imposes a high deal transaction cost on customers. There may be a case for the entry of aggregators in the market, who offer a one-stop solution by aggregating different content from providers in an online offering.

9.3 UNBUNDLING OF MUSIC CONTENT (ITUNES)

The iTunes service was launched by Apple in January 2001 as a complementary service to its iPod product. Initially, the service focused on music, by offering customers a library where they could collect and store their favourite music collections. The complementary iPod was launched the same year to extend Apple's "digital hub" category, which comprised digital cameras, camcorders and organizers. Apple's digital hub concept envisaged the MacBook as the hub with all the other intermediaries working in coordination with the hub to provide customers with digital services that linked cameras, music players, mobile phones and other handhold devices. Over time, iTunes expanded its services beyond music to videos, podcasts and other content like e-books. iTunes implemented a buy-to-own model, which was based on the philosophy that a single piece of software could accommodate all video content including music.[5]

Before iTunes, music content had primarily been sold as a bundled product. In the music industry, the cost of manufacturing labels, distribution and marketing costs were significant. The concept of bundling songs into an album had originally been conceived to cover the costs of creating an album. It was understood that not all songs in the album would become customer favourites, having one or two great numbers in the album could do the trick in terms of customer adoption. Customers would be willing to pay for the album based on just those tracks. Moreover, bundling of songs into albums also increased distribution efficiency and overall market revenue. This meant that songs that were unlikely to be sold on their own could be paired with those that were likely to be sold, to create albums that could bring in good revenue. Also, albums were sold in retail stores, and selling singles on a CD with a large storage space was not a viable option for brick and mortar stores.

With the wider access of the Internet, distribution companies and customers moved from the distribution of physical CDs to online digital music players. The costs of manufacturing, holding inventory and distribution over the Internet was much lower compared to that of selling physical CDs in stores, the easy distribution of singles made the rationale of bundling songs irrelevant. The file sharing model was first introduced by Napster and scaled by iTunes; it eliminated the cost rationale for bundling songs, motivating more and more distribution channels to unbundle the single song and change the way music was distributed. After the launch of iTunes, the low price point and increasing customer demand for singles started to reshape consumption patterns in music. Singles allowed customers the flexibility to cherry-pick the songs they wanted to listen to and not pay for songs they were not interested in. The price point of the flat 99 US cents for every song set by iTunes was attractive to most customers.

---

[5]Elberse, A. (2010). Bye-bye bundles: The unbundling of music in digital channels, *Journal of Marketing*, 74 (3), 107–123. JSTOR, www.jstor.org/stable/27800818, accessed Nov 20, 2020.

In a comparative analysis, the low price point for a preferred song was more desirable than the typical price of $14.99 for a bundled CD. For independent competing music stores, offering the unbundled singles at the price point of 99 cents was not appealing, hence, iTunes changed the dominant business model in the music industry.

Using iTunes, a customer could buy a single track for 99 US cents, organize different songs in their playlist, and synchronize the songs in their iPod. In terms of customer utility, iTunes was the digital jukebox with a wide choice of songs from the world's biggest artists. Customers had easy access to a huge library of tracks from which they could cherry pick their favourites, compared to a comparatively limited stock of bundled music album CDs in a brick and mortar store. While the initial platform of iTunes on Apple was limiting in terms of technology compatibility, in 2003, iTunes for Windows was introduced, removing the dependency of the software on Apple products. This meant that a wider pool of customers with access to digital devices could use iTunes to select their favourite music. iTunes became the blueprint for how people could legally download singles in contrast to the previous unlawful access to singles on file-sharing sites like Napster. However, it was not only the technology behind iTunes that helped create the shift in music consumption patterns. Apple's corresponding cloud offering (iCloud) made it possible for customers to download singles onto the cloud, rather than in cumbersome CDs or USB drives. The capacity of the cloud to support music downloads further helped in forcing the shift to singles.

While the shift from bundled albums to unbundled singles had motivated customers to consume even more music, it had raised concerns about the economic impact it could have on producers and retailers. Although naysayers claimed that unbundling negatively affected the overall sales of music, others argued that the dip in sales of albums had been offset by higher sales of singles on digital platforms. The sales of a bundle and the tracks in it were intertwined since sales of popular tracks as singles could stimulate the sales of the album. This could lead to the lesser known tracks getting more popular over time, leading to higher sales of the album. The pricing was another subject of debate, as industry experts felt that the low price point of 99 cents for a track could lower the perception of the worth of the track. To move beyond the singles-only offering, iTunes provided customers with the flexibility of buying the whole album, albeit at a lower price than a CD album. In December 2006, Interscope Records released pop star Gwen Stefani's new album, The Sweet Escape, on iTunes. The songs were available in iTunes as a bundled album as well as individual singles. Users could purchase the album at $9.99 and individual songs for 99 cents. Gradually, many record labels began to use this hybrid approach to sell music online rather than a purely unbundled approach.

Apple's success in unbundling music offerings laid the groundwork for other business models of unbundled services in the music industry. Pandora and Spotify began offering music in a streaming format, and soon, the streaming format was more popular than Apple's download and storage service. While Pandora offered limited content in the form of select playlists, Spotify provided users an audio streaming platform and access to over 60 million songs. Users could browse Spotify's database by using filters such as the artist, album, or genre, and could create and share playlists with friends. Unlike iTunes which charged a fixed download fee for every song, Spotify charged a monthly subscription fee from customers, and paid royalties to music content providers depending on the number of specific streaming requests as a percentage of the total songs streamed. Spotify had taken the unbundling concept one step further by allowing access to multiple sets of content, thereby eliminating the need of a bundled delivery altogether. Spotify had several advantages over iTunes — the way music was consumed in the subscription model was very different. There was no need for the customer to organize and manage their music collection, as everything they wanted to access could be streamed from the cloud. Second, streaming was not a one-time payment; millions of tracks were being streamed every day, and this could potentially multiply revenues on offer, and create a long-term source of income for artists.

9.3.1 Unbundling of Music Content Services Analysis

General: With the shift of music consumption from albums and records to digitally stored singles to streaming singles, the music industry has indeed come a long way. The introduction of the iTunes unbundled music offerings had a profound impact on the music industry. By working with major records firms like Sony, BMG and Universal, iTunes was able to disrupt the music industry by changing the physical distribution of content to offering the content online. While providers like Napster and Rhapsody had online business models, the lack of integration with the providers in Napster's case and the expensive model in Rhapsody's case had inhibited the digital distribution of music.

Feasibility: The singles distribution model of iTunes enabled the budget impact factor of the iTunes offering to be high, as customers could purchase only content that they desired, rather than having to pay for other content in addition that was not desired. While Apple's pricing was a subject of debate with content providers, the pricing of the song at 99 cents played a very important role in the budget impact factor. Senior executives at Sony had wanted to charge a price of $3 per track, but Warner supported Apple's suggested price point of 99 cents per track, enabling Apple to keep the price down to less than a dollar per track. The psychological impact of paying less than a dollar to acquire a song was a big factor in making the budget impact of the iTunes offering the most significant factor in customer adoption. Previously, customers had to pay more than $12 per CD and they listened to one or two songs on the CD repetitively. The risk impact factor from the customer's perspective is limited, as while there is some unpredictability about how much customers will pay every month, customers pay only 99 cents for each track, so the uncertainty does not have a big price. The online offering of content also meant that the device limitations were overcome — music systems were no longer required, and sound systems on computers, devices like the iPod and later smartphones could be used for music consumption. Since the content is offered online and the devices technology will still be compatible with downloads in future generations, the obsolescence of technology factor works in favour of the iTunes model.

The iPod device itself sold slightly under a million sets in the first year itself, and quickly became the number one MP3 player in the world. However, the iPod was only one piece of the puzzle; by creating the razor and blade model with unbundled songs on iTunes, Apple accelerated the adoption of the iPod device in the market. While the content providers initially signed one-year deals, the sales of iTunes rocketed to more than

$50 million in the first year itself, leading to the content providers extending the contract terms over longer periods. The iTunes model of distributing singles brought down the price of music consumption dramatically, enabling a more widespread distribution and consumption of music content. From the artist's perspective, the iTunes service meant that s/he did not have to create content equivalent to ten to twenty songs to release an album, with one or two lead numbers and many other fillers. The move to singles meant that artists could focus on creating blockbusters each time. However, the content providers like Warner, EMI, BMG and Sony were among the casualties of the move to digital music. Now, artists create singles and offer them directly to distributors like Spotify and Apple for royalties, rather than selling the rights to the records firms, leading to revenue sharing contracts that are based on the sales of the singles. The agility offered by unbundling content in the form of singles is appreciated by customers, as customers can acquire single songs quickly, rather than having to wait and pay for multiple songs in an album. From the artist's and Apple's perspectives, the impact offered by the agility of unbundling singles is indeed an important factor, as they can release impactful content quickly for profitability and growth.

Profitability: The deal transaction costs factor has a moderate impact on the adoption of unbundled services, as customers must download and organize the iTunes collection each time but accessing the song after the download is easy. The frequency of usage can be discriminated on perfectly by Apple with the pay-per-song mechanism, leading to a high degree of profitability. While the expected utility-per-use is extracted to some degree with the 99 cents price, the standard pricing does not differentiate the customers based on the willingness to pay, hence, the expected utility-per-use factor has a moderate impact on the profitability of Apple.

Growth: One of the factors that made the iTunes model successful was the complementarity of offerings from Apple that helped it achieve its dominance in the music industry. The mix of the software, the iTunes service and the iPod contributed to making Apple the biggest player in the distribution of music. More than one billion songs were downloaded on iTunes in less than 3 years from the introduction of the music service, and Apple became the number one music retailer in the US in 2008, and the number one music retailer in the world in 2010. The growth of iPod devices followed suit with iPod sales peaking at 55 million sets in 2008. Apple's proprietary software that enabled iTunes content to be played only on Apple devices meant that customers who wanted to use other MPD players with content acquired on iTunes were not able to do so. The complementarity of the different elements of the music offering created barriers to entry for other device manufacturers, further contributing to Apple's dominant position. The economies of scale factor is also high with the online and cloud storage model of distribution. By offering the software, content and device together, Apple created a solution for music distribution that was hard to replicate, resulting in the rapid growth of the iTunes offering.

By creating its music ecosystem, Apple shut out the competition for a long time. What would it take to challenge Apple's dominant position with the pay-per-song model? As it panned out, the model that would beat the pay-per-song model is the subscription model. Pandora initiated the subscription model with a mix of subscription fees and ad revenues for monetization. Spotify emulated the subscription model of Pandora, but with a broader mix of content, with a royalty model for content creators that enabled content creators to get a broader share of revenues. In the Spotify model, royalties were paid to artists each time customers listened to a song rather than each time customers bought a song. Hence, artists were compensated based on the number of customers that would listen to their songs, and the frequency with which customers listened to the content. Spotify has replicated Apple's successful model of partnering with record companies and artists. While Pandora only offered content in the form of playlists, Spotify offered more flexibility by enabling customers to listen to singles. The unbundling of content has enabled the success of both Apple and Spotify, and it is likely that future leaders in the music industry will adopt similar models for market dominance. The XaaS Staircase for the unbundled music content offering is shown in Figure 9.3.

The XaaS Staircase for unbundled music content shows that Apple built an enviable ecosystem that enabled it to be the dominant player in the music industry for more than a decade. However, while the pay-per-song model enables a high profitability as it can discriminate the frequency of usage, the subscription model of Spotify is better in a competitive market, as it is more attractive for customers owing to a higher customer

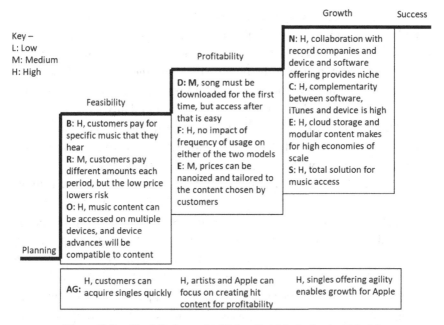

Figure 9.3: XaaS Staircase for Unbundled Music Content Model

surplus. Hence, Spotify's subscription model has given it a higher market share, though Apple's current subscription model is threatening Spotify's pole position in the US market.

9.4 UNBUNDLED COMMUNICATIONS SERVICES (WHATSAPP)

The mobile phone design of all providers was revolutionized by Apple's iPhone offering. While Blackberry was the market leader at the time, the famous Apple interfaces, aesthetics and ergonomics made the iPhone the instant market leader after its launch. The iPhone changed the role of the smartphone from a communications device used for messaging and calls to the primary instrument of access to the Internet, leapfrogging the PC as the instrument of choice for Internet access. Arguably, the most influential factor in propelling the iPhone to the market leadership position was the launch of the app store. The app store enabled customers to buy and use standalone applications, multiplying the functionality and the use of the smartphone many times. The availability of standalone applications in a mobile phone created a new phenomenon of unbundled services that could be provided over the phone directly to the customer. One of the most influential apps in the app store had been the communications app WhatsApp, which had seen ubiquitous adoption globally since its launch. WhatsApp was an unbundled offering for smartphone-based communications, which eliminated the need for messaging and communications services to be bundled with call services on a specific network.[6]

In the early 2000s, voice and SMS-based services were the primary methods of communication available on a mobile phone. These services were delivered by mobile carrier companies and were typically charged as packaged service bundles on a mobile phone connection. However, by 2009, OTT providers like WhatsApp and Skype had started to provide higher quality communication services that included video messaging and group communications for a much lower price. Applications like WhatsApp provided global access to data services, with the added features of saving contacts and data over a cloud. The growth of such unbundled messaging, voice and video services was phenomenal. WhatsApp became the world's leading messaging system in 2015, and had over 2 billion subscribers as of 2020, with about 100 million downloads every month, making it one of the most influential apps globally. WhatsApp was so named as it sounded like 'what's up', which was aligned with the messaging platform's concept of displaying the status of users — the primary feature of the original design. The feature allowed a user to choose his/her status (from several different options) so that everyone in the user's network could be notified. The status feature was further modified in 2009, when WhatsApp decided to send notifications to contacts in the user's network when the user changed his/her status. The application had an exponential growth in adoption rate among mobile phone users, as they could use Internet access for communication that was available for free in most offices and public spaces, and was available in homes for a monthly subscription price.

---

[6]Unbundle products and services, Deloitte University Press, 2014, https://www2.deloitte.com/content/dam/insights/us/articles/disruptive-strategy-unbundling-strategy-standalone-products/DUP_3033_Unbundle-products_v2.pdf, accessed November 20, 2020.

The access of the service over the Internet was preferable to the use of the mobile operator's messaging and calling services, which were typically charged per message or per minute above a certain threshold. By excluding the need for a specific network, WhatsApp eliminated the infrastructure costs that carriers incurred and was able to offer a lower-cost service option.

WhatsApp was a standalone communication solution and offered many additional features that standard messaging services of carrier providers did not provide. WhatsApp was not only more cost friendly; it was also more customer friendly, and an active Internet connection was the only requirement. Moreover, WhatsApp allowed users to send media-rich messages, which included images, video and location. As most carriers charged for SMS services based on per-text-fees, and calling based on prevalent source to destination rates, the cost of messages and calls could add up to a significant amount. Other advantages of WhatsApp included the speed of message transmission, setting up of notifications, information on whether the messages had been received and read, location sharing, and the additional facility of desktop integration to enable seamless communication using different devices and platforms. WhatsApp also had an important security feature in the way it operated — an acquaintance could only be contacted on WhatsApp if the contact was added to the user's contact list. The interoperability features of WhatsApp across platforms and its user friendliness made it a popular tool among users both for social communication and business communication. A WhatsApp message could be shared with various platforms including email applications and other messaging applications. WhatsApp also offered backup options wherein all content could be backed up to Google Drive for Android operating systems or to iCloud for IOS devices. A backup option enabled the restoration of previous communications even when a phone was changed, or factory settings were reset. The private and encrypted nature of usage coupled with enhanced transmission speed enabled WhatsApp to capture the market gradually. Over the years, the unbundling of services like messaging, voice and video had picked up greater pace. Evolving technologies and customer behaviours in the dynamic smartphone market created even greater opportunities for platforms like WhatsApp to flourish and create their own market niche.

9.4.1 Unbundled Communications Service Analysis

General: What is WhatsApp's *raison d'être*? Quite simply, it is the asymmetry between the customer's willingness to pay for different services, the prices charged by mobile phone service providers and the cost structure of the mobile phone service providers. Mobile phone providers charge customers typically a fixed price for a certain number of minutes of calling, a certain number of messages and a certain amount of data. When phone operators began their services in the mid-1990s, they only offered calling and messaging (SMS) services, at price points that reflected the utilization of their communications costs at that time. Over time, the cost of data got much cheaper, but customers were anchored on the calling time and messaging costs from years ago, hence, those prices remained stable. However, the cost of providing data services got much cheaper with the evolution of 3G and 4G networks, and data services today typically offer tens of GB of data in the mobile phone services bundle. By moving calling services, messaging services and communication services to the Internet using VOIP and other technologies, WhatsApp and other communications services lowered the cost of communications dramatically for customers. The primary benefit of WhatsApp is the difference in cost it offers — an SMS can cost a user a few cents depending on the provider, whereas a message on WhatsApp costs 1/300 of that price, based on the average cost of Internet access globally. Why do mobile phone service operators not recognize this trend, and lower their calling and messaging costs dramatically? Several customers are still anchored to the older price models and take the cost of calling services as a given, these customers have not switched yet. Second, the availability of 4G services is not seamless globally yet, hence, in certain areas where the 4G network does not offer Internet services of high quality, the ability to make calls with good sound quality is still valued. With the advent of 5G networks and more global coverage, the mobile phone service providers may be forced to offer data-only services, with calling and messaging services included as free value-add services for the customer. At that stage, the pricing models of mobile phone services providers will have converged to offering data packages, and all other services like calling and messaging will not be bundled for customers, leading to complete unbundled solutions from mobile service providers. The lower costs of WhatsApp and other Internet using communications services like Facebook Messenger and Viber explains their popularity globally. As of 2020, India had 340 million users of WhatsApp, followed by Brazil with 99 million users. The US has 68 million users, out of whom 26 million are active users. Facebook Messenger and Snapchat are more popular in the US with 106 million and 46 million active users. The services are more popular among younger users, and the usage of these unbundled services drops with age.

Feasibility: The lower cost of communication with unbundled services like WhatsApp, Facebook Messenger and Snapchat implies that the budget impact factor of unbundled communications services is high. The advantage of using these unbundled communications services is especially high for frequent international travellers. International roaming rates and messaging costs charged by mobile service providers are prohibitively expensive, as they use partnering contracts with providers in other countries for these services. However, when travelling internationally, hotels in most destinations offer Internet access free of charge as part of the room rental. For international calls and messages, using WhatsApp has enabled customers to significantly lower the costs of calling and messaging by accessing the Internet. The primary risk of using unbundled communications services like WhatsApp is the inability to access these services without an Internet connection. Calls can still be made, and messages can still be sent over the services provider's network if an Internet connection is missing or of bad quality, so that provides some risk mitigation for customers. However, the ability to monitor data usage in real time, and the ability to add more data as offered by most providers, manages the payment risk. Hence, the risk impact factor on the offering of unbundled communications services is moderate. The obsolescence of technology is unlikely to impact unbundled services like WhatsApp; the use of the Internet for enabling communications services is likely to dominate as the pace of improvement of Wi-Fi-enabled calling is faster. Phone network calling services still do not support video calls at reasonable rates compared to the quality of Wi-Fi calls. Hence, the obsolescence of technology factor is in favour of unbundled services. The agility of adding services from the customer's perspective is high with unbundled services, as customers can add apps like WhatsApp later. In contrast, getting those services from mobile service operators is only possible if the applications were chosen at the time of contracting for the service. Given that the provider's phone network is localized, and scaling means the addition of more partnerships globally, where the partners offer similar capabilities, the agility enabling the feasibility of unbundled services is high. From the provider's perspective, WhatsApp is able to offer more services like WhatsApp Business that enables profitability and growth. However, WhatsApp does not have a visible revenue model as of now beyond the WhatsApp Business offering, it used to cost a nominal sum to download, but is now available for free. WhatsApp's equivalent offering in China, WeChat, has online ads and gaming revenues, WhatsApp may add ads in the future to have a sustainable revenue model. As of now, WhatsApp has been growing very fast, so the agility for enabling growth is high.

Profitability: The deal transaction costs do not have an impact on the use of unbundled communications services, as the deal transaction costs are low for the usage of WhatsApp and the provider's calling and messaging services. The frequency of usage can be discriminated perfectly by both the services provider and WhatsApp, as the number of minutes of calling, the number of messages and the data used for downloads can be measured. However, WhatsApp does not charge for any of its services, hence, the expected-utility-per-use has a high impact on the usage of WhatsApp from the customer's perspective. However, since WhatsApp offers all its services for free, from the profitability perspective, WhatsApp has a low expected utility-per-use.

Growth: The space of unbundled communications services is highly competitive, with several players like WhatsApp, Facebook Messenger, Viber and Snapchat having offerings in that space. While WhatsApp managed to get an installed base earlier, the services offered by all of them are similar, and it is hard to create a niche. If WhatsApp moves to the ad revenue model, then it is highly conceivable that customers will switch to other apps that do not have ads. The degree of complementarity between the calling, messaging, and sharing utilities is high, so the complementarity factor in influencing the growth of the unbundled services has been high. The economies of scale are high, as WhatsApp just provides the software for the customer to run it on his/her own device, and access to the app is provided by the app store. WhatsApp can add solutions easily to its suite

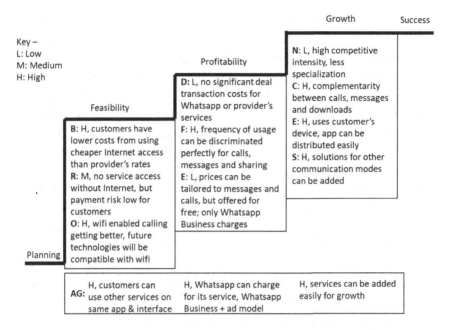

Figure 9.4:   XaaS Staircase for Unbundled Communications Services

based on customer requirements, hence, the solutions factor in accelerating the growth is high. Figure 9.4 shows the XaaS Staircase for unbundled communications services.

The XaaS Staircase for WhatsApp's unbundled communications services shows that the app has indeed been extremely successful in becoming the dominant solution for personal networking. However, the ability to charge with business networking software is new, and the profitability of the model is still a question that must be answered satisfactorily. Facebook has been baulking at adding ads on the platform as customers can switch to other services. Finding a sustainable revenue model that can let WhatsApp continue its path of exponential growth will be the key question for WhatsApp.

9.5 UNBUNDLED AUDIOLOGY SERVICES (WAKE FOREST)

While hearing impairment is not considered to be as serious as the loss of vision, hearing impairment has been a severe problem globally. More than

5% of the world's population, or about 500 million people, suffer from hearing loss to a degree that impairs their ability to have a normal life. This problem is going to be exacerbated over time, with estimates of one in ten people in the world having disabling hearing loss by 2050. In the US, about one in eight people have hearing loss in both ears, and more than 8% of adults aged over 55 have disabling hearing loss. With the improvement in the global economy and increased income over time, the market for hearing aids has been growing steadily, with the global hearing aid market being valued at $6 billion as of 2020. The market had seen a consistent growth over the last decade, with the hearing aid market in the US seeing a jump of 7.2% and 8.7% in 2015 and 2016, respectively. Typically, hearing aids were sold as a package, with the consultation, diagnostic checks, hearing aid device and regular appointments for check-ups being offered in a bundled format by audiology clinics. In May 2017, a legislation was introduced in the US to eliminate medical consultations and associated services from hearing aids to allow them to be sold as over-the-counter devices. The regulations allowed hearing devices to be unbun-dled from a hearing aid package, thereby forcing clinics to consider reinventing their hearing aid offerings.[7]

Wake Forest Baptist Health is an academic health system based in North Carolina U.S. and is operated through two components — the Wake Forest Baptist Medical Centre, which includes a large hospital, five com-munity hospitals, and 350 primary and secondary centres across the state, and the Wake Forest School of Medicine as well as specialty care centres. The audiology department was part of the Medical Centre and offered advanced diagnostic and treatment services for patients with hearing loss. After the new regulations were introduced, the clinic evaluated its existing service-provision model and decided to change its model of hearing aid consultations, fittings, and follow-up to create unbundled services for the practice. Instead of bundling all services into one price as done earlier, Wake Forest shifted its focus to describing each service clearly to customers, and pricing them separately. To execute the unbundling of its services, Wake Forest began by analysing its competition, and its key

---

[7]Meagan Lewis, Audiology Unbundled, Asha Wire, February 1, 2018, https://leader.pubs.asha.org/doi/full/10.1044/leader.AEA.23022018.22, accessed November 20, 2020.

differentiation attributes in the hearing health market. It appointed a task force to brainstorm for solutions to the new regulations and came to the conclusion that its quality of service had created a healthy reputation for its services in the market. Offering audiology services in an unbundled format would enable it to differentiate itself further and afford customers quality hearing healthcare with the ability to make his/her own choices.

Like most audiology clinics, Wake Forest had used the traditional bundled approach to providing its services to customers paired with consultation. The bundled package encompassed device cost, hearing aid fitting, and follow-up appointments for three years. As the consultation was included in the package, the additional variable costs for delivering the package were the device itself and the fitting costs. While brainstorming for an unbundled approach, Wake Forest realized that by not charging for hearing aid evaluations, it was sending a wrong message to its customers — that the consultation was not worth the investment for customers. With the new model, the firm decided to charge for hearing aid evaluations, as they believed that customers would have a higher utility from a hearing aid that fit their loss rather than a more cursory evaluation. The hearing aid recommendations were driven by assessments like LDLS (loudness discomfort levels), quick-SIN (speech-in-noise test), and other patient-reported issues. Such assessments were crucial in interpreting the right hearing solution for the customer. Unbundling the evaluation services allowed Wake Forest to charge the customer for the first 45 days of the services separately from the price of the device. The fee for the evaluation service covered hearing aid evaluation, electroacoustic analysis, real-ear measures, and any additional services required for the complete evaluation. Each service was categorized under a unique code, and patients had the flexibility of choosing which services they wanted to sign up for. Such an unbundled pricing approach offered patients a lower upfront cost and encouraged them to return for fittings when appropriate.

9.5.1 Unbundled Audiology Services Analysis

General: There are major differences between vision and hearing loss, the state-of-the-art diagnostics for both, and the course of correction for the loss of the two kinds of senses. While vision loss can be corrected completely in most cases by eyeglasses or by surgery, hearing loss cannot be corrected completely by using hearing aids. Hearing loss occurs because of damage to the hair cells of the inner ear, and these cells progressively deteriorate over time. While hearing aids can amplify the sound reaching the air, they cannot aid the brain in interpreting the sound signals as the hair cells of the inner ear can. Vision problems are easier to self-diagnose, as people can visually confirm that images of objects are blurred. In contrast, people find it harder to assess if they have disabling hearing loss, leading to delays in most people seeking treatment for hearing loss. After hearing aids are inserted into the ears, the brain needs to get retrained to acclimatize itself to the different sound signals again and interpret them accordingly. These are the reasons that most audiologists bundled the services of consultation, diagnostics, fitting, and follow-up visits: correcting hearing loss is a continuous process, and hearing aids need to be checked and cleaned professionally. Unlike eyeglasses that are easier to self-check by customers, hearing aids need a continuous interaction between audiologists and customers to check if the aids are functioning properly and the customer's hearing loss is being treated adequately. The unbundling of hearing aid services requires the provider to clearly state the fees of the different services included in the package, to enable the customer to evaluate the utility offered by each of the services. Hearing aids are significantly cheaper compared to the prices of the packages, and the unbundling may often lead to customers questioning the need for the associated services with the hearing aid. While the audiologist may have some revenue losses from customers cherry picking the services they want, it also leads to new sources of revenue potentially, as customers who acquire hearing aids over the counter may request consultation and evaluation services. Audiologists can also elaborate on the value of their services by pointing out the pitfalls of using devices that do not fit well or unnecessarily amplify sounds beyond the need of the customer. Further, the prices of each of these services must be set at points that customers are willing to pay for each individual service, rather than having to pay a bundled price to fix their hearing loss.

Feasibility: The move towards unbundled pricing for audiology services does provide customers with the opportunity to pay less for services that they do not require. For example, while many customers still avail of the consultation service with the audiologist and the diagnostic tests, if their hearing ability is enhanced, they may not go to the audiologist for repeat visits. Hence, customers will have an enhanced budget impact factor from the unbundled audiology services. The risk impact factor from the customer's perspective does not have a significant impact on the customer's choice of offering. While customers do not know now the amount that they will pay, they can compare the total prices on the menu from the bundled prices of competitive offerings to know the upper limit of the payment amount. The itemized list of services also enables them to be able to estimate their total payments and make an informed decision of the services that they need. Since hearing aids are fitted to the needs of the customer, there is no risk of capacity from the audiologist's viewpoint, as the audiologist does not need to order hearing aid devices and inventory them ahead of the demand. The obsolescence of technology risk does not have an impact in this case, as the hearing aids and diagnostics will be upgraded to the same level of technology, regardless of the unbundling of the services. However, the data of customer choice patterns can provide the audiologist with valuable feedback about the attractiveness of the services and designing service improvement initiatives. From the customer's perspective, the unbundled services provide a higher degree of agility, as the customer can choose to change the date of the follow-up visits, or not have the follow-up visits, based on his/her experience with the hearing aid devices. The agility of the audiologist is enhanced for profitability, as each service offered will need to be profitable. The audiologist will have to analyze the variable cost structure of the different service offerings and the overhead cost structure of the clinic in detail in determining the prices of the menu. The unbundling of services can also offer the audiologist demand patterns and learning of which services are preferred by customers, whereby the provider can invest in and scale only the services that customers demand on a sustained basis.

Profitability: The deal transaction costs are significant in the choice of unbundled services, as the ticking meter effect potentially influences customers' choice of services when they are offered in an unbundled fashion. While the number of interactions needed can potentially be higher, the average customer will have the same number of interactions if the bundle was designed correctly. However, the ticking meter effect may discourage customers from seeking intervention unless they deem it necessary to have follow-up visits. The frequency of the usage of the service is discriminated better in the unbundled services model, as unlike the bundled flat fee original model, the audiologist gets paid for each visit by the customer. The expected utility-per-use is also in favour of the unbundled service model, as the customer's willingness-to-pay for each service can be used for setting the price for each service, rather than as a bundle.

Growth: The unbundled services model does not have the possibility of creating a niche vis-à-vis the bundled model, as the offering of hearing health services is standard, hence, the competitiveness aspect effect is low. The complementarity offered by both sets of services is standard, hence, the complementarity factor does not offer an advantage to the unbundled offering. The economies of scale of both models are fairly similar, with the caveat that the unbundled services model offers the possibility of specializing in a few services like consultation only, or only the hearing aid device offering with a standardized battery of tests. Further, services like consultation only can be offered online, enabling audiologists to reach out to a wider set of potential customers. The solutions offering in both models is also similar, hence, the solutions offering does not have an impact on the growth of the unbundled services model.

The comparison of the unbundled and bundled models (Figure 9.5) shows that unbundling audiology services by the same set of providers results in a high budget impact factor for feasibility and a high frequency of usage discriminability. However, unbundling services in audiology does not result in a significant impetus for accelerated growth, as there are no significant differences between the unbundled and the bundled models in the growth stage.

9.6 SUMMARY

The unbundling of services helps to improve the transparency of the pricing of each service, and to reach untapped markets which were not accessible earlier as the bundle was not attractive at the corresponding price point. If different services in the bundle are being offered by different

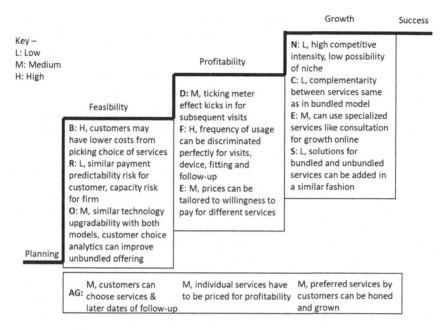

Figure 9.5: XaaS Staircase for Unbundled Audiology Services

resource divisions of the firm, unbundling helps to identify divisions that need a higher efficiency. If the value added by different components of the bundle is not complementary, then the firm may be better off offering the services as standalone offerings. The budget factor impact is the most important factor that influences customer choice of unbundled services. The primary advantage of the unbundling of services from the customer's viewpoint is the ability to pay only for those services that the customer desires. For instance, AirAsia unbundles the flying service from the seating, meals, baggage, and flight insurance services. Customers who intend to travel with only a light carry-on bag for a short period can choose not to buy the baggage service, enabling them to lower their ticket price. While budget airlines are used primarily by price-conscious travellers for personal travel, businesses also can avail of their low-cost services for cost-cutting purposes. Beyond the obvious advantages of choosing only the desired services, budget airlines offer services at multiple service and price points, enabling customers to fine-tune their choice. AirAsia offers baggage services at multiple levels, so if customers want to travel with a small-sized or medium-sized bag, they can choose that particular level for the baggage service. This fine-tuning of the services enables the provider to match the customer needs better with their offerings. Similarly, the older cable channel subscriptions would offer customers bundled choices; HBO Max and other subscription-based models of media offerings have changed that approach. By offering customers the individual choice of channels, customers can pick the channels that they desire to watch and pay a monthly fee to access those channels only. iTunes followed a similar approach in their offering of music, by unbundling music albums, which was the dominant offering in the music industry. By enabling customers to pay for individual tracks, iTunes expanded the market by offering music content to customers who did not want to pay for entire albums to listen to one or two songs only. Wake Forest's model of unbundling audiology services offered customers the choice of the number of interventions for diagnostics, fitting, and follow-on services along with the hearing aid, enabling customers to decide the services that they would access. WhatsApp's model of unbundling communications services from the service provider enabled customers to call and message at much cheaper rates by using the Internet rather than the provider's network as the backbone of the communications infrastructure. The cheaper access of the Internet compared to typical providers' rates made the app's usage more attractive than using the provider's services, especially when used by travelling customers who had to pay exorbitant roaming charges in the past.

The risk impact factor on the adoption of unbundled services is generally low in comparison to the base case of the bundled suite of services. From the customer's perspective, the risk of budget overrun, quality, and reliability is the same as that of the bundled suite of services, as these risks are not impacted by unbundling. From the provider's perspective, the unbundling leads to a nominally higher risk of the adoption of individual elements of the bundle; however, it also enables the provider to focus on creating value within each element of the suite. The risk of complementary assets' (the Internet) availability does exist for WhatsApp, as customers need Internet access when they want to use the app. However, for the other case studies (AirAsia, HBO Max, iTunes and Wake Forest), the risk impact factor does not influence the customer's choice of adoption. The obsolescence of technology and other technology factors also do not have a significant impact on the adoption of unbundled services, as the services offered do not get impacted by technology if they are offered in a bundled or unbundled fashion (AirAsia, Wake Forest). HBO Max and iTunes have the advantage over cable television services and mobile phone provider services of being accessible on multiple devices. While CDs could also be played on multiple devices, streaming services can be accessed more easily while travelling, as there is no need for carrying physical devices like CDs. The HBO Max, iTunes, and WhatsApp services need access to the Internet for either downloading content or watching content. However, given that the Internet is likely to be the backbone of communications infrastructure in the long run, the obsolescence of technology impact is in favour of these unbundled services.

The customer agility that impacts the adoption feasibility is enhanced by many of the case studies of unbundled services. HBO Max's customers can access new niche content on the individual channel more easily than on cable TV. If HBO Max wanted to introduce a new channel on cable TV, it would have to coordinate with the cable TV service providers like Comcast to ensure that it could get compensated for the content on the new channel. However, given that bundle prices are more inflexible as they influence the adoption of the entire service suite, adding new channels had to have a strong business case. In contrast, introducing new channels on HBO Max is easier for HBO; customers who derive utility from the channel will adopt the channel. iTunes's customers can access singles more quickly when artists create new content, rather than having to wait for the creation of other songs to fill an entire album. Similarly, musicians can introduce new content quickly on the iTunes platform. Customers can add apps like WhatsApp at any point of time, while adopting similar services from mobile phone service providers has a higher transaction cost. Wake Forest's customers can make the choice of individual appointments based on their schedule, rather than having to stick to the original schedules of the bundled service. From the perspective of profitability, AirAsia's point-to-point model is more agile than full-service airlines using the hub-and-spoke model, as resources can be moved from one route to the other based on demand. HBO Max can add more channels easily on their platform compared to a cable TV subscription bundle. Apple can add content on the iTunes platform more easily than BMG and Sony could distribute

CDs with new content, which needed an entire physical distribution infrastructure. While WhatsApp can add more chargeable services to their suite easily, their challenge has been in identifying services that customers are willing to pay for. By unbundling its audiology services, Wake Forest can focus on lowering costs and setting prices for individual services, so that each individual service is profitable. The point-to-point model is limiting for growth, as the network does not scale adequately. In contrast, the hub-and-spoke network is ideal for scaling, hence, full-service airlines do better on agility for growth. HBO Max has a higher agility for growth compared to its offerings on cable TV, as there is no revenue sharing with channel partners like Comcast. iTunes's and WhatsApp's app and cloud support model (WhatsApp uses the iCloud and cloud infrastructure of mobile phone manufacturers) is primed for agile growth capabilities. Wake Forest can use customer data analytics to enable it to invest resources in services that have higher demand.

The unbundling of services in general leads to higher deal transaction costs, owing to the increased number of transactions and the ticking meter effect. Hence, unbundled services models lead to a negative impact on the deal transaction costs, leading to bundled services being preferred on this dimension. While customers have the choice of individual services which were only offered as a bundle previously, they have to manage multiple offerings from the same provider (Wake Forest), or multiple providers (HBO Max). The deal transaction costs for unbundled services derive from having to manage multiple subscriptions and bills (HBO Max), and having to manage multiple unbundled appointments, leading to the ticking meter effect (Wake Forest). While budget airlines typically offer different services to customers at the time of buying their tickets, full-service airlines offer loyalty and frequent flyer programs to customers that budget airlines do not. Hence, customers get rewarded for multiple transactions with full-service airlines, but do not reap such benefits with budget airlines. Similarly, in the music industry, the deal transaction costs effect is moderate, as customers must buy songs each time and organize them in their lists. The frequency of usage can be discriminated perfectly by models like Spotify that rely on a pay-per-use model, hence, the frequency of usage can be an advantage for unbundled services if providers use the pay-per-use mechanism. In the airline sector, both budget airlines and full-service airlines use the pay-per-use model, hence, there is no difference in their offerings on the frequency of usage dimension. However, if providers use the subscription model or selling model for both bundled and unbundled services (HBO Max, iTunes), then the frequency of usage is not differentiated for unbundled and bundled services. In the communications industry, both mobile service providers and unbundled service providers like WhatsApp can price their offerings based on usage, hence, there is no distinction between bundled and unbundled services on the usage frequency dimension. However, unbundling services can provide increased revenues in audiology services (Wake Forest), as customers will pay fees each time for repeat consultations on the fitting and testing of hearing aid devices. One of the biggest impacts of the unbundled services offering is on the expected utility-per-use. Since customers choose individual services from the menu, the provider's ability to target specific customer attributes is enhanced. The primary advantage of unbundling services is to make the offerings lean, and optimize value from every service element, by increasing utility on desired services, and eliminating service elements that customers are not willing to pay for. Customers can choose if they want to pay for baggage and meal services in budget airlines (AirAsia) and choose the levels they desire for the baggage service and the individual items on the menu for food services. Hence, prices can be set depending on the value provided to the customer, and costs can be optimized based on the choices made by the customer. Similarly, unbundled media and entertainment services provide customers with the ability to pick the channels they want to watch and enable the firm to eliminate or cut offerings that do not have a high adoption rate. For music content and audiology, prices can be set based on the willingness-to-pay of the customer, and costs can be optimized based on customer choices.

The gold standard in unbundling services in driving growth was undoubtedly set by Apple with its iTunes service. By creating a music ecosystem (iTunes for distribution, iPod as the hardware, and a corresponding software offering), Apple was able to offer a high degree of complementarity to customers. This high degree of complementarity enabled Apple to offer customers the choice of selected content in a cost-effective manner and creating a competitive advantage that was hard to replicate. The online offering along with storage in the device meant that the service was easy to scale with high economies of scale, and the model enabled Apple to offer video content along with audio content, enabling a solutions approach to its offering. Spotify's pay-per-use pricing mechanism and the use of the cloud has meant that it is challenging Apple for dominance in the music industry. Other offerings of unbundled services have not had the roaring success that the unbundling model has had in the music industry, but many offerings have created distinctive niches. By offering customers a lower cost and enabling choice of services, unbundled services offerings in the airlines sector (AirAsia) have managed to create their specific niche with leisure travellers. The niche has been further enabled by the point-to-point model adopted by these providers, in contrast to the hub-and-spoke model of full-service airlines. While HBO Max's strategy of offering its content via both cable and using the OTT model has enabled it to create some niche offerings in the OTT format, the OTT offerings have led to a proliferation of competitors like Netflix and Disney, leading to an intensely competitive market. Unbundling services in the communications and audiology businesses have not had an impact in creating niches, as the service elements like calling and messaging (WhatsApp), and audiology services (Wake Forest), are standardized. The complementarity factor has no impact in airlines (AirAsia) and audiology services (Wake Forest), but has a detrimental effect on OTT offerings, as cable TV bundles offer a wider variety of content than OTT offerings. However, by using a common platform, WhatsApp and HBO Max have been able to get some benefits of complementarity in customer adoption and cost reduction. The economies of scale factor is high for WhatsApp with the online distribution and storage on customer devices. However, the economies of scale impact on the other offerings is mixed. Full-service airlines have higher economies of scale than budget airlines by using the hub-and-spoke model. While HBO Max has reasonably good economies of scale using the cloud, working with cable service providers enabled a better reach for them earlier, as all subscribers of cable TV services had access to their content. Wake Forest can take advantage of online consultation for some economies of scale. The solutions offerings comparison of bundled and unbundled services offers a mixed bag, as bundled services include a larger set of solutions by default. However, enabling customers to pick and choose individual solutions from the bundle provides customers with a higher degree of flexibility.

Chapter 10

Conclusions: The Evolution of XaaS in the Future

The transition of offerings from product-based assets to offering them in the as-a-service mode has been accelerating in the recent future. By offering product asset-based experiences as a service, firms can utilize the principles of successful XaaS models to create value for themselves, customers, and society at large. In this chapter, we will outline our thoughts on the evolution of the XaaS model in the future. To understand why the XaaS model has grown so quickly, we analyze the as-a-service offering using the transaction costs explanation of the theory of the firm. We then identify some societal benefits from the XaaS model, followed by some predictions for the XaaS model in the future.

10.1 XaaS AND THE THEORY OF THE FIRM

At the outset of this concluding chapter, it is worth considering the theory of the firm and the reasons why firms outsource their activities over time. The theoretical underpinnings of the firm's existence help us understand the reasons why the XaaS model will expand in the future. The seminal work of Coase provides a transaction cost basis to the existence of the firm, and explains why the organizational entity of the firm has developed and matured over time.[1] Coase pointed out that in efficient markets, individuals can create contracts with each other for every activity, hence, these contracts between individuals can be used to replicate all relationships within the firm. Entrepreneurs can then identify the most efficient provider (highest value for lowest cost) for any product, component, or service, and contract with those individuals. However, the existence of transaction costs precludes this contracting approach for individuals, thereby facilitating the formation of the firm as a long-term entity.

These transaction costs take the form of search and information costs, bargaining costs, and enforcement costs, and these costs can make the approach of designing contracts with multiple individual agents inefficient.[2] Search and information costs relate to the cognitive burden that entrepreneurs undertake when searching for a better component, service, or set of employee skills. Entrepreneurs conduct such a search until the costs of search and information are higher than the marginal benefit provided by the component, service, or more skilled labour. These search costs include the opportunity costs of time and energy of the entrepreneur in conducting the search, advertising costs, the costs of evaluating different options and conducting research, or the costs of outsourcing the search to third parties. Bargaining costs include the costs incurred in multiple iterations of negotiating contracts, the costs associated with research into the criticality of the value added by different parties, and the costs of designing appropriate contracts that align the incentives of the contracting parties. Once contracts have been designed, individual parties may deviate from these contracts unless these contracts can be effectively enforced. The transaction costs of enforcement include the costs of monitoring the efforts and behaviour of individual parties, the costs of litigation when contracts are not adhered to, and the costs of contract renegotiation if required.

Williamson built upon the transaction costs framework, by explaining that the drivers of transaction costs are uncertainty, bounded rationality,

---

[1] Demsetz, H. (1988). The theory of the firm revisisted. *The Journal of Law, Economics, & Organization.*, 4, 141.

[2] Transaction Costs, CFI, https://corporatefinanceinstitute.com/resources/knowledge/economics/transaction-costs/, accessed December 2, 2020.

repeated transactions, asset specificity, and opportunistic behaviour.[3] Uncertainty is an important driver of transaction costs, as a high degree of uncertainty of the quality and valuation of different kinds of assets would inhibit frequent contracting with different parties. Similarly, the bounded rationality of individual entrepreneurs would limit their ability to conduct multiple searches. A high number of repeated transactions would induce entrepreneurs to internalize activities, as bargaining repeatedly imposes higher bargaining costs. A high degree of asset specificity leads to the inability of the entrepreneur to exit contracts for these assets, and the opportunistic behaviour of individuals implies higher costs of monitoring.

In the past, these transaction costs were higher, as the technologies and processes for assisting the search, bargaining, and enforcement activities were primitive, leading to the creation of more value-added activities within firms to avoid these transaction costs. Coase noted that when search and information gathering activities are tedious and costly, firms that are formed are more likely to conduct activities internally with existing resources. Internalizing activities enabled firms to avoid these expensive searches for more efficient methods of production, services, or employees. Similarly, when bargaining costs and policing and enforcement costs were high, existing firms tended to avoid bargaining with external parties, owing to potentially high bargaining and enforcement costs. The number of activities performed internally by the firm and the number of activities that are performed by outsourced parties are a function of the transaction costs from dealing with external parties and the overhead costs within the firm. As firms get larger, there are higher overhead costs and an increased cognitive inability to perform functions efficiently internally. Hence, firms tend to outsource activities that they have found reliable suppliers for (reducing the need for search and information gathering). They can design long-term contracts with these partners (reducing the need for repeated bargaining), and they work towards having a collaborative relationship with them (reducing the need for policing and enforcement). Outsourced activities also tend to be of lower value to

---

[3] Williamson, O. (1981). The economics of organization: The transaction cost approach. *American Journal of Sociology*, 87(3), 548–577.

the firm, enabling firms to focus on their core activities, and outsourcing activities that are non-core to long-term reliable suppliers. In such cases, firms tend to form ecosystems of collaborative enterprise, where they contribute their expertize in their core activities to provide complete goods and services to end customers. Using the collaborative history with their partners and building stronger ties with reliable partners enable firms to avoid the transaction costs as postulated by Coase.

Why does the XaaS model enable the customer to be lean and support outsourcing by lowering transaction costs? First, let us examine the drivers of the transaction costs, viz., uncertainty, bounded rationality, repeated transactions, asset specificity, and opportunistic behaviour. When asset valuations were uncertain with repeated transactions in the past, the customer preferred to internalize activities supported by those assets to minimize the associated search and bargaining costs. However, the advent of free trials on low-cost online access mechanisms has enabled customers to ascertain the value of those assets and lower the corresponding valuation uncertainty. Similarly, customers exhibited bounded rationality when they had several external options to choose from in their evaluation process. The degree of standardization in market offerings over time has enabled the evaluation of the offerings to impose a lower cognitive burden on the customer. The asset specificity associated with tasks has been addressed by XaaS providers by the ownership transfer scheme, enabling access to specific assets to the customer in an outsourced fashion. Finally, the potential for opportunistic behaviour on the part of the provider that could result in higher enforcement costs for repeated outsourced interactions is mitigated by the larger number of customers that could enforce the standard contract on the provider. Another mitigating factor for the enforcement costs is the ease of switching providers in the XaaS model. The XaaS model has a unique mix of properties from the asset ownership transfer, technology driven value, the solutions provider approach, the nanonization of utility, and a continuous innovation culture (Figure 1.1). The search and information costs in the XaaS model are lowered from the use of digital technology access to the terms and conditions of the offering, and in the actual delivery of the value for IT-based XaaS offerings. Customers can access multiple related services from the same provider as providers adopt the solutions approach, leading to lower search costs.

Since providers typically offer a standardized menu of solutions with the ability to pick nanonized elements of the product or service, the bargaining costs are lowered. The need to avoid enforcement and policing costs is eliminated in the XaaS model as providers continuously strive to provide more value with a continuous innovation culture to maximize customer retention.

10.2 SOCIETAL VALUE OF XaaS MODEL

The societal value of the XaaS should not and cannot be understated; the XaaS model can make a significant impact on society and help achieve societal goals. The importance of serving the needs of customers in the base of the pyramid (BoP) has been widely discussed; people in this section constitute a majority of the world's population, and do not have access to a large set of products and services.[4] At the same time, the sheer size of potential customers in the BoP makes it an attractive market, and firms that can use innovative models to meet the needs of such customers will find it financially rewarding if the right model of access can be designed. It has been well documented that the challenges of serving customers at the BoP arise from the lack of buying power and transactional capacity; both issues can be addressed by the XaaS model. The five characteristics of successful XaaS offerings as enunciated in Chapter 1 illustrate the benefits of XaaS offerings for the BoP. The XaaS model enables customers at the bottom of the pyramid to access various products and services with lower cash outlays; this is enabled by the asset ownership transfer feature of XaaS models. The ability to consume only the needed components of utility enables customers to match the offering with their needs, thereby keeping their costs low. Having the solutions provider approach and the continuous innovation features enables providers to continuously understand shifting customer needs and meeting them with a cost-conscious focus. Finally, the ingenious use of technology can make the firm's offering more accessible to customers, help in monitoring transactions, as well as adding utility to customers. With some innovative

---

[4] Hart, S. L. & Christensen, C. M. (2002). The great leap: Driving innovation from the base of the pyramid. *MIT Sloan Management Review*, 44(1), 51.

financing help like payments due after the agricultural produce is sold, firms can create significant impact for customers in the BoP in agriculture, fishing, and other traditional occupations. The use of the XaaS model in meeting the needs of smallholders in agriculture has been documented in Chapter 7 in the TAFE case study, which illustrates the use of the XaaS model in enabling access to mechanized agricultural equipment to small-holders. In the industrial context, SMEs often lack the ability to invest upfront in new technologies that could potentially unlock significant value. The XaaS model can serve the purpose of adding SMEs to the customer base of larger organizations by providing products, services, and software to them in the XaaS mode, thereby alleviating the need for initial cash outlays.

The XaaS model can be a very useful tool in adding individual customers to the customer portfolio, as individual customers often face the same issues as SMEs in being able to access firm offerings. For the provider, another important stakeholder to be considered is their own set of employees; what is the impact of the XaaS model on employee satisfaction? By aligning the HR practices to continuous engagement with the employee, XaaS providers enable employee satisfaction to a higher degree. By having a culture of continuous innovation, providers enable employees to be consistently engaged with customers, thereby increasing the value provided to customers. The XaaS model also needs a more elaborate set of skills from employees, including the ability to work with IoT and other field service technologies. The constant reskilling of employees helps keep them engaged and the virtuous cycle of learning and development leads to higher employee satisfaction. Another interesting societal benefit of using the XaaS model for IP is demonstrated by RPX (Chapter 1), which buys patents and then licenses them to multiple industry players. The practice of defensive patent aggregation reduces the litigation and patent-trolling activity in research-intensive industry sectors, shares the impact of innovation with multiple players, and leads to the innovation being diffused to a larger set of customers.

The environmental benefits of the XaaS model have been alluded to before in the Ahrend case study; these benefits extend to the application of the XaaS model to IT assets as well. It is well known that the operation of IT assets like data centres is energy intensive. The use of the XaaS model can enable businesses to reduce their energy consumption, lower utility costs, and help attain their sustainability goals. While the data centres used to serve large corporations burn a lot of electricity, by centralizing IT operations for multiple firms, data centres also serve an important social purpose in reducing the energy needs for IT applications for their customers. Large organizations can achieve significant economies of scale in their own operations by centralizing IT applications. However, the economies of scale achieved are specific to the location, hence, they are limited in effectiveness. They also have the added issue that the use of energy in such centralized facilities has a high degree of variability based on the time of the day. On the other hand, cloud providers achieve much higher economies of scale, and hence, their energy consumption is lower. Further, by operating the data centre to serve customers across different sectors, these cloud providers can achieve a more uniform loading of the grid, leading to more predictable power usage that can be planned. Cloud providers can also design their infrastructures in a way that reduces energy consumption further, owing to their scale. The agency costs of monitoring the energy usage and the corresponding carbon footprint can be daunting for individual organizations. However, cloud providers find it easier to manage energy usage and the carbon footprint by using systemic measures across different locations. Similarly, for disposal and lifecycle management of IT assets, the XaaS model makes it easier for cloud providers to manage this process systemically and at scale, compared to corresponding ad hoc processes at individual organizations.

At its root, the XaaS model is similar to the sharing economy, with the difference that the provider owns the assets in the XaaS model, whereas in the sharing economy, a different set of partners own assets that are distributed by platforms. The benefits of the sharing economy in meeting societal needs of customers and partners, as well as in meeting sustainability goals have been well understood. A number of apparel manufacturers in the fast fashion sector like Zara, H&M, and Mango have been criticized for the proliferation of apparel beyond acceptable needs, and highlighted the need for sustainability in the apparel sector.[5] CaaStle

---

[5] Rashmila Maiti, "Fast Fashion: Its Detrimental Effect on the Environment", *Earth.Org.*, Jan 29, 2020, https://earth.org/fast-fashions-detrimental-effect-on-the-environment/, accessed December 2, 2020.

offers a clothing-as-a-service platform, where retailers can use the platform to rent apparel for specific occasions.[6] The clothing-as-a-service model has indeed been used historically to distribute apparel for specific occasions, e.g., tuxedos for graduation or weddings, or graduation gowns. Similar offerings in the past included Rent the Runway and Nuuly. CaaStle offers customers the choice of four outfits a month for $89, or unlimited items for a monthly fee of $159. These XaaS models for apparel reduce the proliferation of apparel globally and enable customers to access the latest fashions in a sustainable manner.

10.3 THE FUTURE OF XaaS FOR PRODUCT ASSETS

How will the XaaS model evolve in the future for product assets? As the XaaS model gains traction, we expect that the access to products meant for customers in the BoP should grow with the XaaS model. The Food and Agriculture Organization (FAO) of the United Nations has an Advisory Committee on Fishery Research (ACFR), which suggests that the poorer sections of society should have access to fishery equipment using innovative means.[7] The XaaS model can alleviate the issues of the lack of capital and knowhow for fisherfolk in the lower economic rungs of society. The OECD (2017) report on the need for new technologies in fisheries to make fishing more sustainable highlights the need for the diffusion of new technologies in fishing, and the need for social entrepreneurship models for this diffusion.[8] Providing access to new technologies like IoT and big data along with access to sophisticated fishing equipment using the XaaS model can provide an impetus to the global fishing industry. Similarly, the

---

[6] Tim Hirsch, "Clothing as a service will disrupt consumption habits", Leaders League, June 5, 2019, https://www.leadersleague.com/en/news/tim-hirsch-clothing-as-a-service-will-disrupt-consumption-habits, accessed December 10, 2020.

[7] Regional Fishery Bodies Summary Descriptions, Food and Agriculture Organization of the United Nations, http://www.fao.org/fishery/rfb/acfr/en, accessed December 2, 2020.

[8] Pierre Girard & Thomas Du Payrat, "An inventory of new technologies in fisheries", *OECD*, November 21, 2017, https://www.oecd.org/greengrowth/GGSD_2017_Issue%20Paper_New%20technologies%20in%20Fisheries_WEB.pdf, accessed Dec 20, 2020.

global manufacturing industry relies heavily on SMEs for the manufacturing of small parts, which are assembled by larger suppliers into modular components for OEMs. SMEs have highly variable cash flows and are hit harder by global boom and bust cycles; hence, large initial investments in equipment are risky for SMEs as they find it hard to survive during economic downturns. The use of the XaaS model for access to manufacturing equipment would be a useful tool for OEMs who partner with SMEs in the supply chain and equipment manufacturers. ORIX has XaaS solutions for SMEs to enable smooth operations for them on equipment needed for continuing operations, or for turnkey projects. The technology risk and the costs associated with equipment disposal and waste management are borne by ORIX. SMEs have the choice of buying the equipment at the end of the contractual period of use for a pre-specified price.[9]

There is a well-known product classification scheme in marketing that classifies customer products into one of four categories: convenience goods (bought frequently without comparison and significant buying effort), shopping goods (low frequency of purchase, with significant comparisons on price and quality), specialty goods (unique products with a significant buying effort), and unsought goods (not considered usually by customers, only bought under special circumstances).[10] How will the XaaS model for convenience goods evolve? Examples of convenience goods are FMCG goods like coffee and consumer staples. Convenience goods do not make a good case for the XaaS model, with some notable exceptions. After reading the coffee-as-a-service example in the beginning of the book, we suspect that some readers may have begun searching for alcohol-as-a-service offerings. While we have conducted exhaustive searches, there are no comparable subscription services for alcoholic beverages at similar price points. However, there are innovative service-based offerings for alcoholic beverages as well. You can buy a subscription to the HipBar in India, where you buy the rights to a bottle of an alcoholic

---

[9] ORIX, Leasing, https://www.orixindia.com/equipment-leasing.php, accessed December 20, 2020.

[10] Maximilian Claessens, 4 Types of Consumer Products and Marketing Considerations — Convenience, Shopping, Speciality and Unsought Products, Marketing-Insider, June 20, 2017, https://marketing-insider.eu/4-types-of-consumer-products/, accessed December 30, 2020.

beverage, and then consume drinks equal to the volume of that bottle at any participating bar or restaurant of your choice until the bottle is consumed.[11] The service is provided with an app, which keeps tabs in real time on the volume of the bottle that has been consumed. After software on the cloud and infrastructure on the cloud, welcome to the bold new world of whisky on the cloud!

We expect the use of the XaaS model for shopping and specialty goods to grow significantly in the future. Residential and commercial properties are either classified as shopping products or specialty products depending on the nature of the property. The co-living offering using the XaaS model has seen a mixed adoption in the past: while renting residential properties was always preferred by select market segments, the co-living offering goes beyond offering the rental of the property alone. The concept of mixed residential offerings with some private and some communal residential space has found a reasonable degree of acceptance as a means of achieving enhanced social interaction. Young professionals dominate the current market segment that has adopted co-living spaces, but there are other demographics like retirees that are also latching on to the co-living concept. As communications technology improves and organizations grow more decentralized, the fluidity of mobility is expediting the adoption of the co-living concept. The flexibility of co-living beats the need for signing long rental leases for mobile professionals who desire a higher degree of freedom in their career choices. For retirees, the co-living option enables them to have access to a social circle without having to completely compromise on their private space. The budget impact combined with the greater flexibility offered by co-living seems to suggest that the model will continue growing as an attractive option for mobile professionals and other select segments in larger cities, where the affordability of accommodation is a concern. Hence, we expect to see a growth in the co-living market over time in larger cities, and cities with a higher proportion of technology companies that attract a young and digitally savvy set of workers. Similarly, in our opinion, while the diffusion of

---

[11] Patel, D., "Introducing AaaS — Alcohol as a Service", https://medium.com/@darshipatel/introducing-aaas-alcohol-as-a-service-daf64a90dd71#:~:text=HipBar%2C%20allows%20liquor%20connoisseurs%20to, 30%20ml% 20in%20any%20bar., accessed January 4, 2021.

co-working spaces has got off to a rocky start, we are sanguine about the future of co-working spaces. First, there is a wide body of evidence that businesses that will be successful in the future will depend a lot on business ecosystems; it will be hard for firms to operate as an island in the future. Being a part of an ecosystem necessitates a continual interaction with other constituents of the ecosystem. Co-working spaces provide a supporting environment for employees of different organizations to collect and collaborate in these spaces. While Allen's research has shown that communication is more effective with co-location, the competitive advantage in the future will be with firms that offer co-location and collaboration opportunities outside the boundaries of the firm.[12] Given the aspirations of work flexibility of millennials, it will be harder to expect them to move to a centralized location to co-work with all other employees of the organization. The flexibility offered for remote work by co-working spaces can go a long way in providing millennials with the ability to add value to organizations while working in a decentralized fashion. The COVID-19 pandemic has also shown that working in a decentralized manner can be efficient using communications tools like Zoom, Microsoft Teams, and Slack. The diffusion of these technologies will enable the diffusion of co-working spaces in the future. The growth of the gig economy has also demonstrated that organizations are increasingly using freelancers as an integral part of their workforce strategy. Freelancers do not neatly fit into the boundaries of the organization, yet they need to interact intermittently with employees to build a cohesive work environment. Co-working spaces are a bridge between the need for a higher degree of location flexibility and the human need for connection and social interaction. Co-working spaces facilitate community building and create a collaborative environment for holding workshops and networking, thereby enabling successful organizations for the future.

The future of mobility in the form of personal and commercial vehicles is also showing signs of a XaaS-led renaissance. Deloitte found that in the US, there are about 20 million registrations of new light vehicles annually, out of which about 18% are from the corporate sector and 82%

[12] Allen, M. (Ed.). (2017). *The SAGE Encyclopaedia of Communication Research Methods*. Sage Publications, California. https://dx.doi.org/10.4135/9781483381411

are from the retail sector.[13] Out of the corporate registrations, about 11% of the vehicles are operated on the XaaS model, while in the retail sector, about 24% of the vehicles are operated based on the XaaS model. In the commercial vehicle segment, the proportion of vehicles operated using the XaaS model is significantly higher.[14] The future of mobility is in a state of flux, with electrical vehicles, autonomous vehicles, and vehicle sharing advancing at a rapid clip. In the commercial vehicle space, technologies such as big data analytics, IoT, and track-and-trace technologies like cloud-based GPS are revolutionizing the commercial mobility world. The constant churn of new technologies and access models in the mobility sector makes the purchase of vehicles a risky proposition. In the light vehicles market, while many customers chose to purchase their vehicles, they outsourced the maintenance to service providers. The fleet management of commercial vehicles has been dominantly outsourced for more than two decades, hence, the XaaS model has already had a hold on this market for a long time. The capital costs of fleet acquisition and the needs for financing, maintenance, and insurance resulted in most OEMs outsourcing fleet management to 3PL and 4PL providers, as the logistics function was not considered to be a core competence. For the logistics providers, the costs of acquiring their own fleet was a big source of cash flow burn, hence, many of them chose to access vehicles using the XaaS model.

While the adoption of electrical vehicles has been growing rapidly, a key hurdle for more ubiquitous adoption is the range of electrical vehicles. Currently, the Tesla Model S Long Range Plus has a range of about four hundred miles on a full battery charge.[15] While this is sufficiently attractive for city driving, the sales data of fossil fuel cars show that the

---

[13] Deloitte, Future of Mobility, January 2018, https://www2.deloitte.com/content/dam/Deloitte/us/Documents/consumer-business/us-cp-fleet-leasing-and-management-in-north-america.pdf, accessed January 4, 2021.

[14] Fortune Business Insights, Transportation & Logistics, https://www.fortunebusinessinsights.com/commercial-vehicle-rental-and-leasing-market-102988, accessed January 4, 2021.

[15] Tesla, Model S Long Range Plus: Building the First 400-Mile Electric Vehicle, Tesla Blog, June 15, 2020, https://www.tesla.com/blog/model-s-long-range-plus-building-first-400-mile-electric-vehicle, accessed January 4, 2021.

exponential growth phase in fossil fuel cars was preceded by the building of the interstate highway network and the fuel station infrastructure in the US. There have been a number of significant battery technology advances in the recent past; QuantumScape's solid-state battery technology promises to increase the range of electric vehicles by more than 80 percent, with a higher charge retention period and a higher energy density compared to lithium ion batteries.[16] Tesla and other manufacturers are also predicting rapid advancements in their battery technologies. Another potential path for electric vehicle manufacturers is battery swapping: manufacturers can adopt a standardized battery design, with the potential for customers to exchange discharged batteries with freshly charged batteries at charging stations. Innovations such as solid-state batteries and battery swapping make the adoption of electric vehicles risky unless vehicles are designed to be upgradeable. Given the high prices of electric vehicles and the uncertainty associated with the dominant design in the future, the XaaS model will enable a faster diffusion of vehicles with new technologies. The demand for electrical vehicles has outstripped the production capacity of manufacturers like Tesla thus far. As Tesla's manufacturing capacity ramps up and the competitive intensity increases in the EV market, manufacturers may adopt the XaaS model to mitigate the adoption risk of customers. The XaaS model aligns the kilometres driven to the price charged in the pay-per-use pricing mechanism, hence, the incentive for customers for a higher range and the incentive for manufacturers will be aligned. Similarly, when autonomous vehicles become commercially viable, there will be an extended period when the technology will improve rapidly, leading to customers preferring a wait-and-see approach by using the XaaS model for accessing autonomous vehicles. Autonomous vehicles also need the development of complementary assets like inter-vehicle and traffic control connectivity, which will result in a probe and learn phase for several years. The combination of a high budget impact, rapid churn in technology, the need for continuous technology-based

---

[16] Green Car Congress, "QuantumScape releases performance data for its solid-state battery technology", December 9, 2020, https://www.greencarcongress.com/2020/12/20201209-qs.html, accessed January 4, 2021.

innovations for efficient operations, and the uncertainty of the primary customer needs makes the XaaS model an increasingly attractive option in the future.

Other prominent classes of products in the shopping category are household furniture and appliances like white goods and kitchen appliances. While technology can be used for creating value in these product categories as well, the advancement of technologies in these categories is relatively slow. The clock speed of industry change in these categories is slow, as customer preferences for products in these categories are stable. Hence, the continuous innovation prevalent in more fast-paced industries is not as salient in firm offerings in these categories. Customers typically mix and match individual products and create their own solutions; the offering of products in a solutions suite does not differ significantly between the purchasing and XaaS modes. Since products in these categories offer functional utility, the nanonization of utility over time or utility-per-use is not a differentiating feature. The budget impact of these categories is moderate. While the price of high-end furniture can meet and exceed any level of customer aspirations, the choice of products in these categories depends on the customer's budget. Accessing products in these categories for a long period of time may result in much higher payments compared to purchasing, without the corresponding benefits of the XaaS model that is evident for other product categories. In the retail sector, young professionals who are highly mobile and tend to move quickly from one location to another will prefer the XaaS mode of offering in these product categories. Similarly, in the office furniture sector, some firms may prefer this model if they value the flexibility of office layouts, having a more predictable cash flow, or if they intend to use the furniture for shorter periods of time. When the image of the firm is influenced by the ambience of its office space, the XaaS model can enable the firm to change its furniture and layout to project a new image if needed. There could be tax deductions accruing from using the XaaS model to acquire office furniture as well. The sustainability advantages of the office furniture as a service offering have been alluded to earlier in this book in the Ahrend example. Steelcase is the leader in the office furniture category and has introduced the servitization mode with other associated services like financing.[17] In the household appliances category, there have been significant improvements in the energy efficiency of products. However, the energy efficiency dimension is not important enough for customers to want to use the XaaS mode for these products. Large players in the household appliances category like Whirlpool, LG, and Samsung offer their products in the XaaS mode, but for customers with longer horizons, purchasing remains the preferred mode.[18] Overall, in these categories, we expect that the XaaS model will have niche segments that will grow over time, but we do not expect the XaaS mode to have a significant market share in these categories.

In shopping categories such as sport equipment and sports apparel, there has been a spurt in the growth of the XaaS mode in the recent past, and we expect this trend to continue, especially with customers who want to "experience" different sporting avenues. On the other hand, customers who specialize in certain sports will prefer to purchase their own equipment and apparel. For customers who participate in seasonal sports and want to experience high-end equipment, the XaaS mode will be the preferred mode of equipment and apparel access. The ski, biking, sailing, and hiking sports industries will lead this trend, as the frequency of usage is limited owing to weather patterns, and the budget impact of sports equipment in these categories can be significant. Globetrotter has introduced a servitized mode of access to its equipment like tents, bikes, and outdoor cooking equipment.[19] Similarly, Decathlon has introduced its own brand, Forclaz, which offers products like technical equipment, tents, and sleeping bags in the XaaS mode. In central Europe, Schöffel has started offering its skiwear range via the online channel as a service, and deliveries of rented equipment are made directly to the ski resort chosen by the

---

[17] Tan, A. R. (2010). Service-oriented product development strategies (Doctoral dissertation, Rozprawa doktorska. Technical University of Denmark, 2010, dokument elektroniczny. http://orbit. dtu. dk/fedora/objects/orbit: 82986/datastreams/file_5177222/ content (dostęp: 18.05. 2016 r.)).

[18] Rentacenter, Rent to own refrigerators, https://www.rentacenter.com/appliances/ refrigerators/c/2002, accessed January 7, 2021.

[19] Henkel, R., "Renting Instead of Buying: How Sports Equipment Rental Opens up New Target Groups", April 8, 2020, https://www.ispo.com/en/companies/renting-instead-buying-how-sports-equipment-rental-opens-new-target-groups, accessed January 7, 2021.

customer.[20] In France, Ski-Chic specializes in the XaaS model, and like Schöffel, rented products are offered online and delivered directly to the ski resort. In general, in the sports apparel market, outerwear is a popular category for accessing in the XaaS mode, while innerwear is typically purchased by customers. We expect the growth of the XaaS mode in the sports equipment and apparel market to be moderate, and the growth segment coming from customers who desire new experiences in sports.

An interesting application of the XaaS model is the growth in the luxury market of product categories such as jewellery and luxury watches. Luxury products were considered as collectibles by most customers in the past, but there is an increase in the number of customers who are keen to access these products using the as-a-service model. The easy access to luxury products on online channels has helped the acceleration of the as-a-service model, as the consumption of these products has moved from a collector's model to that of an experiential model, and the growth is being driven by millennials. Millennials often do not have the time to invest in purchasing jewellery with the associated comparisons for price and quality, and find that the XaaS model has many advantages in being able to access high-end luxury items without having to worry about incurring the shopping effort. In the luxury market of jewellery and high-end watches, both the subscription and the pay-per-use models are gaining traction. Glitzbox is one example of an online jewellery store in the UK that provides customers the choice of three jewellery pieces from their collection for a monthly subscription fee of fifty pounds.[21] The high budget impact of luxury goods is obviously a contributing factor in the growth of the XaaS model; however, there are also significant risks associated with security and fraud, which have been alleviated by technologies such as blockchain and AI in the recent past.[22] In Singapore, Acquired Time offers a monthly subscription offering to luxury watches, where customers can

---

[20] Henkel, R., "Schöffel Expands Ski Clothing Rental", May 3, 2020, https://www.ispo.com/en/companies/schoffel-expands-ski-clothing-rental, accessed January 7, 2021.

[21] Goodfellow, C., "How jewelry subscription startup Glitzbox's improved its pricing strategy", April 17, 2018, https://thepitch.uk/startup-glitzboxs-marketing-and-pricing/, accessed January 8, 2021.

[22] Lazazzera, M., "Why buy jewellery when you can rent it?" September 1, 2018, https://www.ft.com/content/2dcb5fce-7eac-11e8-af48-190d103e32a4, accessed January 8, 2021.

get one luxury watch every month for a cost of a few hundred dollars. Acquired Time follows a process of collecting a deposit first and has a pre-specified fee for damage or loss. The firm operates a platform where owners of luxury watches can offer their timepieces on the site and have a revenue sharing model with Acquired Time. In the US, Flont operates a subscription model for jewellery, with a varying subscription fee depending on the type of jewellery. In the past, the adoption of the XaaS model was difficult, owing to the lack of generalized vetting processes for customers, and the potential for theft or fraud. With modern technological advances, many of these issues have been alleviated. Product categories such as graduation gowns and wedding tuxedos also have a low frequency of usage, and the nanonization of utility has driven the growth of the XaaS model in these categories. We expect the use of the XaaS model to grow in the luxury segment, and products such as high-end bags and dresses are also being offered using this model.

The growth of the XaaS model in the customer electronics sector over the next few years is expected to be moderate. The device-as-a-service model has been growing over the last few years in the corporate market. Devices such as computers and smartphones are being contracted by organizations in the as-a-service mode to reduce the need for IT staff to focus on the procurement and maintenance of these devices for employees. The budget impact of this move is moderate, as devices are replaced within a period of a few months to a couple of years anyway, owing to the clock speed of technology in devices. In general, the XaaS model is preferable during industry downturns as it conserves cash flow, and vice versa, the acquisition mode is preferred when the economy is doing well. The pace of technology change in customer electronics favours the XaaS model; smartphones are typically offered by most providers in the XaaS model now with a long-term contract. Customer electronics products are typically mass-market products, hence, the cycle of continuous innovation and the solutions provided are not customer specific usually. The software loaded onto these devices can be customized for the needs of individual customers and organizations, and the choice in the hardware is typically offered in the form of bundles. Hence, the nanonization of utility is better under the XaaS model; however, individual customers also have similar choices when purchasing products. Quantum jumps in the technology behind devices can be expected with the commercialization of healthcare technology in wearables; at that stage, the XaaS model may be more suitable for the wearables market. Given that there is a balance between the purchasing and XaaS options for customer electronics, we expect the offering of the XaaS mode to grow in market share to a moderate degree.

In the industrial products sector, one of the segments with a high growth in the XaaS offering is the medical devices and medical technology sector. Healthcare technology is a focus area for many large organizations, and customer electronics firms like Apple are investing large amounts in the integration of healthcare technology with customer products. At the same time, healthcare administrators are increasingly conscious of the costs of medical devices and equipment, as they contribute significantly to overall healthcare costs. The need for efficient management of capital is one of the drivers of the move to the XaaS mode in the healthcare sector.[23] A second reason is the lack of visibility of the dominant technology or brand in the future, as the XaaS model enables hospitals to hedge their risk and make the decision to acquire devices based on a detailed study of the usage of devices and patient characteristics. Medical devices also need to have a high degree of reliability and low downtime, and often have a significant share of consumables. This makes the periodic servicing of medical equipment imperative, and providers almost always include servicing in their contracts. Medical devices such as infusion, smart, and volumetric pumps and ventilators may have variable needs; the demand for ventilators has shot up dramatically during the COVID-19 pandemic. The XaaS mode offers healthcare providers the ability to scale their equipment based on current demand patterns. We expect the growth of the XaaS model in the medical device and technology sector to continue, as the advantages over the acquisition mode are indeed significant. As a technology, additive manufacturing is increasingly being used in the healthcare sector, and the pay-per-use model or the subscription model to access 3D printing technology is going to grow in the future. Additive manufacturing has many properties like personalization and integration of different materials that are getting popular in

---

[23] Med One Group, "Top Reasons to Consider Renting Medical Equipment", November 18, 2019, https://www.medonegroup.com/aboutus/blog/top-reasons-to-consider-renting-medical-equipment, accessed January 8, 2021.

healthcare. Unfortunately, the cost of additive manufacturing is still high; hence, several customers do not have access to these services. The XaaS mode can be used effectively to scale additive manufacturing as a service in healthcare and other fields in the future.

The XaaS mode is expected to grow in other B2B sectors as well. The use of construction equipment in the XaaS mode has been increasing recently; the American Rental Association (ARA) reports that over 90% of their members have rented equipment in the last two years.[24] Construction equipment has a rapid clock speed, which is one of the drivers of the increased XaaS market share. Cash flow conservation owing to volatile market conditions coupled with boom and bust cycles makes XaaS an attractive proposition in the construction sector. Seasonality also plays an important role in the construction sector and renting equipment for short cycles that align with the timing of construction projects makes better financial sense than owning equipment. Equipment such as scissor lifts, large booms and cranes, generators, and other bigger items that require significant upfront investments if purchased are popular items to adopt in the XaaS mode. The use of IoT and big data technologies has been booming in the construction sector, with telematics and analytics enabling the monitoring and usage of equipment. A lot of the equipment is available online with short delivery lead times, thereby lowering the incentive to acquire the equipment. Manufacturers are making a push to integrate the technology used in their equipment with the software used by contractors, thereby enabling seamless adoption and operation of their equipment.

We also wanted to analyze Xerox's XaaS strategy in this concluding chapter; after all, while Salesforce is widely credited as the originator of the design of the as-a-service concept, Xerox introduced the XaaS model earlier with the 914 copier. What were the reasons for Xerox's fall from grace? Many analyzes have concluded that the reasons for Xerox's inability to commercialize subsequent innovations were strategic in nature.[25]

---

[24] Ingle, S., "Equipment Rental Industry Trends of 2019 and 2020", December 2, 2019, https://www.forconstructionpros.com/rental/article/21103920/equipment-rental-industry-trends-of-2019-and-2020, accessed January 8, 2021.

[25] Damer, B., "HCI Review of the Xerox Star", https://xeroxstar.tripod.com/#:~: text=Even%20though%20innovation%20is%20good,image%20as%20a%20copier%20 company, accessed January 8, 2021.

Xerox PARC indeed designed the first GUI, which was the precursor to the operating systems of the Macintosh and Windows. While Xerox tags itself as "The Document Company", its efforts at commercializing the Xerox Star workstation were not executed with the flexibility that it showed in its commercialization of the 914 product. The Xerox Star was meant to be a system to automate office work, but the high price and lack of a complementary software products meant that the Star's sales never really took off.[26] However, the laser printer that was offered with the Star was a successful product until HP designed printers in the 90s that were more commercially and functionally attractive. Xerox could not become the dominant player in all aspects of documents, and with the advent of document processing software from Microsoft and Adobe, Xerox was relegated to the world of hardware in documents processing and sharing. We would like to add that in a competitive market, pricing pressures on the pay-per-use model dictate that the subscription model may be better. The XaaS model also relies heavily on servicing, and the cost of maintaining a service network globally can be detrimental to financial gains from the model. The XaaS model needs firms to have a continuous innovation culture, technology leadership along with a solutions approach, and while Xerox nominally had all three, it had a number of key people leave at critical points and design alternative innovations. In our view, Xerox had all the right ingredients for a successful XaaS offering in perpetuity, but things never fructified for Xerox systemically at the right time. Interestingly, most analysts refer to the Xerox Star as a great offering that was ahead of its time.

10.4 THE FUTURE OF XaaS FOR IT ASSETS

The global XaaS market for IT assets (cloud computing revenues) is expected to grow at a CAGR of 17.5% annually for the next five years.[27]

---

[26] Johnson, J., Roberts, T., Verplank, W., Smith, D., Irby, C., Beard, M. Mackey, K. (1989). The Xerox Star: A Retrospective. Computer. 22. 11– 26. 10.1109/2.35211.

[27] Research and Markets, "Cloud Computing Industry to Grow from $371.4 Billion in 2020 to $832.1 Billion by 2025, at a CAGR of 17.5%", August 21, 2020, https://www.globenewswire.com/news-release/2020/08/21/2081841/0/en/Cloud-Computing-Industry-to-Grow-from-371-4-Billion-in-2020-to-832-1-Billion-by-2025-at-a-CAGR-of-17-5.html, accessed February 11, 2021.

The growth of the as-a-service model for IT assets is like the industrial growth post the centralization of electricity generation. When manufacturing units were rid of the need to generate their own electricity with the centralization of the utility distribution system, they focused on their core manufacturing competency, and grew dramatically in scale. The ability to access IT infrastructure externally from XaaS providers can have a similar impact. The outsourcing of IT began before the evolution of the XaaS model, but the advent of the XaaS offering has hastened the pace of digital transformation of organizations. We expect the IT support outsourcing model to be affected significantly by the rise of the XaaS model, and IT outsourced support services will work with XaaS providers in the future.[28] This will provide IT support firms with economies of scale, but will result in a higher degree of pressure on their margins. Firms offering IT support services will also work closely with customers to align the as-a-service offering with their business offering, leading to a greater integration of their services with the XaaS providers. Hence, IT support services will work closely with customers on PaaS offerings to customize the software with the tools available on the platform and will need to offer more value-added services higher up on the technology pole. One of the challenges faced by XaaS providers is the incentivization of their sales force when selling the XaaS model to customers. If the provider uses a commission-based model, salespeople naturally gravitate to the selling of the product rather than a subscription or pay-per-use model, as they can pocket the commission instantaneously in their next paycheck. Providers must align the incentives for salespeople so that they market the XaaS offering with the same intensity as they hawked IT products to customers.

Basic services will be acquired increasingly by customers in a commoditized form from XaaS providers. From the customer's perspective, the availability of different infrastructure needs, platforms, and software as a service has enabled organizations to focus on the transformation of their own operations to digital platforms. The XaaS model gives customers the ability to avail of transparent payment schemes like the subscription or pay-per-use models. The XaaS model provides both customers the

[28] Toesland, F., "XaaS models are reshaping the future of outsourcing", May 8, 2019, https://www.computerweekly.com/feature/XaaS-models-are-reshaping-the-future-of-outsourcing, accessed February 11, 2021.

ability to scale their IT applications and providers the ability to scale their IT resources. The scalability feature of cloud computing distinguishes the XaaS offerings of IT assets from offerings with product assets or unbundled services.

In the IaaS domain, we expect the future to continue to be dominated by the larger firms like AWS, Microsoft, Google, and Alibaba. The complementarity of offerings on these larger platforms makes it easier for customers to choose the larger players, compared to smaller providers with more niche offerings. The increasing scale of the larger players will also lead to increasing economies of scale and lowered costs, resulting in a market where the larger players will dominate. There are competing forces at play in choosing a mix of providers. While most organizations today have a mix of IT asset XaaS providers, there will be a tendency to rationalize the number of providers for administrative efficiency. On the other hand, having a mix of providers can enable firms to choose best-in-class offerings from each of these providers, and hence, have a mix of providers. Having a mix of providers has the added benefit of risk diversification and lowering the lock-in risk and being able to choose specific offerings from each provider. We expect that between these competing forces, the advantages of centralized procurement of IT resources and the benefits of one-stop shopping will dominate. This implies that customers will choose their favourites from among these providers, and increase their procurement volume from their chosen provider, but will choose other providers when there is a clear difference in competence of the other provider. Apart from these larger firms, we expect that other providers will focus on niche offerings and invest more in the innovation of the services in these offerings to differentiate themselves and incentivize customers to avail of their offerings.

Hitherto, providers have had to price their offerings competitively as the competitive intensity increases. This competitive pressure on pricing will continue, and providers will have to demonstrate visibly the value of their offerings. However, they will also focus on their specific areas of expertize and innovate in those areas so that they can keep pricing power in their favour for those offerings. This scenario will lead to the development of clear areas where specific providers will define core areas of competence. Basic services will be commoditized over time with relatively low pricing power, and providers will have pricing power in their core areas of competence. The increased competitive intensity for basic services will result in more firms offering subscription-based pricing compared to pay-per-use pricing for these basic services. Subscription-based pricing is better for customers with higher frequencies of usage, which would mean that larger customers gravitate towards the providers who offer subscription-based pricing. On the other hand, for services within the areas of competence, providers will prefer usage-based pricing, as it enables them to extract customer utility more efficiently. While these pure models of subscription and pay-per-use will still continue, we expect providers to adopt more sophisticated forms of blended pricing, where frequencies of usage below a certain threshold will be available for a flat fee, and a higher frequency of usage than the threshold will be charged a pay-per-use price.

The competitive intensity in the PaaS market is significantly lower than in the IaaS market, as by definition, PaaS providers offer a more customized set of options compared to IaaS and SaaS providers. There are many niche players in the PaaS market, and we expect that these niche players will continue to dominate in specific segments in the future. While the likes of AWS and Microsoft Azure will be the larger players in the market, we do not expect to see these larger players dominating in the PaaS market to the extent that they have in the IaaS and SaaS domains, since the standardization strategy will not be feasible. The key strengths for continued relevance in the PaaS market are understanding how current platforms can be refined for providing functionality in adjacent applications and keeping abreast of needs for current applications. The application of mass customization techniques will indeed grow, and the evolution of PaaS offerings will mirror the growth of ERP applications. ERP applications evolved from integrating manufacturing information needed by different functions and units within the firm and using relational database management systems for sharing data to a more comprehensive basic unit of data storage and analysis for enterprise-wide coordination. Today, organizations can enhance the functionality of their ERP systems by building additional modules. PaaS offerings will also evolve in a similar fashion, and the niche players will always exist, either by adding modules to the offerings of the larger players like AWS and

Microsoft Azure, or by retaining their own distinctive platform for specific markets.

The set of SaaS offerings is understandably the leader of the pack in the cloud computing market in terms of revenue. Gartner predicts that the SaaS market will eclipse 140 billion dollars by 2022, which will be twice the revenue of the IaaS and PaaS markets.[29] The growth rate will be more than 10% annually, which will be lower than the growth rate of the IaaS and PaaS offerings. A report from Blissfully shows that the fastest growth in SaaS offerings comes from cybersecurity, customer support, and HR, while the slowest growth comes from sales and marketing-oriented offerings.[30] The report also shows that while larger customers have more applications that they contract for on the cloud, the usage of these applications per person is fewer in larger organizations than smaller organizations. This shows that larger organizations use a wider suite of applications, but these applications are used by dedicated employees within the organization. In contrast, smaller organizations use a smaller suite of applications, but their employees multitask and perform a larger range of roles for which they use more applications. The report also indicates that there is a growth amount of redundancy within organizations in duplicating software applications with similar functionality. Hence, there is a lot of potential for customers to enhance their efficiency on their app spend, which should result in a more rationalized market potential in the future.

As in the IaaS domain, we expect the top firms in SaaS to be the larger providers like Microsoft, Google, and Salesforce. Again, in a similar vein to the IaaS domain, complementarity, one-stop shopping, and integration are desirable features. The integration issue is a bigger asset for the SaaS than the IaaS; having integrated solution suites that are inter-operable will mean that larger firms with a broader suite of offerings will be market leaders. The winner-take-all feature of the SaaS market will be the most

---

[29] Gartner, "Gartner Forecasts Worldwide Public Cloud Revenue to Grow 6.3% in 2020", July 3, 2020, https://www.gartner.com/en/newsroom/press-releases/2020-07-23-gartner-forecasts-worldwide-public-cloud-revenue-to-grow-6point3-percent-in-2020, accessed February 11, 2021.

[30] Diaz, A., "2020 Annual SaaS Trends — Blissfully Report", October 23, 2019, https://www.blissfully.com/saas-trends/2020-annual-report/, accessed Feb 11, 2021.

pronounced. However, there will still be adequate room for agile developers to have focused best-in-class offerings. Firms with a suite of offerings will have a relatively lower competitive pressure on pricing, while firms with offerings of generic functionality will have to go the white label route, and their focus will be on efficiency and continuous improvement in their offerings. As in the IaaS domain, we expect that subscription pricing gains traction over pay-per-use pricing in competitive areas, with more sophisticated hybrid pricing models also getting popular. We expect some of the biggest growth in applications in the domains of AI and its subsets of machine learning and deep learning in industry applications, specifically in the PaaS segment. AI software can be used for a myriad number of applications, including process analysis and improvement, productivity gains, forecasting and trend analysis, and enabling business decisions. AI software also enables personalized services by analysing different elements of interaction in real time, and the use of natural language processing can be used for customer service and marketing in real time. Machine learning can be used for the automation of responsiveness in customer service and to design self-improving processes. The most promising usage of AI and machine learning techniques is in healthcare, where personalized diagnosis and treatment options analysis can help medical professionals use the SaaS mode for keeping pace with advancements. In the B2C market, we are already seeing a trend of offering software in the SaaS mode, with Microsoft offering its office suite in Basic, Standard, and Premium bundles. We expect this trend to continue for other firms' offerings as well.

An interesting struggle for dominance is unfolding in the CRM domain, where Microsoft Dynamics is challenging Salesforce's Numero Uno position in the market. In the past, Microsoft had entered the browser market relatively early, even though it did not have first-mover advantage. Likewise, its search engine Bing was late to the market compared to first movers like Yahoo, Infoseek, and later, Google. However, Microsoft Dynamics is trying to challenge for the pole position at a point of time when CRM software is relatively mature. While Salesforce is well established as the market leader, other large firms such as Adobe, Oracle, and SAP are well entrenched in the market. Oracle and SAP also have complete ERP systems, of which the CRM system is a module. Salesforce has pioneered the SaaS concept, while Dynamics also has the on-premises version.[31] Given that most users have used Microsoft's software like Windows and the Office Suite, the learning barriers are relatively lower for Dynamics compared to the other offerings. Dynamics also integrates with the other Microsoft offerings that are leaders in office applications, while other firms' offerings have a lower degree of complementarity and integration. Dynamics is priced to be a high-end service, while Salesforce's standard offering is priced modestly. Dynamics' growth in market share over the last few months and the complementarity of Microsoft's offerings suite make it a formidable competitor. Which firm will come out on top in the new CRM wars? The safe answer would be "it depends"; however, in our opinion, Salesforce has a deeper knowledge of the CRM market and an expertize in the area of B2B offerings that Microsoft has lacked so far. Microsoft's traditional strength has been mass market products, while Salesforce has had a better understanding of the needs for customized solutions. Unlike in the past where customers had significant shared utility (cross-individual and cross-firm) in adopting the dominant software (Microsoft), CRM software is used more internally within the organization by a dedicated set of employees. Given Salesforce's focused approach, it will continue to concentrate on customer analytics, and include more functionality related to market analysis in the future. The game in the future will be about understanding user data at the personal level, and personalizing products and marketing campaigns at the level of the individual. Microsoft will continue to convert larger firms to its Dynamics offering and will use its vaunted development team to develop a smaller portfolio of add-on modules that are targeted at these larger firms. While Microsoft has shown a learning ability and a survival and growth instinct that are evidenced by its successful pivoting of its offerings in the past, the CRM market has different characteristics compared to Microsoft's past success stories. We expect both firms to be market leaders, with Salesforce maintaining its leadership position in CRM revenue, with a larger customer base and having a higher market share from

---

[31] Wright, N., "Head to head: Microsoft Dynamics vs Salesforce", https://www.nigelfrank.com/blog/head-to-head-microsoft-dynamics-vs-salesforce/, accessed Feb 11, 2021.

medium-sized enterprises, while Microsoft will have a higher market share from larger firms.

10.5 THE FUTURE OF XaaS FOR UNBUNDLED SERVICES

The unbundling of services in the XaaS mode will continue to change the world of services in the future. Blogs unbundled opinion and editorial content in the news media sector and made content accessible either in a pay-per-use or a subscription format. Airlines are already unbundling their services in different classes, with Emirates pioneering the unbundled offerings trend in 2019.[32] Emirates offers business class fares in three classes: flex, saver, and special. Unlike passengers in the flex and saver classes, passengers who buy tickets at special fares will not have the chauffeur pickup service at the origin and the destination. They will also not have lounge access (passengers who buy tickets at special fares but have Emirates Skywards membership will still be able to access lounge services), upgrades to first class if available, and unrestricted seat selection. Passengers in the special class will also earn fewer Skywards miles. Finnair joined the bandwagon in 2020, but with lounge access still offered in the lower-priced category.[33] The lower-priced ticket takes away the checked baggage amenity offered to passengers, the ability to change travelling dates without a change fee, and offers fewer points compared to the full-fare ticket. Zipair, which is owned by Japan Airlines, also introduced an unbundled business class seat offering, with meals, checked baggage, lounge access, and other services as optional items.[34]

---

[32] McWhirter, A., "Emirates to 'unbundle' business class fares", June 13, 2019, https://www.businesstraveller.com/business-travel/2019/06/13/emirates-to-unbundle-business-class-fares/, accessed February 11, 2021.

[33] Ott, G., "'Unbundled' Business Class: The Growing Travel Trend", October 20, 2020, https://www.godsavethepoints.com/airline-unbundled-business-class/, accessed Feb 11, 2021.

[34] Miller, S., "Basic Business Class now on sale", October 9, 2020, https://paxex.aero/zipair-basic-business-class/, accessed Feb 11, 2021.

The COVID-19 pandemic has disrupted all industry sectors, but perhaps it has accelerated the trend towards unbundled education services most significantly. The pandemic forced educational institutions towards online learning exclusively, raising questions about the value that traditional educational institutions like universities offer over pure play content offerings like Coursera.[35] The unbundling of the education-as-a-service model forces traditional institutions to rethink their model, as technological advances replicate the classroom setting in distributed environments. The pandemic has made stark the need for differentiation between the offerings of traditional institutions and the technology-based mass content players. However, the encroachment of the education-as-a-service model into the traditional degree-granting institution's space has been developing steadily over two decades. Platforms such as Coursera, Udacity, and Udemy have been increasingly popular among both working professionals and aspiring university graduates, and many universities have collaborated with these platforms to disseminate their course content more openly. Indeed, many universities also co-opt online learning modules in their own offerings, and cost savings is one feature that is attractive for universities. More than two-thirds of students in state universities have taken an online course before the pandemic, while only a third of students in private universities have taken a course online. The face-to-face learning experience in a co-located group still has advantages like inductive learning from group interaction, networking, peer-to-peer sharing, and learning methods. However, these advantages are being progressively lowered by the judicious use of technology in the education-as-a-service model. Initially, many universities struggled with the remote model of learning, with many faculty members using the same methods online as they adopted in in-class settings. This led to mixed student experiences, as the requirements of the online learning model are vastly different from the in-class setting. Universities have begun to adapt to the needs of online education with a mix of synchronous and asynchronous content that is offered in bite-sized chunks, compared to the contiguous modules of

---

[35]Yao, R., "The Future of Education: Unbundled & Content-Driven", July 31, 2020, https://medium.com/ipg-media-lab/the-future-of-education-unbundled-content-driven-b13b93519839, accessed Feb 11, 2021.

in-class learning. In terms of market access, the education-as-a-service model with its online delivery has access to a much larger clientele, compared to the geographical co-location constraint of the in-class setting.

Universities have been adapting to the new education-as-a-service model by unstacking course content, along with offering content with varying levels of certification. Many universities now offer flexible mini-degree programs like certificates, diplomas, and other methods of recognition of learning in addition to the traditional degree certification. These courses can be counted towards degree programs at a later stage in these universities, leading to the unstacking of degree programs. The shorter modules also lead to the personalization of learning compared to the traditional model of core courses for basic skills along with electives for the personalization of learning. Universities also have other strengths like certifying admissions quality (you can get a set of skills akin to what a degree at a top university offers, but students at top universities had solid academic records that enabled them to get into that top university), peer socialization and network building, placement services, and alumni networks. The assessment of students, while flawed, is still a service that is hard to replicate for online education providers. However, those strengths are not invulnerable, and the evolution of education will see a convergence towards a mix of functional skill-developing content along with soft skills. The traditional model will co-exist with the MOOC-based model, and the choice of students towards either model will be dictated by the adaptation to change of both models.

The unbundling of services can also revolutionize the structural bases of operations for many industries; in the first chapter, we highlighted the innovation-sharing model of RPX and other innovation aggregators. The RPX offering of subscriptions to patent portfolios to protect against patent litigation can offer the unbundling of the patent portfolio over the entire spectrum of patents owned by RPX. The availability of the subscription or the pay-per-use mechanism can give firms access to patent portfolios that are matched to customer requirements in scope, and over time. Customers can choose to access a limited set of patents in RPX's portfolio that is relevant to their set of offerings, and hence, the pricing of the subscriptions can be negotiated with individual customers. Customers can also access the patent protection of these defensive aggregators for limited periods of time and discontinue their access when the patent protection is no longer required. In the field of legal services, there is a move towards the unbundling of different components of the services so that the incentives of lawyers and clients are better aligned. In the pay-per-billing hour model of legal services, the misaligned incentive of extensive trial time for the legal services provider has been well documented. By moving to an unbundled service model of separate mediation, arbitration, and litigation services, the interests of law firms and clients can be aligned better.

10.6 CONCLUDING THOUGHTS

The XaaS model is here to stay. The XaaS model will grow in the future. The data on the adoption and growth of the XaaS model across industries support these statements. The growth of the sharing economy supports these statements. The strengths of the XaaS model are the principles needed for its successful implementation: the transfer of asset ownership to the provider, the adoption of a solutions provider approach, the adoption of the lean model by the nanonization of offerings in attribute space and time, the continuous innovation approach, and the use of technology for enabling the XaaS model. The pace of change of technology is getting quicker every year; the XaaS model enables customers to overcome the rapid obsolescence problem of products, software, and services. Customer expectations and requirements are changing quickly, and the attention spans of millennials and Generations X, Y, and Z are getting shorter. In this fast-paced environment, the XaaS model enables customers to access the latest offerings with low risk. The XaaS model has definitive strengths from the customer's perspective and the firm's perspective. These strengths are summarized in the BROAD FENCES analysis with the three stages of the XaaS model (feasibility, profitability, and growth). The BROAD FENCES analysis should be useful to business leaders in the design stage of the service, and at different stages of the improvement of the service. The models developed in this book should help business leaders design, assess, and improve their offerings.

The XaaS model also has a notable weakness: the pricing strength, the revenue base, and the attractiveness of the XaaS model are based on having a differentiated offering. In an intensely competitive market, the XaaS model generates weak returns for the provider if the offering is commoditized. The use of the XaaS model by firms is like riding the proverbial tiger: once you adopt the XaaS model, you commit to riding it by continuously innovating and matching your offering to customer requirements. Any attempt to dismount the tiger will cause catastrophic consequences; herein lies the beauty of the XaaS model. It forces the provider to commit to a strategy of providing customers with a better offering continuously. And, it signals the provider's commitment to the customer, thereby making the adoption decision for the customer easier. Can you ask for a better model?

Printed in the United States
by Baker & Taylor Publisher Services